business solutions

Automating
Microsoft® Access
with VBA

Susan Sales Harkins

Mike Gunderloy

800 E. 96th Street
Indianapolis, Indiana 46240

Contents at a Glance

I Laying the Foundation

1 Why Access? Why VBA? 9
2 Getting Around in the Visual Basic Editor 17
3 Using Variables, Constants, and Data Types 33
4 Using Procedures 45
5 Choosing the Right VBA Function 57
6 Using Flow-of-Control Statements 91
7 Working with Arrays 105
8 Understanding Objects 113
9 Understanding Scope and Lifetime 131

II Working with the Access User Interface

10 Working with Forms 145
11 Analyzing the Access Event Model 161
12 Working with List and Combo Boxes 175
13 Working with Other Controls 195
14 Working with Reports 209
15 Working with the Application Collections 223

III Working with Access Data

16 Retrieving Data with ADO 237
17 Manipulating Data with ADO 253
18 Creating Objects with ADOX 273
19 Performing Advanced Data Operations 287

IV Using Advanced VBA Techniques in Access

20 Working with Data Files 301
21 Automating Other Applications 313
22 Working with XML Files 325
23 Using the Windows API 337

V Appendix

A Review of Access SQL 347

Index 359

D0731107

Automating Microsoft Access with VBA

Copyright © 2005 by Que Publishing

International Standard Book Number: 0-7897-3244-0

Library of Congress Catalog Card Number: 2004109548

Printed in the United States of America

First Printing: September, 2004

07   06   05   04   4   3   2   1

Trademarks

Warning and Disclaimer

Bulk Sales

Que Publishing offers excellent discounts on this book when ordered in quantity for bulk purchases or special sales. For more information, please contact

U.S. Corporate and Government Sales
1-800-382-3419
corpsales@pearsontechgroup.com

For sales outside of the U.S., please contact

International Sales
1-317-428-3341
international@pearsontechgroup.com

Associate Publisher
Michael Stephens

Acquisitions Editor
Loretta Yates

Development Editor
Songlin Qiu

Managing Editor
Charlotte Clapp

Project Editor
George E. Nedeff

Copy Editor
Kezia Endsley

Indexer
Erika Millen

Proofreader
Linda Seifert

Technical Editor
Dana Christine Jones

Publishing Coordinator
Cindy Teeters

Multimedia Developer
Dan Scherf

Book Designer
Anne Jones

Page Layout
Cheryl Lynch

Table of Contents

Introduction **1**

    Who This Book Is For 1

    What's in This Book 2

    Conventions Used in This Book 4

    The Sample Code for This Book 5

    Contacting the Authors 5

I LAYING THE FOUNDATION

1 Why Access? Why VBA? **9**

    Understanding the Place of Access in Office 9

        Choosing Between Access and Excel 9

        Choosing Between Access and OneNote 11

    Understanding Access Programming Choices 11

        Using Macros 12

        Using SQL 12

        Using VBA 13

    Case Study 13

        Using the TimeTrack Sample Database 13

2 Getting Around in the Visual Basic Editor **17**

    Your First Glance at the Visual Basic Editor 17

    Introducing the VBA Modules 21

    Entering and Running VBA Code 22

        Saving the Code 24

    Getting Help on Code 25

        Helpful Shortcuts for Entering Code 26

Establishing Good Habits in Coding 28

Using a Naming Convention 28

Indenting Your Code 30

Commenting Your Code 30

3 Using Variables, Constants, and Data Types **33**

Declaring Variables and Constants 33

Declaring Variables 33

Using Option Explicit 34

Naming Variables 37

Declaring Constants 37

Intrinsic Constants 38

VBA Data Types 39

The `Boolean` Data Type 40

The `Byte` Data Type 40

The `Currency` Data Type 40

The `Date` Data Type 41

The `Decimal` Data Type 41

The `Double` Data Type 41

The `Integer` Data Type 41

The `Long` Data Type 41

The `Object` Data Type 41

The `Single` Data Type 41

The `String` Data Type 42

The `Variant` Data Type 42

Referencing Syntax 42

4 Using Procedures **45**

Understanding Procedure Types 45

Creating and Using Sub Procedures 45

Creating and Using Function Procedures 47

Declaring Procedures as Public or Private 48

Passing Arguments 49

Using Optional Arguments and Default Values 50

Passing Arguments by Reference 50

Passing Arguments by Value 51

Giving a Function a Data Type 51

Implementing Error Handling 52

    Using On Error Resume Next 53
    Using On Error Goto 53

Debugging Code 54

    Using Run and Break Mode 54
    Single-Stepping 55
    Setting Breakpoints 56

5 Choosing the Right VBA Function **57**

Introducing VBA's Built-in Functions 57

Converting Data Types with VBA Functions 58

    Converting to a `Boolean` Data Type 59
    Converting to a `Byte` Data Type 60
    Converting to a `Date` Data Type 61
    Converting to an `Integer` Data Type 62
    Converting to a `String` Data Type 62
    Converting to a `Variant` Data Type 62
    Converting Null Values 63

Working with Date Functions 65

    Returning the Date 65
    Adding to and Subtracting from Dates 66
    Determining the Difference Between Two Dates 66
    Extracting Date Components 68
    Creating a Date from Individual Components 68
    Creating a Date from a String Expression 69
    Returning a Specific Date or Time Component 69

Using Mathematical and Financial Functions 70

    The `Abs` Function 70
    The `Int` Function 71
    The `Rnd` Function 71
    The `Ddb` Function 72
    The `FV` Function 72
    The `IPmt` Function 73
    The `NPer` Function 73
    The `Pmt` Function 73

The PPmt Function 73

The Rate Function 74

The Syd Function 74

Using String Functions 75

The Asc Function 76

The Chr Function 76

The Case Functions 77

The Len String Function 77

The Left, Right, and Mid Functions 77

The Replace Function 78

The Space Function 78

The Split String Function 79

The StrComp Function 79

The Three Trimming Functions 79

Using the Format Function 81

Applying User-Defined Formats 82

Using the Is Functions for Flawless Processing 85

Interacting Functions 85

The InputBox Function 86

The MsgBox Function 86

Case Study 88

Business Days 88

6 Using Flow-of-Control Statements **91**

Branching and Looping 91

Using If...Then...Else 91

The Simple If Statement 91

Creating More Complex Conditions 92

Adding the Else Statement 93

Using the ElseIf Statement 93

Using Select Case 94

Using For...Next 95

    Looping in Reverse 96

    Using a Variable for the Loop Counter 97

    Nesting For...Next Loops 98

    Aborting a For...Next Loop 99

Using Do Loops 99

    Creating a Simple Do Loop 99

    Varieties of the Do Loop 100

    Aborting a Do Loop 101

Using GoTo 101

Case Study 102

    Billing for Work in Progress 102

7 Working with Arrays **105**

Introducing Array Variables 105

Declaring an Array Variable 105

Understanding the Array's Index 106

    Using Option Base 107

Working with Array Elements 107

    Defining Array Elements 108

    Referencing Array Elements 109

Arrays with Multiple Dimensions 110

Expanding to Dynamic Arrays 110

    About ReDim 110

8 Understanding Objects **113**

Introducing Objects 113

    Digressing into the Real World 113

    An Object Example from Access 114

    Creating Objects in Code 114

Reading and Setting Properties 116

Invoking Methods 117

Working with Collections 119

Working with an Object Model 121
    Using an Object Model 121
    Using References 122
    The Object Browser 123

Creating Your Own Objects 124

Working with Events 126

Case Study 128
    Opening Forms and Handling Errors 128

9 Understanding Scope and Lifetime **131**

What's Scope? 131
    Procedure-Level Variables 131
    Module-Level Variables and Constants 133
    Public Variables and Constants 134

Measuring the Lifetime of a Variable or Constant 136
    The Lifetime of a Procedure-Level Variable 137
    The Lifetime of a Module-Level Variable 137
    The Lifetime of a Public Variable 138

Using Static Variables 139

II WORKING WITH THE ACCESS USER INTERFACE

10 Working with Forms **145**

Opening and Closing Forms 145
    Opening a Form 145
    Closing a Form 146

The Form Module and Event Handling 147

Performing Common Tasks 148
    Checking for a Form's Existence 148
    Determining Whether a Form Is Loaded 149
    Resizing a Form 150
    Passing Arguments Using OpenArgs 151
    Populating the Form 152

Handling Errors at the Form Level 154

Working with Multiple Form Instances 157

Case Study 158
    Working with Two Instances of the Same Form 158

11 Analyzing the Access Event Model **161**

Responding to Events 161

The Event Sequence for Controls 162
    Focus Events 163
    Data Events 165
    Control-Specific Events 167

The Event Sequence for Forms 167
    Navigation Events   168
    Data Events   168
    Behind the Scenes: Data Buffers 169

The Event Sequence for Reports 170

Canceling Events 171

Case Study 172
    Validating Data Before Saving It 172

12 Working with List and Combo Boxes **175**

Populating a List Control 175
    A Simple Filtering List Control 177

Adding to the List—or Not 181
    Updating a Value List 181
    Updating a Table/Query List 183

Working with Multiselect Controls 187
    Determining What's Selected and What's Not 187

Considering Callback Functions 189

Case Study 191
    Using List Box Controls as Drill-Down Controls 191

13 Working with Other Controls **195**

Working with Text Boxes 195
    Key Properties of Text Boxes 195
    Tracking the Focus 197
    Working with Unbound Text Boxes 198

Using Controls in Option Groups 200

Working with Subforms 202

Working with the `Tag` Property 202

Case Study 203
    Creating a Master Viewing Form 203

14 Working with Reports **209**

Introducing the Report Module and Events 209

Opening and Closing Reports 210
    Opening a Report 210
    Closing a Report 211

Passing Arguments Using OpenArgs 212

Populating the Report 213
    Applying a Filter and Sort Order 214

Handling Report-Level Errors 215
    What to Do When There's No Data 217

Using VBA to Determine Group Properties 218

Case Study 220
    Adding a Daily Report 220

15 Working with the Application Collections **223**

Investigating the Application Collections 223

Retrieving Lists of Objects 225

Working with Object Properties 226

Programmatically Determining Dependencies 229

Case Study 232

Enhancing the Master Form 232

III WORKING WITH ACCESS DATA

16 Retrieving Data with ADO **237**

What's ADO and Why Do You Need It? 237

The ADO Object Model 237

Using the ADO Connection Object 238

Opening the Connection 239

About Connection Strings 240

Closing a Connection 242

Working with Command Objects 242

Creating a Command Object 243

Executing the Command Object 243

Understanding the Different Types of Recordsets 244

Creating and Opening a Recordset 245

Filtering Recordsets 247

Using the `Recordset` Property 248

Case Study 250

Who's Connected to the Database? 250

17 Manipulating Data with ADO **253**

   Moving Through a Recordset 253

      Referencing Recordset Fields 256

   Finding Data in a Recordset 256

      An Alternative to `Find`—the ADO `Seek` Method 258

   Adding Data Using a Recordset 260

   Deleting Data in a Recordset 262

   Updating Data in a Recordset 263

   Using Transactions to Commit Groups of Records—or Not 266

   Case Study 268

      Using a Recordset Object to Add Items to a Combo Box 268

18 Creating Objects with ADOX **273**

   What Is ADOX? 273

   Creating Tables 274

      Creating a Table and Columns 275

      Creating Indexes 277

      Creating Relationships 278

   Securing Objects 279

      Creating a New Group 279

      Creating a New User 280

      Changing Object Ownership 281

      Setting Object Permissions 282

   Case Study 284

      Creating a Data Dictionary 284

19 Performing Advanced Data Operations **287**

   Coding for Concurrency 287

      Understanding Concurrency 287

      Optimistic Locking in ADO 289

      Pessimistic Locking in ADO 291

Retrieving a User Recordset 293

Using Other Schema Recordsets 294

Case Study 296

Using the Form Error Event to Resolve Locking Errors 296

IV USING ADVANCED VBA TECHNIQUES IN ACCESS

20 Working with Data Files **301**

Understanding File I/O 301

Opening Files 302

About mode 302
About access 303
About locking 303
A Simple Open Example 303

Reading from Files 304

Using Input 304
Using Line Input # 306
Using Input # 306

Writing to Files 307

Printing to Files 309

Case Study 310

Using I/O to Number Lines in a Text File 310

21 Automating Other Applications **313**

Understanding Automation 313

Setting Object References 314

Creating Objects in an Automation Server 315

Using CreateObject 316
Using GetObject 316
Using Early Binding 317

Talking to Excel from Access 318

Talking to Word from Access 320

Case Study 322
  Using Excel Chart Features from Inside Access 322

22 Working with XML Files **325**

An Introduction to XML 325

Using ExportXML 326
  An Export Example 327
  Exporting a Web-Ready File 329
  Exporting Related Data 329

Using ImportXML 330
  An Import Example 331

Case Study 334
  Exporting Up-to-Date Project Information 334

23 Using the Windows API **337**

Declaring API Calls 337

Using API Calls 338

API Calls That You Can Use From Access 340
  Determining Whether an Application Is Running 340
  Retrieving the Current Username 341
  Getting the Executable for a Data File 342

Knowing When to Use the Windows API 343

V APPENDIX

A **Review of Access SQL** **347**

An Introduction to SQL 347

SQL Structure and Syntax 348

Retrieving with SQL SELECT 350

    The SQL Predicates 350

    The SQL FROM Clause 351

    The SQL WHERE Clause 352

    The SQL ORDER BY Clause 353

    The SQL GROUP BY Clause 353

    The SQL HAVING Clause 354

Modifying with SQL UPDATE 354

Deleting with SQL DELETE 355

Appending With SQL's INSERT INTO 355

Making Tables With SQL SELECT INTO 356

Creating a Crosstab Query with SQL TRANSFORM 357

Index **359**

About the Authors

Mike Gunderloy is an independent developer and author who has been working with computers for 25 years. His experience with Microsoft Office dates back to Office 4.3, which, despite the number, was the very first version of the integrated suite. In the intervening years, he's worked closely with the Office product team, participating in focus groups and even contributing some code to the finished product. Mike has written or contributed to more than 20 books on development topics. He's currently the editor of the weekly *Developer Central* newsletter. You can reach Mike at MikeG1@larkfarm.com or visit his Web sites at http://www.larkware.com and http://www.codertodeveloper.com.

Susan Sales Harkins is an independent consultant with an expertise in Access. With Mike, Susan's latest Office book is *Upgrader's Guide to Microsoft Office System 2003*. Currently, Susan writes for a number of technology-based publishers and magazines, including *Element K Journals*, builder.com, and devx.com. Her most recent books, also with Mike, include *Exam Cram 2 ICDL* and *ICDL Practice questions Exam Cram 2*, *Absolute Beginner's Guide to Access 2002*, and *Absolute Beginner's Guide to Access 2000*, all from Que.

Dedication

This one's for Thomas, whose parents both worked on it

—Mike Gunderloy

To Lexie for keeping me young and Bill for keeping me grounded

—Susan Sales Harkins

Acknowledgments

One of the pleasant things about finishing a book manuscript is that you finally get to write one of the easy parts: the acknowledgments. Or rather, one of the nontechnical parts. It's not easy to find the right words to thank everyone who helped make this a better book. We'll start with Loretta Yates, who first approached us with the idea of contributing a book in a new series. We also had great help from the rest of our editorial team, Songlin Qiu and George Nedeff at Que Publishing, as well as technical editor Dana Jones. Thanks also to the production team who took the hard work that all these people did and turned it into a physical book.

Of course, if any inaccuracies or flat-out mistakes made it into print, it's despite these fine people, not because of them. We've done our best to write the book that we think you want to read, and we thank you for buying a copy.

As always, Mike appreciates the forbearance of his family while he was writing yet another book. Dana managed to help run a household while pursuing her own business and tech editing my mistakes, not to mention growing a baby. Adam and Kayla continually rewarded me with smiles and hugs, when they weren't making me a better man by testing my patience. And Thomas had the sense to gestate until the last chapter was in manuscript form.

Susan would like to thank the Que folks for continuing to support great book projects *and* for continuing to call upon her to fulfill those projects. Most especially, Susan thanks her family for supporting her decision to work from home in her pajamas so she can grow young with her granddaughter.

We Want to Hear from You!

As the reader of this book, *you* are our most important critic and commentator. We value your opinion and want to know what we're doing right, what we could do better, what areas you'd like to see us publish in, and any other words of wisdom you're willing to pass our way.

As an associate publisher for Que Publishing, I welcome your comments. You can email or write me directly to let me know what you did or didn't like about this book--as well as what we can do to make our books better.

Please note that I cannot help you with technical problems related to the topic of this book. We do have a User Services group, however, where I will forward specific technical questions related to the book.

When you write, please be sure to include this book's title and author as well as your name, email address, and phone number. I will carefully review your comments and share them with the author and editors who worked on the book.

Email: feedback@quepublishing.com

Mail: Michael Stephens
            Associate Publisher
            Que Publishing
            800 East 96th Street
            Indianapolis, IN 46240 USA

For more information about this book or another Que Publishing title, visit our Web site at www.quepublishing.com. Type the ISBN (0789732440) or the title of a book in the Search field to find the page you're looking for.

INTRODUCTION

Welcome to *Automating Microsoft Access with VBA!* This book is designed to build on the Access skills that you have already developed in a business setting, and help you take them to the next level—using a programming language to automate things you currently do manually. Access includes the Visual Basic for Applications (VBA) programming language, and even if you've never programmed before, you can learn how to use it to make your use of Access more productive than ever before.

Who This Book Is For

We've written this book for professionals who use Microsoft Access in a business setting. We don't expect that you're a software developer by profession, but we do think you probably sit in front of a computer much of the day. You've got real work to get done, and you can't spend all day sitting around reading a computer book. This has shaped our coverage. We aim to teach you the essential skills involved in automating your databases as quickly as possible, so that your time investment in this book is paid back rapidly. We've also tried to expose you to many different techniques. As a result, you might find that you reference some subjects more than others, but everything will be of interest to the beginning VBA developer.

This book was written using Access 2003, the version that ships as part of the Microsoft Office System 2003. But you don't have to worry about upgrading to this latest version to use the information we've provided. The VBA language that you use has not changed substantially in recent years. You should be able to follow all the examples equally well with Access 2000 or Access 2002, although some things (such as toolbar icons) might look a bit different in earlier versions.

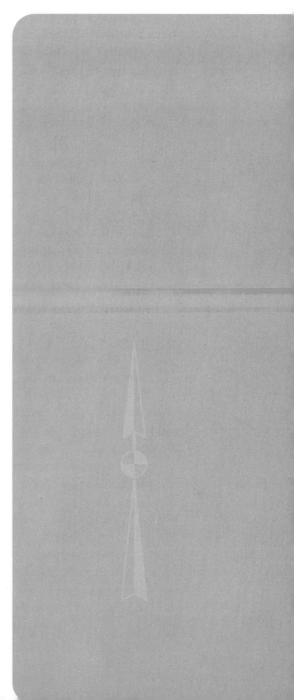

What's in This Book

The book has 23 chapters divided into four parts, plus one appendix.

- Part I, "Laying the Foundation," teaches you the syntax and programming structures that you need to understand before you can do useful work with VBA.

  Chapter 1, "Why Access? Why VBA?," is designed to get you oriented. Access isn't the only application in Office, and VBA isn't the only way to program Access. By the time you finish this first chapter, you should understand why we think using VBA to automate Access is a useful skill to have.

  Chapter 2, "Getting Around in the Visual Basic Editor," shows you the user interface that you use to write VBA code. We also show you some good coding practices in this chapter.

  Chapter 3, "Using Variables, Constants, and Data Types" introduces the first set of basic concepts that you need to understand to write VBA code.

  Chapter 4, "Using Procedures," gives you the tools to organize your VBA code. Procedures are independent units of code that can be executed one at a time to do useful work. You'll find many more procedures over the course of the book.

  Chapter 5, "Choosing the Right VBA Function," tours some of the support that VBA gives your code. Financial and date calculations, text manipulation, and mathematical functions are a few of the things that are built into VBA. Using these functions helps you get more done while writing less code of your own.

  Chapter 6, "Using Flow-of-Control Statements," demonstrates the tools that VBA provides for making decisions. For example, you can write a procedure that does one thing when a number is positive and another when the number is negative.

  Chapter 7, "Working with Arrays," discusses a way to store many pieces of information in a single variable. Arrays are useful when you're tracking a group of similar items.

  Chapter 8, "Understanding Objects," covers some of the most powerful concepts in VBA programming. Objects enable you to create structures in your VBA code that represent things. VBA and Access include a number of built-in objects that you can use in your code to represent things like forms open on the screen.

  Chapter 9, "Understanding Scope and Lifetime," introduces some remaining fine points of variable handling in Access.

- Part II, "Working with the Access User Interface," builds on the foundation of Part I to show you how to work with the Access user interface from code. Just about anything you can do manually, from opening a form to running a query, you can also do with code. This is where VBA meets Access to provide a true automation tool, replacing and extending anything that you can do with Access macros.

  Chapter 10, "Working with Forms," shows you how to use VBA to automate Access forms. You learn how to open and close forms, open multiple copies of the same form, and pass information to a form, among other things.

Chapter 11, "Analyzing the Access Event Model," drills into event handling in Access. Events enable you to run code when something happens onscreen. For example, you can have a bit of VBA code attached to a form so that the code runs every time a database user opens the form.

Chapter 12, "Working with List and Combo Boxes," shows you how to use VBA to populate and manipulate these two important controls.

Chapter 13, "Working with Other Controls," shows you how to use VBA with a variety of other controls on Access forms. These controls include text boxes, option buttons, and subforms.

Chapter 14, "Working with Reports," demonstrates the use of VBA code with Access reports. You have almost complete control over the data and layout of reports from code, if you know what you're doing.

Chapter 15, "Working with the Application Collections," tells you how to use VBA to get information about Access objects such as forms, reports, tables, and queries.

- Part III, "Working with Access Data," turns from the Access user interface to the data stored in Access. Here, you learn about using the ActiveX Data Objects (ADO) library to read and change data.

Chapter 16, "Retrieving Data with ADO," begins the process by demonstrating how to get data from tables and queries and put it into recordset objects in memory. You learn how to get just the data that your VBA code needs to work with.

Chapter 17, "Manipulating Data with ADO," looks at the other half of the process: adding, deleting, and updating data. ADO enables you to perform all these operations easily.

Chapter 18, "Creating Objects with ADOX," deals with a specialized area of ADO that enables you to create your own data-bearing objects. For example, you can use ADOX to create an entirely new Access table without ever touching the Access user interface.

Chapter 19, "Performing Advanced Data Operations," digs into a few more corners of ADO. This chapter is primarily about working with a database that's used simultaneously by more than one user.

- Part IV, "Using Advanced VBA Techniques in Access," touches on some advanced VBA techniques. You might never need any of these techniques, but they show you some of the powerful operations that VBA is capable of.

Chapter 20, "Working with Data Files," demonstrates techniques for working with data stored in regular text files. Even though Access stores its own data within databases, VBA makes it possible to work with all sorts of other files.

Chapter 21, "Automating Other Applications," shows you how you can use VBA code in Access to manipulate applications such as Microsoft Word or Microsoft Excel. You learn how easy it is to use this technique to make use of functionality from other applications.

Chapter 22, "Working with XML Files," teaches you how VBA and Access support Extensible Markup Language (XML). XML is a current darling of the software industry, so it's likely that you'll run across XML files sooner or later.

Chapter 23, "Using the Windows API," rounds out the book. Here, you see how to use powerful functions supplied by Microsoft Windows itself to do things that are otherwise impossible.

■ Finally, Appendix A, "Review of Access SQL," includes a review of the SQL language used to retrieve and manipulate data in Access. Although SQL itself isn't a part of VBA, you need to know SQL to use some of the other functions you see in this book.

Conventions Used in This Book

The following typographic conventions are used in this book:

■ Code lines, commands, statements, variables, and any text you type or see onscreen appear in a `monospace` typeface.

■ *Italics* highlight technical terms when they're being defined.

■ You'll come across a lot of syntax statements where arguments are italicized and often enclosed in brackets. The italicized text values are arguments. You replace these with values that are relevant to the task at hand. Brackets denote optional arguments.

Throughout the book we've included some helpful features to make it easier for you to learn to use VBA quickly and effectively:

→ Cross-references show you where to find related information in other chapters of the book.

CAUTION

Cautions warn you of potentially confusing or damaging side effects to running code. This might be anything from unexpected behavior when you do things in the wrong order to a new way to lose data.

TIP

Tip paragraphs offer our tips and tricks for making effective use of VBA in Access 2003. If you apply the knowledge from these paragraphs, we think you'll find VBA to be a productive language.

NOTE

Notes provide additional notes or background on VBA features. These tidbits of information can help you understand what's going on when you run VBA code, or point you to additional resources when you want to learn more.

Many of the chapters in this book end with a case study. These case studies are extended examples that show you how to apply the tools and techniques from the chapter in a business setting. We've designed the case studies to help you understand why you're learning VBA, and to provide inspiration for automating your own databases.

The Sample Code for This Book

We designed the case studies in this book around a sample database named TimeTrack. TimeTrack starts the book as a very simple database with no automation. It keeps track of consulting projects, employees, and hours worked for a variety of customers. You can read more about the basic structure of the database in Chapter 1.

Each chapter's sample code is added to the TimeTrack database to produce a new version. For example, `TimeTrack5.mdb` contains all the code from the first five chapters of the book. By the time you reach the end of the book, we hope you'll have some appreciation of what VBA automation can do for a database.

You can download all the versions of the TimeTrack database from the Que Publishing Web site at `www.quepublishing.com`. Enter this book's ISBN (without the hyphens) in the Search box and click Search. When the book's title is displayed, click the title to go to a page where you can download the code.

Contacting the Authors

One of the best things about writing a book is the opportunity to hear from readers. We can't upgrade Office for you, but we'd be happy to hear from you if something's not clear, or if you just want to tell us how much you liked the book. You can email Susan at `ssharkins@bellsouth.net`, or Mike at `MikeG1@larkfarm.com`.

Laying the Foundation

IN THIS PART

1 Why Access? Why VBA? 9

2 Getting Around in the Visual Basic Editor 17

3 Using Variables, Constants, and Data Types 33

4 Using Procedures 45

5 Choosing the Right VBA Function 57

6 Using Flow-of-Control Statements 91

7 Working with Arrays 105

8 Understanding Objects 113

9 Understanding Scope and Lifetime 131

Why Access? Why VBA?

Understanding the Place of Access in Office

Welcome to *Automating Microsoft Access with VBA*. In this book, you'll learn how to make your Access databases much more than just a convenient place to keep track of information. Visual Basic for Applications—VBA—is the core automation language that's built in to every copy of Microsoft Access. You'll see how you can speed up data entry, perform complex business processes, and even send data to other Windows applications. Even if you have no prior programming experience, by the end of the book you'll be writing code with the pros.

Before we dive into automating Access, though, we're going to take a few pages to understand the place of Access and VBA in the office automation landscape. That's what this chapter is about. Although VBA and Access are both popular and versatile tools, they're not the perfect tool for every job, and you need to be aware of the alternatives.

Presumably you're using (or thinking about using) Access to store information. But Microsoft Office 2003 offers three different applications that are suitable for storing information:

- Microsoft Office Access 2003
- Microsoft Office Excel 2003
- Microsoft Office OneNote 2003

Your first task is to choose the appropriate application for your own information storage needs.

Choosing Between Access and Excel

The most difficult choice for many users is whether to use Excel or Access for their business information.

IN THIS CHAPTER

Understanding the Place of Access in Office . .9

Understanding Access Programming Choices 11

Spreadsheets have been around since before most of us were working with computers, and they offer a familiar and accessible interface for storing information. Access, on the other hand, can be a bit harder to approach; there's a certain feeling that databases are harder to understand than spreadsheets. Microsoft encourages this separation by not including Access in the least-expensive versions of the Office suite.

Although it's true that both Access and Excel can store information in tables with rows and columns (see Figure 1.1), there are serious differences between the two. Understanding these differences will help you decide which application is right for your information.

Figure 1.1
Tables in Access and Excel.

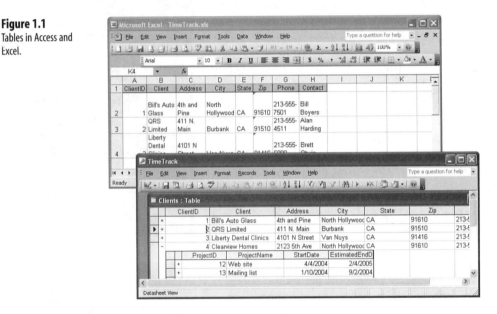

The big advantage that Excel has over Access is the relative simplicity of its interface. Excel is a large and complex application, but it only stores things in one place: on worksheets in a workbook. By contrast, when you first open Access, you're faced with the database window, and no obvious place to type in your data. The many object types in Access (tables, queries, forms, reports, and so on) can also be overwhelming for beginners.

But Access offers a big advantage over Excel after you get past that initial learning curve: It takes better care of your information. For example, if you tell Access that a particular column in a database table will only contain dates, it won't let you type a customer name in that column by mistake. Excel, on the other hand, will let you type pretty much anything anywhere.

Access also understands the concept of relations between data. For example, you can tell Access what the connection is between a table of clients and a table of projects. This lets Access enforce business rules, such as the rule that each project must belong to a customer.

> **NOTE**
>
> Throughout this book, we'll assume that you already have a good understanding of the Access user interface and the basics of building a relational database. If you need to brush up on these subjects, we suggest reading *Absolute Beginner's Guide to Microsoft Office Access 2003*, by Mike Gunderloy and Susan Sales Harkins (Que, 2004).

Choosing Between Access and OneNote

Microsoft also released another information-storage application with Office 2003: Microsoft Office OneNote 2003, shown in Figure 1.2. Although aimed mainly at Tablet PC users, it also offers an interesting alternative for data storage on the desktop.

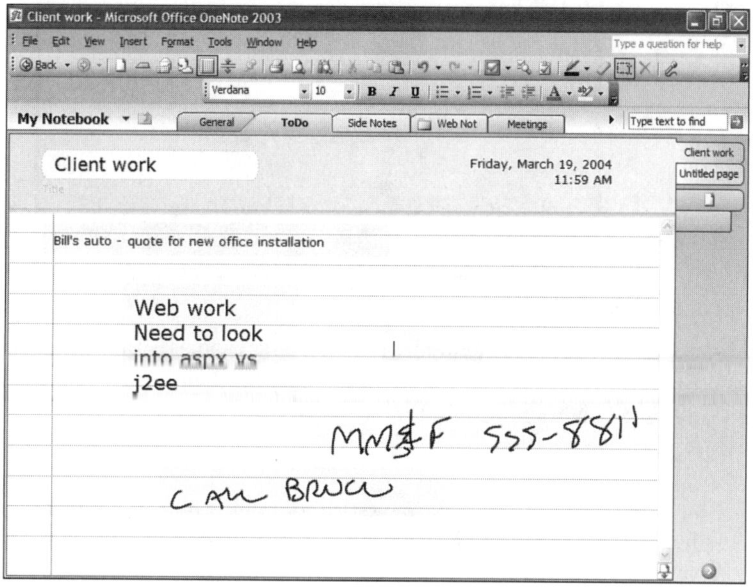

Figure 1.2
OneNote 2003 offers freeform information storage.

OneNote is designed to offer a flexible way to record and organize all sorts of information. You can type in it, hand-write notes, paste or drag in pictures and other rich content, and even make audio recordings a part of your notes. But it imposes even less structure on your information than Excel does. If you're having trouble figuring out how something could fit into Access or Excel because it's too unstructured, then you should take a look at OneNote as an alternative.

Understanding Access Programming Choices

After you've settled on Access as the place where you'll store your information, you still have decisions to make. One of these is which programming language to use with Access.

VBA is not the only means available to automate your Access solutions; depending on the situation, you might also want to make use of Access macros or Structured Query Language (SQL) for some or all of your work.

Using Macros

You may already be familiar with the Access macro programming language, which provides a limited (though still useful) set of tools for automating database actions. For example, Figure 1.3 shows a simple macro that opens a single form. You can run this macro directly from the database container, or attach it to a button on another form.

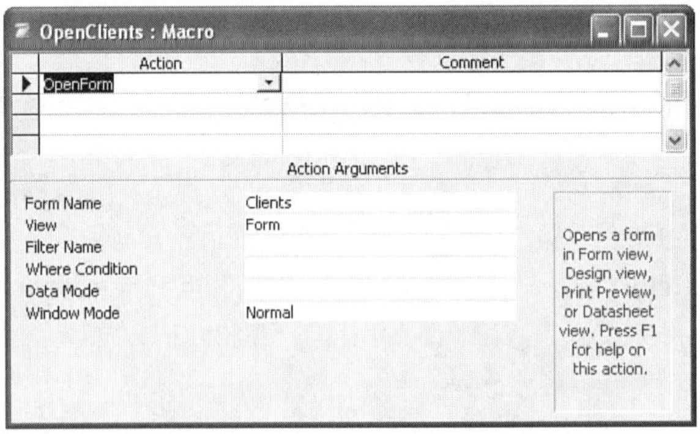

Figure 1.3
Access macros provide a limited means of automating database actions.

Macros are useful but limited. We've seen some databases that do amazing things with macros, but if you're a power user, you'll soon hit their limits. In particular, macros have only a limited ability to respond to errors or other conditions out of the ordinary.

> **TIP**
> There's no need to remove working macros from a database if you've decided to switch to VBA. Access is perfectly able to mix the two automation languages in a single database.

Using SQL

You might also have heard of Structured Query Language, more commonly called SQL. SQL is the language that Access uses to store database queries. For example, you might want to find all the Web-related projects in a database of tasks. Figure 1.4 shows an Access query to perform this task.

Although most users prefer to work with queries in design view, this isn't how Access saves your queries. Instead, it uses SQL for this purpose. Here's the SQL statement that corresponds to the query shown in Figure 1.4:

```
SELECT Projects.*
FROM Projects
WHERE (((Projects.ProjectName) Like "*Web*"));
```

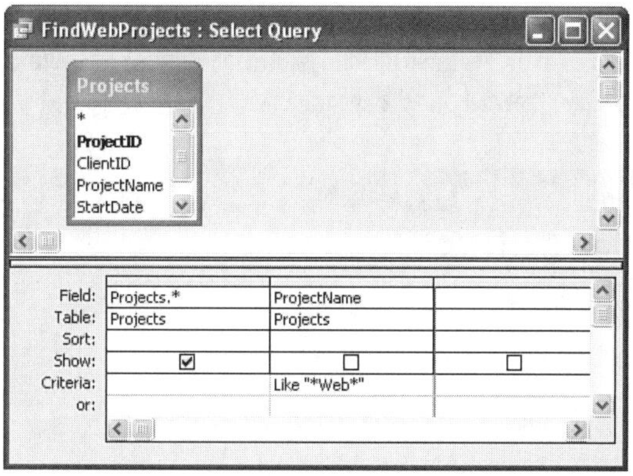

Figure 1.4
The design view of an Access query is just a pretty face atop the query's SQL.

FindWebProjects : Select Query

Projects
*
ProjectID
ClientID
ProjectName
StartDate

Field:	Projects.*	ProjectName	
Table:	Projects	Projects	
Sort:			
Show:	☑	☐	☐
Criteria:		Like "*Web*"	
or:			

Although SQL isn't a general-purpose programming language, you'll need to understand the basics to work with Access. That's because many automation tasks in Access involve retrieving particular data, and SQL is the way to do that.

→ If you're not familiar with SQL, you'll find a primer in Appendix A, "Review of Access SQL," page 347.

Using VBA

Finally, there's VBA, the focus of this book. VBA can automate just about any operation that you can perform in an Access database. Here are some of the things that we'll teach you to do throughout this book with VBA:

- Streamline data entry on Access forms
- Add new items to list boxes
- Customize the data that appears on reports
- Work with data without even opening a form
- Automate other applications from within Access
- Import and export XML files

That's just a small sample; the possibilities are nearly limitless. To demonstrate the power of VBA, we'll start with a simple database and gradually make it more complex (and useful).

CASE STUDY

Using the TimeTrack Sample Database

Of course, you'll eventually want to use the techniques that you learn from this book in your own databases. But to demonstrate them, we're going to use a sample database named TimeTrack.mdb. At this point, there's no VBA code at all in the TimeTrack database. It handles the basic activities involved in keeping track of billable time for a small software development company, but it's pretty bare bones.

When you open the database, you'll see the Switchboard form, shown in Figure 1.5. This form provides an interface to the other four forms and the single report that make up the application.

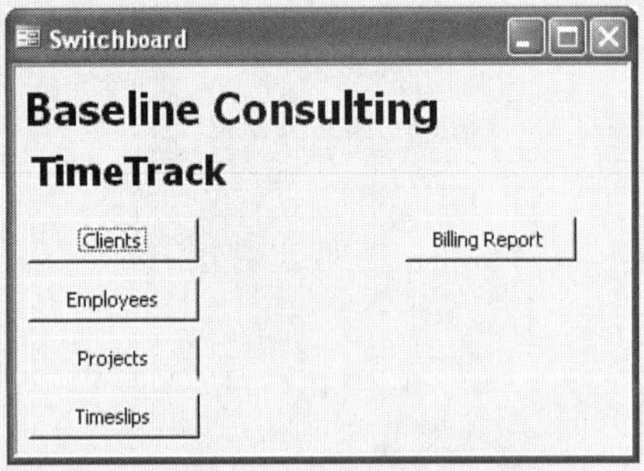

Figure 1.5
The Switchboard form is the starting point for the TimeTrack application.

Clicking the Clients button will show you the list of the firm's clients as well as the projects that are underway for each client. Figure 1.6 shows the form that displays this information.

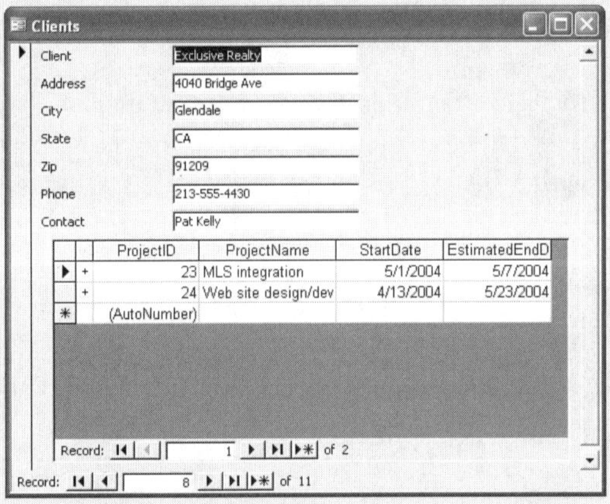

Figure 1.6
You can work with both clients and projects from the clients form.

Figure 1.7 shows the Employees form, which tracks basic information for each employee who can be assigned to work on a task.

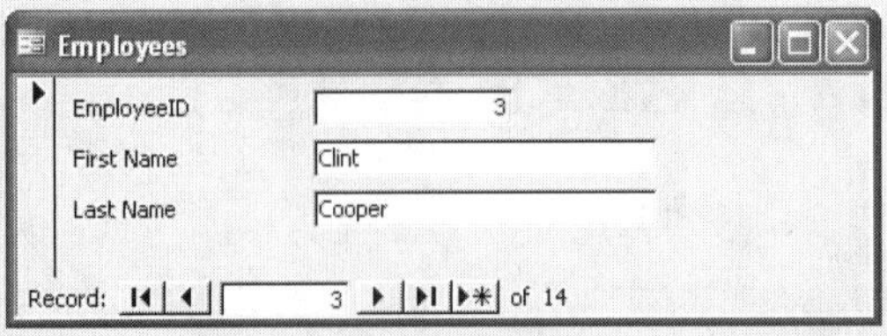

Figure 1.7
The Employees form displays basic information on each employee.

The Projects form is central to working with projects. For each project, you can choose the appropriate client. You can also enter the various tasks that make up the project and the billing rate associated with each one, as shown in Figure 1.8.

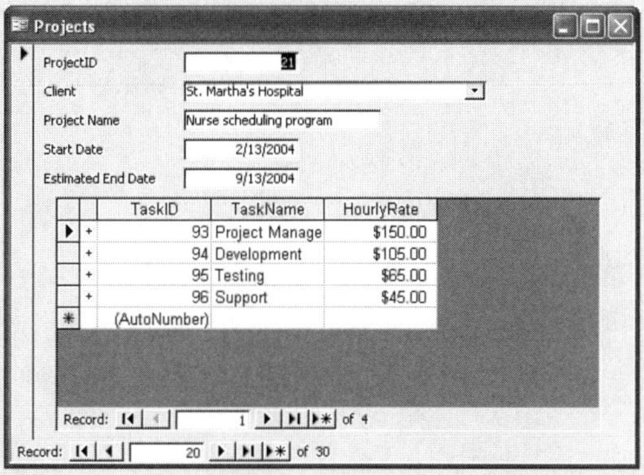

Figure 1.8
Projects contain tasks, which can be billed at different rates.

The last form in the application, shown in Figure 1.9, tracks timeslip information. After choosing an employee and a task, you can enter the date and the number of hours worked. This ensures that those hours are properly billed to the customer.

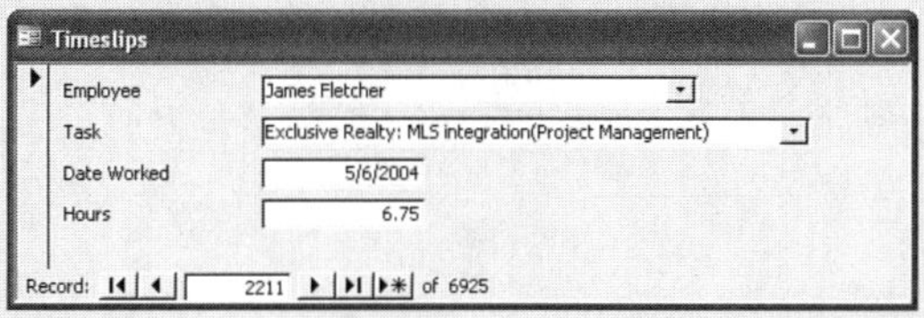

Figure 1.9
Timeslips record billable time.

Finally, Figure 1.10 shows the Billing Report, which is used to calculate charges for a client. When you run the report, it will prompt you to select a client as well as a starting date and an ending date.

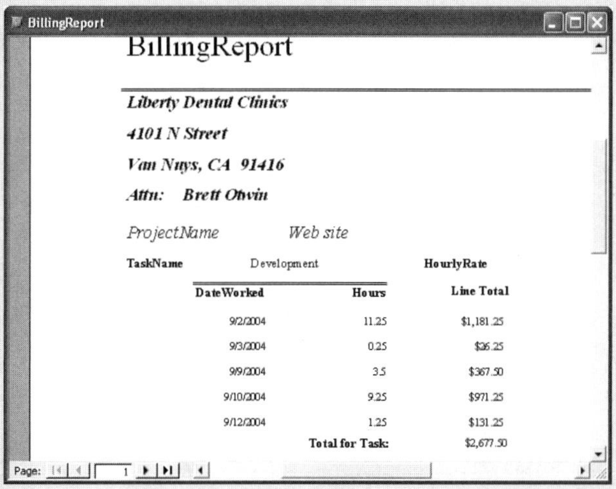

Figure 1.10
The Billing Report calculates the amount due from a client for a period of time.

Right now, all the automation in this database is done with macros. But it won't stay that way!

Getting Around in the Visual Basic Editor

Your First Glance at the Visual Basic Editor

The Visual Basic Editor (VBE) is the interface you'll use to write VBA code. Figure 2.1 shows the VBE window for the TimeTrack sample database. The easiest way to launch the VBE is to open Access, load the database, and then press Alt+F11. (If you're following along with an existing database, the VBE may display some code when you first open it.)

In this chapter, we'll introduce you to the many components you'll be working with and even let you enter a bit of code. We won't spend a lot of time learning about every single element, tool, and menu command in the VBE—you'll learn about them later by actually using them as you produce example code. For now, just familiarize yourself with the development environment so you'll be on friendly ground later.

2

IN THIS CHAPTER

Your First Glance at the Visual Basic Editor . .17

Introducing the VBA Modules 21

Entering and Running VBA Code 22

Getting Help on Code 25

Establishing Good Habits in Coding 28

By default, the VBE displays the following components:

- The menu is the default menu.
- The Standard toolbar is the default toolbar.
- Project Explorer displays a hierarchical list of the items contained and referenced in the current database.
- The Properties Window is a simple interface for displaying and modifying object properties.
- The Immediate window displays the results of code.

Figure 2.1
Welcome to the Access
Visual Basic Editor.

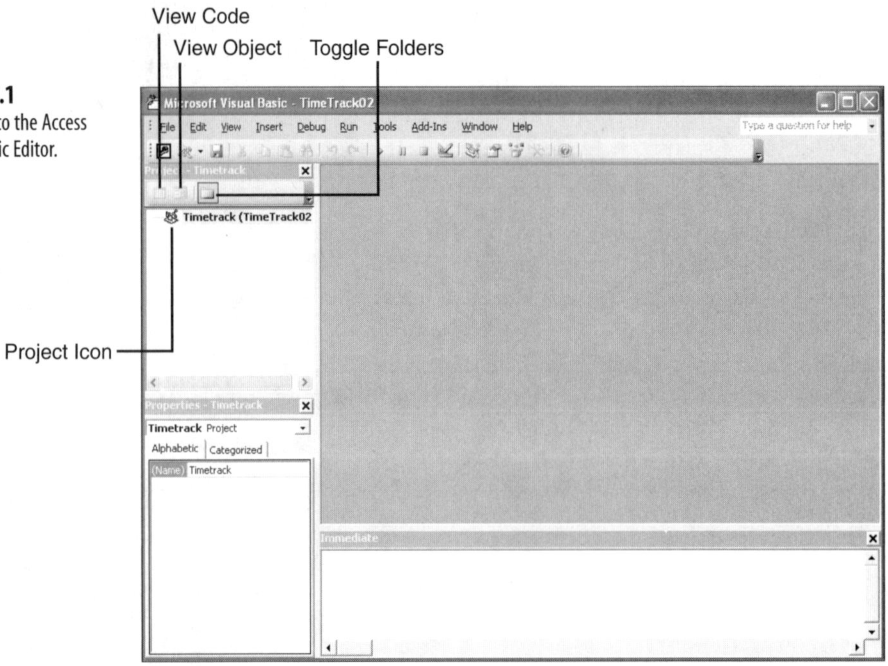

> T I P
> Individual windows in the VBE are dockable, just like most menus and toolbars. Double-click the title bar of a window to toggle docked and floating.

Table 2.1 describes the tools on the VBE's standard toolbar, which is shown in Figure 2.1. These are the tools you'll use most of the time.

Table 2.1 The Standard Toolbar

Name	Purpose	Keystroke Combination	Menu
View Microsoft Office Access	Displays the Access 2003 window without closing the VBE window.	Alt+F11	View, Microsoft Office Access
Insert Module	Creates a new and empty module. Choose a module type from the tool's drop-down list.		Insert, Module
Find	Searches for a specific word or phrase in the module.	Ctrl+F	Edit, Find
Undo	Cancels the last keyboard stroke or the last mouse operation (when possible).	Ctrl+Z	Edit, Undo
Redo	Cancels the last Undo action (when possible).		Edit, Redo
Run Sub/ UserForm	Executes the current procedure or continues execution after a procedure has been paused by a break condition.	F5	Run, Run Sub/UserForm
Break	Halts a procedure.	Ctrl+Break	Run, Break
Reset	Terminates a procedure and reinitializes all variables to their default values.	Shift+F5	Run, Reset
Design Mode	Toggles to UserForms design mode.		Run, Design Mode
Project Explorer	Opens the Project Explorer.	Ctrl+R	View, Project Explorer
Properties Window	Opens the Properties window.	F4	View, Properties Window
Object Browser	Opens the Object Browser window.	F2	View, Object Browser
Toolbox	Displays the Toolbox.		View, Toolbox
VBA Help	Opens the VBA online Help window.	F1	Help, Microsoft Visual Basic Help

2

Other tools are available on the three additional toolbars, two of which are shown in Figures 2.2 and 2.3. You'll learn more about the tools on these toolbars as you work through the examples in this book. A fourth toolbar, UserForm, is available, but we won't cover UserForms or the toolbar in this book.

> **NOTE**
>
> We won't be using UserForms because Access has its own forms, with which you should already be familiar. Access forms are more powerful and flexible than UserForms. Why, then, do UserForms even exist? The answer is that the VBE, and VBA itself, are shared components. You'll find VBA implemented in dozens of software packages, including other Microsoft Office applications, Autodesk's AutoCAD drawing package, Peachtree Office Accounting, and more. These other products, which lack their own forms interface, benefit from the inclusion of UserForms in VBA.

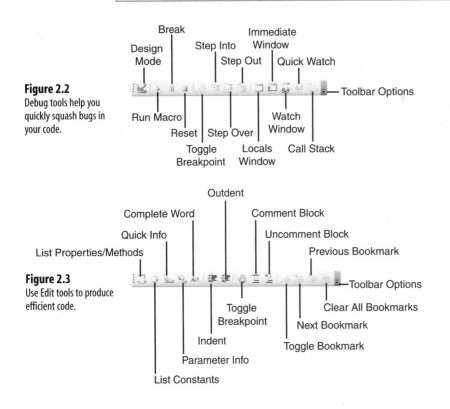

Figure 2.2
Debug tools help you quickly squash bugs in your code.

Figure 2.3
Use Edit tools to produce efficient code.

To display a toolbar, choose <u>V</u>iew, <u>T</u>oolbars and click the appropriate toolbar item: Debug, Edit, or Standard. (Uncheck an item to hide the toolbar.)

Introducing the VBA Modules

After launching the VBE, you'll probably want to view existing code or enter new code. All VBA code is contained in one of three types of modules:

- Standard—Contains code that's independent of a specific object.
- Object—Contains code that responds to the attached form or report. If you're already writing event procedures, you're doing so in these modules. Each form and report in an Access database can have its own object module.
- Class—Contains code that defines custom objects. You'll learn about class modules in Chapter 8, "Understanding Objects"

To insert a standard or class module, choose Insert, Module or Insert, Class Module, respectively. Access responds by inserting the appropriate type module.

Figure 2.4 shows a standard module in the VBE. Notice how inserting a new module updates the contents of both the Project Explorer and the Properties window. Enter procedures that are independent of any objects or events in a standard module. You can use objects and events in the code, but the module itself isn't defined by an object nor does it contain any predefined events.

Figure 2.4
Modules contain the VBA code that automates your database

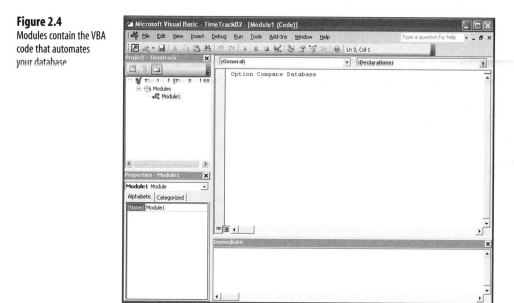

Object modules come with the forms or reports you create. They're really a type of class module, but you don't have to reinvent the wheel every time you want to add code to a form or report. These modules come with your forms and reports. The code in an object module is usually triggered by and responds to the object's events. However, an object module can contain a procedure that's not related to an event.

> **TIP**
>
> There are a number of keyboard shortcuts for moving around the VBE. Many of these are listed in Table 2.1, but there are many others. For instance, pressing Shift+F10 displays the active window's shortcut menu. (You can also display this menu by right-clicking the window.) To learn more shortcuts, search in the special VBA Help files for "Keyboard Shortcuts."

Entering and Running VBA Code

Enter code the same way you would enter data in a text editor—just start entering the appropriate declarations, variables, and statements into a module.

Once you're proficient with VBA code, that's probably exactly how you'll do it. Until then, you might want a little help. That's what the Insert Procedures dialog box is for.

→ A *procedure* is a self-contained, executable collection of code statements. Read "Understanding Procedure Types" in Chapter 4 (p. 45) for an in-depth discussion of procedures.

Follow these steps to create a new procedure:

1. If you don't already have a new open module (refer to Figure 2.4) in which to enter a procedure, choose Insert, Module to create one.

2. Choose Insert, Procedure to display the Insert Procedure dialog box.

3. Enter a descriptive but short name for the new procedure. In this case, use the name `OpenClientForm`.

4. Click a Type and a Scope option. When creating static variables, click the All Local Variables as Statics option. For this example, choose Sub and Public and ignore the static variable option.

5. Click OK when you're ready to create the procedure.

Don't worry if you don't know which options to choose yet. Figure 2.5 shows us creating a public sub procedure named `OpenClientForm`.

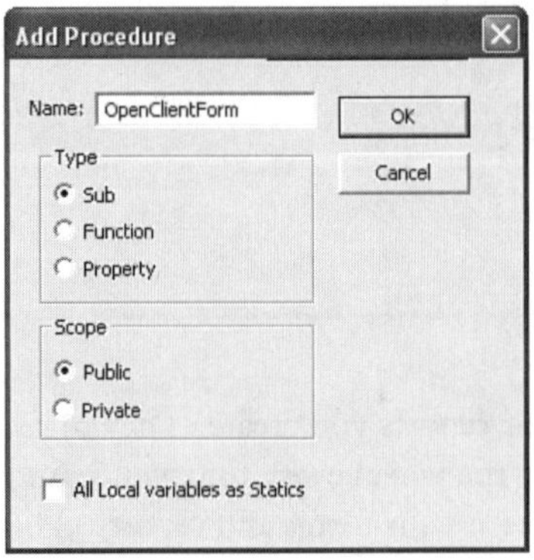

Figure 2.5
Set these options to define a new procedure.

→ You'll learn more about scope in "Declaring Procedures as Public or Private," p. 48.

When you click OK, the VBE enters what's known as a stub, as shown in Figure 2.6. A stub identifies the procedure as either a sub or function procedure, contains the procedure's name, and provides the procedure's required End statement. The stub doesn't contain any executable code—that's your job.

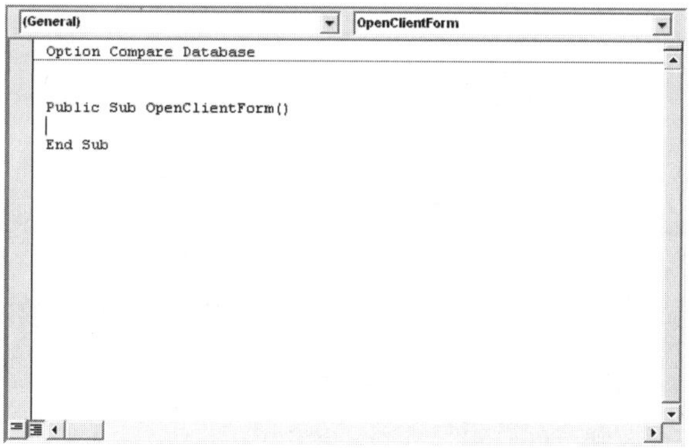

Figure 2.6
The VBE enters the new procedure's stub.

```
(General)                          OpenClientForm
    Option Compare Database

    Public Sub OpenClientForm()

    End Sub
```

Whether you start with a VBE generated stub or enter it yourself, it's your job to add the code. That's what you'll be learning to do throughout this book. For now, you're probably itching to actually accomplish something, so complete the procedure by inserting the additional code between the two provided statements as follows:

```
Public Sub OpenClientForm()
  ' Open the client form
  DoCmd.OpenForm "Clients"
  Debug.Print "The form is open"
End Sub
```

If the Immediate Window isn't already open at this point, open it by pressing Ctrl+G. Now, run the procedure by inserting the mouse pointer anywhere inside the actual procedure (in the module) and pressing F5. Two things will happen. First, Access will open the Clients form shown in Figure 2.7 in the Access window, just as if you'd opened it by hand—even though you won't readily see it. (Switch to the Access window to view the opened form if you like, but it isn't necessary.) Second, the procedure will print the message shown in Figure 2.8 in the Immediate window.

Normally, you won't display values in the Immediate window. Instead, you'll use them in your code somehow. For now, it's enough to see that you can display results in the Immediate window, which is a great way to debug your code.

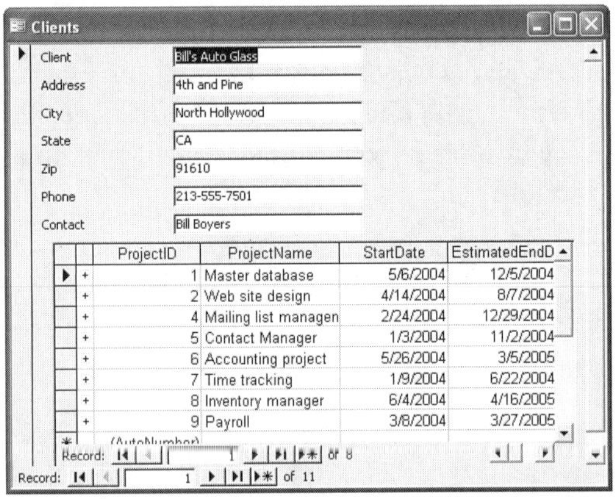

Figure 2.7
Running the procedure
opens an Access form.

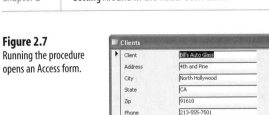

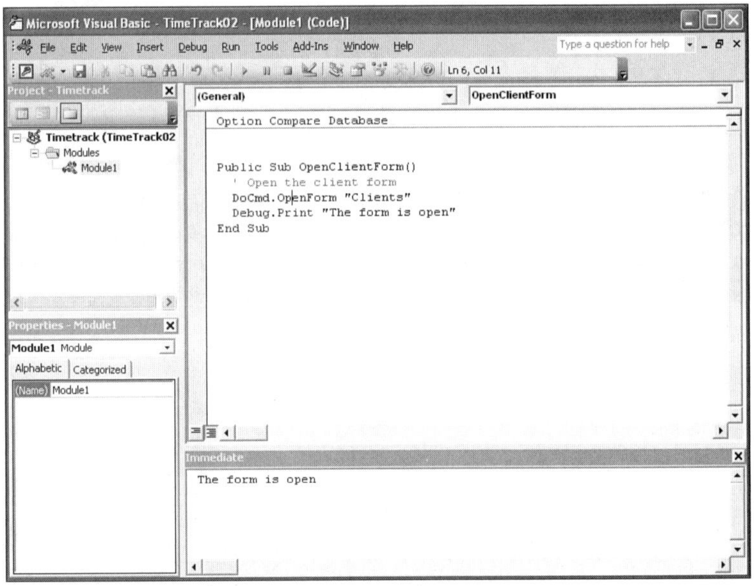

Figure 2.8
The procedure displays a
message in the
Immediate window.

Saving the Code

To save a new module or to save changes made to an existing module, click the Save tool on
the Standard toolbar or choose File, Save *project*. When saving a new module, Access 2003
displays the Save As dialog box. Accept the default name or enter a new one, as shown in
Figure 2.9, and choose OK.

CAUTION

You can close the VBE without losing unsaved code, although it isn't advisable. However, once you
close a module any unsaved code is lost.

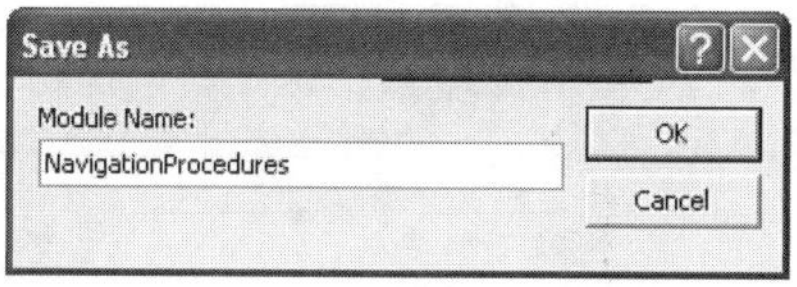

Figure 2.9
Be sure to save a new module.

Notice that the new module is listed in the Project Explorer as shown in Figure 2.10. (It was there as Module1.) It's also worth noting that highlighting the new module (Chapter2) in the Project Explorer updates the contents of the Properties window. Currently, there are no properties to display other than the name of the module. You'll become accustomed to working with and even depending upon these windows.

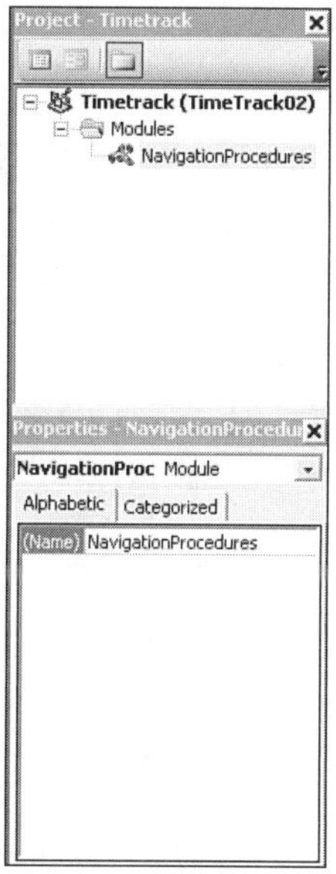

Figure 2.10
Saving the module updates its name in the Project Explorer.

Getting Help on Code

Few of us ever get so good at writing code that we stop making mistakes. In fact, most of us spend a lot of time perfecting (fixing) code. Fortunately, the VBE provides a powerful and flexible Help system that's completely separate from the Access 2003 Help system.

Open the Visual Basic Help task pane shown in Figure 2.11 to access all this information. There are two ways to do so. Choose <u>H</u>elp, Microsoft Visual Basic <u>H</u>elp or choose <u>V</u>iew, <u>T</u>oolbars, Task Pane.

This task pane works similar to the old Help system but doesn't usurp your entire VBE container window. Enter a word or phrase in the Search control to return a list of links in the Search Results task pane.

Figure 2.11
Search for help on VBA topics in the new Visual Basic Search task pane.

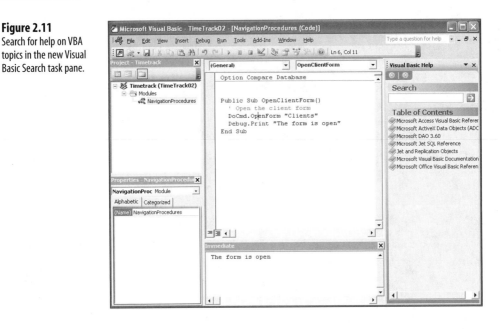

> **TIP**   The quickest way to get help is to position the cursor in the middle of a keyword (function, property, method) and then press F1. The Help system displays the most appropriate topic on the selected term.

Helpful Shortcuts for Entering Code

You can rely on the VBA Help topics for quick information about the VBA language, but sometimes, you don't need quite so much information. As you enter code into a module, a special feature called *IntelliSense* kicks in. When the VBE can guess what you might be about to type, it displays a pop-up window with appropriate values to help you complete the statement.

The list is always context-sensitive. You may have noticed this happening when you were entering the first bit of example code. To illustrate this feature, let's work through another example.

1. On a fresh line in the Immediate Window, type **DoCmd.** (including the period character). As soon as you enter the period character, the VBE displays the pop-up shown in Figure 2.12.

2. Choose OpenForm from the list. You can use the scroll bar to find it, or you can press the Down arrow until it's visible. Highlight OpenForm and then press Tab (or double-click).

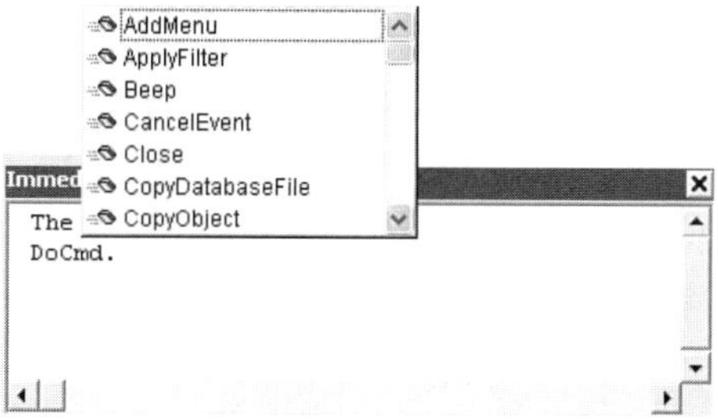

Figure 2.12
The pop-up list limits its contents to values that are relevant to the word you're entering.

3. Enter a space character and the VBE displays a new list. This time the list contains the OpenForm's arguments as shown in Figure 2.13.

Figure 2.13
This feature can display a method's arguments.

4. The first argument is the form's name. After entering an appropriate reference and the following comma, the VBE displays the next argument constants, as shown in Figure 2.14. You haven't been introduced to arguments or constants yet. In this case, they both represent values used by the OpenForm method. You'll learn more about arguments and constants throughout this book.

Figure 2.14
Choose from a limited list of constants.

If you need help but the list isn't visible, right-click the keyword to display the list shown in Figure 2.15. Click the appropriate option for additional help. (This action in the Immediate window is less useful because the resulting list is much shorter.)

Figure 2.15
Right-click a keyword to
get additional help.

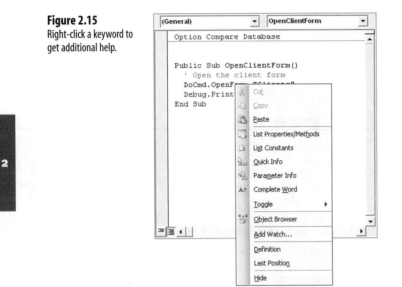

Establishing Good Habits in Coding

Getting the job done is rarely your only goal when customizing your database using VBA code. From the very beginning, you should think like a professional developer by writing readable code that's easy to follow with little effort. We offer three recommendations:

- Name variables and objects consistently.

- Indent your code to show structural flow.

- Comment your code so you can remember what your code does later—because you will forget. Besides, you might not be the one updating your code.

Using a Naming Convention

As you write VBA code, you'll create variables and objects, which need a name. You can name them any way you please, but we recommend that you use a consistent convention.

→ You'll learn how to create and use variables in "Declaring Variables and Constants" in Chapter 3 (p. 33) You'll learn more about objects in Chapter 8 (p. 113).

A *naming convention* is a set of rules that determine the names of variables and objects. Your company or organization may have a convention, and if that's the case, you'll apply those rules. If you have to choose one, don't let the task overwhelm you because the key is to consistently apply a convention—any convention, even if it's your own.

A good convention will indicate the type of object or variable you're creating. A fairly common form using the following syntax:

classObjectName

where *class* is a three-letter prefix that identifies the type of object or a variable's data type, and *ObjectName* is a purposeful, descriptive name. Notice the strange letter case in the form:

- *class* is lowercase.
- *ObjectName* uses camel or title case—the first letter of each word is uppercase.

Also, notice that the name contains no spaces.

Throughout this book we'll work with a common convention that's based on the Hungarian convention. This convention adheres to the preceding rules. In addition, we'll use what's known as the *natural* naming system, whereby the object and variable names identify their purpose or the data they contain.

Tables 2.2 and 2.3 list the most common prefixes. Neither list is complete by any means, but these are the tags that we'll use throughout this book and that you'll probably encounter most often.

Table 2.2   Object Tags

Access Object	Prefix
table	tbl
query	qry
form	frm
report	rpt
check box	chk
combo box	cbo
command button	cmd
label	lbl
list box	lst
option button	opt
subform/subreport	sub
text box	txt

Table 2.3 Variable Tags	
Data Type	**Tag**
byte	byt
integer	int
single	sng
long integer	lng
double	dbl
text	str
currency	cur
date/time	dtm
Boolean	boo

At first, you might wonder what all the fuss is about, but as you produce more code, you'll begin to appreciate a consistent naming scheme. Most importantly, you can tell at a glance what type of variable or object you're dealing with, and that can mean a lot when you're debugging or maintaining code.

Indenting Your Code

You may have noticed that the code in the earlier example is indented. This is another good habit you should establish early because the indentations help indicate the code's structural flow.

For example, each line is our earlier sample procedure (refer to Figure 2.8) in indented two spaces from the procedure's name and End statements. These indents simply make it easier to read the code. After awhile you'll indent code automatically.

You can insert an indent using the VBE's interface. To do so, highlight the code in the module, and then choose Edit, Indent or Outdent, appropriately. The Indent command enters one tab; Outdent removes a tab. By default, these tabs are equal to four characters.

> **TIP**
>
> Indents are a clue to the code's structure and flow. Another way to distinguish individual steps is to add a blank line at logical points. Whether you do so is up to you, but you'll probably find that a blank line helps you locate specific sections of code much quicker.

Commenting Your Code

Adding comments that describe your code's purpose is always a good idea. To add a comment, simply preface it with the apostrophe character ('), as you did in earlier in the chapter:

```
Public Sub OpenClientForm()
  ' Open the client form
  DoCmd.OpenForm "Clients"
  Debug.Print "The form is open"
End Sub
```

Each procedure should have an introductory comment that describes the procedure's purpose. Code composed of many lines and tasks will require more comments. There's a knack that comes to knowing just when and just what to say, but here are a few guidelines that should help:

- Be as succinct as possible.

- Be as descriptive as possible.

- Use grammatically correct sentences and phrases.

- Use punctuation when appropriate.

- Avoid comments that simply restate the code.

- Comment passed arguments if attributes aren't obvious in the code.

- Comment revisions—who made the change, when it was made, and why. (Not all developers include these comments.)

- Write comments as you write the code and the task and any problems worth commenting are still clear in your mind.

Another commenting format places comments in line and to the right of the actual code. We won't use this format in this book, but you'll probably encounter it when reviewing existing code.

The Edit toolbar contains commenting tools that can help you comment or uncomment a large block of code. To illustrate, display the toolbar by choosing View, Toolbars, Edit. Then, highlight a block of code and click Comment Block on the Edit toolbar. Figure 2.16 shows the results of commenting an entire procedure with one quick click. Click Uncomment Block on the Edit toolbar to remove comments.

Figure 2.16
Quickly comment out an entire procedure.

Using Variables, Constants, and Data Types

Declaring Variables and Constants

The key to learning VBA is the same as if you were learning a foreign language. You must learn the basics first. VBA, like any language, has its own syntax and components that you must combine in just the right way for Access to understand your message and respond. Until you learn these rules, you'll find it difficult, if not impossible, to speak to Access.

VBA uses variables and constants to represent a value. Technically, a *variable* is a small portion of memory that stores a piece of information, but people tend to think of them as names that represent data. Constants are similar to variables in that they store a value. What the two have in common is that both represent values or objects. The main difference between the two is that a constant represents a value that doesn't change, whereas variables can be updated at any time.

IN THIS CHAPTER

Declaring Variables and Constants 33

Referencing Syntax 42

Declaring Variables

Variables are a representation of a value or an object. You assign a descriptive name using your naming convention, declare a data type for the variable and then use it, reuse it, and even change it.

Before you use a variable, declare it using the `Dim` statement in the form

```
Dim variablename As [New] datatype
```

where *variablename* identifies the variable by name, and *datatype* is one of many VBA data types. If you omit *datatype*, VBA defaults to a Variant. It's best to always explicitly declare a variable's data type. Variant variables require slightly more memory and are slightly slower than other types of variables. On the other hand, they don't limit the type of data you store. But you are unlikely to have the requirement to store many types of data in a single variable, which is the only good use for a variant.

→ The New keyword is optional and can only be used when declaring an object variable. To learn more about this issue, read Chapter 8, "Understanding Objects" (p. 113).

> **TIP** Generally, Dim statements appear at the beginning of a procedure. This arrangement isn't required, but you'll find most developers adhere to this guideline. By grouping them at the beginning, you can find them much quicker.

You can declare a number of variables in a single line by separating them with commas, as follows:

```
Dim variable1 As datatype, variable2 As datatype
```

> **TIP** Declared variables are supported by IntelliSense. That means you can choose the variable from the completion drop-down list rather than enter it from the keyboard—thus avoiding typos.

Using Option Explicit

By default, VBA lets you enter undeclared variables in your code. To illustrate, open a standard blank module and enter the following code:

```
Private Function DeclarationTest()
  varValue = "Undeclared variable"
  Debug.Print varValu
End Function
```

Be sure to open the Immediate window if necessary by pressing Ctrl+G. Next, position the cursor inside the procedure and press F5 to execute it. Did you expect to see the string, "Undeclared variable" in the Immediate window? The reason you don't see the string is because varValue is misspelled in the Debug.Print statement. The variable varValue does equal the string "Undeclared variable;", but the variable varValu equals Empty at this point. Finding the problem can be difficult, especially in a long and complex procedure.

VBA can force you to declare variables to avoid such problems—which is a good practice. To do so, enter the Option Explicit statement in the module's General Declarations area. After doing so, execute the procedure again. This time, VBA returns the error shown in Figure 3.1.

The Option Explicit statement can mean the difference between errors and no errors—and all you have to do is turn it on. We strongly recommend that you enable this feature and leave it on to avoid the almost unavoidable typos that occur when writing code.

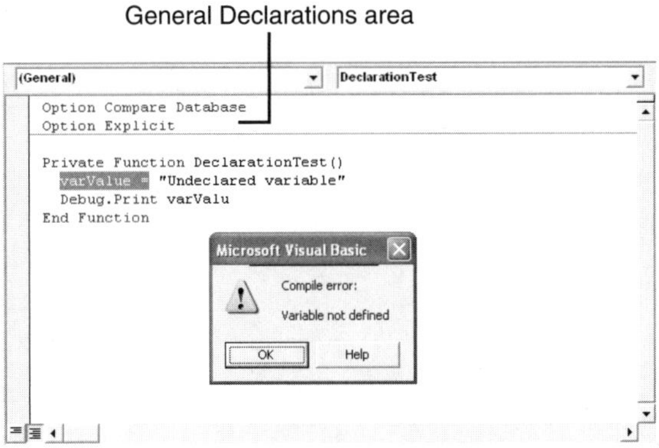

Figure 3.1
Undeclared variables return an error when you're using Option Explicit.

General Declarations area

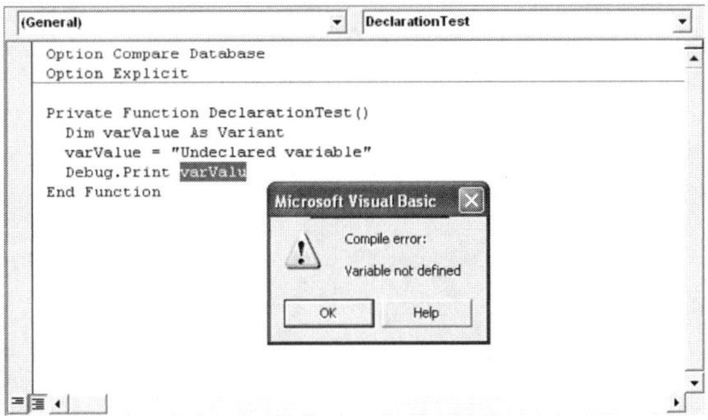

Figure 3.2
VBA catches a misspelled variable.

Click OK to close the error message, and then click Reset to clear the error. Declare the variable by adding the following `Dim` statement to the beginning of the procedure:

```
Dim varValue As Variant
```

Next, run the procedure a third time. This time, VBA catches the misspelled variable varValu, as shown in Figure 3.2. Click OK and then click Reset to clear the error and fix the misspelled variable. At this point, if you run the procedure, you'll see the expected string in the Immediate window, as shown in Figure 3.3.

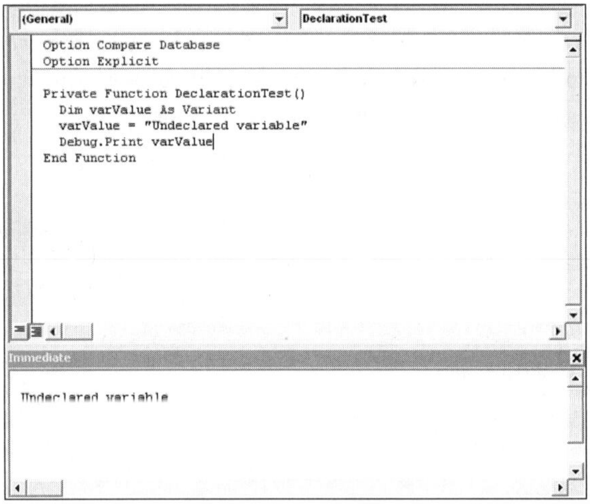

Figure 3.3
After fixing the misspelled variable, VBA runs the procedure as expected.

```
(General)                          ▼   DeclarationTest                    ▼

   Option Compare Database
   Option Explicit

   Private Function DeclarationTest()
     Dim varValue As Variant
     varValue = "Undeclared variable"
     Debug.Print varValue
   End Function



Immediate                                                             ☒

   Undeclared variable

```

The previous method enables the automatic variable declaration feature for only the current module. To enable this feature for all new modules, do the following:

1. In the VBE, choose Tools, Options.

2. Click the Editor tab.

3. Check the Require Variable Declaration option shown in Figure 3.4.

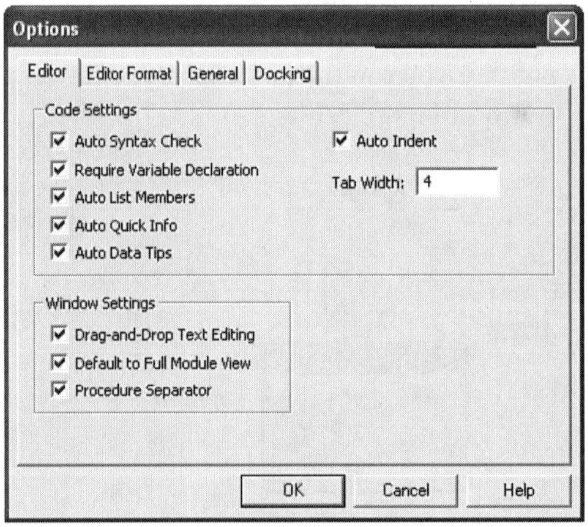

Figure 3.4
Enable the automatic variable declaration feature.

```
Options                                                    ☒

 Editor │ Editor Format │ General │ Docking │

 ┌─ Code Settings ─────────────────────────────────────┐
 │   ☑ Auto Syntax Check          ☑ Auto Indent        │
 │   ☑ Require Variable Declaration                     │
 │   ☑ Auto List Members          Tab Width:  4        │
 │   ☑ Auto Quick Info                                  │
 │   ☑ Auto Data Tips                                   │
 └──────────────────────────────────────────────────────┘

 ┌─ Window Settings ───────────────────────────────────┐
 │   ☑ Drag-and-Drop Text Editing                      │
 │   ☑ Default to Full Module View                     │
 │   ☑ Procedure Separator                             │
 └──────────────────────────────────────────────────────┘

              OK          Cancel          Help
```

4. Click OK to close the Options dialog box.

CAUTION

Enabling the Require Variable Declarations feature for all modules affects only new modules inserted after enabling the feature. You must update any existing modules by adding the Option Explicit statement manually.

Naming Variables

Your naming convention should also cover variables. Aside from your naming convention, there are a few inherent rules you need to consider:

- A variable name must begin with an alphabetic character.
- Don't use the following special characters in a variable name: ., %, $, !, #, @, and $.
- Variable names must be unique. It really isn't as simple as all that, but for now, knowing that you can't give two variables in the same procedure the same name is sufficient.
- A variable name can consist of up to 255 characters.

→ Naming conventions are covered in Chapter 2, in the section "Establishing Good Habits in Coding," (p. 28).

Declaring Constants

You'll find that the term *constant* has many meanings in VBA. A constant represents a literal value, much in the same way a variable represents a value or an object. The difference is, the value of a constant can't be changed while the code is executing—not even by mistake.

Use the Const statement to declare a constant in the form

```
[Public ¦ Private] Const constantname As datatype = expression
```

Items in square brackets are optional, and the vertical bar indicates a choice. So a constant declaration can start with Public, or Private, or just Const. In any case, *constantname* identifies the constant by name, *datatype* specifies the constant's data type, and *expression* is the literal value that the constant equals. The *expression* argument can't refer to a variable, a result of a function procedure, or include one of VBA's many built-in functions.

The following example illustrates the use of a constant:

1. In a standard module, enter the following statement in the General Declarations area:

```
Const conMessage As String = "Undeclared variable"
```

2. Enter the following procedure using the Insert Procedure dialog box or from the keyboard:

```
Private Function ConstantTest()
    Dim varValue As Variant
    varValue = conMessage
    Debug.Print varValue
End Function
```

3. With the insertion point somewhere inside ConstantTest(), press F5 to execute the procedure. As you can see in Figure 3.5, the Debug.Print statement prints the contents of the variable varValue, which refers to conMessage (the constant).

Change the string expression in the Const statement to "Constant" and run the procedure again. This time, varValue equals "Constant", as shown in Figure 3.6. Now imagine several references to conMessage throughout your module. Instead of updating each and every reference, you change just the value of conMessage in the Const declaration statement.

Figure 3.5
The `varValue` variable equals the constant named `conMessage`.

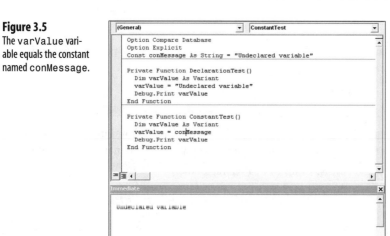

```
Option Compare Database
Option Explicit
Const conMessage As String = "Undeclared variable"

Private Function DeclarationTest()
    Dim varValue As Variant
    varValue = "Undeclared variable"
    Debug.Print varValue
End Function

Private Function ConstantTest()
    Dim varValue As Variant
    varValue = conMessage
    Debug.Print varValue
End Function
```

Immediate

```
Undeclared variable
```

Figure 3.6
Change the constant value in the `Const` declaration statement.

```
Option Compare Database
Option Explicit
Const conMessage As String = "Constant"

Private Function DeclarationTest()
    Dim varValue As Variant
    varValue = "Undeclared variable"
    Debug.Print varValue
End Function

Private Function ConstantTest()
    Dim varValue As Variant
    varValue = conMessage
    Debug.Print varValue
End Function
```

Immediate

```
Undeclared variable
Constant
```

Intrinsic Constants

In addition to letting you define your own constants, VBA offers a number of predefined constants, known as *intrinsic constants*, that you can use to specify specific data types (and other values).

There are two advantages to using these constants. First, you don't have to define them yourself. Second, they improve the readability of your code. The intrinsic constant's name describes its value or purpose, thus making it instantly recognizable. To assign one of these subtypes to a variable, use that subtype's corresponding intrinsic constant as follows:

```
varValue = vbEmpty
```

Intrinsic constants are predefined by VBA; you don't define them in your code, you simply refer to them in expressions and statements. You revisit intrinsic constants in the next section.

VBA Data Types

When you declare a variable, you should also identify its data type. You're probably already very familiar with data types because you assign data types to table fields. VBA uses the same data types to define a variable.

The most important job of a data type is to ensure the validity of your data. Specifying a data type won't keep you from entering an invalid value, but it will keep you from entering an invalid *type*. If you omit the data type, VBA applies the Variant data type to your variable—it's the most flexible and VBA won't guess at what the data type should be. Table 3.1 compares VBA's many data types.

Table 3.1 VBA Data Type Comparison

Data Type or Subtype	Required Memory	Default Value	VBA Constant	Range
Integer	2 bytes	0	`vbInteger`	–32,768 to 32,767
Long Integer	4 bytes	0	`vbLong`	–2,147,483,648 to 2,147,486,647
Single	4 bytes	0	`vbSingle`	–3402823E38 to –1.401298E–45 or 1.401298E–45 to 3.402823E38
Double	8 bytes	0	`vbDouble`	–1.79769313486232E308 to –4.94065645841247E–324 or 1.79769313486232E308 to 4.94065645841247E–324
Currency	8 bytes	0	`vbCurrency`	–922,337,203,477.5808 to 922,337,203,685,477.5807
Date	8 bytes	00:00:00	`vbDate`	January 1, 100 to December 31, 9999
Fixed String	String's length	Number of spaces to accommodate string	`vbString`	1 to 65,400 characters
Variable String	10 bytes plus the number of characters	Zero-length string ("")	`vbString`	0 to 2 billion characters
Object	4 bytes	Nothing (`vbNothing`)	`vbObject`	Any Access object, ActiveX component or Class object

continues

3

Table 3.1   Continued

Data Type or Subtype	Required Memory	Default Value	VBA Constant	Range
Boolean	2 bytes	False	vbBoolean	−1 or 0
Variant	16 bytes	Empty (vbEmpty)	vbVariant	Same as Double
Decimal	14 bytes	0	vbDecimal	−79,228,162,514,264,337,593,543,950,335 to 79,228,162,514,264,337,593,543,950,335 or −7.2998162514264337593543950335 to 7.9228162514264337593543950335
Byte	1 byte	0	vbByte	0 to 255

The Boolean **Data Type**

Use the Boolean numeric data type to store logical data that contains only two values: on and off, true and value, yes and no, and so on. The keywords True and False are predefined constants and are interchangeable with the values −1 and 0, respectively. To illustrate these keywords, enter the following statements, one at a time in the VBE's Immediate window, as shown in Figure 3.7:

```
?True = 0
?True = -1
?False = 0
?False = -1
?True = False
```

Figure 3.7
True and False
equal −1 and 0, respec-
tively.

```
?True = 0
False
?True = -1
True
?False = 0
True
?False = -1
False
?True = False
False
```

The Byte **Data Type**

Byte is VBA's smallest numeric data type and holds a numeric value from 0 to 255. This data type doesn't include any negative values. If you attempt to assign one, VBA returns an error.

The Currency **Data Type**

Use the Currency numeric data type to store monetary values from −922,337,203,477.5808 to 922,337,203,685,477.5807. A Currency data type results in a scaled value with accuracy to 15 digits to the left of the decimal point and 4 digits to the right. Use this data type to avoid rounding errors when precision is of the utmost importance.

The Date **Data Type**

The Date data type stores a specially formatted numeric value that represents both the date and time. You don't have to store both the date and time value. The Date data type accepts either the date or the time, or both. Possible values range from January 1, 100 to December 31, 9999.

The Decimal **Data Type**

The Decimal data type is a subtype of Variant and not a truly separate data type all its own, accommodating values from –79,228,162,514,264,337,593,543,950,335 to 79,228,162,514,264,337,593,543,950,335 if the value contains no decimal places. The data type maintains precision up to 28 decimal places with values from –7.9228162514264337593543950335 to 7.9228162514264337593543950335.

The Double **Data Type**

Use the Double data type to store precision floating point numbers from –1.79769313486232E308 to –4.94065645841247E-324 or 1.79769313486232E308 to 4.94065645841247E-324.

The Integer **Data Type**

This is probably the most common data type in use, besides String. Use this data type to store only whole numbers that range from –32,768 to 32,767.

The Long **Data Type**

The Long data type is also an Integer data type storing only whole numbers, but the range is much larger than the traditional Integer data type. Use Long to store values from –2,147,483,648 to 2,147,486,647.

The Object **Data Type**

An Object variable is actually a reference to an Access object, such as a form, report, or control. Or, the data type can reference an ActiveX component, or a class object created in a class module.

→ Class modules are covered briefly in "Introducing the VBA Modules," in Chapter 2 (p. 21) and in more depth in "Introducing Objects," in Chapter 8 (p. 113).

→ You'll learn more about Object variables in " in Chapter 8, "Understanding Objects" (p. 113).

The Single **Data Type**

The Single data type stores precision numbers—numbers with decimal places or fractional numbers. The data type is similar to Double, but the range is smaller. Use this data type to store values from –3402823E38 to –1.401298E–45 or from 1.401298E–45 to 3.402823E38.

The `String` **Data Type**

`String` is another very common data type; it stores values or numbers, but treats them as text. There are two varieties: fixed and variable. A fixed string can handle from 1 to 65,400 characters. To declare a fixed string, use the `Dim` statement in the form

```
Dim variablename As String * stringlength
```

In contrast, the variable `String` data type grows and shrinks as required to fit its stored value. By default, all `String` variables are of this type. To declare this type, use the `Dim` statement in the form

```
Dim variablename As String
```

The `Variant` **Data Type**

The `Variant` data type stores numeric and non-numeric values. This data type is the most flexible of the bunch because it stores very large values of almost any type (matches the Double numeric data type). Use it only when you're uncertain of the data's type or when you're accommodating foreign data and you're not sure of the data type's specifications.

The Variant data type is VBA's default, so the following code interprets `varValue` as a Variant:

```
Dim varValue
```

Although the Variant data type is flexible, VBA processes these data types a little slower because it must determine the most accurate data type for the assigned value. However, most likely, you'll never notice the performance hit.

The biggest disadvantage is the data type's lack of readability. By that, we mean that you can't easily determine the appropriate data type by viewing the code, and that can be a problem.

Referencing Syntax

A great deal of your code will reference Access objects—forms and controls for the most part. Knowing how to reference objects and data correctly is one of the basics you need to master. You can start by learning a few new terms:

- *Identifier*—An expression that identifies the value of a control, property, or another expression.

- *Operator*—Within this context, an operator is a symbol used to separate an identifier's individual components. An identifier can have several layers. There are two identifier operators: the dot and the bang—the period and exclamation characters, respectively. You read about just the bang operator in this section.

- *Qualifier*—Identifies an object's collection.

→ Learn more about the dot operator in "Reading and Setting Properties," in Chapter 8 (p. 116).

When referencing objects, VBA needs to know not only what object to reference but also what kind of object it is. At this point, `TimeTrack.mdb` (the sample database you customize throughout this book) has several objects—tables, forms, reports, and even a VBA module. In addition, more than 60 controls comprise the application's forms and reports. There are a lot of possible references.

To reference any of these objects, use the form

`qualifier![objectname]`

where `qualifier` identifies the object's collection and `objectname` identifies the object. Notice that the bang character (!) separates the two components. For instance, to refer to the Clients form in `TimeTrack.mdb`, you use the following expression

`Forms![Clients]`

`Forms` refers to the form collection, and `Clients` is the name of the form. To reference the billing report, you use the expression

`Reports![BillingReport]`

Controls are a little different because a control belongs to the form or report (the *parent* object). That means you have to work through two layers of objects (identifiers in this case) using the form

`qualifier![objectname]![controlname]`

where `qualifier` is either `Forms` or `Reports`.

> **CAUTION**
>
> Controls display data retrieved from a field in a specific table or query. The term *field* refers to the column in the table or query where the data is stored. A *control* is an object that displays that data in a form or report. Often, you will see controls that share the same name as the underlying field that supplies the data, which can cause confusion. Most developers try to differentiate between the two elements by using a prefix tag in the control's name. As a result, `txtFirstName` becomes the name of a control that displays data stored in a field named `FirstName`.

To illustrate this syntax, look at the Employees form shown in Figure 3.8. This form has three controls, `EmployeeID`, `FirstName`, and `LastName`. Each control's full name contains a qualifier, the form's identifier, and the control's identifier:

```
Forms![Employees]![EmployeeID]
Forms![Employees]![FirstName]
Forms![Employees]![LastName]
```

All three controls belong to the Controls collection for this form, which is the form object's default collection. Consequently, you can omit the Controls collection reference.

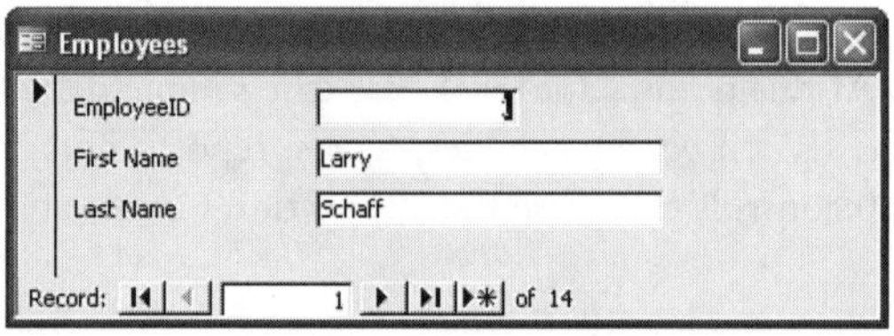

Figure 3.8
A collection of controls belongs to the form or report.

TIP

You probably noticed that each object is enclosed in brackets ([ ]). The brackets keep VBA from returning an error if the name contains a space character. When there's no space character, you can omit the brackets. However, if you forget about the rule and omit the brackets when the name does contain spaces, VBA will return an error. That's why many developers include them out of habit rather than need—just in case. The best solution is to omit space characters in object names.

Using Procedures

Understanding Procedure Types

VBA code is organized into *statements*. A statement is a single line of code, for example:

```
intCount = 6
```

This statement sets the value of the `intCount` variable to 6. Although you can execute individual statements in the Immediate window, you can't store individual statements in a VBA module. Within a module, statements must be organized into *procedures*: groups of statements that perform a task together. Although you've already seen a few procedures in the brief bits of code demonstrated in earlier chapters, this chapter gives you a much more in-depth look at creating and using procedures.

To start, you need to understand the difference between two types of procedures:

- Sub procedures
- Function procedures

→ There are also two specialized types of procedures that aren't covered in this chapter: property procedures and event procedures. For information on these types of procedures, see "Reading and Setting Properties," p. 116 and "Working with Events," p. 126.

Creating and Using Sub Procedures

A *sub procedure* is a procedure that does not return a value (you learn more about returning values in the next section of this chapter). Here's a very simple sub procedure:

```
Sub Procedure1()
  ' Print a message to the immediate window
  Debug.Print "Hello"
End Sub
```

A sub procedure starts with the keyword `Sub`, followed by the name of the procedure (in this case, `Procedure1`) and an empty pair of parentheses.

Understanding Procedure Types 45

Declaring Procedures as Public or Private . . .48

Passing Arguments 49

Giving a Function a Data Type 51

Implementing Error Handling 52

Debugging Code 54

The sub procedure ends with the keywords End Sub. In between, you can have as many statements as you like. In Procedure1, there's a comment followed by a Debug.Print statement (recall that Debug.Print prints whatever follows on the line to the Immediate window).

You can run a sub procedure from the Immediate window simply by typing the name of the procedure and pressing Enter, as shown in Figure 4.1.

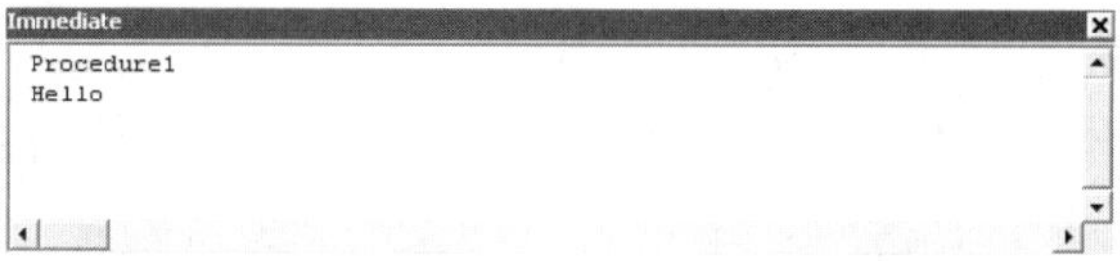

Figure 4.1
Running a sub procedure
from the Immediate
window.

Procedures can contain more than one statement. In this case, VBA executes each statement in turn, starting at the top of the procedure. For example, consider this sub procedure:

```
Sub Procedure2()
  ' Add two numbers together
  Dim intFirst As Integer
  Dim intSecond As Integer
  intFirst = 4
  intSecond = 7
  Debug.Print intFirst + intSecond
End Sub
```

If you run this procedure from the Immediate window, you'll see that it prints 11, the sum of the two numbers.

Procedures wouldn't be much use if they could only be run from the Immediate window, though. Fortunately, there are two other ways to run a procedure:

- From another procedure
- From the Access user interface

To run a sub procedure from another procedure, you include the name of the called procedure as a statement within the calling procedure, as in this example of two procedures:

```
Sub Procedure3()
  ' Display execution of another procedure
  Debug.Print "In Procedure3"
  Procedure4
  Debug.Print "Back in procedure3"
End Sub


Sub Procedure4()
  ' Print a message
  Debug.Print "In Procedure4"
End Sub
```

Figure 4.2 shows the result of running Procedure3 from the Immediate window. As you can see, it prints the first message in Procedure3, and then switches to Procedure4. When Procedure4 is done with its work, execution returns to Procedure3.

Figure 4.2
A sub procedure calling
another sub procedure.

→ You learn about calling procedures from the Access user interface in Chapter 10, "Working with Forms," p. 145.

Creating and Using Function Procedures

The second type of procedure you'll use is the *function procedure*. Function procedures are almost identical to sub procedures, except that function procedures return a value. Here's a simple function procedure to introduce the idea:

```
Function Procedure5()
    Procedure5 = "Hello"
End Function
```

Notice that a function procedure begins with the keyword Function and the name of the procedure, and ends with End Function. Between these two lines, as in a sub procedure, you can have any number of statements. But there's a new type of statement that can appear only in a function procedure: one that specifies the *return value* of the procedure. In this case, the only statement in the procedure gives the procedure the return value of "Hello" by assigning that string to the name of the procedure. Every function procedure has a return value. If you don't assign a return value explicitly, the return value is the special value Null, which is a sort of empty value.

Figure 4.3 shows how you can call this function procedure from the Immediate window.

Figure 4.3
Calling a function proce-
dure from the Immediate
window.

Note the use of the question mark before the function procedure name. This tells VBA that you want it to run the procedure and then print the return value. As you can see, the Immediate window shows the return value from the procedure even though it does not contain a Debug.Print statement.

> **TIP**
> You can use the question mark operator in the Immediate window to perform simple calculations. For example, if you type ?12 * 12 in the Immediate window and press Enter, it prints the answer (144).

4

Like sub procedures, function procedures can contain more than one statement, and can be called from other procedures, as in this example:

```
Function Procedure6()
    ' Display execution of another procedure
    Debug.Print "In Procedure6"
    Procedure7
    Debug.Print "Back in Procedure6"
End Function

Function Procedure7()
    ' Print a message
    Debug.Print "In Procedure7"
End Function
```

One of the more useful things that you can do with a function procedure is to use its return value within another procedure, as in this example:

```
Function Procedure8()
    ' Use a value from another procedure
    Dim i As Integer
    i = Procedure9
    Debug.Print i
End Function

Function Procedure9()
    Procedure9 = 5
End Function
```

If you run Procedure8 from the Immediate window, it prints the return value of 5. This happens because Procedure8 assigns the return value from Procedure9 to the variable i, and then prints the value contained in that variable.

Declaring Procedures as Public or Private

You won't always see procedures declared with just the Sub or Function keyword. There are various modifiers that can go in front of these keywords. Two of the important modifiers are Public and Private. A public procedure can be called from anywhere within your Access VBA code. A private procedure can only be called from within the module where it is declared. Here's how these declarations look, in procedures that don't actually do anything:

```
Public Sub Procedure10()
    ' Can be called from anywhere
End Sub

Private Sub Procedure11()
    ' Can only be called from this module
End Sub

Public Function Procedure12()
    ' Can be called from anywhere
End Function

Private Function Procedure13()
    ' Can only be called from this module
End Function
```

CAUTION

Private procedures can't be called from the Immediate window.

Passing Arguments

So far, the procedures that you've seen do the exact same thing every time that they're executed. But that doesn't have to be the case. You can use a procedure *argument* to pass information to a procedure. When you define a procedure (by using either the Sub keyword or the Function keyword), you can also specify a list of arguments that the procedure will accept. Here's a sub procedure that accepts a single integer argument:

```
Sub Procedure14(intInput As Integer)
  ' Double the input argument and print the result
  Debug.Print (intInput * 2)
End Sub
```

The declaration of Procedure14 specifies that you must pass it a single value of the Integer data type. This value is assigned to the variable named intInput, which is available within the procedure. The procedure prints the result of multiplying this value by two. Figure 4.4 demonstrates that calling the procedure with different arguments prints different values.

Figure 4.4

Calling a procedure with a single argument.

→ For a list of the data types that you can use for arguments, see "VBA Data Types," p. 39.

A procedure can have more than one argument. Here's a function procedure that accepts two string arguments and then returns the result of concatenating them together:

```
Function Procedure15(strIn1 As String, strIn2 As String)
  ' Concatenate a pair of strings
  Procedure15 = strIn1 & strIn2
End Function
```

NOTE

The *concatenation* operator, &, takes two strings and combines them into a single string.

When you declare more than one argument for a procedure, separate the declarations by commas.

Using Optional Arguments and Default Values

You can specify that some or all the arguments to a procedure are optional. For example, here's a procedure that accepts a single optional argument:

```
Sub Procedure16(Optional strIn As String)
  ' Print the input argument, if any
  Debug.Print (strIn)
End Sub
```

As Figure 4.5 shows, you can call this procedure with or without an argument value. If you don't supply a value, there's simply nothing assigned to the corresponding argument within the procedure.

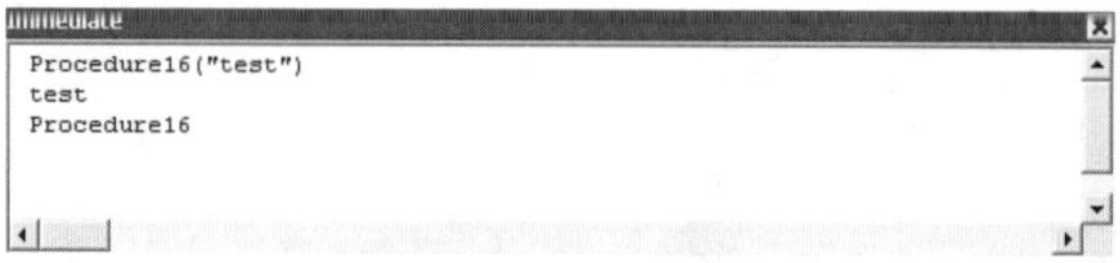

Figure 4.5
Calling a procedure with an optional argument.

```
Procedure16("test")
test
Procedure16
```

An optional argument can also have a default value, which is used if the user does not supply a value when calling the procedure. Consider this procedure:

```
Sub Procedure17(Optional strIn As String = "Missing")
  ' Print the argument or a default value
  Debug.Print strIn
End Sub
```

If you don't supply a value for the strIn argument when you call the procedure, it is assigned the default value "Missing".

> **NOTE**
> Passed values are treated like any other value, meaning that you must delimit them properly. For instance, strIn in the accompanying example is a String value. You must enclose the actual value in quotation marks in the procedure call to pass it properly to the procedure.

Passing Arguments by Reference

By default, arguments in VBA are passed *by reference*. This means that when you pass a variable from one procedure to another, the called procedure is working with the exact same copy of the variable as the calling procedure. This example shows how passing by reference works:

```
Sub Procedure18()
  ' Demonstrate passing by reference
  Dim i As Integer
  i = 5
  ' Pass by reference to another procedure
  Procedure19 i
  ' And print the result
  Debug.Print i
End Sub
```

```
Sub Procedure19(intInput As Integer)
   intInput = 12
End Sub
```

If you run `Procedure18` from the Immediate window, you'll see that the ultimate result is 12. That's because the actual variable named i is passed to `Procedure19`, where its value is changed. The variable retains the changed value when control returns to `Procedure18`.

> **TIP** When passing arguments to a sub procedure, you don't need to enclose the arguments in parentheses.

Passing arguments by reference is fast, but it can have unintended side effects if you aren't expecting the called procedure to have an effect on the calling procedure. That's why there's an alternative: passing arguments *by value*.

Passing Arguments by Value

When you pass a variable from one procedure to another by value, VBA makes a copy of the variable and hands the copy to the called procedure. Thus, any changes made by the called procedure don't affect the variable in the calling procedure. You use the `ByVal` keyword to indicate that you're passing a variable by value. Here's the previous example, changed to pass the variable by value:

```
Sub Procedure20()
   ' Demonstrate passing by value
   Dim i As Integer
   i = 5
   ' Pass by reference to another procedure
   Procedure21 i
   ' And print the result
   Debug.Print i
End Sub

Sub Procedure21(ByVal intInput As Integer)
   intInput = 12
End Sub
```

Now if you run `Procedure20` from the Immediate window, it prints the value 5. The change made to the variable in the called procedure, `Procedure21`, affects only a copy of the variable instead of the original.

Giving a Function a Data Type

You learned in Chapter 3 that variables can have data types. Function procedures, too, can have data types to indicate the data that they return. Here's a function procedure that explicitly returns an integer value:

```
Function Procedure22(intInput As Integer) As Integer
   ' Multiple the input by ten and return it
   Procedure22 = intInput * 10
End Function
```

As you can see, declaring a return data type for a function procedure uses the same syntax as declaring a data type for a variable: the As keyword followed by the data type.

You can use any of the VBA data types for a function procedure's return value. If you don't specify a data type for the function, the return value will be a variant. Just as with a variable, this means that the return value can be of any data type.

Implementing Error Handling

There's a potential problem with the procedure that you just saw: because it uses integers for both input and output, it's possible for it to calculate a value greater than an integer will hold. For example, Figure 4.6 shows the result of trying to call Procedure22 with an input value of 20,000. Because this calculates an output value of 200,000, which is larger than an Integer variable can hold, a VBA overflow error occurs.

Figure 4.6
A procedure with an overflow error.

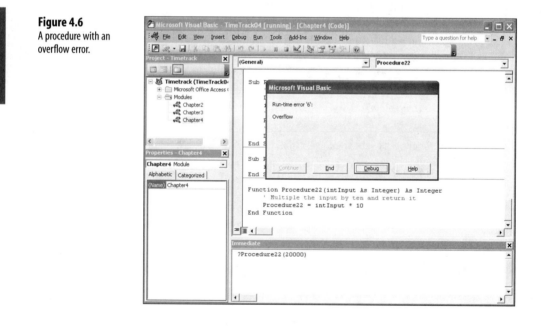

Errors in your VBA code can cause major problems with your applications. That's because VBA stops running code when it encounters an error. But that's only the default behavior of VBA. VBA also supplies several ways for you to monitor your running code for errors, and to recover from those errors.

Using `On Error Resume Next`

The simplest way to handle an error in VBA is to tell VBA that you don't want to be bothered. The mechanism for doing this is the `On Error Resume Next` statement:

```
Function Procedure23(intInput As Integer) As Integer
  ' Multiple the input by ten and return it
  On Error Resume Next
  Procedure23 = intInput * 10
End Function
```

If you call `Procedure23` with an input that will lead to an overflow (such as 20000), you won't see an error onscreen. Instead, the value zero is returned. That's because the line that calculates the return value still raises an overflow error, but the `On Error Resume Next` statement tells VBA to ignore the error and proceed to the next line of code—in this case, the `End Function` statement. The function returns zero because that's the default value for an integer that doesn't have anything else assigned to it.

`On Error Resume Next` takes effect as soon as it is executed, and remains in effect until you tell VBA to remove or change the error handling.

Using `On Error Goto`

Although `On Error Resume Next` is easy to use, it might not be the safest way to handle errors. In many situations, you'll find `On Error Goto` to be a better choice. `On Error Goto` lets you execute a special section of code when something goes wrong. Here's how you might use it:

```
Function Procedure24(intInput As Integer) As Integer
  ' Multiple the input by ten and return it
  On Error GoTo HandleErr
  Procedure24 = intInput * 10

ExitHere:
  Exit Function

HandleErr:
  Debug.Print Err.Description
  Resume ExitHere
End Function
```

There are several new things to note in this procedure:

- The `On Error Goto HandleErr` statement tells VBA that if any error occurs, execution should continue at the point marked `HandleErr`.

- `ExitHere` and `HandleErr` are *labels*, which are places within a procedure where execution can continue.

- The `Exit Function` statement tells VBA to quit running the function without executing any more code.

- `Err.Description` is a special variable that contains the description of the most recent error.

4

- `Resume ExitHere` is an instruction to clear the error and resume executing code at the indicated label.

If all goes well in this function, it prints 10 times its input and then exits at the `Exit Function` line. If anything goes wrong, it jumps to the `HandleErr` label, prints the description of the error, and then exits from the function. Figure 4.7 shows several calls to this function in the Immediate window.

Figure 4.7
Calling a procedure with error trapping.

```
Immediate
?Procedure24(2000)
 20000
?Procedure24(20000)
Overflow
 0
```

There are two other statements that you might use after an error has occurred:

- The `Resume` statement tells VBA to begin executing the code again, starting at the statement that caused the error. You can use this if a transient error occurs that you can correct in your error-handling code.

- The `Resume Next` statement tells VBA to begin executing the code again, starting at the statement after the statement that caused the error. You can use this if you decide that a particular error is harmless enough to ignore.

Debugging Code

No matter how thorough you are with error handling, there will probably still be mistakes lurking somewhere in your code. Fortunately, the VBE offers a few tools for helping you debug (find) these mistakes so you can resolve them.

Using Run and Break Mode

After writing a procedure, you need to test it before actually setting it free upon your application, and you do this testing in the VBE. Your first step is to simply run the procedure and see what happens within the controlled VBE environment.

There are a number of ways to execute a procedure, but the quickest and easiest is to position the cursor in the procedure and press F5 or choose Run, Run Sub/UserForm. If it works, great.

If a runtime error occurs, and the problem isn't immediately apparent, you have a bit more work ahead. To expose the clues you need to find the problem, you need to temporarily suspend the procedure within the controls of the development environment (the VBE). This temporary suspension is called *break mode*. You can switch from run mode to break mode by doing any of the following:

- Inserting a breakpoint in your code.
- Inserting a `Stop` statement where you want the code to stop.

- Inserting a watch expression.
- Pressing Ctrl+Break during execution (probably the least preferable method because you can't really control where the code stops).
- Clicking the Debug button in the runtime error dialog box when it occurs.
- Clicking the Break tool on the toolbar.

After execution is suspended, you have the opportunity to modify the code. Afterward, you can test your modifications by pressing F5 again. Sometimes, you'll want to continue without restarting. To do so, choose Run, Reset *project* or click the Reset toolbar button.

> **NOTE**
> Watch expressions are an advanced developer's topic that aren't covered in this book. For details, search the VBA help file for "watch expression."

Single-Stepping

Often, the only way to find a problem is to sift through the code, line by line. When this is the case, press F8 or choose Debug, Step Into to highlight the first line of your procedure, as shown in Figure 4.8. Press F8 to advance to the next statement. You can continue pressing F8 to execute the procedure one statement at a time.

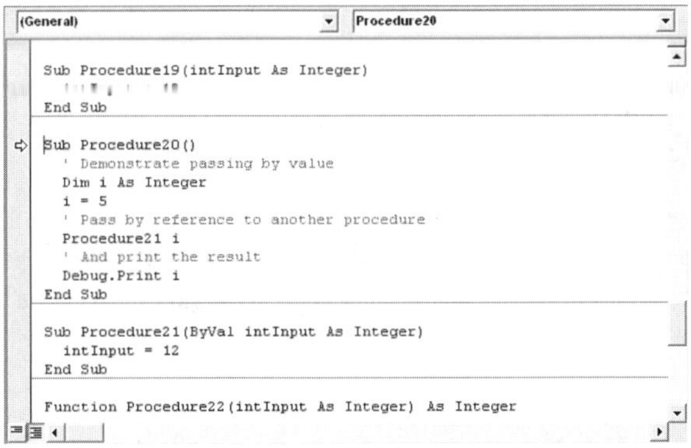

Figure 4.8
The arrow and highlighting indicate the next statement that will be executed in break mode.

```
(General)                          ▼   Procedure20                    ▼

    Sub Procedure19(intInput As Integer)

    End Sub

⇨   Sub Procedure20()
        ' Demonstrate passing by value
        Dim i As Integer
        i = 5
        ' Pass by reference to another procedure
        Procedure21 i
        ' And print the result
        Debug.Print i
    End Sub

    Sub Procedure21(ByVal intInput As Integer)
        intInput = 12
    End Sub

    Function Procedure22(intInput As Integer) As Integer
```

At any time during this single-step process, you can get information about a variable by hovering the mouse pointer over the reference right in the code. The VBE will display the reference's current value. You can review code at any point in the process, including review references that have been resolved and those that you've yet to reach.

There are other steps you can take while single-stepping through your code:

- Press Shift+F8 (choose Debug, Step Over) to skip the next statement.
- Press Ctrl+Shift+F8 (choose Debug, Step Out) to skip the procedure entirely. This isn't the same as resetting or breaking the process because Step Out returns control to a calling procedure (if applicable).

■ Press Ctrl+F8 (choose Debug, Run to Cursor) to execute the code from the current statement to the statement that contains the cursor. This command lets you process several statements automatically while controlling where execution stops.

Setting Breakpoints

Setting a breakpoint is another good way to control where run mode stops. Position the cursor in the statement where you want execution to stop. Then, choose Debug, Toggle Breakpoint or press F9 to set a breakpoint. Doing so places a marker in the margin of the module, as shown in Figure 4.9.

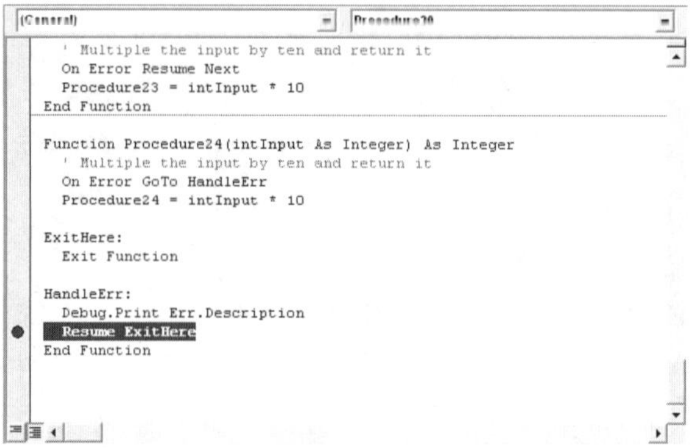

Figure 4.9
Set a breakpoint to better control execution.

```
(General)                    ▼   Procedure24                ▼

        ' Multiple the input by ten and return it
        On Error Resume Next
        Procedure23 = intInput * 10
    End Function

    Function Procedure24(intInput As Integer) As Integer
        ' Multiple the input by ten and return it
        On Error GoTo HandleErr
        Procedure24 = intInput * 10

    ExitHere:
        Exit Function

    HandleErr:
        Debug.Print Err.Description
        Resume ExitHere
    End Function
```

Run the procedure as you normally would. You'll find that execution stops at the breakpoint. You can then single-step from there or use any of the other available debugging tools to determine what's going wrong.

> **TIP**
>
> To remove a breakpoint, place your cursor on the line of code with the breakpoint and press F9 again. Or, you can just click in the margin of the module to set or remove a breakpoint.

Choosing the Right VBA Function

5

Introducing VBA's Built-in Functions

VBA is considered a high-level language, which means it can take a while to master. On the other hand, the combination of Access and VBA is flexible enough that you can start using VBA to automate your Access applications right out of the box, with just a little reading and preparation.

There are a number of functions that perform dozens and dozens of tasks and calculations for you. While you're learning, don't make the mistake of re-inventing the wheel—use the functions VBA provides. You'll find them easy to use, flexible, and dependable.

Like the function procedures that you write yourself, the built-in functions return a value. In addition, most functions rely on both required and optional arguments. Thanks to IntelliSense, there's not much guesswork. As you enter the function, the VBE displays a list of context-sensitive suggestions. Keep in mind the following when working with VBA functions:

- Functions expect arguments of a certain data type. If you supply the wrong type of data, VBA will return an error.
- The values returned by each function are of a specific data type. Be familiar with the type of data returned so you don't introduce unintentional errors into your code.

IN THIS CHAPTER

Introducing VBA's Built-in Functions 57

Converting Data Types with VBA Functions . .58

Working with Date Functions 65

Using Mathematical and Financial
Functions 70

Using String Functions 75

Using the Format Function 81

Using the Is Functions for Flawless
Processing 85

Interacting Functions 85

TIP Knowing which function to use, or if there even is an appropriate function available can be one of the biggest hurdles for new VBA users. Fortunately, help is close at hand. In the VBE, choose Help, Microsoft Visual Basic Help to open the Help task pane. In the Table of Contents list, click the first item, Microsoft Access Visual Basic Documentation. Click the Functions or the Statements link in the expanded list and then click the alphabetized listing links to view what's available.

TIP You might find the terms *function* and *statement* used interchangeably. Technically, statements have been around for the duration and are much older than any VBA functions. As Access and VBA have matured with an expanding object model, many statements have been replaced with functions. I recommend that you use functions whenever possible, because they represent the most up-to-date functionality. Seemingly similar statements are usually included for backward compatibility. However, not all statements are obsolete.

Throughout this chapter (and the entire book), I use the most up-to-date functions, not the older statements, even if they exist. Nor do I bother to tell you when there are older, comparable statements. There's simply no reason for you to use them unless you inherit an application that uses them.

Converting Data Types with VBA Functions

At some point, you'll probably have to import data from a foreign source or you might be forced to use existing data in a manner not originally intended. When this happens, you might need to convert data from one data type to another, and VBA provides many functions for converting data types. Just remember that you're not changing the stored value's data type.

→ For a more in-depth review of the VBA data types, read "VBA Data Types," in Chapter 3 (p. 39).

For a complete list of functions that force a specific data type, open the Help task pane in the VBE and search for "Type Conversion Functions." In this chapter, you learn how to use several of the most common conversion functions:

- CBool—Converts a value to a Boolean data type.
- CByte—Converts a value to a Byte data type.
- CDate—Converts a value to a Date data type.
- CInt—Converts a value to an Integer data type.
- CStr—Converts a value to a String data type.
- CVar—Converts a value to a Variant data type.

TIP There are a few older conversion statements, such as `Str`, still included in the most recent versions of VBA. The most up-to-date conversion functions start with the letter C. It's best to use these later functions because they consider your system's date, time, and number settings, whereas the older statements don't.

The conversion functions all use the same simple syntax

```
CBool(variable)
```

where *variable* is the name of a variable, constant, or an expression that evaluates to a specific data type. The functions convert *variable* to the appropriate data type so you can use the converted value elsewhere. Nothing happens to the stored value. However, not every data type can be converted to any other data type. You learn more about these conversion pitfalls in the following sections dedicated to specific functions.

Converting to a `Boolean` Data Type

Use `CBool` to convert a value to a `Boolean` data type. The *variable* argument is required and can be a string or a number. You might think that means the value being converted must be implicitly or explicitly, −1 or 0, but the value being converted can be any number or string that can be interpreted as a number.

When the value is a numeric or string 0, `CBool` returns `False`. Any other value or string returns `True` (−1). For instance, all the following expressions return `True` because *variable* can be interpreted as a numeric value and that value is a number other than 0.

```
CBool("1")
CBool(1+0)
CBool(2)
CBool(-300)
```

On the other hand, both of the following expressions return `False`. In both cases, *variable* is interpreted as the numeric value 0. Therefore, both return `False`.

```
CBool(0)
CBool("0")
```

`CBool` can't handle every character. VBA must be able to express the value you're converting as a numeric value. That includes digits stored as strings, but not alphabetic characters. Figure 5.1 shows such an example in the Immediate window returning a mismatch data type error. The expression `CBool("one")` returns a mismatch error because VBA can't interpret the string `"one"` as the numeric value 1.

5

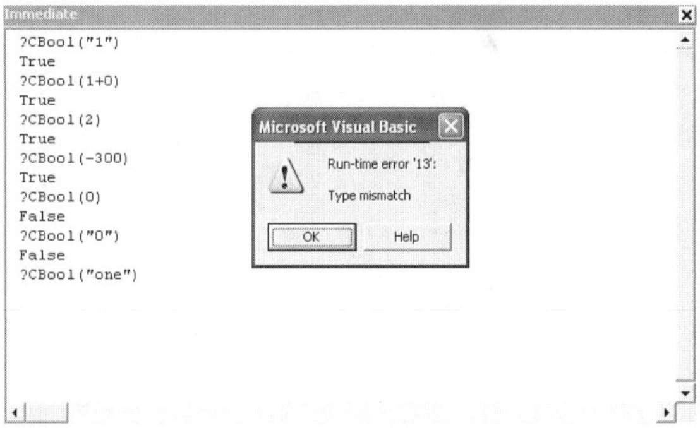

Figure 5.1
CBool returns an error when VBA can't interpret a numeric value.

```
Immediate
?CBool("1")
True
?CBool(1+0)
True
?CBool(2)
True
?CBool(-300)
True
?CBool(0)
False
?CBool("0")
False
?CBool("one")
```

Microsoft Visual Basic

Run-time error '13':

Type mismatch

OK   Help

C A U T I O N

CBool converts any value or expression that evaluates to 0 to False and any non-zero value to True. Consequently, a False value can be converted back to its original value of 0. A True value can be restored to its original value only when it was originally −1.

Converting to a Byte Data Type

The Byte data type stores numeric values from 0 to 255. The *variable* argument is required and can be a Numeric or String data type. CByte converts a value from 0 to 255 or any variable or constant that can evaluate to a value from 0 to 255 to the Byte data type. The following functions return the Byte values 0, 255, and 1, respectively:

```
CByte(0)
CByte(255)
CByte("1")
```

When the value being converted is out of the Byte data type's range (from 0 to 255), CByte returns an *overflow* error message, as shown in Figure 5.2.

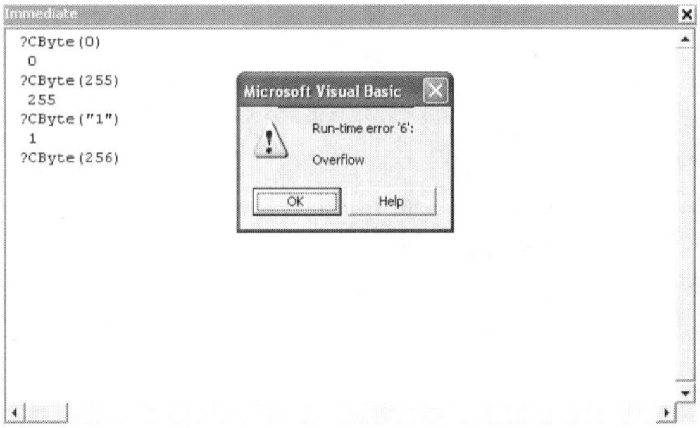

Figure 5.2
A value out of the Byte range generates an overflow error.

```
Immediate
?CByte(0)
0
?CByte(255)
255
?CByte("1")
1
?CByte(256)
```

Microsoft Visual Basic

Run-time error '6':

Overflow

OK   Help

> **TIP**
>
> CByte rounds a floating point number to the nearest integer *before* converting to the Byte data type. As long as the rounded integer is from 0 to 255, CByte converts it.

Converting to a Date **Data Type**

The CDate function converts a value to a Date data type. The *variable* argument is required and the value can be a String or Numeric data type or any valid date expression. CDate uses your system's locale settings to determine the order of the three date components, day, month, and year. The following guidelines might help when converting to the Date data type:

- CDate converts the integer portion to the date represented by the same number of days that have passed since December 31, 1899. The fraction is converted to the time of day, where .01 represents 14 minutes and 24 seconds (864 seconds) past midnight.

- CDate accepts both numeric and string values. For instance, CDate can correctly interpret the following string values: "3/1/04", "March 1, 2004", "1 Mar 04", and 38046 (the date serial value equal to March 1, 2004).

- The Date data type supports dates from January 1, 100 to December 31, 9999. Any value out of that range generates an error.

- Two-digit year values that are less than 30 are converted to 21st century dates. Year values that are greater than or equal to 30 are converted to 20th century dates. When the year value is omitted, CDate uses the current year.

Figure 5.3 shows the evaluated result of a CDate function that returns an unexpected result. CDate interprets 3/1/04 as an equation and works the math as follows (because there are no parentheses, the equation is evaluated from left to right):

```
3/1 = 3
3/04 = .75
```

5

No delimiters

Figure 5.3
Be sure to properly
delimit a date string.

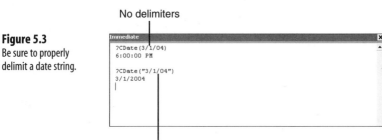

```
Immediate                                    ☒
  ?CDate(3/1/04)
  6:00:00 PM

  ?CDate("3/1/04")
  3/1/2004
  |
```

Delimited properly

The resulting fractional value of .75 is processed as a time value where .75 is three quarters through the day, or 6:00:00 PM. The key here is to remember to delimit a date string as a string. Then, CDate will convert the date value properly.

Converting to an `Integer` Data Type

Use `CInt` to convert a numeric or string value to an `Integer` data type. The *variable* argument is required and its range can be any variable, constant, expression, or literal value from –32,678 to 32,767. When the fractional component is exactly 0.5, `CInt` rounds to the nearest even number. For example, 0.5 rounds to 0 and 1.5 rounds to 2. Both of the following functions return the integer value `1000`:

```
CInt(1000)
CInt("1000")
```

If *variable* evaluates to anything other than a numeric value, the function returns an error. If *variable* evaluates to a numeric value outside of the `Integer` data type range, the function generates an overflow error.

> **TIP**
> `CInt` is more flexible than the `Val` function because it uses the system's regional settings and can recognize the thousands separator. For instance, `CInt` correctly converts a `String` value of "1,234" to 1234. `Val` converts the same value to 1.

Converting to a `String` Data Type

Use `CStr` to convert almost any value to a `String` data type. The *variable* argument is required, but it can equal any variable, constant, expression, or literal value that can evaluate to a string. Although that covers a lot, prepared for a few unexpected results:

- Uninitialized `Numeric` data types return `"0"`
- Unintialized `Date` data types return `"12:00:00 AM"`

> **TIP**
> The term *uninitialized* describes a variable that has not been defined by a value. In other words, it's a variable's state between the time it's declared and when you give it a value to store.

Converting to a Variant Data Type

The section "VBA Data Types" in Chapter 3 introduces the `Variant` data type as the most versatile because it can store almost any value. Using `CVar`, you can convert almost any numeric or string value to the `Variant` data type. Numeric values are restricted to the same range as the `Double` data type; there are no restrictions on non-numeric values.

> **CAUTION**
> It's best to use `CVar` only when the data type isn't important (which is almost never) or when there's no doubt as to the value's data type.

Converting Null Values

Few functions can handle a Null value, so if a variable is Null, it's probably going to cause you trouble—even though a Null value isn't inherently incorrect. For instance, the simple equation

```
varResults = value1 + value2
```

returns a runtime error if either `value1` or `value2` is Null.

You can avoid runtime errors caused by Null values by using the `Nz` function to convert the Null value to 0, a zero-length string (`""`), or a specific string value. After wrapping both *value1* and *value2* in an `Nz` function as follows, the expression no longer returns an error when *value1* or *value2* is Null:

```
varResults = Nz(value1) + Nz(value2)
```

The `Nz` function uses the form

```
Nz(value, [valueifnull])
```

where *value* is any data type that represents the evaluated value or expression and *valueifnull* is the value you want the `Nz` to return when *value* is Null. If the optional argument is omitted, `Nz` returns either 0 or a zero-length string, based on *value*'s data type.

A Conversion Example

Now let's look at a quick example that solicits a date from a user and then performs some simple date arithmetic. Suppose users need a rough estimate of the number of days to complete a new project that's starting today. To get started, launch the VBE by pressing Alt+F11. Then, complete the following steps:

1. Open a new blank module by choosing Insert, Module.

2. Next, enter the following procedure:
   ```
   Public Sub GetDate()
       Dim varDate As Variant
       varDate = InputBox("Please enter date")
       MsgBox Now - varDate
   End Sub
   ```

→ Learn how to enter a function procedure in "Entering and Running VBA Code," in Chapter 2 (p. 22).

3. With the insertion point inside the procedure, press F5 to run the code.

4. When the input box shown in Figure 5.4 appears, enter a date using any valid date string and click OK.

Figure 5.4
Enter a valid date string.

5. When VBA displays the mismatch error, click Debug to return to the procedure. Figure 5.5 shows the line where the error occurs—VBA highlights it.

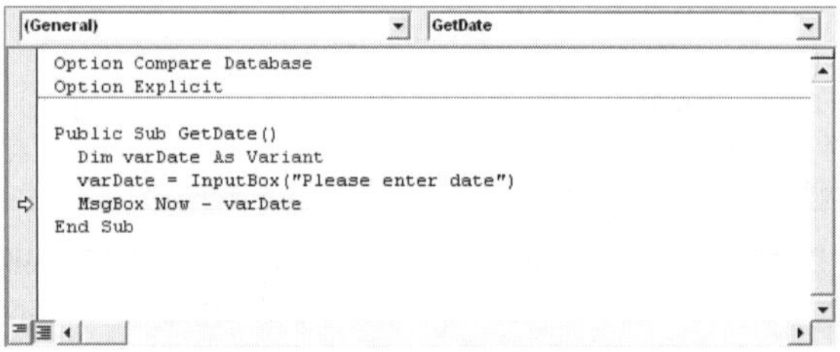

Figure 5.5
The MsgBox line is returning an error.

```
(General)                           ▼   GetDate                          ▼
    Option Compare Database
    Option Explicit

    Public Sub GetDate()
        Dim varDate As Variant
        varDate = InputBox("Please enter date")
    ⇨   MsgBox Now - varDate
    End Sub
```

6. Click Reset on the standard toolbar.

> **NOTE**
> A few of the examples use the VBA InputBox function to display a dialog box that prompts the user to enter data. Like the MsgBox function, you'll see this function several times in this book. In its simplest form, this function requires only the prompt text that the dialog box displays to remind the user what type of data is needed. The function returns that variable as a Variant String subtype. In this context, a subtype is simply one of several data types that Variant accepts.

The problem is the equation that subtracts your date string from the Now function, which returns the current date. VBA can't do the math because the variable that's storing the input date is a Variant. VBA needs a Date data type to do the date arithmetic. One way to eliminate the error is to convert the passed data.

1. Between the InputBox line and the MsgBox line, enter the function
   varDate = CDate(varDate)
2. With the insertion point in the procedure, press F5.
3. Enter the same date in the input box and click OK.
4. This time the MsgBox can return the results of the simple equation Now—varDate, as shown in Figure 5.6.

Figure 5.6
After changing the data type of the input date string value, the equation works.

Microsoft Office Access

33.8462037037025

OK

5. Click OK to clear the message box and save the module, if you like, as Chapter5.

After you change the date string's data type from Variant to Date, VBA can calculate the number of days between the two dates. There's a simpler way to solve the problem.

Instead of declaring varDate as a Variant, declare it as a Date to begin with. Then you won't need to convert the input date value because VBA forces the data type for you.

Solutions won't always be that simple because changing a variable's data type is seldom convenient or practical. In fact, most of the time, you will not want to do so, unless you can determine, as in this case, that the variable is simply not the most appropriate data type to begin with.

Working with Date Functions

Working with dates can be difficult if you don't know what you're doing. VBA won't help you use dates correctly if you don't know the basics. However, if you use dates in Access expressions (queries, calculated controls, and so on) without trouble, you should experience the same success using VBA. This section reviews a number of functions that work with dates.

> **CAUTION**
>
> All the date functions in this section are limited to the Date data type range restrictions. The first date value recognized is January 1, 100, and the last is December 31, 9999. Any date out of this range returns an error.

Returning the Date

VBA's Date function takes the simplest form of all

```
Date
```

and returns a Variant Date subtype that equals the system's current date. (The Date$ function returns a String data type.)

> **TIP**
>
> The Date function returns only the system's current date. If you need both the date and time, use the Now function.

To reset the system's current date, use the Date statement, in the following form

```
Date = newdate
```

where *newdate* is a String, Date, or Variant Date subtype. For example, the statement

```
Date = "March 1, 2004"
```

sets your system's date to March 1, 2004. However, it's better not use this method unless you have a specific reason for doing so. Changing your system's date can have far-reaching and unintended consequences.

5

Adding to and Subtracting from Dates

Use the DateAdd function to add or subtract a given number of time periods to or from a specific date. For instance, you might calculate the date that's 10 days or 10 months into the future (or in the past). Or, you might return the date and time 36 hours into the future.

This function takes the form

DateAdd(*interval, number, date*)

where *interval* is a String value or expression that denotes the type of time period (day, week, or month) that you want to add or subtract. Table 5.1 lists the predefined *interval* settings. The *number* argument is a numeric value that specifies the number of times *interval* should be added or subtracted and *date* is a Date Variant that represents the date to which you're adding or subtracting *interval*.

Table 5.1 Interval String Settings

String Setting	Description
yyyy	Year
q	Quarter
m	Month
y	Day of year
d	Day
w	Weekday
ww	Week
h	Hour
n	Minute
s	Second

A negative *interval* value returns a date from the past; a positive value returns a date in the future. If *number* contains a fractional component, DateAdd rounds that value to the nearest whole number before actually calculating the function's results.

Determining the Difference Between Two Dates

To determine the number of time intervals between two dates, use VBA's DateDiff function. This function returns a Variant Long subtype and takes the form

DateDiff(*interval, date1, date2*[, *firstdayofweek*[, *firstweekofyear*]])

where *interval* is a String value that represents the type of time period to calculate between *date1* and *date2* (refer to Table 5.1). The two optional arguments, *firstdayofweek* and *firstweekofyear*, are numeric constants that define the first day of the week and the first day of the year, respectively. See Tables 5.2 and 5.3 for a list of constants. If omitted, these arguments default to Sunday and January 1, respectively.

Table 5.2   First Day of Week Constants

Constant	Description	Integer Value
vbSunday	Sunday (the default)	1
vbMonday	Monday	2
vbTuesday	Tuesday	3
vbWednesday	Wednesday	4
vbThursday	Thursday	5
vbFriday	Friday	6
vbSaturday	Saturday	7

Table 5.3   First Week of Year Constants

Constant	Description	Integer Value
vbFirstJan1	Use the week in which January 1 occurs (the default)	1
vbFirstFourDays	Use the first week that has at least four days in the new year	2
vbFirstFullWeek	Use the first full week of the new year	3

This function might not always yield the expected dates:

- When *date2* falls before *date1*, the returned value is negative.
- Even though there's only one day between December 31 of one year and January 1 of the next, DateDiff knows there's an entire year between the two dates. This also happens when calculating the number of months and quarters.

Figure 5.7 shows these guidelines in action in the Immediate window.

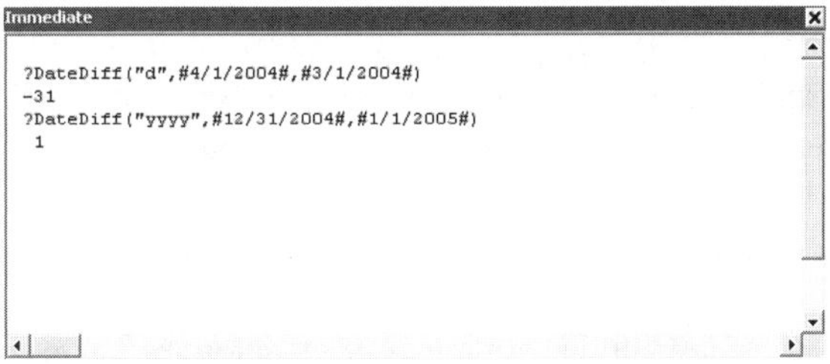

Figure 5.7
Be mindful of DateDiff's specific calculation behaviors.

```
Immediate
?DateDiff("d",#4/1/2004#,#3/1/2004#)
 -31
?DateDiff("yyyy",#12/31/2004#,#1/1/2005#)
  1
```

> **NOTE**
> The dates in Figure 5.7 are enclosed by two pound sign characters (#). This character is the appropriate delimiter for date values, just as the quotation mark is the delimiter for string values. When using dates, you must delimit the value or Access will return an error or return erroneous data.

Extracting Date Components

It's easy to determine a specific date component using the `DatePart` function. For instance, the following functions return the values 4, 1, and 2004, respectively:

```
DatePart("m",#4/1/2004#)
DatePart("d",#4/1/2004#)
DatePart("yyyy",#4/1/2004#)
```

This function returns a variant of the `Integer` subtype and takes the form

```
DatePart(interval, date[, firstdayofweek[, firstweekofyear]])
```

where *interval* is a `String` value that specifies the component you want to extract and *date* is a variant of the `Date` subtype and equals the date from which you're extracting *interval*. (Refer to Table 5.1 for the *interval* values.) The two optional arguments, *firstdayofweek* and *firstweekofyear*, are numeric constants that define the first day of the week and the first day of the year, respectively (see Tables 5.2 and 5.3 for a list of constants). If omitted, these arguments default to Sunday and January 1, respectively.

Creating a Date from Individual Components

In the last section, you learned how `DatePart` extracts a date component from a date. Similarly, you can use `DateSerial` to combine date components to create a date. This function returns a variant of the `Date` subtype using the form

```
DateSerial(year, month, day)
```

where *year*, *month*, and *day* represent integer values that represent the corresponding date part. There are a few rules about the values you can use for each argument:

- *year* is required and must equal a numeric value from 100 to 9999.
- *month* is required and must be a numeric value from 1 to 12.
- *day* is required and must be a numeric value from 1 to 31.

> **TIP**
>
> Like most date functions, `DateSerial` assumes a year value between 0 and 29 is a 21st century date. Likewise, a year value between 30 and 99 is a 20th century date. To be safe, it's best to use four-digit values to express year values. It's always better to explicitly force date values rather than letting VBA guess.

If any of the argument values fall out of their respective ranges, `DateSerial` will just keep going into the next time period. For instance, the function

```
DateSerial(2004, 15, 3)
```

returns March 3, 2005 because the 15th month of 2004 is March 2005. That is, `DateSerial` uses up the 12 months in 2004 and then goes three more months into 2005. Similarly,

```
DateSerial(2005, 4, 45)
```

returns May 15, 2005. VBA uses up the 30 days in April and then goes 15 days more into May.

Creating a Date from a String Expression

VBA lets you create a date from a string expression. The `DateValue` function returns a `Variant` (Date subtype) and uses the form

`DateValue(stringexpression)`

where *stringexpression* is required and uses the system's short date setting. In addition, the date separators must conform to those used by the system's settings. Time information is ignored; if only time values are used, the function returns an error. All three of the following functions return the same date, March 1, 2004:

```
DateValue("3/1/2004")
DateValue("March 1, 2004")
DateValue("1 Mar 04")
```

> **TIP** The `TimeSerial` and `TimeValue` functions work similarly to the `DateSerial` and `DateValue` functions with time components.

Returning a Specific Date or Time Component

There are several functions that return specific date and time components. They're easy to use because all you need to specify is the date. Table 5.4 lists these functions.

Table 5.4 Date Component Functions

Function	Result
`Day(date)`	Returns an `Integer` value between 1 and 31 that represents a day of the month.
`Hour(time)`	Returns an `Integer` value between 0 and 23 that represents an hour of the day.
`Minute(time)`	Returns an `Integer` value between 0 and 59 that represents a minute.
Second(*time*)	Returns an `Integer` value between 0 and 59 that represents a second.
`Month(date)`	Returns an `Integer` value between 1 and 12 that represents a month.
`Year(date)`	Returns an `Integer` value that represents a year.

A Date Function Example

Have you ever needed to know the number of days you have to complete a project? Using the following function procedure, you can enter the project's beginning and ending dates and get an immediate response:

```
Public Function GetDays() As Integer
  Dim dteStart As Date
  Dim dteEnd As Date
  Dim varDays As Variant
  dteStart = InputBox("Enter beginning date")
  dteEnd = InputBox("Enter ending date")
```

```
    varDays = DateDiff("d", dteStart, dteEnd)
    GetDays = varDays
End Function
```

1. First, enter the preceding function procedure in Chapter 5's example module.

2. In the Immediate window, enter the following statement and press Enter:

   ?GetDays

3. When VBA displays the first input box, enter 3/1/2004 and click OK.

4. In the second input box, enter 4/1/2004 and click OK.

Figure 5.8 shows your answer—you've planned 31 days to complete your project.

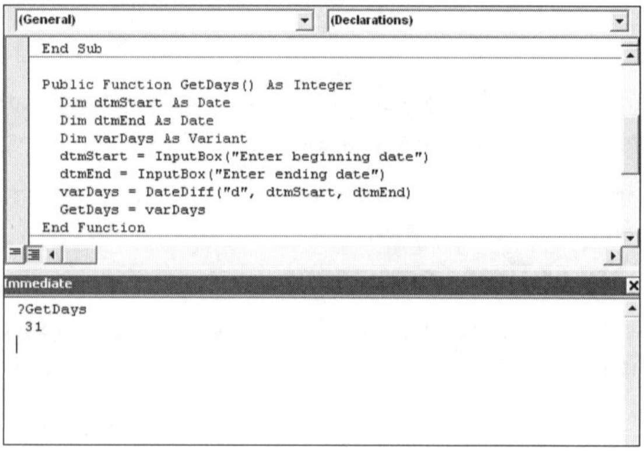

Figure 5.8
Determining the number of days between two dates.

Using Mathematical and Financial Functions

There are more mathematical, financial, and statistical functions than could possibly be covered in one short section. For the most part, these functions use operands and operators to evaluate numeric data. This section doesn't attempt to completely cover each, but rather provides a succinct review of those most often used.

The Abs Function

The Abs function returns the absolute value of a numeric value. This function uses the form

Abs(*number*)

where *number* is any valid numeric expression or a literal numeric value. The returned value is the same as *number*, but without the sign. For instance, the function

Abs(intValue)

where intValue is an Integer variable that stores the value –3, returns the Integer value of 3.

The `Int` **Function**

The `Int` function returns the integer portion of a numeric value. This function takes the form

`Int(number)`

where *number* is required and can be any valid `Numeric` data type. The `Int` function does no rounding; it simply removes the fractional portion of *number*, if one exists. For instance, the function

`Int(10.9)`

returns 10, not 11. If *number* is negative, `Int` returns the first negative integer less than or equal to *number*. For instance, the function

`Int(-10.9)`

returns –11.

When converting values, consider using `CInt` instead of `Int`, but keep in mind that the two functions aren't entirely interchangeable. The `Int` function won't convert *number*'s data type. Although `CInt` is often the better choice, it won't return the same results. Consider the task and use the most appropriate function.

The `Rnd` **Function**

Use the `Rnd` function to return a random number. This function's optional argument is any valid numeric expression. The function takes the form

`Rnd[(seed)]`

where *seed* determines the range of the returned random number as follows:

- When *seed* is less than 0, `Rnd` returns the same random number.
- When *seed* is greater than 0, `Rnd` returns the next number in the sequence of random values as determined internally.
- When *seed* equals 0, `Rnd` returns the most recently generated random number.
- When *seed* is omitted, `Rnd` returns the next number in the sequence of random values, as determined internally.

5

TIP

Sometimes you must work with values that don't generate random values as required. For instance, suppose you're working with values that are less than 0, but you don't want to generate the same value over and over. When this is the case, use the `Randomize` statement to reset the internal *seed* value so the `Rnd` function can return seemingly unique random values that don't repeat.

A Mathematical Function Example

The first example used the CDate function to convert a Variant data type to a valid Date data type. You might also remember that the result wasn't a whole number. You can display a whole number by adding an Int function to the equation. To do so:

1. Return to the Chapter5 module and find GetDate().

2. Comment out the MsgBox statement by selecting that statement and clicking the Comment Block tool on the Edit toolbar. Or, simply insert an apostrophe character (') at the beginning of the statement.

3. Enter the following new code
   ```
   MsgBox Int(Now - varDate)
   ```

4. With the insertion point in the Sub procedure, press F5.

5. Enter 3/1/2004 in the input box and click OK. This time, the message box displays a whole number, as shown in Figure 5.9. Click OK to clear the message box.

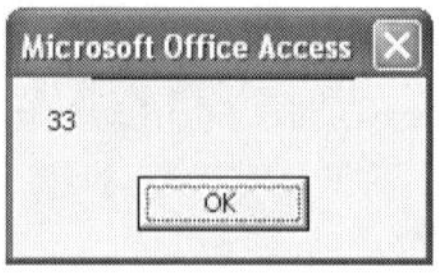

Figure 5.9
Adding the Int func-
tion improves your
message's display.

The Ddb Function

The Ddb function returns a Double data type that represents the depreciation of an asset for a specific time period using the predefined double-declining balance method. This function takes the form

```
Ddb(cost, salvage, life, period[, factor])
```

where *cost* is a Double value or expression that represents the asset's initial cost, and *salvage* is a Double value that specifies the asset's value at the end of *life*, which is a Double value that expresses the length of the asset's life. Likewise, *period* is a Double that expresses the period for which the depreciation is to be calculated. The optional *factor* argument is a Variant that determines the rate at which the asset balance declines. When omitted, the double-declining method is assumed (although documentation doesn't seem to support any other values).

The FV Function

When you need to calculate the future value of an annuity, use the Fv function. This function returns a Double value and uses the form

```
Fv(rate, nper, pmt[, pv [, type]])
```

where *rate* is a Double value that specifies the interest rate per period, *nper* is an Integer value that specifies the number of payment periods in the annuity, and *pmt* is a Double value that specifies the payment made each period. The two optional arguments, *pv* and *type*, are Variant data types that represent the present value and whether payments are due at the start or the end of the period, respectively.

The IPmt Function

Calculate the interest payment for a given period of an annuity using the IPmt function. This function returns a Double and takes the form

```
IPmt(rate, per, nper, pv[, fv[, type]])
```

where *rate* is a Double that states the period's interest rate, *per* is any numeric expression that specifies the period for which the payment is to be calculated, *nper* is a Double that represents the total number of payments, and *pv* is any valid numeric expression that specifies the present value. The two optional arguments, *fv* and *type*, are Variant data types that indicate the future value or cash balance after the final payment and whether the payments are due at the start or the end of the period.

The NPer Function

The Nper function calculates the number of periods for an annuity as a Double. Use the form

```
NPer(rate, pmt, pv[, fv [, type]])
```

where *rate* is a Double that represents the interest rate per period, *pmt* is a Double that specifies the payment made each period, and *pv* is a Double that identifies the present value. The two optional arguments, *fv* and *type*, are Variant data types that identify the future value of the series of payments and whether the payments are due at the start or the end of the period.

The Pmt Function

Use the Pmt function to calculate the payment for an annuity as a Double. This function takes the form

```
Pmt(rate, nper, pv[, fv[, type]])
```

where *rate* is a Double that represents the interest rate per period, *nper* is an Integer that specifies the total number of payments, and *pv* is a Double that identifies the present value. The two optional arguments, *fv* and *type*, are Variant data types that identify the future value of the series of payments and whether the payments are due at the start or the end of the period.

The PPmt Function

Use the PPmt function to calculate the principal payment for an annuity as a Double. This function takes the form

```
PPmt(rate, per, nper, pv[, fv[, type]])
```

5

where *rate* is a Double that represents the interest rate per period, *per* is a Double that represents the period for which a payment is to be calculated, *nper* is a Double that specifies the total number of payments, and *pv* is a Double that identifies the present value. The two optional arguments, *fv* and *type*, are Variant data types that identify the future value and whether payments are due at the start or the end of the period.

The Rate Function

The Rate function calculates the interest rate per period for a loan or annuity. This function returns a Double and requires the form

```
Rate(nper, pmt, pv[, fv[, type[, guess]]])
```

where *nper* is a Double that specifies the total number of periods, *pmt* is a Double that specifies the payment amount per period, and *pv* is a Double that identifies the present value. The three optional arguments, *fv*, *type*, and *guess*, specify the future value, determine whether the payments are due at the start or the end of the period, and present an estimate of the function's resulting value. The first two optional arguments, *fv* and *type* are Variants; *guess* is a Double.

The Syd Function

The Syd function calculates the sum-of-years' digits depreciation of an asset for a specific period. This function returns a Double and uses the form

```
Syd(cost, salvage, life, period)
```

where *cost* is a Double that specifies the asset's initial cost, *salvage* is a Double that indicates the asset's value at the end of its useful life, *life* is a Double that identifies the length of the asset's useful life, and *period* is a Double that represents the period for which the depreciation is being calculated.

A Financial Function Example

Access users often forget that the financial functions even exist and reach for Excel when they need to analyze some figures. Depending on your needs, Excel might very well be the best tool for the job, but Access uses the same functions—it just presents the data differently.

Let's suppose you want to take out a small business loan to purchase new computer equipment so you can expand the business. A flexible function procedure can calculate your monthly payments on any loan. You plug in the numbers and VBA does the work. To create this function, return to the VBE and the Chapter5 module (or open a new module if you like). Then, complete the following steps:

 1. Enter the following procedure
```
Public Function CalPayment(rate As Double, _
  nper As Integer, pv As Double) As Currency
   CalPayment = Int(Pmt(rate / 12, nper, pv))
End Function
```

NOTE The code in the accompanying example includes an underscore character (_) at the end of the first line. That's what is known as the line continuation character. Use this character at the end of a line when you want to continue a line of code to the next line. Including this character lets VBA know that the current line and the next are part of the same statement and should be evaluated as such.

2. In the Immediate window, enter the following statement and press Enter:

```
?CalPayment(.07, 48, 10000)
```

Figure 5.10 shows the approximate monthly payment (without fees) of $240. Are you curious how VBA knew to display the amount as a currency? Look at the function's first line

```
Public Function CalPayment(rate As Double, _
  nper As Integer, pv As Double) As Currency
```

The As Currency phrase returns the function's value as a Currency data type. The Int function forces a whole number.

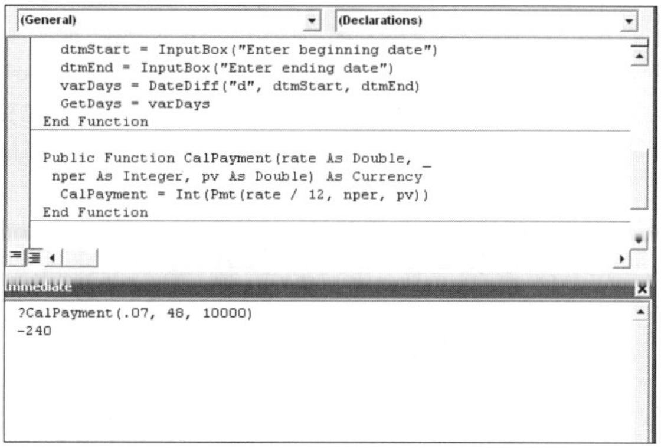

Figure 5.10
A quick procedure can calculate a monthly payment.

A quick function procedure can help you determine whether to go loan shopping. Simply pass different values to the function to change the payment amount. Perhaps you think you can get a better interest rate and consequently, borrow more money. If this were a task you were going to incorporate into your database, you'd create a form to gather all those values, but for now, the VBE does the trick without any special interface objects.

Using String Functions

String functions help you work with text data. For instance, you might want to replace one string with another or you might need to determine whether a string contains a specific character or a set of characters. In this case, and more, you'll rely on many of the string functions reviewed in this section.

The Asc **Function**

Oddly enough, string characters can be represented by an integer value, which can come in handy occasionally. What you're really working with are American National Standards Institute (ANSI) and American Standard Code for Information Interchange (ASCII) codes. When you need to work with that integer value, use the Asc function using the form

```
Asc(string)
```

where *string* is the literal string value or an expression that evaluates to a string that contains at least one valid character. A Null or zero-length string returns a runtime error. The returned value is an Integer data type from 0 to 255.

> **NOTE**
>
> The American National Standards Institute, or ANSI, is a private, nonprofit organization that administers and coordinates voluntary standardization in the United States.
>
> The American Standard Code for Information Interchange, or ASCII, is a numerical representation of characters that computers can't process as is.

> **CAUTION**
>
> The Asc function returns the integer value for only the first character in a string, regardless of the total number of characters in the string. All characters other than the first are ignored.

Usually, string values must be properly delimited using the apostrophe or double quotation character. This isn't the case with Asc. For instance, the two functions both return the value 49:

```
Asc("1")
Asc(1)
```

> **TIP**
>
> A *delimiter* is any character used to separate a value. For instance, VBA requires that you enclose a string in a set of apostrophe characters or double quotation marks, as follows: 'Harkins' or "Harkins". Dates must be properly delimited as well, using the pound sign (#).

The Chr **Function**

Just as Asc returns the ANSI value of a character, the Chr function returns the character equivalent of the ASCII character code. This simple function returns a variant of the String subtype and takes the form

```
Chr(charactercode)
```

where *charactercode* is a Long data type or expression that evaluates to an ASCII character. In the last section, you learned that 49 was the ANSI code for the value 1. On the flip side, use the Chr function to determine the character 49's corresponding character, which is of course, 1:

Chr(49)

> **TIP**
>
> Many string functions return a variant of the String subtype. To specifically force the function to return a String data type, use the $ form of the function. For instance, Chr returns a variant of the String subtype, but Chr$ returns a literal String value. The latter performs better in subsequent evaluations because VBA doesn't have to evaluate its data type before processing.

The Case **Functions**

There are two functions used to change letter case: LCase and UCase. Both functions take the form

LCase(*string*)
UCase(*string*)

where *string* is a literal string value or an expression that returns a string value. The return value is a Variant String subtype, but both functions have a $ format alternative that return a literal string value. If *string* is Null, the function returns Null. LCase returns the input string converted to all lowercase letters, and UCase returns the input string converted to all uppercase letters.

The Len **String Function**

Use Len to count the number of characters in a string value. This function takes the form

Len(*string*)

where *string* is a literal string value or an expression that returns a string value. The character count is returned as a Long Integer unless *string* is Null. In the case of a Null string, the function returns Null.

The Left, Right, **and** Mid **Functions**

Three functions, Left, Right, and Mid, return a subset of characters from a string. All three return a Variant Long subtype and support a $ version to force a String data type.

The Left function takes the form

Left(*string*, *length*)

where *string* represents the string being evaluated and *length* indicates the number of characters to return, beginning with the first character in *string*. The Right function takes the same form as Left, but Right returns characters from the end of *string*.

5

The Mid function requires three arguments, using the form

Mid(*string, start*[, *length*])

where *start* is a Variant Long subtype that determines where the count starts (from the left) and *length* is a Variant Long subtype that determines how many characters are counted.

In all three functions, if *string* is Null, the function returns Null. Figure 5.11 shows all three functions parsing different pieces of the same string.

Figure 5.11
Use Left, Right, and Mid to parse string values.

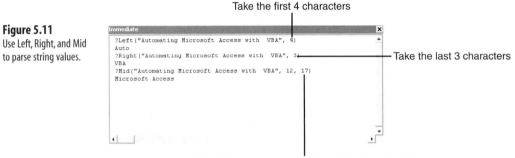

Take the first 4 characters

Take the last 3 characters

Take 17 characters beginning with character 12

The Replace **Function**

You can use the Replace function to replace a character or a subset of characters with another set of characters. This function uses the form

Replace(*string, stringtoreplace, replacementstring*[, *start*[, *count*[, *compare*]]])

where *string* is the complete String value, *stringtoreplace* is a string that represents the set of characters you plan to replace, and *replacementstring* is that String value that replaces *stringtoreplace*. There are three optional arguments: *start* identifies where Replace starts, *count* specifies how many characters in *stringtoreplace* to replace, and *compare* specifies the method used to compare *stringtoreplace* with *string*. Remember, a simple Replace can totally change the string. For instance, the following function changes the word block to black:

Replace("block","o","a")

The Space **Function**

Use Space to return a string consisting of a specific number of space characters as a Variant String subtype. Use the form

Space(*number*)

where *number* is an integer value that specifies the number of space characters to return. This function supports the $ format that forces the String data type.

The Split **String Function**

The Split function parses a single string into an array of delimited values. Basically, you're breaking the string into more than one piece. This function takes the form

```
Split(expression[, delimiter[, count[, compare]]])
```

where *expression*, a String data type that represents the string to be parsed, is the only required argument. The optional *delimiter* argument is a Variant that specifies the delimiting character. Use the optional *count* argument to specify the number of strings to return. The last optional argument, *compare*, is a tad more complex, specifying the type of comparison method. The possible vbCompareMethod constants follow:

- vbBinaryCompare—Comparisons are based on a sort order derived from the internal binary representations of the characters.
- vbTextCompare—Comparisons are based on a case-insensitive text sort determined by your system's locale settings.
- vbDatabaseCompare—This setting is unique to Access; the comparison is based on a sort order determined by the locale ID of the database.

The StrComp **Function**

Determine whether two strings are equal using the StrComp function. Use the form

```
StrComp(string1, string2[, compare])
```

where *string1* and *string2* are strings or string expressions. The optional *compare* argument is one of the vbCompareMethod constants reviewed for the String function in the previous section. The returned value is one of the following Variant Integer subtype values:

- –1—*string1* < *string2*
- 0—*string1* = *string2*
- 1—*string1* > *string2*
- Null—*string1* or *string2* is Null

A string is less than another string if it comes before the second string in alphabetical order. StrComp comes in handy any time you want to sort arbitrary data alphabetically.

The Three Trimming Functions

Trim, LTrim, and RTrim remove leading or trailing spaces from a specific string. They all use the same form

```
Trim(string)
LTrim(string)
RTrim(string)
```

5

where *string* is a String data type or an expression that evaluates to a string. All three functions return a Variant String subtype and support the $ format for forcing the result to a String data type. If *string* is Null, all three functions return Null.

LTrim removes leading space characters from the beginning of *string*; RTrim removes leading space characters from the end. Trim removes unnecessary spaces from both the beginning and the end of *string*.

> **NOTE**
>
> If you're an experienced Access user, you might be wondering where the section on domain or aggregate functions is. You won't find one in this book because neither are part of the VBA object model. Domain and aggregate functions both have similar functions in that they evaluate the values in a field. Domain functions enable you to specify criteria to limit the records that are evaluated, but they're native to Access, not VBA. Aggregate functions are very similar in functionality to domain functions; however, you can't limit the records to be evaluated. In addition, aggregate functions are provided by SQL—not by Access or VBA.

A String Function Example

Apostrophe characters within a string throw VBA for quite a loop. Unfortunately, they're everywhere. The sample database, TimeTrack.mdb, has a customer with an apostrophe character in its company name—Bill's Auto Glass.

I don't go into the specific problems that these embedded apostrophes create, but do show you a simple function that deletes them. First, return to the VBE and the Chapter5 module (or any standard module). Then, do the following:

1. Enter the following function procedure into the module:

```
Public Function StripApostrophe(str As String) As String
   StripApostrophe = Replace(str, "'", "")
End Function
```

2. In the Immediate window, run the following statement:

```
?StripApostrophe("Bill's Auto Glass")
```

Figure 5.12 shows the results. The function procedure removed the apostrophe character. Your users don't have to be burdened with too many data entry rules when you can clean up the values for them. I'm not suggesting that you actually change the stored value. Rather, you can use this function when a stored value doesn't conform to the requirements. You can manipulate the value—in the form you need—without changing the stored value.

Figure 5.12
Use Replace to
remove a troublesome
character.

```
(General)                              ▼    StripApostrophe                    ▼
  End Function                                                                 ▲

  Public Function CalPayment(rate As Double, _
    nper As Integer, pv As Double) As Currency
      CalPayment = Int(Pmt(rate / 12, nper, pv))
  End Function

  Public Function StripApostrophe(str As String) As String
      StripApostrophe = Replace(str, "'", "")
  End Function
                                                                              ▼
≡▤ ◀                                                                     ▶
Immediate                                                                    ☒
  ?StripApostrophe("Bill's Auto Glass")                                      ▲
  Bills Auto Glass
  |
```

Using the Format **Function**

Formatting data can consume a lot of your time. Fortunately, the Format function provides a
number of predefined formatting options. In addition, you can create user-defined formats
for custom formatting needs. The possibilities are too numerous to adequately cover, but
this section lists the tools you have at your disposal.

> **CAUTION**
>
> The most important thing to remember about the Format function is that the resulting value is a
> Variant String subtype—the resulting value's data type does *not* remain the same. That
> means that although the Format function can make your data look good, you won't want to use it
> with values used in other calculations. When a value needs manipulating before calculating, look to
> the conversion functions for help.

The Format function uses the form

```
Format(expression[, format[, firstdayofweek[, firstweekofyear]]])
```

where *expression* is a String or Numeric data type that represents the value you're formatting. The optional arguments determine how *expression* is formatted. The *format* argument is one of many predefined or custom format expressions. You saw the last two,
firstdayofweek and *firstweekofyear*, in the earlier section, "Extracting Date
Components."

Numbers, including date and time values and serial numbers, as well as strings, can all be
formatted using the Format function. You use a unique set of named and user-defined format expressions, defined in Tables 5.5 and 5.6.

5

Table 5.5   Numeric Named Formats

Format	Example	Result
General Number	Format(1234.5678, "General Number")	1234.5678
Currency	Format(1234.5678, "Currency")	$1,234.57
Fixed	Format(0.1, "Fixed")	0.10
Standard	Format(1234.5678, "Standard")	1,234.57
Percent	Format(.5678, "Percent")	56.78%
Scientific	Format(1234.5678, "Scientific")	1.23E+03
Yes/No	Format(0, "Yes/No") Format(2, "Yes/No")	No Yes
True/False	Format(0, "True/False") Format(2, "True/False")	False True
On/Off	Format(0, "On/Off") Format(2, "On/Off")	Off On

Most of the format expressions are self-explanatory, but a few deserve a bit more information. Currency relies on your system's locale settings for the appropriate symbols and thousand separators. Fixed always displays at least one digit to the left and two digits to the right of the decimal point. Standard is similar to Fixed except it also includes the thousands separator, as determined by the system's locale settings. Percent simply multiples the value by 100 and adds the percent symbol.

Table 5.6   Date/Time Named Formats

Format	Example	Result
General Date	Format("04/01/04", "General Date")	4/1/2004
Long Date	Format("04/01/04", "Long Date")	Thursday, April 01, 2004
Medium Date	Format("04/01/04", "Medium Date")	01-Apr-04
Short Date	Format("04/01/04", "Short Date")	4/1/2004
Long Time	Format("13:41:02", "Long Time")	1:41:02 PM
Medium Time	Format("13:41:02", "Medium Time")	1:41 PM
Short Time	Format("13:41:02", "Short Time")	13:41

Applying User-Defined Formats

The named formats listed in Table 5.5 and Table 5.6 won't always be adequate. When they don't suffice, you can use the user-defined format characters to create your own. These formats are listed in Tables 5.7, 5.8, and 5.9.

Table 5.7   Numeric User-Defined Formats

Format	Explanation	Example	Result
0	Existing digit or 0 is displayed for each 0	`Format(12.3456, "000.00000")`	012.34560
	Rounds if more digits than placeholder characters	`Format(12.3456, "000.00")`	012.35
#	Displays existing digit or nothing	`Format(12.3456, "###.#####")`	12.3456
	Rounds if more digits than placeholder characters	`Format(12.3456, "###.##")`	12.35
%	Multiples value by 100 and adds the percentage symbol	`Format(.3456, "##%")`	35%
E- E+ e- e+	Converts to scientific notation	`Format(1.234567, "###E-###")`	123E-2
		`Format(1.234567, "###e-###")`	123e-2
- + $ ( )	Displays a literal character	`Format(123.45, "$#####.##")`	$123.45
\	Displays following character as a literal character	`Format(.3456, "##.##\%")`	.35%

Table 5.8   Date User-Defined Formats

Format	Explanation	Example	Result
d	Displays day of month without a leading zero	`Format("04/01/04", "d")`	1
dd	Displays day of month with a leading zero when month is one character value	`Format("04/01/04", "dd")`	01
ddd	Displays day of week by abbreviated name	`Format("04/01/04", "ddd")`	Thu
dddd	Displays day of week by full name	`Format("04/01/04", "dddd")`	Thursday
ddddd	Displays short date	`Format("04/01/04", "ddddd")`	4/1/2004
dddddd	Displays long date	`Format("04/01/04", "dddddd")`	Thursday, April 01, 2004
m	Displays month value without a leading zero	`Format("04/01/04", "m")`	4
mm	Displays month value with leading zero when month is single digit value	`Format("04/01/04", "mm")`	04

5

continues

Table 5.8 Continued

Format	Explanation	Example	Result
mmm	Displays month as abbreviated name	`Format("04/01/04", "mmm")`	Apr
mmmm	Displays month as full name	`Format("04/01/04", "mmmm")`	April
q	Displays yearly quarter	`Format("04/01/04", "q")`	2
h	Displays hour of the day without leading zeros	`Format("9:41:02", "h")`	9
hh	Displays hour of the day with leading zeros when hour is single digit value	`Format("9:41:02", "hh")`	09
n	Displays minute without leading zeros	`Format("9:03:02", "n")`	3
nn	Displays minute with leading zeros when minute is single digit value	`Format("9:03:02", "nn")`	03
s	Displays second without leading zeros	`Format("9:03:02", "s")`	2
ss	Displays second with leading zero when second is single digit value	`Format("9:03:02", "ss")`	02
ttttt	Displays 12-hour clock using locale settings	`Format("13:41:02", "ttttt")`	1:41:02 PM
AM/PM	Displays 12-hour clock using uppercase AM/PM	`Format("13:41:02", "hh:mm AM/PM")`	01:41 PM
am/pm	Displays 12-hour clock using lowercase am/pm	`Format("13:41:02", "hh:mm am/pm")`	01:41 pm
A/P	Displays 12-hour clock with uppercase A or P	`Format("13:41:02", "hh:mm A/P")`	01:41 P
a/p	Displays 12-hour clock with lowercase a or p	`Format("13:41:02", "hh:mm a/p")`	01:41 p
ww	Displays the week value, 1 to 54	`Format("04/01/04", "ww")`	14
w	Displays the weekday value, 1 to 7	`Format("04/01/04", "w")`	5
y	Displays a day value from 1 to 366	`Format("04/01/04", "y")`	92
yy	Displays a two-digit year value from 00 to 99 that represents the date's year	`Format("04/01/04", "yy")`	04
yyyy	Displays a four-digit year value from 0100 to 9999 that represents the date's year	`Format("04/01/04", "yyyy")`	2004

5

Table 5.9 String User-Defined Formats

Format	Explanation	Example	Result
@	Displays existing character or space	`Format("VBA", "@@@@@")`	VBA (includes two spaces before the string)
&	Displays existing character or nothing	`Format("VBA", "&&&&&")`	VBA
<	Displays all characters in lowercase	`Format("VBA", "<<<")`	vba
>	Displays all character in uppercase	`Format("vba", ">>>")`	VBA

Using the `Is` Functions for Flawless Processing

All functions are prone to errors if you don't reference the right type of data. Most of these errors can be avoided by a simple check using one of VBA's many `Is` functions:

- `IsArray`—Tests for an array
- `IsDate`—Tests for a valid date value
- `IsEmpty`—Determines whether variable has been initialized (by having stored a value)
- `IsError`—Determines whether an expression is a valid error value
- `IsMissing`—Determines whether an optional argument has been passed to a procedure
- `IsNull`—Determines whether an expression contains a Null value
- `IsNumeric`—Determines whether an expression can be evaluated as a valid number
- `IsObject`—Indicates whether a variable contains a reference to an object

→ You learn about arrays in Chapter 7, "Working with Arrays," (p. 105).

All the `Is` functions use the same simple form

`Isfunction(value)`

where *value* represents the actual value, variable, argument, or expression being checked. Each function returns a Boolean value. If the value meets the condition being checked for the function returns `True`. Each function returns a `False` value if the condition isn't met. For instance, if the variable `varValue` is Null, the following function returns `True`:

`IsNull(varValue)`

Interacting Functions

Often, you'll need to prompt the users to enter relevant data or to simply share information. Either way, the application is interacting with the users. The two most frequently used functions in this area are the `InputBox` and `MsgBox` functions.

5

The InputBox **Function**

Earlier in this chapter, you worked with a few examples that gathered information from you in order to finish a task. This type of interaction can really come in handy because you won't always know every possible value when you're coding the solution. In addition, this type of solution lets you use one procedure over and over—in the same way you might use a parameter query.

The InputBox function takes the form

```
InputBox(prompt[, title][, default][, xpos][, ypos][, helpfile, context])
```

The only required argument is *prompt*—it's a String data type that represents the message the dialog box displays and is usually some kind of query that describes the type of data the users need to enter in response to the dialog box. The maximum number of characters allowed in *prompt* is 1,024. You can use the *title* String argument to display a title for the dialog box. If you omit this argument, VBA displays the application's name. Specify a string default value for the dialog box using the *default* option. The *xpos* and *ypos* arguments are both Numeric data types that specify the dialog box's position in relation to the screen. Specifically, *xpos* specifies the distance from the left side of the screen to the left side of the dialog box and *ypos* specifies the distance from the top of the screen to the top of the dialog box. You'll seldom use *helpfile* and *context*, but they go together; use them both or not at all. The *helpfile* argument is a String value that specifies the help file to use if the user clicks the dialog box's Help button and *context* is a Numeric value that specifies the context number to use within *helpfile*. (Note that creating Help files is beyond the scope of this book.)

The MsgBox **Function**

Use MsgBox to display information to users in a dialog box. You control the type of dialog box and how the users can respond. This function returns an integer value and uses the form

```
MsgBox(prompt[, buttons][, title][, helpfile, context])
```

where *prompt* is the only required argument. It's a String data type and represents the message displayed in the message box. You control how the users respond by specifying the type of buttons offered in the message box using *buttons*. Table 5.10 lists the button possibilities. Use *title* (a string) to display text in the dialog box's title bar. Both *helpfile* and *context* are the same for MsgBox as they are for InputBox (see the previous section for information on these two optional arguments).

Table 5.10   MsgBox Button Constants

Constant	Button Description	Integer Value
vbOKOnly	OK only	0
vbOKCancel	OK and Cancel	1
vbAbortRetryIgnore	Abort, Retry, and Ignore	2
vbYesNoCancel	Yes, No, and Cancel	3
vbYesNo	Yes and No	4
vbRetryCancel	Retry and Cancel	5

Table 5.11 lists the icons you can display in the *buttons* argument in the form

```
buttonsconstant + iconconstant
```

For instance, the function

```
MsgBox "You are about to delete records. Do you wish to continue?", vbOKCancel +
vbCritical, "Warning!"
```

resembles the message box shown in Figure 5.13. There are two buttons: OK and Cancel. The critical icon is the white x in the red circle. The plus sign combining vbOKCancel and vbCritical lets you display more than one element along with the message.

Table 5.11   Icon Constants

Constant	Icon	Integer Value
vbCritical	Critical Message	16
vbQuestion	Warning Query	32
vbExclamation	Warning Message	48
vbInformation	Information Message	64

5

Figure 5.13
You determine the type of message and the available buttons in a message box.

The function's returned value comes from the user's actions—the clicked button. Table 5.12 lists the possible values.

Table 5.12 Button Values

Button Clicked	Returned Value	Integer Value
OK	vbOK	1
Cancel (or Esc)	vbCancel	2
Abort	vbAbort	3
Retry	vbRetry	4
Ignore	vbIgnore	5
Yes	vbYes	6
No	vbNo	7

The message box in Figure 5.13 has two buttons, OK and Cancel. That means the MsgBox function returns either 1 or 2, accordingly.

CASE STUDY

Business Days

Part of managing all the projects tracked in TimeTrack.mdb is estimating the number of business days you have to get a particular job done. VBA's DateDiff function can quickly calculate the number of actual days, but there's no built-in function that excludes weekend days from the count.

In the following solution, you'll add a command button and a text box to the Projects form. Clicking the command button displays the number of business days between the project's start and end dates in the new text box. That way, you'll have a more accurate workday count for the project.

1. Open the Projects form in Design view and add a command button and a text box to the right of the Estimated End Date control. Name the command button cmdCalculate and the text box txtBusinessDays and set the text box control's Visible property to No.

2. Click the Code button on the Form Design toolbar to open the form's module in the VBE.

3. Enter the following event procedures:

```
Private Sub cmdCalculate_Click()
    'Determine the number of business days
    'allotted for the project
    'This procedure does not allow for holidays
    Dim dtmStart As Date
    Dim dtmEnd As Date
    Dim intTotalDays As Integer
    Dim intWeekendDays As Integer
    Dim intBusinessDays As Integer
    If IsNull(StartDate) Then
      MsgBox "Please enter a start date", _
        vbOKOnly, "Error"
      Exit Sub
    End If
```

```
            If IsNull(EstimatedEndDate) Then
              MsgBox "Please enter an end date", _
                vbOKOnly, "Error"
              Exit Sub
            End If
            dtmStart = StartDate
            dtmEnd = EstimatedEndDate
            Select Case DatePart("w", dtmStart, vbMonday)
              Case Is = 6
                dtmStart = DateAdd("d", dtmStart, 2)
              Case Is = 7
                dtmStart = DateAdd("d", dtmStart, 1)
            End Select
            Select Case DatePart("w", dtmEnd, vbMonday)
              Case Is = 6
                dtmEnd = DateAdd("d", dtmEnd, -1)
              Case Is = 7
                dtmEnd = DateAdd("d", dtmEnd, -2)
            End Select
            intTotalDays = DateDiff("d", dtmStart, dtmEnd) + 1
            intWeekendDays = DateDiff("ww", dtmStart, dtmEnd, vbMonday) * 2
            intBusinessDays = intTotalDays - intWeekendDays
            txtBusinessDays = intBusinessDays
            txtBusinessDays.Visible = True
          End Sub
          Private Sub Form_Current()
            'Reset txtBusinessDays control
            txtBusinessDays = ""
            txtBusinessDays.Visible = False
          End Sub
```

4. Save the code and return to Access by clicking the View Microsoft Office Access button on the VBE's standard toolbar or by clicking the form button on the Windows taskbar.

5. Click the View button to see the modified form in Form view, as shown in Figure 5.14.

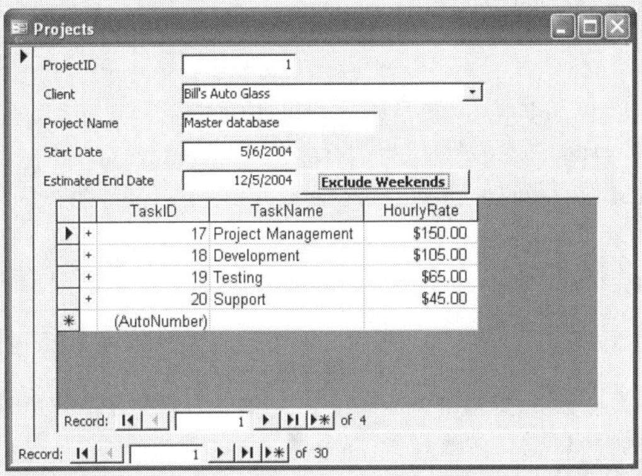

Figure 5.14
You can't see the new text box because its Visible property is set to False.

6. Click the Exclude Weekends command button to display the number of business days between the project's start and end dates, as shown in Figure 5.15. Don't worry if your answer differs from the example. The actual number of days depends on the actual day (not the day on which this example was evaluated).

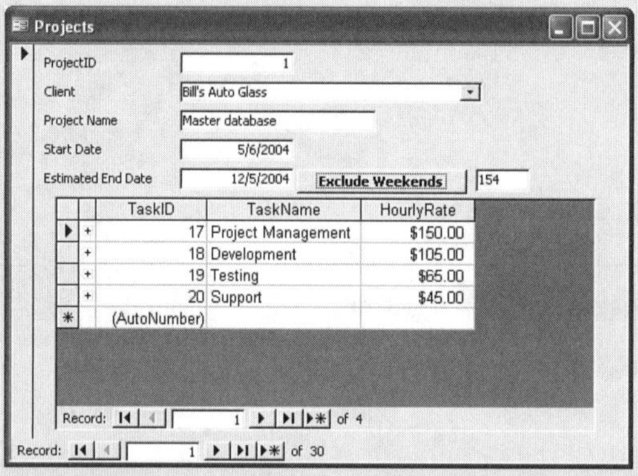

Figure 5.15
Click the new command button to calculate and display the number of estimated working days for the current project.

After declaring and defining a number of variables, the `IsNull` function checks for a start and end date. If either is missing, the procedure alerts the user and exits the procedure.

When both dates are present, the first `Select Case` statement adjusts the start date if it falls on a Saturday or Sunday by adding 1 or 2, as appropriate. The second `Select Case` statement adjusts the end date by subtracting 1 or 2, accordingly.

→ Learn about the Select Case and If End statements in "Using Select Case," p. 94, and "Using If . . . Then . . . Else," p. 91.

→ The procedure in this case study responds to a control's event procedure. Learn more about this process in "Responding to Events," p. 161, and "The Event Sequence for Controls," p. 162.

The remaining calculations determine the total number of days and the total number of weekend days (Saturday and Sunday) between the two adjusted dates. The number of business days between the two dates is the difference between the total number of days and the total number of weekend days.

There's nothing in this procedure to prevent you from entering an end date that's earlier than the start date. You probably won't want to do this, but occasionally this type of calculation is warranted. You have to decide for yourself if you want to add the necessary functionality to limit date values.

> **TIP**
>
> You might remember that Chapter 3 stressed the importance of using appropriate data types for each field. Now you can see at least one benefit of that rule. You don't have to worry about invalid date entries because the underlying table field is a `Date/Time` data type. If you try to enter anything but a date, Access rejects the entry. That's one error-handling task you can skip because you eliminated the possibility of that error at the application's very foundation—the table.

You might be wondering what the `Current` event procedure does. That simple procedure resets the contents of the text box and sets its `Visible` property back to `False` when you move to another record.

The procedure itself incorporates many of the good coding practices you learned about in Chapter 2. Specifically, each line is indented appropriately and there's a descriptive comment at the beginning of both procedures that describes their purpose. In addition, the procedure declares and uses several variables of various types.

Using Flow-of-Control Statements

Branching and Looping

So far, nearly all the code that you've seen in this book has been strictly sequential. That is, execution starts at the top of each procedure, continues line-by-line through the procedure, and stops at the end of the procedure. The one exception to this rule that you've seen so far has been in error-handling code.

→ Error handling in VBA was covered in "Implementing Error Handling," p. 52.

VBA is capable of more complex patterns of program execution than this, though. To write flexible VBA code, you need to understand the concepts of *branching* and *looping*. Branching lets VBA make a decision and then execute one of several statements depending on that decision. Looping lets VBA execute a statement or a set of statements more than once. As you'll see in this chapter, there are several variations on each of those themes. Together, branching and looping structures are referred to as *flow-of-control* statements, because they determine the order in which your program's executing flows.

IN THIS CHAPTER

Branching and Looping 91

Using If . . . Then . . . Else 91

Using Select Case 94

Using For . . . Next 95

Using Do Loops 99

Using GoTo 101

Using If...Then...Else

The first branching statement that you should know about is the If statement. As you might guess from the word, the If statement executes code if something is true.

The Simple If Statement

To begin with, you can use If to control the execution of one or more statements. Here's an example:

```
Function IsSunday(dtmDayToCheck As Date) As Boolean
  ' Returns true if the specified date is a Sunday
  IsSunday = False
  If DatePart("w", dtmDayToCheck) = 1 Then
    IsSunday = True
  End If
End Function
```

This function accepts a single date argument, and returns a Boolean value. If the `DatePart` function returns 1 when queried for the day of the week, the function returns `True`. Otherwise, it returns `False`, which is set as the function's default value by the first line of code.

Schematically, this simple form of the `If` statement looks like this:

```
If condition Then
  statements
End If
```

The condition can be anything that returns a `True` or `False` value. If the condition returns `True`, all statements until the `End If` statement are executed in order. Otherwise, the entire block is skipped, and the first statement after the `End If` is executed next.

> **TIP**
> If a condition returns a numeric value, the value 0 is considered to be the same as `False`, and any other value is considered to be the same as `True`.

Creating More Complex Conditions

Conditions can use complex logic together with parentheses to group things if need be. For example, this function tests whether a date is Saturday or Sunday:

```
Function IsWeekend (dtmDayToCheck As Date) As Boolean
  ' Returns true if the specified date is on a weekend
  IsWeekend = False
  If ((DatePart("w", dtmDayToCheck) = 1) Or _
    (DatePart("w", dtmDayToCheck) = 7)) Then
    IsWeekend = True
  End If
End Function
```

Here the condition is spread across two lines. If the `DatePart` function returns `True` in either case, `IsWeekend` is set to `True`. Otherwise, it remains at the default value of `False`.

You'll frequently see one or more of the three logical keywords in a condition:

- The `Or` keyword is used when one or more conditions should be true. If you join two conditions with `Or`, the whole is true if either (or both) of the parts is true.

- The `And` keyword is used when all the conditions must be true. If you join two conditions with `And`, the whole is true only if all the parts are true.

- The `Not` keyword reverses true to false and vice versa.

Table 6.1 shows some examples of these logical keywords.

Table 6.1   Logical Keywords in Action

Condition	Explanation
(intDays = 4) Or (intWeeks = 3)	True if either intDays is 4, or intWeeks is 3, or both.
(intDays = 4) And (intWeeks = 3)	True if both intDays is 4 and intWeeks is 3.
Not (intDays = 4)	True if intDays has any value other than 4.

Adding the Else Statement

There are some optional parts to the If...End If structure. The first of these is the Else statement.

```
Function IsWeekday(dtmDayToCheck As Date) As Boolean
  ' Returns true if the specified date is a weekday
  If ((DatePart("w", dtmDayToCheck) = 1) Or _
  (DatePart("s", dtmDayToCheck) = 7)) Then
    IsWeekday = False
  Else
    IsWeekday = True
  End If
End Function
```

Adding Else lets you return something if the condition is false. Schematically, it works like this:

```
If condition Then
  statements1
Else
  statements2
End If
```

If the condition is True, the first set of statements is executed. Otherwise, the second set of statements is executed.

Using the ElseIf Statement

The other optional part to the If...End If structure is the ElseIf statement. Here's an example of this statement in action:

```
Function GetDayName(dtmDayToCheck) As String
  ' Returns the day of the specified date
  If DatePart("w", dtmDayToCheck) = 1 Then
    GetDayName = "Sunday"
  ElseIf DatePart("w", dtmDayToCheck) = 2 Then
    GetDayName = "Monday"
  ElseIf DatePart("w", dtmDayToCheck) = 3 Then
    GetDayName = "Tuesday"
  ElseIf DatePart("w", dtmDayToCheck) = 4 Then
    GetDayName = "Wednesday"
```

6

```
   ElseIf DatePart("w", dtmDayToCheck) = 5 Then
     GetDayName = "Thursday"
   ElseIf DatePart("w", dtmDayToCheck) = 6 Then
     GetDayName = "Friday"
   Else
     GetDayName = "Saturday"
   End If
End Function
```

Be sure to pass a valid date variable or a properly delimited date string using the # delimiting character. Otherwise, the function returns Saturday, regardless of the passed value. When VBA executes this function, it evaluates each of the conditions in turn, starting with the one following the `If` and continuing with each `ElseIf`. When it finds one that evaluates to `True`, it executes the corresponding statements and then skips to the `End If` statement. The main difference between `Else` and `ElseIf` is that you can state many different conditions instead of just one.

Using `Select Case`

The `If` statement can get quite cumbersome to read and understand if there are many `ElseIf` clauses. To simplify your code while maintaining the same basic structure, you can use the `Select Case` statement. Here's the previous example rewritten as a `Select Case`:

```
Function GetDayName(dtmDayToCheck) As String
  ' Returns the day of the specified date
  Select Case DatePart("w", dtmDayToCheck)
    Case 1
      GetDayName = "Sunday"
    Case 2
      GetDayName = "Monday"
    Case 3
      GetDayName = "Tuesday"
    Case 4
      GetDayName = "Wednesday"
    Case 5
      GetDayName = "Thursday"
    Case 6
      GetDayName = "Friday"
    Case Else
      GetDayName = "Saturday"
  End Select
End Function
```

To use the `Select Case` structure, you place an expression that returns a value in the `Select Case` statement itself. After that, you can have any number of `Case` statements, each containing a value. VBA matches the result of the expression against each `Case` value in turn, and when it finds a match, it executes the statements immediately following that `Case` statement, stopping at the next `Case` or at the `End Select`. Note that you can also use `Case Else` to match anything that's not matched by an earlier case.

It's best to end a `Select Case` statement with a `Case Else`. That way, if anything goes wrong and none of the `Case` conditions are matched, the `Case Else` can alert you to the fact that no condition was matched. This approach can probably avoid data errors or even a runtime error.

Using For...Next

Sometimes it's convenient to execute a set of statements more than once. That's why VBA includes looping statements. The first looping statement you should know about is `For...Next`.

To see why such statements are useful, let's start with this example, which does not include any looping statements:

```
Sub PrintWeek(dtmStart As Date)
  ' Print out a week's worth of dates
  ' starting at dtmStart
  Debug.Print dtmStart
  Debug.Print DateAdd("d", 1, dtmStart)
  Debug.Print DateAdd("d", 2, dtmStart)
  Debug.Print DateAdd("d", 3, dtmStart)
  Debug.Print DateAdd("d", 4, dtmStart)
  Debug.Print DateAdd("d", 5, dtmStart)
  Debug.Print DateAdd("d", 6, dtmStart)
End Sub
```

Figure 6.1 shows this procedure in action. As you can see, it prints a set of seven dates starting at a specific date to the Immediate window. In real life, you'd probably store this information somewhere, or print it to a printer, but you don't yet have the VBA tools to perform these tasks.

Figure 6.1
Printing dates without a loop.

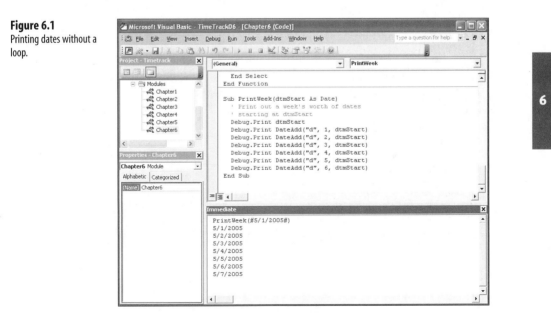

Although this procedure works as advertised, there are two problems with it. First, the code is very repetitive; it takes a lot of code to do such a simple task. Second, it's inflexible. What if you want to print three dates, or 30? You have to actually change the code to do so.

You can overcome both of these problems with the For...Next looping structure. First, here's the original procedure converted into a loop:

```
Sub PrintWeek(dtmStart As Date)
  ' Print out a week's worth of dates
  ' starting at dtmStart
  Dim intI As Integer
  For intI = 0 To 6
    Debug.Print DateAdd("d", intI, dtmStart)
  Next intI
End Sub
```

In this procedure, the variable intI is called the *loop counter*. The For...Next structure assigns the values from 0 through 6 to this variable and executes the statements between the For and the Next statements once for each of those values. Here there's just a single statement in the body of the loop, but you can have more than one statement within the loop.

> **NOTE**
> Traditionally, loop counters are named with short variable names such as i, j, and k. If you're using a naming convention, you might prefer (as I do) intI, intJ, and intK. Some people use a meaningful counter name (such as intDays) instead.

> **TIP**
> You can omit the loop variable from the Next statement, simply writing Next instead of Next intI. I prefer to include the variable, but don't get confused if you see code without it.

Looping in Reverse

The first loop that you saw uses the values 0, 1, 2, 3, 4, 5, and 6 in that order for the loop counter. The default behavior of the For...Next loop is to increment the loop counter by 1 each time that it executes the loop. But you can actually change the loop counter by a different value. Here's a version that counts backward:

```
Sub PrintWeekReverse(dtmStart As Date)
  ' Print out a week's worth of dates
  ' ending at dtmStart
  Dim intI As Integer
  For intI = 6 To 0 Step -1
    Debug.Print DateAdd("d", intI, dtmStart)
  Next intI
End Sub
```

The Step part of the For statement tells VBA to (in this case) subtract 1 from the loop counter each time it executes the loop. You can use Step to change the loop in other ways as well. For example, to count by threes, you set up your loop this way:

```
For intI = 0 to 9 Step 3
  statements
Next intI
```

In this case, the statements in the loop are executed four times, with intI having the values 0, 3, 6, and 9.

Using a Variable for the Loop Counter

In the second version of the PrintWeek procedure, the loop counter ranges over a fixed set of values from 0 to 6, but those values can be variables as well. Here's a more flexible procedure:

```
Sub PrintDays(dtmStart As Date, intDays As Integer)
  ' Print out a week's worth of dates
  ' starting at dtmStart
  Dim intI As Integer
  For intI = 0 To intDays - 1
    Debug.Print DateAdd("d", intI, dtmStart)
  Next intI
End Sub
```

Now the number of days to print is controlled by the second argument to the procedure. Figure 6.2 shows how you might call this version to print four successive dates.

Figure 6.2
Printing dates with a loop.

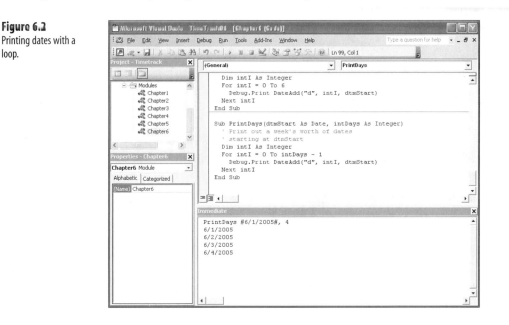

Nesting For...Next **Loops**

Loops can also contain other loops. Nesting loops let you write even more condensed code under some circumstances. Suppose you want to print timecards with slots for every hour during the work day across a week. You can do this by using one loop for the days and another inner loop for the hours:

```
Sub PrintTimecard(dtmStart As Date)
  ' Print out hourly timecard for a week
  Dim intI As Integer
  Dim intJ As Integer
  For intI = 0 To 6
    Debug.Print DateAdd("d", intI, dtmStart)
    For intJ = 0 To 8
      Debug.Print "   " & DateAdd("h", intJ, #9:00:00 AM#)
    Next intJ
  Next intI
End Sub
```

A little thought will show you how this works. The outer loop, using intI as the loop variable, walks through the seven days of the week. For each value of intI, it prints the day, and then calls the inner loop. The inner loop is executed nine times before control returns to the outer loop. In case you're having trouble visualizing the results, Figure 6.3 shows how this works.

Figure 6.3
Using nested loops.

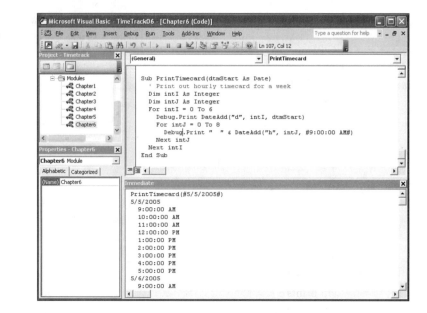

This procedure prints 70 lines of output. By using nested loops, it achieves this task with 8 lines of code rather than 70 Debug.Print statements.

You're not limited to nesting two loops; you can nest three, four, five, or even more loops if you've got a good use for such code.

Aborting a For...Next **Loop**

Sometimes you might change your mind and not want to complete all the cycles through a For...Next loop. For those times, the VBA language contains the Exit For statement. Consider this procedure, which returns the date of the Monday that most closely follows the given date:

```
Function GetNextMonday(dtmDateStart As Date) As Date
  ' Returns the date of the next Monday
  Dim intI As Integer
  Dim dtmDayToCheck As Date
  For intI = 1 To 7
    dtmDayToCheck = DateAdd("d", intI, dtmDateStart)
    If DatePart("w", dtmDayToCheck) = 2 Then
      GetNextMonday = dtmDayToCheck
      Exit For
    End If
  Next intI
End Function
```

It's obvious that there is always a Monday no more than seven days after the given date. The function uses a For...Next loop to create each of those seven dates, using the DateAdd function. Each time, it determines whether the date is a Monday. If it is, that date can be returned, and there's no point in completing the For...Next loop. The Exit For statement tells VBA to move to the next statement after the entire For loop and to continue execution there; in this case, that's the End Function statement.

→ A second form of loop, the For...Each loop, is used with object variables. For information on For...Each loops, see "Working with Collections," p. 119.

Using Do **Loops**

For...Next loops are useful when you can specify the number of times that you need to repeat an action. But sometimes you don't know in advance how many times you want to repeat something. For those times, there's the Do looping structure.

Creating a Simple Do **Loop**

This first Do loop prints a chart showing the amount to be billed for one hour, two hours, and so on through eight hours at a specific hourly rate:

```
Sub PrintBilling(curHourlyRate As Currency)
  ' Print out a billing chart
  Dim intHours As Integer
  intHours = 1
```

```
    Do
        Debug.Print intHours * curHourlyRate
        intHours = intHours + 1
    Loop Until intHours = 9
End Sub
```

The lines between `Do` and `Loop` constitute the `Do` loop. When VBA executes the `Do` statement, it starts executing the statements in the body of the loop, and continues executing them until the condition in the `Loop` statement is `True`. In this particular example, VBA continues adding one to the `intHours` variable and executing the statements in the loop until `intHours` is equal to 9, at which time it proceeds to the next statement.

> **TIP**
> If you make a mistake in programming a `Do` loop—for example, if you forget to change anything that affects the ending condition—you can set up an infinite loop that executes forever, locking up your computer. If this happens, press Ctrl+Break to enter Debug mode and suspend the loop.

> **NOTE**
> In many cases, a `Do` loop can be replaced by an equivalent `For...Next` loop. In the PrintBilling example, you could have used `For intHours = 1 to 8` as the loop structure. Choose whichever statement you think is more clear to read when building your own loops.

Varieties of the Do Loop

The `Do` Loop comes in four slightly different varieties. You can perform the check for termination at the start or the end of the loop, and you can loop while something is true or until it becomes true. You've already seen the first version, which checks at the end of the loop and proceeds until a condition is true:

```
Do
    statements
Loop Until condition
```

If you prefer, you can execute the statements in the loop while a condition is true. In this case, the condition is still checked at the end of each run through the loop, and execution continues past the loop when the condition returns `False`:

```
Do
    statements
Loop While condition
```

You can also perform the check at the start of the loop instead of at the end. You can do this with an `Until` condition:

```
Do Until condition
    statements
Loop
```

Finally, you can check at the start of the loop with a `While` condition:

```
Do While condition
  statements
Loop
```

Choosing between these four ways of constructing a `Do` loop can be a bit tricky. If you find that your code isn't executing the loop the number of times that you were expecting, one thing to consider is whether your `Do` loop is not the right type. The debugging tools that you learned about in Chapter 4 can be a big help here; by single-stepping through the loop, you can see exactly what's going on.

> **CAUTION**
>
> If you put the check at the end of the loop, the statements in the loop are always executed at least once, regardless of the initial value of the condition.

Aborting a Do **Loop**

When you want to jump out of the middle of a `Do` loop, you can use the `Exit Do` statement, which works very much like `Exit For`. Here's an example:

```
Sub PrintLimitedBilling(curHourlyRate As Currency)
  ' Print out a billing chart, limited to $200
  Dim intHours As Integer
  intHours = 1
  Do
    Debug.Print intHours * curHourlyRate
    If intHours * curHourlyRate >= 200 Then
      Exit Do
    End If
    intHours = intHours + 1
  Loop Until intHours = 9
End Sub
```

This procedure works much the same as the `PrintBilling` procedure that you saw earlier in the chapter. However, each time VBA executes the statements within the loop, it determines whether the calculated value is greater than or equal to 200. If it is, VBA executes the `Exit Do` statement to terminate the loop.

Using GoTo

There's one final flow-of-control statement that you should know about: the `GoTo` statement. `GoTo` produces an unconditional change in the flow of your program. Here's an example of the `GoTo` statement in action:

6

```
Sub CalculateBill(curRate As Currency, intHours As Integer)
  ' Calculate the bill for this line item
  If intHours > 100 Then
    GoTo ExitHere
  End If
  Debug.Print curRate * intHours
ExitHere:
End Sub
```

In this code, ExitHere is an example of a *label*. A label is not executed by VBA. Rather, it is a bookmark within the code that VBA can refer to by name.

The GoTo statement transfers the program flow to the specified label. So in this particular procedure, the effect is to exit from the entire procedure if the intHours variable has a value of more than 100.

The GoTo statement has been a subject of debate for many years. Most professional developers agree that using GoTo can make your code harder to read and understand, because you have to jump around to follow the code when you're reading it. And in most cases, you can rewrite code to avoid the GoTo statement. For example, here's another version of the CalculateBill procedure:

```
Sub CalculateBill(curRate As Currency, intHours As Integer)
  ' Calculate the bill for this line item
  If intHours <= 100 Then
    Debug.Print curRate * intHours
  End If
End Sub
```

This version has exactly the same effect as the first version, but it does not use the GoTo statement.

On the whole, I agree with those who feel that the GoTo statement should be avoided. You might occasionally find that using GoTo makes your code seem more clear, and in those cases, there's nothing wrong with using GoTo. For example, if there are many places within a complex procedure where you want to execute cleanup code and then terminate the procedure, you might use GoTo statements to avoid having to repeat the cleanup code. But don't leap to use GoTo as your first tool in all cases.

→   The GoTo statement is necessary as a part of the On Error GoTo error-trapping statement, and you shouldn't avoid using that statement just because it includes a GoTo. See "Using On Error GoTo," on p. 53.

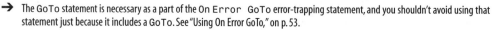

CASE STUDY

Billing for Work in Progress

One thing that consultants tend to be concerned with is the amount of revenue that they're generating. Often, one consultant is juggling multiple projects, working a few hours per day on each one. In these cases, it's useful to be able to generate a chart showing the amount to be billed for, say, three hours a day across four days at a particular rate.

To generate such a chart, we've developed the procedure named PrintBillingChart. This procedure puts together several of the flow-of-control statements that you've seen in this chapter. Here's the text of the procedure:

```
Sub PrintBillingChart(curBaseRate As Currency, _
 intMaxDays As Integer)
  ' Show hourly billings for up to the
  ' specified number of days
  Dim intDays As Integer
  Dim intHours As Integer

  If intMaxDays > 6 Then
    Debug.Print "This procedure is limited to 6 days"
  Else
    ' Create the chart title
    Debug.Print "Billing Chart for " & _
     Format(curBaseRate, "Currency")

    ' Create the chart header
    Debug.Print vbTab;
    intDays = 0
    Do Until intDays = intMaxDays
      intDays = intDays + 1
      Debug.Print CStr(intDays) & " days" & vbTab;
    Loop
    Debug.Print

    ' Create the chart body
    For intHours = 1 To 8
      Debug.Print CStr(intHours) & vbTab;
      intDays = 0
      Do Until intDays = intMaxDays
        intDays = intDays + 1
        Debug.Print Format(intDays * intHours * curBaseRate, _
         "Currency") & vbTab;
      Loop
      Debug.Print
    Next intHours
  End If
End Sub
```

Before dissecting this code, let's look at the output. Here's what you see in the Immediate window if you execute PrintBillingChart 25, 4:

```
Billing Chart for $25.00
   1 days   2 days   3 days   4 days
1 $25.00   $50.00   $75.00   $100.00
2 $50.00   $100.00 $150.00 $200.00
3 $75.00   $150.00 $225.00 $300.00
4 $100.00 $200.00 $300.00 $400.00
5 $125.00 $250.00 $375.00 $500.00
6 $150.00 $300.00 $450.00 $600.00
7 $175.00 $350.00 $525.00 $700.00
8 $200.00 $400.00 $600.00 $800.00
```

So, for example, if you bill three hours a day for three days at the specified rate of $25, the total bill is $225.

The procedure starts by declaring the variables that it will use (remember, it's a good idea to declare all variables in one spot so they're easy to find). Then it checks to make sure it's not being asked to print a chart that's too wide. The If...Else...End If structure provides a handy way to abort the procedure if the arguments are unreasonable.

Within this structure, there are three major pieces of code. Note that I've used comments to make it easier to see what's going on. Printing the chart title is easy; this just requires executing a single Debug.Print statement.

Printing the chart header uses one bit of code that you haven't seen before. Note that some of the Debug.Print statements end with a semicolon. This tells VBA to continue printing on the same line, rather than always returning to the next line. So to print the chart header, it prints each separate column header, and then executes a blank Debug.Print statement to return to the first column of the next line of the output. Also note the use of the vbTab constant. This is a built-in constant that represents the Tab character.

Printing the chart body nests a Do loop within a For...Next loop. Thus, the Do loop is executed eight times, once for each row of the chart. Within the Do loop, VBA does the work of formatting the amount to be billed, and then prints it.

Although this code is more complex than the procedures you've seen up to this point in the book, it makes use of the same building blocks. If you look at each block in turn, you can see how it all fits together. If you have any doubts, you can set a breakpoint and single step through the procedure.

Working with Arrays

IN THIS CHAPTER

Introducing Array Variables 105

Declaring an Array Variable 105

Understanding the Array's Index 106

Working with Array Elements 107

Arrays with Multiple Dimensions 110

Expanding to Dynamic Arrays 110

Introducing Array Variables

So far, the variables you've encountered have been straightforward in that all variables have a purpose, a data type, and eventually, a value. Sometimes variables aren't quite so simple. Sometimes a variable can equal more than one value at the same time. In this chapter, you learn how array variables store more than one value.

In general terms, an array refers to a large group of similar items. In mathematical terms, an array is rectangular set of values in rows and columns. A VBA *array* is a set of fixed values, called *elements*, that share the same data type and name. VBA interprets and processes the group of values as one variable.

Array variables are useful anytime you have a set of related values that you need to store. For instance, if you loop through the same code, grabbing values and storing them in a temporary table, you might consider an array to store those values instead. Temporary tables require additional code to create, maintain, and then destroy. Whatever your reason, anytime you find yourself thinking in terms of storing a set of related values, consider using an array.

Declaring an Array Variable

Because an array is a type of variable, you must declare it and specify a data type, as you must any other variable. When declaring an array, specify the array's upper and lower bounds. In other words, let the array know the smallest and largest values it can store.

To declare an array variable, use the following syntax:

```
Dim arrayvariable([lower to ]upper) [AS datatype]
```

where *arrayvariable* is the variable's name, *lower* is the array's smallest index, *upper* is the array's largest index, and *datatype* defines the type of data the array can store. If you omit the *datatype* argument, VBA declares the array as a Variant array.

In its simplest form, you can omit *lower* and VBA will assume it's 0. We recommend that you specify both bound arguments unless you have a specific reason to delay their definition.

Now, let's look at a simple example of an array declaration statement:

```
Dim arrInteger(1 To 4) As Integer
```

Right away you know a few things about this array:

- arrInteger can contain up to four elements. Think of each element as a "slot" within the array where you can store a value.
- arrInteger can store only Integer values.
- The elements (slots) in arrInteger are numbered 1, 2, 3, and 4.

Understanding the Array's Index

At this point, you might be wondering how VBA—and you—differentiate between all the possible elements (values) in an array. Internally, VBA assigns an *index* to each element in the array. Simply put, the index is a type of identification value for each element.

The index values depend on the *lower* and *upper* bounds. For instance, the statement

```
Dim arrInteger(1 To 4) As Integer
```

accommodates four Integer values. These four values are stored in the four array elements, each identified by one of the four index values—1, 2, 3, and 4. The first element's index value is 1, the second element's index value is 2, and so on.

Table 7.1 lists several simple arrays that can also store up to four Integer values, but the index values would be different. As you can see, the numbering of the elements is determined by the upper and lower bounds in the array declaration.

Table 7.1   Array Examples

Array Declaration	Index Values
`Dim arrInteger(0 To 3) As Integer`	0, 1, 2, 3
`Dim arrInteger(2 To 5) As Integer`	2, 3, 4, 5
`Dim arrInteger(-4 To -1) As Integer`	–4, –3, –2, –1
`Dim arrInteger (-3 to 0) As Integer`	–3, –2, –1, 0
`Dim arrInteger (3) As Integer`	0, 1, 2, 3

> **TIP**
>
> Occasionally, the index value relates to the stored value in some way, but don't confuse the two. The index is simply VBA's way of finding the value—it identifies the position of the element in relation to the other elements. For example, the first element in an array of integers can contain the value 1, or 17, or −257, or any other integer value. Don't try to find a way to relate the index values to the actual stored values unless the relationship just naturally exists, which probably won't happen very often.

Using `Option Base`

By default, the lowest bound value is always 0 unless one of the following conditions apply:

- You explicitly specify a different lower bound value.
- The module includes an `Option Base` statement.

You've already seen the first condition at work, which leaves the `Option Base` statement. You enter this statement in a module's General Declarations section using the form

```
Option Base 0 | 1
```

This statement sets the default lowest bound for arrays within that module, and only that module. You can set the default bound to 0 or 1, not to any other value.

→ The general declarations section of a module is reviewed in "Introducing the VBA Modules," p. 21.

> **TIP**
>
> Although the `Option Base 1` statement automatically sets the lower bound of all arrays within the module to 1, consider explicitly specifying the lower bound for each individual array instead. Doing so creates a more readable array statement. You'll also prevent those possible (and likely) errors after you forget that the default lower bound has been set to 1 by the `Option Base` statement.

Working with Array Elements

After declaring an array variable, there are two ways to manipulate that array's elements:

- You can define the array elements
- You can refer to the array elements

Defining and referencing array elements is similar to doing so with any other variables. Just remember, you have to work within the context of the array's index values.

7

Defining Array Elements

Declaring an array is only half the job. The next step is to actually store the elements in it. To do so, use the simple syntax

```
arrayvariable(index) = value
```

where *index* identifies the element's position within the array and *value* is any valid value or expression that fits the declared data type. Following the previous example

```
Dim arrInteger(1 To 4) As Integer
```

index can be only the values 1, 2, 3, and 4, but *value* can be any valid integer. For instance, all the following statements are valid:

- `arrInteger(1) = 100`
- `arrInteger(2) = -200`
- `arrInteger(3) = 3`
- `arrInteger(4) = 40`

The previous statements set arrInteger's four elements to the values 100, –200, 3, and 40, respectively.

Similarly, the following procedure sets the value of four array elements to . 1, . 2, . 3, and . 4:

```
Public Sub ArrayExample1()
  Dim intCounter As Integer
  Dim arrExample(1 To 4) As Variant
  For intCounter = 1 To 4
    arrExample(intCounter) = intCounter * 0.1
  Next
End Sub
```

The lower bound is 1 and the upper bound is 4. The For…Next statement loops once for each intCounter value (1 through 4). During each loop, intCounter equals an index value. (This won't always be the case.) The procedure multiples the index value by .10 and assigns the resulting value to the corresponding element. For instance, the first time through, intCounter equals 1, so the definition statement evaluates as follows

```
arrExample (1) = 1 * 0.1
arrExample (1) = .1
```

The second time through the loop, intCounter equals 2, so arrExample(2) equals .2 (2 * 0.1), and so on.

→   To learn how to use the For…Next statement, see "Using For…Next," p. 95.

Referencing Array Elements

The previous Sub function assigned a value to each of the array's four elements. What you need to know now is how to access those values. You access array elements similarly to the way you defined them—you use the index values in the form

```
variable = arrayvariable(index)
```

For instance, to refer to any of the elements in arrExample from the previous example, refer to the appropriate element index value as follows:

```
arrExample(1)
arrExample(2)
arrExample(3)
arrExample(4)
```

To illustrate referencing an element, use the following Sub procedure to pass a value to the procedure and then display the corresponding array element in a message box:

```
Public Sub ArrayExample2(ele As Integer)
  Dim intCounter As Integer
  Dim arrExample(1 To 4) As Variant
  For intCounter = 1 To 4
    arrExample(intCounter) = intCounter * 0.1
  Next
  MsgBox "The value of array element " & _
    ele & " is " & arrExample(ele), vbOKOnly
End Sub
```

To see the procedure in action, launch the VBE, open a blank module, and enter the procedure. Or, open Chapter7 in the TimeTrack.mdb sample database. Then, enter the following statement in the Immediate window

```
arrayExample2(x)
```

where *x* is the value 1, 2, 3, or 4, and then press Enter. (There's no error-handling in this procedure, so if you enter a value other than 1 through 4, the message box will display an incomplete message.) The procedure sets all four array elements, but returns only the value of the element represented by the passed value. Figure 7.1 shows the result of passing the value 2 to the procedure. Click OK to clear the message box and return to the VBE.

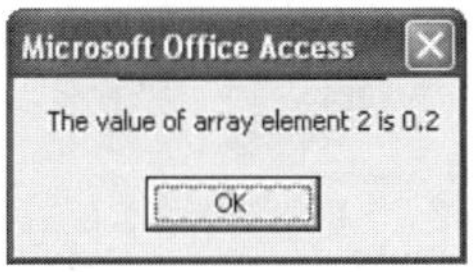

Figure 7.1
Use the index value to reference an array's elements.

Microsoft Office Access

The value of array element 2 is 0.2

OK

→ To learn how to include error handling in your VBA procedures, see "Implementing Error Handling," p. 52.

7

Arrays with Multiple Dimensions

Arrays can also use more than one index to locate an element. For example, a two-dimensional array assigns two indexes to each element. To declare a two-dimensional array, you specify the range of each index, separated by commas. For example, this statement defines an array of 10 elements by 10 elements:

```
Dim arrTaxAmount(1 To 10, 1 To 10) As Double
```

When defining or retrieving values from a two-dimensional array, you must supply both index values, as in this procedure:

```
Public Function GetTaxAmount(intPercent As Integer, _
 intAmount As Integer) As Double
  ' Return a tax amount for the specified
  ' tax percentage and purchase amount
  ' Inputs are limited to the range of 1 to 10

  Dim i As Integer
  Dim j As Integer
  Dim arrTaxAmount(1 To 10, 1 To 10) As Double
  ' Build the array
  For i = 1 To 10
    For j = 1 To 10
      arrTaxAmount(i, j) = (i * j) / 100
    Next j
  Next i

  ' Now look up the amount
  GetTaxAmount = arrTaxAmount(intPercent, intAmount)
End Function
```

Arrays can have up to 60 dimensions, which is far more than you're ever likely to need.

Expanding to Dynamic Arrays

So far, all the array examples have specified the array's lower and upper bounds when declared. Doing so creates what's known as a *fixed-size* array. If you don't specify the size of the array when you declare it, you create a *dynamic* array. To size the array, you must use the ReDim statement as follows:

```
Dim arrExample() As datatype
...
ReDim arrExample([lower] To upper) As datatype
```

Because VBA insists on an explicit value when declaring an array using Dim, this is the only way to control the value of the lower and upper bounds using a variable.

About ReDim

The ReDim statement changes the dimensions and reallocates storage space for a dynamic array. Use this statement to define an array's bounds after you've declared the array and before you use the array.

The `ReDim` statement takes the form

```
ReDim [Preserve] arrayvariable([lowerTo] upper) As datatype
```

where `Preserve` is a VBA keyword that preserves an array's data when changing the only or last dimension value (bound). Without the `Preserve` keyword, `ReDim` erases an array's existing values.

The following procedure uses a dynamic array:

```
Public Sub ArrayExample3(l As Integer, u As Integer)
  Dim intCounter As Integer
  Dim arrExample() As Variant
  ReDim arrExample(l To u)
  For intCounter = l To u
    arrExample(intCounter) = intCounter * 0.1
  Next
  For intCounter = l To u
    Debug.Print arrExample(intCounter)
  Next
End Sub
```

In this procedure, the array's dimensions aren't set by the original `Dim` statement, but by the `ReDim` statement. Consequently, you can pass the lower and upper values to the procedure, which makes the procedure much more flexible.

You can use the procedure provided in `TimeTrack.mdb`'s `Chapter7` module. Or, you can open a blank module and create it yourself. Either way, execute the procedure by entering the following statement in the Immediate window:

```
ArrayExample3 1, 4
```

Figure 7.2 shows the results—0.1, 0.2, 0.3, and 0.4. Try again, but this time pass the values 2 and 6, as shown in Figure 7.3.

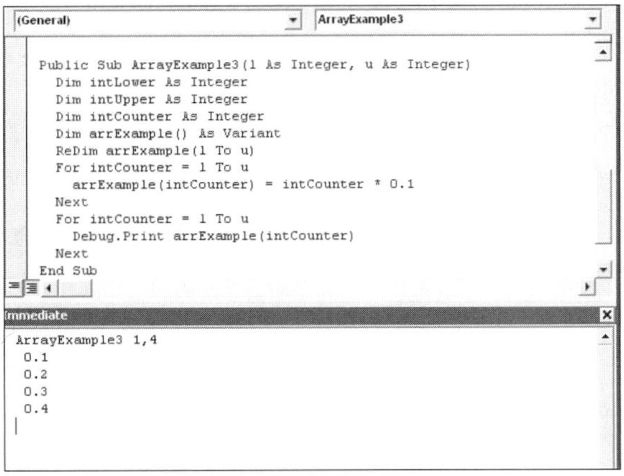

Figure 7.2
Pass the lower and upper dimensions via procedure arguments.

Figure 7.3
Change the array's
dimensions by passing
different values.

Understanding Objects

Introducing Objects

You've seen quite a few variables so far in this book. Recall that a *variable* is a named part of VBA code that holds a single value (for example, a number or a string of characters). Or in the case of an array variable, the variable can store multiple related values. But so far you've been exposed to only one type of variable, which you might call a *simple variable* (sometimes you'll see the technical term *scalar variable* used for this type). There's actually a second type called *object variables*, or just *objects*. An object variable is a variable that also includes behavior. This concept is often tough for beginners to grasp, so this section starts by exploring an analogy that will help you understand how objects work.

IN THIS CHAPTER

Introducing Objects .113

Reading and Setting Properties 116

Invoking Methods 117

Working with Collections 119

Working with an Object Model 121

Creating Your Own Objects 124

Working with Events 126

Digressing into the Real World

To understand objects, you're going to look at a real-world object. Specifically, this section discusses the sort of toy radio-controlled car that has been popular with kids (and software developers!) for many years. Here are three key facts about a typical such car:

- The plastic cars are mass-produced from a single mold. One mold can make many cars.

- Any given car is described by a set of adjectives such as "blue." Every car can be described by characteristics like its color, but different cars can have different colors.

- When you manipulate the control box, the car does things such as go forward, turn, or go backward. You don't have to know anything about how the car does these things; you just send it the appropriate commands.

All that probably seems perfectly obvious, which was the point. If you keep these little cars in mind when learning about objects, it will help you sort out the key concepts.

An Object Example from Access

There are objects in VBA and in the applications that it manipulates, just like there are objects in the real world. For example, each Access form is actually an object. Here's how the analogy plays out:

- Form objects are mass-produced from a single template called a *class*. Making an object from a class is called *instantiating* the class (an object is an *instance* of a class). One class can instantiate many objects.

- Any given form is described by a set of *properties* such as a caption, for example, "Switchboard." Every form can be described by properties like its caption, but different forms can have different captions.

- The form can do things like open or close. You don't have to know anything about how the form does these things; you just invoke the appropriate *methods*.

Of course, analogies break down after a while, and there are some aspects of objects (such as events, which you learn about later in this chapter) that don't fit neatly into this particular analogy. But on the whole, if you start to feel confused about VBA objects, thinking about real objects might help.

Creating Objects in Code

Although you can create some objects (such as Access forms) through a user interface, most VBA objects are completely abstract and can only be created in code. Before you can do anything else with objects, you need to know how to create them. Here's an example of VBA code that creates a new object, in this case an instance of the Projects form in the sample database:

```
Sub CreateObject1()
  ' Create and display a form object
  Dim frm As Form_Projects
  Set frm = New Form_Projects
  frm.Visible = True
  MsgBox "Click OK to continue"
End Sub
```

If you run this code, you'll discover that it creates an instance of the Projects form and displays it, along with a message box, as shown in Figure 8.1. When you click OK, both the message box and the form vanish.

The code starts by declaring the object variable named `frm`. Rather than being a simple variable such as a string or an integer, this variable is declared to be of the `Form_Projects` type. For each form in your Access application, Access creates a matching class named `Form_form-name`.

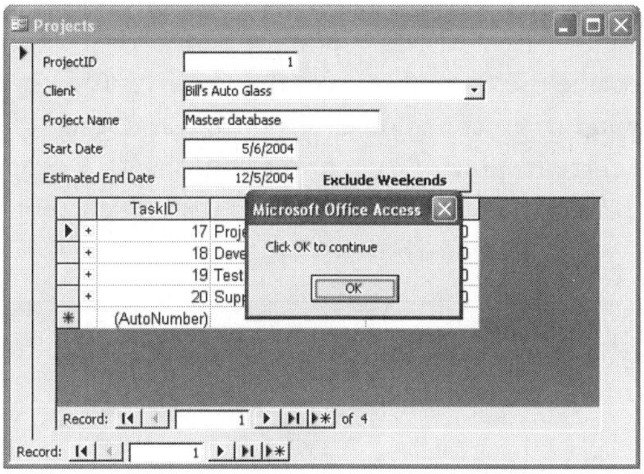

Figure 8.1
Form object created with VBA code.

8

Remember, though, that the class is not itself an object. To actually use the object, you need to instantiate the class. That's what the second line of code (the Set statement) does. This line tells VBA to create a new instance of the Form_Projects class, and to use the frm variable to refer to that object in the future.

By default, new Access forms are hidden when they are created. The next line of code sets the Visible property of the form to True, so that it will be visible onscreen.

Next comes the MsgBox statement to generate the message box. Remember, when you create a message box, your code pauses until the user responds to the message.

After you click OK, you'll see the form vanish. That's because VBA destroys all the variables declared in a procedure at the end of the procedure. When the frm variable is destroyed in code, the corresponding form ceases to exist onscreen.

→ It is possible to declare variables slightly differently so that they are available outside of a single procedure. For details, see "Understanding Scope and Lifetime," p.131.

There's a second way to create an object that takes slightly less code:

```
Sub CreateObject2()
  ' Create and display a form object
  Dim frm As New Form_Projects
  frm.Visible = True
  MsgBox "Click OK to continue"
End Sub
```

The line of code

```
Dim variablename As New classname
```

both declares and instantiates the variable in a single line.

> **CAUTION**
>
> When you declare and instantiate an object in a single statement, the object isn't actually created until the first time that you use the object variable in code. If you want to make it easy to tell when the object is created, use the two-statement format.

Reading and Setting Properties

An object's properties describe the current state of the object. Any class can have zero or more properties. When you instantiate an object from the class, each of these properties has a value. You can read the current value of each property from VBA code, or assign new values to properties from VBA code. Here's an example of reading current values of a form object's properties:

```
Sub ReadProperties()
  ' Display some properties of an object
  Dim frm As New Form_Projects
  frm.Visible = True
  Debug.Print frm.Caption
  Debug.Print frm.RecordSelectors
End Sub
```

When you run this procedure from the Immediate window, you get output that looks this:

```
Projects
True
```

To get the value of a property from an object, you refer to it by using the object name and the property name, with a dot in between:

object.property

You can assign this value to a variable, or (as in the example you just saw) print it, or use it as an argument to a procedure; in fact, you can use a property value anywhere that you can use a simple variable of the same type. In this case, the caption of the form is "Projects" and the form's record selectors (the vertical bar at the left side of the form) are turned on.

To change the value of a property, you assign a value to the property using very similar syntax:

```
Sub WriteProperties()
  ' Change some properties of an object
  Dim frm As New Form_Projects
  frm.Visible = True
  frm.Caption = "Project details"
  frm.RecordSelectors = False
  MsgBox "Click OK to continue"
End Sub
```

Running this procedure results in a display like that shown in Figure 8.2. Note that the form's caption is set to the value specified in the code, and the record selectors have been hidden by the VBA code. (Compare Figures 8.1 and 8.2 and you'll see that the small black triangle at the upper-left portion of the form is missing in Figure 8.2—that's the record selector.)

> **NOTE**
> If you run the WriteProperties procedure and then re-open the form from the regular Access user interface, you'll discover that the property changes made through VBA don't persist. By default, any changes you make in VBA are thrown away by Access when you're done with the object. You can override this default by calling the form's Save method; you learn about methods in the next section of this chapter.

Figure 8.2
Changing property values with VBA.

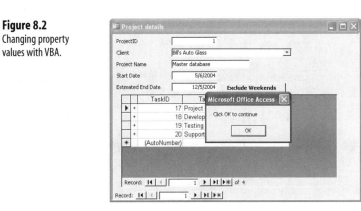

Any object can have three types of properties:

- Read/write properties, which you can both read and change in code
- Read-only properties, which you can read, but not change, in code
- Write-only properties, which you can change, but not read, in code

Most properties are read/write. Read-only properties are often used for properties that can't change after you create an object; for example, a Form object has a Name property that returns the name of the class. Write-only properties are rare. You might run across a class with a password property that is write-only, enabling you to set a new password but not to read an existing password.

Invoking Methods

The things that an object knows how to do are called the object's methods. Invoking a method uses syntax very similar to setting a property. You separate the method name from the object name with a dot. Here's an example of invoking a method:

```
Sub InvokeMethod()
  ' Invoke a method of an object
  Dim frm As New Form_Projects
  frm.Visible = True
  frm.Move 0, 0, 1440, 1440
  MsgBox "Click OK to continue"
End Sub
```

This code calls the Move method of the Form class. Methods can have arguments, which follow the method name and are separated by commas; in this case, there are four arguments to the Move method, in this order:

- The *left* argument specifies the new position of the left edge of the form relative to the Access workspace.
- The *top* argument specifies the new position of the top of the form relative to the Access workspace.

- The *width* argument specifies the new width of the form.

- The *height* argument specifies the new height of the form.

Figure 8.3 shows the result of running the InvokeMethod procedure. As you can see, the form is scrunched up to the top-left side of the workspace, and has its width equal to its height.

Figure 8.3
Form after invoking the Move method.

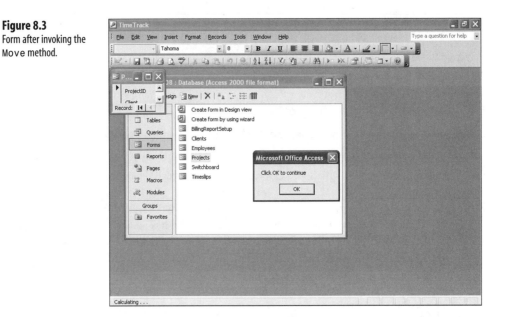

N O T E

In VBA, distances and sizes are measured in *twips*. There are 1440 twips in one inch.

Many methods have optional arguments. In fact, the last three arguments of the Move method are all optional. If you don't supply a value for one of these arguments, the corresponding property of the form doesn't change. You can skip over optional arguments by just putting nothing between the commas. For example, if you want to supply values for just the *left* and *width* arguments, you can use this line of code:

```
frm.Move 0, , 1440
```

As you can see, you don't have to even supply the commas if you're leaving out an optional argument at the end of the list. You can also refer to arguments by name, in which case you can supply them in any order:

```
frm.Move Width:=1440, Top:=0
```

The := characters separate an argument's name and its value.

Working with Collections

Many objects are grouped into *collections*. A collection is a special object that contains other objects. For example, Access maintains its own collection of open forms, and you can use this collection in VBA. Because Access maintains this collection object, you don't need to instantiate it yourself. In this section of the chapter, you learn the basic syntax to work with collections. Collections are most useful for listing and finding instances of the objects that they contain.

Here's the first way to list the objects in a collection:

```
Sub ListCollection1()
  ' List the items in a collection

  ' First, open three forms
  Dim frmClients As New Form_Clients
  Dim frmProjects As New Form_Projects
  Dim frmSwitchboard As New Form_Switchboard
  frmClients.Visible = True
  frmProjects.Visible = True
  frmSwitchboard.Visible = True

  ' Now go through the built-in Forms
  ' collection to list them
  Dim i As Integer
  For i = 0 To Forms.Count - 1
    Debug.Print Forms.Item(i).Name
  Next i

End Sub
```

This code starts its work by opening three forms, using the syntax you've already seen to instantiate the form objects. It then declares a variable i to act as a loop counter. The loop sets i equal to each value, from 0 to one less than Forms.Count. Forms.Count is a property that returns the number of objects in the built-in Forms collection (that is, the number of open forms). The numbering here is *zero-based*: that is, if the collection contains three objects, they are numbered 0, 1, and 2.

→ To review the details of looping, see "Using For…Next," p. 95.

Each iteration of the loop retrieves the name of one of the objects in the collection. Item is a property of the Forms collection that returns a particular member of the collection. For example, Forms.Item(1) returns the second member of the collection. Because the collection contains forms, this member is a form object, and the code can retrieve and print the Name property of the form. When you run the procedure, you see this result in the Immediate window:

```
Clients
Projects
Switchboard
```

There are two ways to simplify this code. First, the `Item` property is the *default property* of the `Forms` collection. This means that you don't actually have to include the property name in the code. So this procedure still works to list the open forms:

```
Sub ListCollection2()
  ' List the items in a collection

  ' First, open three forms
  Dim frmClients As New Form_Clients
  Dim frmProjects As New Form_Projects
  Dim frmSwitchboard As New Form_Switchboard
  frmClients.Visible = True
  frmProjects.Visible = True
  frmSwitchboard.Visible = True

  ' Now go through the built-in Forms
  ' collection to list them
  Dim i As Integer
  For i = 0 To Forms.Count - 1
    Debug.Print Forms(i).Name
  Next i

End Sub
```

Finally, because looping through all members of a collection is such a common operation, there's a special looping statement just for this purpose. The `For…Each` loop goes through a collection, setting an object variable to each member of the collection in turn:

```
Sub ListCollection3()
  ' List the items in a collection

  ' First, open three forms
  Dim frmClients As New Form_Clients
  Dim frmProjects As New Form_Projects
  Dim frmSwitchboard As New Form_Switchboard
  frmClients.Visible = True
  frmProjects.Visible = True
  frmSwitchboard.Visible = True

  ' Now go through the built-in Forms
  ' collection to list them
  Dim frm As Form
  For Each frm In Forms
    Debug.Print frm.Name
  Next frm

End Sub
```

When you use the `For…Each` syntax, your loop counter variable must be an object variable of the appropriate type. As VBA goes through the loop, it instantiates this object variable to refer to each member of the collection in turn. With this syntax, you don't have to worry about retrieving the collection's `Count` and setting an integer appropriately; VBA takes care of the details.

Every collection has a Count property and an Item method. You might also find methods such as Add and Remove on many collections. These methods adjust the membership of the collection. Because the Forms collection is maintained by Access, it does not have Add or Remove methods.

Working with an Object Model

Collections and the items that they contain are often arranged into an *object model*. An object model is a diagram that shows the objects in an application and their relationships. For example, Figure 8.4 shows a portion of the object model supplied by Access.

Figure 8.4
A portion of the Access object model.

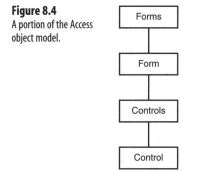

The diagram indicates that the Forms collection contains individual Form objects. Each Form object contains a Controls collection. The Controls collections each contain Control objects. As you undoubtedly guessed, the Control objects each represent a control on a form.

Using an Object Model

Here's some code that uses this portion of the object model:

```
Sub ListControls()
  ' List the controls on all open forms

  ' First, open three forms
  Dim frmClients As New Form_Clients
  Dim frmProjects As New Form_Projects
  Dim frmSwitchboard As New Form_Switchboard
  frmClients.Visible = True
  frmProjects.Visible = True
  frmSwitchboard.Visible = True

  ' Use collections to list their controls
  Dim frm As Form
  Dim cnt As Control
  For Each frm In Forms
    Debug.Print frm.Name
```

```
      For Each cnt In frm.Controls
        Debug.Print "   " & cnt.Name
      Next cnt
   Next frm

End Sub
```

Here, the nested For...Each loops go through both levels of the Access object model for forms and controls. The net effect is to list every control name on the three specified forms.

Using References

Many applications supply object models that VBA can use. For example, every application in the Microsoft Office suite has its own object model. To use the object model from an application other than the one where VBA is running, you must first set a *reference* to the object model. A reference tells VBA that you intend to use objects from a particular object model.

To set a new reference, select Tools, References in the VBA editor. This opens the References dialog box, shown in Figure 8.5. The references that are already set for the current VBA project are listed at the top of the dialog box, followed by all the available references on your computer, in alphabetical order.

Figure 8.5
The References dialog box.

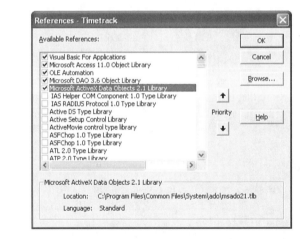

To set a reference to an object model, scroll to the model in the list and select its check box. Then click OK. After you set a reference to an object model, you can use the objects in that model. For example, if you set a reference to the Microsoft Excel 11.0 Object Library, this code runs perfectly well in Access:

```
Sub TestExcel()
   ' Use the Excel object model
   Dim objExcel As New Excel.Application
   objExcel.Visible = True
   MsgBox "Excel should be visible"
End Sub
```

Because Access and Excel both have objects named `Application`, it's necessary to specify that the code use the `Application` object from the `Excel` object model rather than the one from Access. This is done by specifying the name of the library followed by a dot and the name of the object, as in these examples:

```
Access.Form
Excel.Application
```

In this book, you mainly use objects from two object models. The `Access` object model includes `Forms`, `Controls`, `Reports`, and other objects specific to Access. The `ADO` object model includes objects for working with data. You learn more about these object models in Parts II and III of this book.

The Object Browser

When you start working with objects, you quickly discover that there are hundreds of available objects, properties, and methods. The Object Browser tool makes it easier to navigate this often confusing forest.

To open the Object Browser, select <u>V</u>iew, <u>O</u>bject Browser or press F2. This opens the Object Browser as a window in the VBA editor, as shown in Figure 8.6.

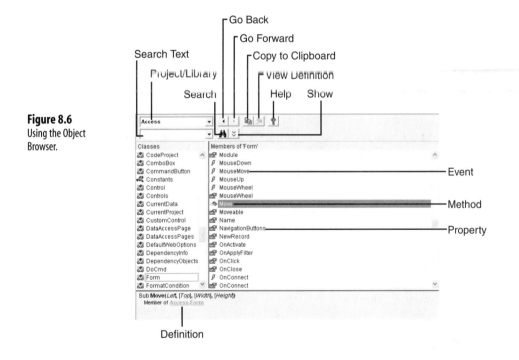

Figure 8.6
Using the Object Browser.

Here are some of the things that you can do with the Object Browser:

- Select a library or object model to work with in the Project/Library drop-down list. You can also select <All Libraries> to have Object Browser look at everything that you have currently loaded.

- Locate a class by scrolling down the list on the left side. You can also enter part or all the name of the class in the Search Text box and click the Search button to quickly find the class.

- When you select a class, the right side of the Object Browser shows all the properties, methods, and events of the class. Collectively, properties, methods, and events are known as *members*. You learn about events later in this chapter.

- When you select a member of a class, the Definition window shows brief details on the member.

- Click the Help button to see detailed help on the currently selected member.

- Use the Go forward and Go back buttons to move back and forth in the list of members that you've viewed recently.

- Use the Copy to Clipboard button to copy the current member to the Clipboard.

> **TIP**
> When you're writing code that uses objects, you'll probably find that the Object Browser is a faster way to get help than digging through the help files.

Creating Your Own Objects

In addition to using objects from existing libraries, VBA enables you to build your own classes and objects. This section shows you how to build a simple class that represents a weekly timecard summary. To get started, select Insert, Class Module. In the VBA window, an empty class module looks just like an empty regular module. But the Properties window shows that it's a class module, and you'll see a different icon in the Project window. Use the Properties window to name the class TimeWeek.

Now enter this code to implement the class:

```
Option Compare Database
Option Explicit

' Expose some simple properties
Public MondayHours As Integer
Public TuesdayHours As Integer
Public WednesdayHours As Integer
Public ThursdayHours As Integer
Public FridayHours As Integer
Public SaturdayHours As Integer
Public SundayHours As Integer
```

8

```
' Expose a property backed with a private variable
Private strEmployeeName As String
Public Property Let EmployeeName(NewName As String)
  strEmployeeName = NewName
End Property
Public Property Get EmployeeName() As String
  EmployeeName = strEmployeeName
End Property

' Calculate three read-only properties
Public Property Get TotalHours() As Integer
  TotalHours = MondayHours + TuesdayHours + _
  WednesdayHours + ThursdayHours + FridayHours + _
  SaturdayHours + SundayHours
End Property

Public Property Get RegularHours() As Integer
  If TotalHours > 40 Then
    RegularHours = TotalHours
  Else
    RegularHours = 40
  End If
End Property

Public Property Get OvertimeHours() As Integer
  If TotalHours > 40 Then
    OvertimeHours = TotalHours - 40
  Else
    OvertimeHours = 0
  End If
End Property

' Implement a simple method
Public Function PrintTimeReport()
  Debug.Print "Monday " & MondayHours
  Debug.Print "Tuesday " & TuesdayHours
  Debug.Print "Wednesday " & WednesdayHours
  Debug.Print "Thursday " & ThursdayHours
  Debug.Print "Friday " & FridayHours
  Debug.Print "Saturday " & SaturdayHours
  Debug.Print "Sunday " & SundayHours
End Function
```

This code demonstrates two ways to implement properties, and one way to implement a method. The easy way to create a property for a class is to simply give the class a public variable; all such variables are visible as properties of the class.

A more complex way to create a property is to write *property procedures*. The EmployeeName property is implemented using a Property Let procedure and a Property Get procedure. When someone sets a value for the property, the Property Let procedure is called with the new value. When someone reads the value of the property, the Property Get procedure is called to return the value. In the case of the EmployeeName property, the value is simply stored in an internal private variable; in this case, the property procedures behave exactly the same as a public string variable would.

The other three properties (TotalHours, RegularHours, and OvertimeHours) are all implemented using Property Get procedures without corresponding Property Let procedures. This makes them read-only properties, because there's no way for outside code to set these values.

PrintTimeReport is a method of the class. Any public Function procedure or public Sub procedure becomes a method of the class.

After saving this code, you can use the TimeWeek class just like any other class. Here's an example of calling the TimeWeek class:

```
Sub UseTimeWeek()
    ' Demonstrate the TimeWeek class
    Dim tw As New TimeWeek
    tw.MondayHours = 8
    tw.TuesdayHours = 9
    tw.WednesdayHours = 8.5
    tw.ThursdayHours = 8
    tw.FridayHours = 7.5
    tw.SaturdayHours = 4
    tw.SundayHours = 3.5
    Debug.Print "Regular: " & tw.RegularHours
    Debug.Print "Overtime: " & tw.OvertimeHours
    Debug.Print "Total: " & tw.TotalHours
    Debug.Print "-------------------"
    tw.PrintTimeReport
End Sub
```

And here's the output that the UseTimeWeek procedure produces in the Immediate window:

```
Regular: 49
Overtime: 9
Total: 49
-------------------
Monday 8
Tuesday 9
Wednesday 8
Thursday 8
Friday 8
Saturday 4
Sunday 4
```

Working with Events

There's one more part of working with objects that you haven't read about yet: dealing with events. You're probably familiar with events from working in the Access user interface. Events provide "hooks" that let you run your own code when something happens. For example, buttons have a Click event, and when the user clicks a button in your application, you can run a macro in response.

However, it turns out that running macros in response to events is a shortcut invented by the Access team to make it possible to construct reasonably complex applications without writing any code. Most professional developers avoid the use of macros for several reasons (notably that macros do not implement any error trapping). Instead of using macros to respond to events, you can use *event procedures*, which are special pieces of VBA code.

In the TimeTrack sample application, all the buttons use macros to perform their work. Let's convert one of these to use an event procedure so that you can see the syntax involved.

1. Open the Switchboard form in Design view.

2. Select the Clients button and display its properties.

3. Change the name of the button to cmdClients. When you're writing event procedures, it's helpful to use meaningful names for controls, so that it's obvious in code which control you are referring to.

4. Change the On Click property from OpenClients (the name of the macro that the click event currently calls) to [Event Procedure] (you can find this choice, including the square brackets, in the drop-down list for the property).

5. Click the ellipsis button next to the property to construct the event procedure. Access then opens the VBA editor with the code for the form loaded and constructs an empty event procedure for you.

6. Fill in the body of the event procedure with this code:
   ```
   Private Sub cmdClients_Click()
     DoCmd.OpenForm "Clients"
   End Sub
   ```

7. Save the form and switch back to Access. Click the button and it will still open the Clients form. You can set a breakpoint in the event procedure to verify that the code is doing the work.

VBA hooks up event procedures to events based on a naming convention and the location of the code. In this case, the code is in the module for the Switchboard form, and the procedure is named using the pattern *objectname_eventname*. As Figure 8.7 shows, there are also cues in the VBA user interface that let you know when you're working in an event procedure. If you want to construct a new event procedure without using the Access interface, you can select the appropriate object and event from the drop-down lists in the VBA editor.

This event procedure introduces one more of the built-in Access objects: the DoCmd object. You can think of the DoCmd object as a bridge between the world of Access macros and that of VBA code. The DoCmd object has no properties, but it implements one method for each of the actions that you can include in an Access macro. Anything that you can do with an Access macro, you can do in VBA code with the DoCmd object.

Containing Form | Object | Event

Figure 8.7
An event procedure in
the VBA editor.

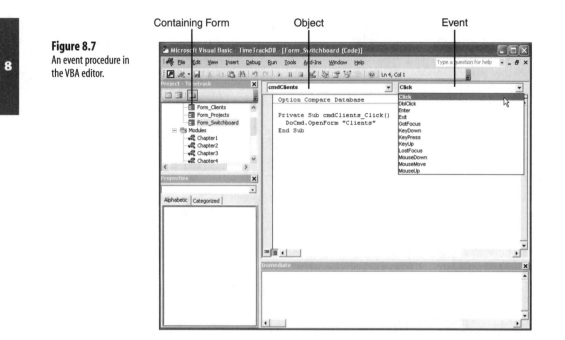

Opening Forms and Handling Errors

As you get comfortable with VBA, you'll want to start using event procedures to handle events. You might also want to convert existing macros to event procedures. Doing so helps you catch any errors in event handling moving forward, and places all your code in one place (the VBA editor) instead of spreading it around multiple macros.

The `TimeTrack` application contains six macros; five of them are called from the `Switchboard` form and they all open various other forms. Here's the code to use VBA in place of these macros, with some basic error handling added:

```
Option Compare Database
Option Explicit

Private Sub cmdBillingReport_Click()
  On Error GoTo HandleErr
  DoCmd.OpenForm "BillingReportSetup"
ExitHere:
  Exit Sub
HandleErr:
  MsgBox "Error " & Err.Number & ": " & _
   Err.Description & " in cmdBillingReport_Click"
  Resume ExitHere
End Sub

Private Sub cmdClients_Click()
  On Error GoTo HandleErr
```

8

```
  DoCmd.OpenForm "Clients"
ExitHere:
  Exit Sub
HandleErr:
  MsgBox "Error " & Err.Number & ": " & _
  Err.Description & " in cmdClients_Click"
  Resume ExitHere
End Sub

Private Sub cmdEmployees_Click()
  On Error GoTo HandleErr
  DoCmd.OpenForm "Employees"
ExitHere:
  Exit Sub
HandleErr:
  MsgBox "Error " & Err.Number & ": " & _
  Err.Description & " in cmdEmployees_Click"
  Resume ExitHere
End Sub

Private Sub cmdProjects_Click()
  On Error GoTo HandleErr
  DoCmd.OpenForm "Projects"
ExitHere:
  Exit Sub
HandleErr:
  MsgBox "Error " & Err.Number & ": " & _
  Err.Description & " in cmdProjects_Click"
  Resume ExitHere
End Sub

Private Sub cmdTimeslips_Click()
  On Error GoTo HandleErr
  DoCmd.OpenForm "Timeslips"
ExitHere:
  Exit Sub
HandleErr:
  MsgBox "Error " & Err.Number & ": " & _
  Err.Description & " in cmdTimeslips_Click"
  Resume ExitHere
End Sub
```

CAUTION

If you're entering this code yourself, remember that you need also to change the control names to match those in the code.

This code demonstrates a simple error-handling pattern that you can use by default whenever you don't need to implement more complex error handling. Each procedure starts by using On Error GoTo to identify a label where errors will be trapped. At the end of the normal code in the procedure, a labeled Exit Sub statement is used to finish the procedure without entering the error handler. Within the error handler, the code uses a message box to display some properties of the built-in Err object, which contains information about the most recent error. It then uses a Resume statement to return to the same exit point used by the normal code.

→ To review the basics of error-handling code, see "Implementing Error Handling," p. 52.

The final macro in the sample database is used by the BillingReportSetup form to open the report. Converting this one to VBA is slightly trickier, because the code needs to specify that the report opens in Print Preview mode:

```
Private Sub cmdOpenReport_Click()
  On Error GoTo HandleErr
  DoCmd.OpenReport "BillingReport", acViewPreview
ExitHere:
  Exit Sub
HandleErr:
  MsgBox "Error " & Err.Number & ": " & _
    Err.Description & " in cmdBillingReport_Click"
  Resume ExitHere
End Sub
```

If you use the Object Browser to look at the OpenReport method of the DoCmd object, you'll see that it has one parameter corresponding to each argument of the matching macro action. The second parameter to the OpenReport method is a constant that indicates the initial view to use for the report. In this case, the built-in constant acViewPreview specifies Print Preview mode. In general, you'll find that the arguments for DoCmd methods are in the same order as the arguments for the corresponding macro actions, which makes converting macros to VBA code fairly easy.

Understanding Scope and Lifetime

What's Scope?

In this chapter, you add an important building block to your programming foundation. Specifically, this chapter discusses when a variable or procedure is accessible to code in another procedure. Two interlocking concepts control which variables a procedure can use: the *scope* of a variable dictates its visibility to other code, and the *lifetime* of a variable dictates when it contains valid data. Although the examples use variables, the information in this chapter also applies to constants.

Most variables work within the confines of the procedure in which they're declared. Sometimes you need a variable that can be seen by (is accessible to) other procedures. A variable's visibility is known as its *scope*. Variable scope is similar to the concept discussed in "Declaring Procedures as Public or Private" in Chapter 4. Just as a procedure can be called from another module, a variable can be seen by other procedures. There are three levels of variable scope:

- Local—Variables exist only within the procedure that declares them.
- Module—Variables are available to all procedures in the module in which they're declared.
- Public—Variables are available to the entire application.

IN THIS CHAPTER

What's Scope? 131

Measuring the Lifetime of a Variable
or Constant 136

Using Static Variables 139

Procedure-Level Variables

At this point, you've seen plenty of procedure-level variables. These are variables that are available to only the procedure that declares them. What that means is that the variable can be referenced only by the procedure that defines it.

Because procedure-level variables are limited to just the one procedure, you can have several variables with the same name in the same module (as long as they're in different procedures). However, you can't have more than one variable with the same name in the same procedure.

To illustrate procedure-level scope, launch the VBE (press Alt+F11), open a blank standard module, and enter the following procedures:

```
Function ProcedureLevel1()
  Dim strScope As String
  strScope = "Procedure Level Variable"
  Debug.Print strScope
End Function


Function ProcedureLevel2()
  strScope = "No procedure level declaration here"
  Debug.Print strScope
End Function
```

Or use the Chapter 9 sample module in the TrackTime sample database.

> **NOTE** The sample database includes some changes made over the course of the chapter. If you want to follow along with the code from start to finish, you should re-create the samples in your own database.

With the insertion point somewhere in ProcedureLevel1, press F5. The procedure assigns the string "Procedure Level Variable" to strScope and then prints the variable's value to the Immediate window. There's nothing new here—you've seen this many times by now.

Notice that ProcedureLevel2 refers to a variable by the same name. However, this procedure doesn't declare the variable. With the insertion point in ProcedureLevel2, press F5. Doing so returns the error shown in Figure 9.1. That's because the variable strScope doesn't exist for ProcedureLevel2. Click OK, and then click Reset to clear the error.

Figure 9.1
Referring to a variable that doesn't exist returns an error.

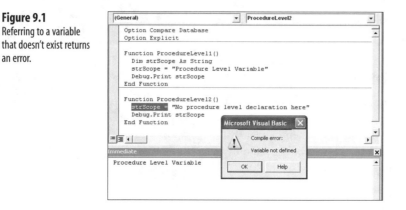

There are two ways to fix this error:

- Declare strScope in both procedures.
- Make strScope a module-level variable.

Module-Level Variables and Constants

Module-level variables can be seen by all the procedures in the module. The key to creating a module-level variable (or constant) is to declare the variable in the module's Declarations section—not in a procedure.

We can easily illustrate a module-level variable by moving the Dim statement from ProcedureLevel1 from the previous example to the Declarations section. After doing so, both procedures run without producing an error. To make the switch, complete the following steps:

1. Using Figure 9.2 as a guide, delete the Dim strScope As String statement in ProcedureLevel1 and copy it to the General Declarations section.

General Declaration Section

Figure 9.2
Copy the declaration statement from the procedure to the General Declarations section.

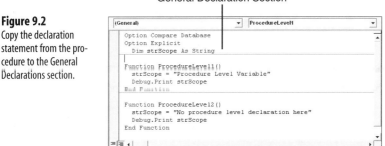

2. After moving the declaration statement, position the insertion point in ProcedureLevel1 and press F5 to print strScope's value in the Immediate window. (The procedure prints the string "Procedure Level Variable".)

3. Now, position the insertion pint in ProcedureLevel2 and press F5. This time, the procedure runs properly and assigns a string value to strScope and then prints that value, "No procedure level declaration here" to the Immediate window, as shown in Figure 9.3. That's because strScope is now available to all the procedures in the module.

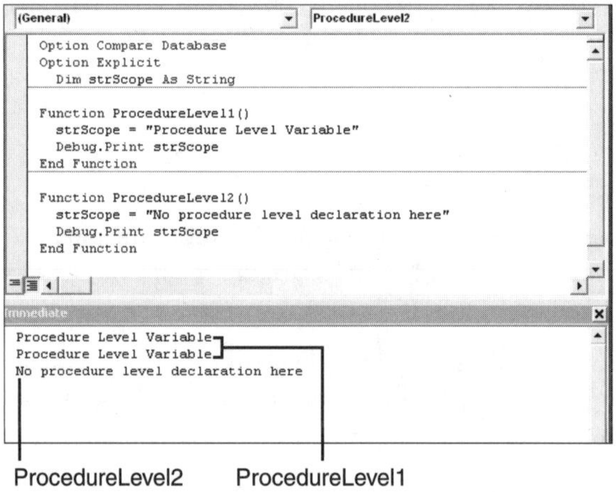

Figure 9.3
Both procedures use the module-level variable declared in the module's General Declarations section.

ProcedureLevel2   ProcedureLevel1

Public Variables and Constants

Public is the third and last level of scope in this discussion. A public variable is accessible from outside the module where it's created. Let's test `strScope` to determine whether it's currently a public variable. To do so:

1. Create a new standard module by choosing Insert, Module.

2. Enter the following procedure in the empty module:

```
Function PublicVariableTest()
  strScope = "Now the variable's public"
  Debug.Print strScope
End Function
```

Or, open the module `Chapter9PublicExample` in the TrackTime sample database.

3. With the insertion point in `PublicVariableTest`, press F5. The result is the same error you saw earlier (refer to Figure 9.1). The variable `strScope` doesn't exist within the scope of the current module.

4. Click OK and then click Reset to clear the error.

There are two ways to fix this error:

- Declare a procedure- or module-level variable in the new module.
- Make `strScope` a public variable in the first module (Chapter 9's sample module).

To create a public variable, return to the Chapter 9 sample module without closing the new module. In the Chapter 9 sample module's General Declaration's section, change `Dim` to `Public`, as shown in Figure 9.4.

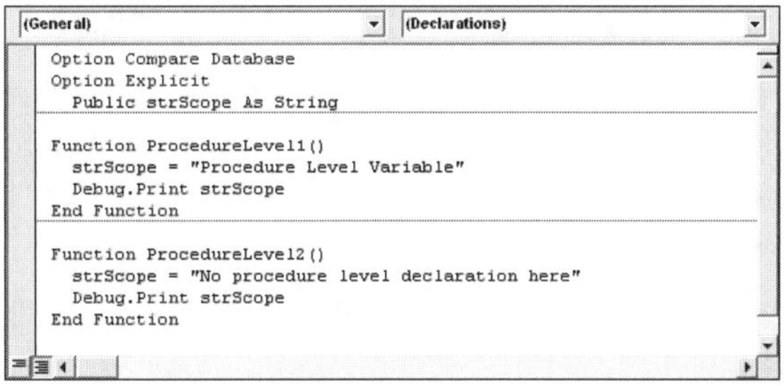

Figure 9.4
Change the variable's
scope from module level
to public.

```
(General)                              (Declarations)
  Option Compare Database
  Option Explicit
    Public strScope As String

Function ProcedureLevel1()
  strScope = "Procedure Level Variable"
  Debug.Print strScope
End Function

Function ProcedureLevel2()
  strScope = "No procedure level declaration here"
  Debug.Print strScope
End Function
```

After changing the declaration to public, return to the second module (the one with
`PublicVariableTest`). With the insertion point somewhere in `PublicVariableTest`, press F5.
This time, the procedure works fine, printing the string as shown in Figure 9.5. The variable, `strScope`, is now a public variable. That means `PublicVariableTest` can use `strScope`
even though it's actually created (seemingly) by another module.

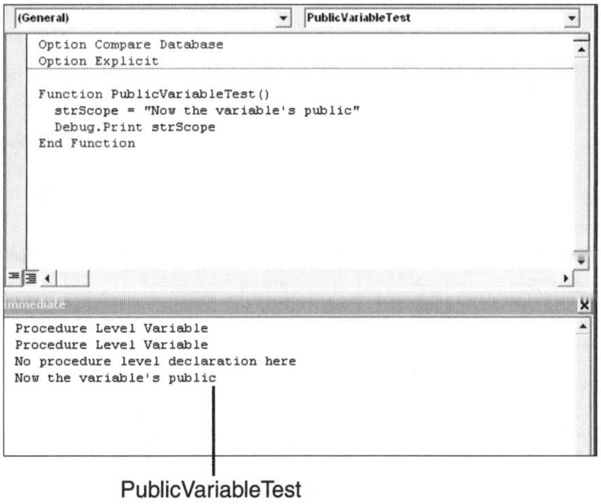

Figure 9.5
A public variable can be
accessed from any
module.

```
(General)                              PublicVariableTest
  Option Compare Database
  Option Explicit

Function PublicVariableTest()
  strScope = "Now the variable's public"
  Debug.Print strScope
End Function
```

```
Procedure Level Variable
Procedure Level Variable
No procedure level declaration here
Now the variable's public
```

PublicVariableTest

Measuring the Lifetime of a Variable or Constant

Scope determines which procedures can access a variable or procedure. A variable's *lifetime* determines when and for how long that variable is live (active in memory) and can therefore be accessed. To help clarify lifetime, within the context of a variable, here are a few guidelines that will help:

- Lifetime refers to the time during which a variable retains its value.
- A variable's value can change over its lifetime, but the variable retains some value.
- When a variable loses scope (that is, when the scope where it is defined vanishes) it loses its value, so there is a relationship between scope and lifetime, but they aren't the same thing.

When a procedure is executed, VBA initializes all the variables within that procedure's scope. That means each variable has a value, as listed in Table 9.1, even before the code assigns one. These initial values remain intact until the code explicitly assigns a value to the variable.

Table 9.1   Value of Initialized Variables

Data Type	Initialized Value
Numeric	0
Variable-length string	" " (zero-length string)
Fixed-length string	The result of Chr(0), which is a non-printable character
Variant	Empty
Object	Nothing

Now, let's look at the relationship between a variable's scope and its lifetime:

- A procedure-level variable that's declared with the Dim keyword has a lifetime that equals the procedure's lifetime. In other words, the variable retains its value only as long as the procedure is running.
- A module-level variable defined in a standard module retains its value until the database is closed and all code stops running. This is called the *application lifetime*.
- A module-level variable defined in a class module retains its value in an instance of the class as long as the instance remains open. This is called the *object lifetime*.
- A public variable retains its value until code stops running. Public variables always have application lifetime.

The Lifetime of a Procedure-Level Variable

You've already experienced a procedure-level variable's lifetime—it's the same as the procedure's scope. When you execute the procedure, VBA initializes the variables. When the procedure quits, the variables lose their value. At procedure level, the scope is limited to the procedure itself and the lifetime lasts only as long as the procedure is running.

The following procedure shows a variable that's changing values throughout the lifetime of the procedure (see Figure 9.6):

```
Function ProcedureLT1()
  Dim strPLT As String
  strPLT = "Variable is alive"
  Debug.Print strPLT
  strPLT = strPLT & " and well"
  Debug.Print strPLT
End Function
```

This example defines and then redefines the `strPLT` variable. Notice that the variable doesn't disappear after it's used. You don't have to redeclare it each time you define it or modify it. In fact, you can redefine the variable as many times as you like. It's available as long as the code's running.

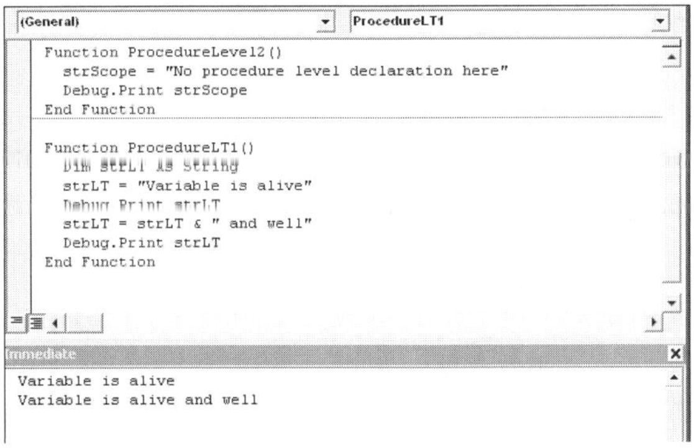

Figure 9.6
Procedure-level variables maintain a value as long as the procedure is running.

The Lifetime of a Module-Level Variable

Now let's take the next step and examine the lifetime of a module-level variable. Let's use the existing procedures in the Chapter 9 sample module as follows:

1. Enter the following declaration statement in the Chapter 9 sample module's General Declarations section:

   ```
   Dim intMLT As Integer
   ```

2. Enter the following functions in the Chapter 9 sample module:

   ```
   Function ModuleLT1()
     Debug.Print intMLT
   End Function
   ```

```
Function ModuleLT2()
    intMLT = 100 * 3
    Debug.Print intMLT
End Function
```

3. Position the insertion point inside `ModuleLT1` and press F5. The procedure prints the value **0** to the Immediate window because `intMLT` equals **0** after it's initialized but before a value is assigned to it.

4. Execute `ModuleLT2` to print the value **300** to the Immediate window.

5. Execute `ModuleLT1` a second time. This time, as shown in Figure 9.7, the procedure prints the value **300**, and not **0**, to the Immediate window. Not only is the variable accessible to both procedures, the variable retains its value between calling procedures. The variable doesn't die in between calls as a procedure-level variable does.

Figure 9.7
The module-level variable is alive and well as long as code is running.

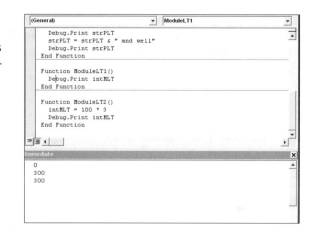

If you try to access `intMTL` from another module, VBA will not see it and will return a run-time error. However, the variable is still alive—and useable—within the scope of its own module. Don't confuse this behavior with the variable's lifetime. This behavior is a scoping issue and not a matter of the variable's life or death.

The Lifetime of a Public Variable

Public variables are accessible by any procedure. After they are initialized, they live until destroyed. You can change the variable's value, but the variable itself still returns a value.

To illustrate the long life of a public variable, change the declaration for `intMTL` in the General Declarations section of your Chapter 9 module to a `Public` declaration. Then, enter the following procedure in your second Chapter 9 sample module (the one with just `PublicVariableTest`):

```
Function PublicLTTest()
    Debug.Print intMLT
End Function
```

Figure 9.8 shows the result of executing `PublicLTTest`. Because the variable is public, `PublicLTTest` can refer to it from your second module. In addition, the variable's value remains intact. A module-level variable and a public variable can have the same lifetime, but not share the same scope. That means a variable might not be available to all procedures in the application, even though it is residing alive and well in memory.

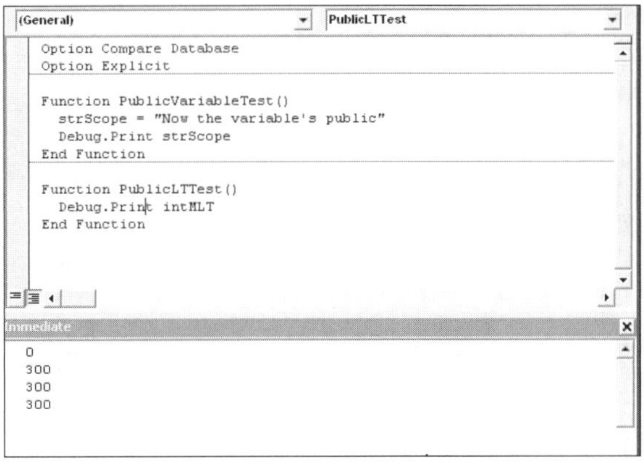

Figure 9.8
A public variable lasts as long as the code is running.

```
(General)                          PublicLTTest

    Option Compare Database
    Option Explicit

    Function PublicVariableTest()
       strScope = "Now the variable's public"
       Debug.Print strScope
    End Function

    Function PublicLTTest()
       Debug.Print intMLT
    End Function
```

```
Immediate
    0
    300
    300
    300
```

Using Static Variables

Earlier, you saw that a procedure-level's variable has no life outside of that procedure. But there's an exception to this rule: you can extend a procedure-level's variable beyond the procedure by declaring the variable as a static variable using the `Static` statement in the form

```
Static variablename [As datatype]
```

A *static variable* is a procedure-level variable that retains its value between calls to the procedure that declares it. In that way it's similar to a module-level variable. If you don't specify *datatype*, VBA makes it a variant. Thus, `Static` works just like `Dim`—except that static variables have application lifetime.

> **CAUTION**
>
> Although a static value persists between calls to the procedure, it doesn't have scope outside of the procedure that declares the static variable.

The following procedure is a simple example of a static variable:

```
Function StaticVariableTest()
  Dim intValue As Integer
  intValue = intValue + 1
  Debug.Print intValue
End Function
```

You can probably guess what the Debug.Print statement prints to the Immediate window the first time you execute this statement. Figure 9.9 shows the results the first time around. The procedure prints the value 1 because intValue = 0 until the statement

```
intValue = intValue + 1
```

evaluates to 1.

Figure 9.9
The variable
intValue equals 1
each time.

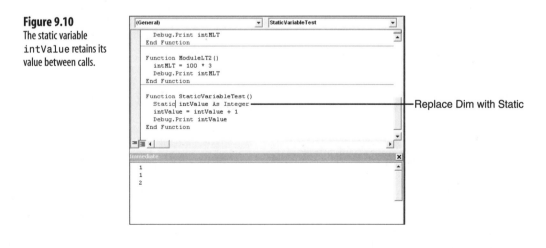

Run the procedure a second time, and the procedure still prints the value 1 to the Immediate window. That's because intValue loses its value after the procedure is done. When you execute the procedure a second time, intValue equals 0 until the same statement as before evaluates to 1. As is, this statement will never return any value other than 1.

Now, change the Dim keyword to Static and run the procedure. Again, the procedure returns the value 1. Execute the procedure a second time using the static variable. This time, the procedure prints the value 2, as shown in Figure 9.10. That's because intValue retains its value between the two calls. If you execute the procedure again, intValue will equal 3, and so on.

Figure 9.10
The static variable
intValue retains its
value between calls.

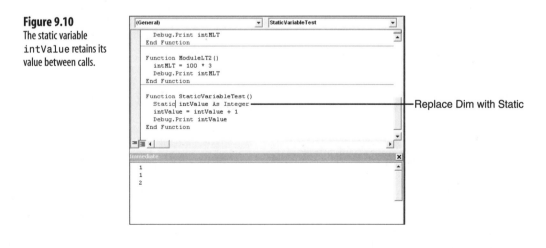

Replace Dim with Static

> **NOTE**
>
> After creating an object variable and then defining it with a reference to an object, you might think you're done, but you're not. Always include code that sets all object variables to `Nothing` using the syntax
>
> ```
> Set objectvariable = Nothing
> ```
>
> Include a set-to-nothing statement in code when you're done with the variable, or add all such statements to the end of your procedure. In addition, be sure to include a set of these statements to any error-handling routine. That way if the procedure exits early because of an error, the object variables are still handled correctly.
>
> The `Nothing` keyword is used only with object variables to determine whether the variable has a valid object reference.

9

Working with the Access User Interface

IN THIS PART

10	Working with Forms	145
11	Analyzing the Access Event Model	161
12	Working with List and Combo Boxes	175
13	Working with Other Controls	195
14	Working with Reports	209
15	Working with the Application Collections	223

II

Working with Forms

10

Opening and Closing Forms

In the first part of this book, you learned the basics of the VBA language. Now it's time to start applying your skills to Access. This chapter covers the use of VBA with one of the most commonly used Access objects: the form. You're no doubt familiar with Access forms from developing applications. As a first step, you learn how to open and close forms using VBA.

IN THIS CHAPTER

Opening and Closing Forms 145

The Form Module and Event Handling 147

Performing Common Tasks 148

Handling Errors at the Form Level 154

Working with Multiple Form Instances 157

Opening a Form

You already saw the code to open a form in Chapter 8's case study. But it's worth reviewing again, to make sure you understand what's going on. The DoCmd object is the key to unlocking many of VBA's capabilities to automate Access. There is one DoCmd object open at all times; you can neither create it nor destroy it. What you can do is use its methods. These methods let VBA code interact directly with Access-specific objects.

To open a form, you invoke the DoCmd.OpenForm method, which has a number of optional arguments:

```
DoCmd.OpenForm formname, [view], [filtername],
[wherecondition], [datamode], [windowmode],
[openargs]
```

As you might assume, you must supply the form name when invoking the OpenForm method. The optional arguments let you control the behavior of the newly opened form in more detail:

- The *view* argument specifies the initial view (form, datasheet, and so on) of the form.

- The *filtername* argument lets you supply the name of a query to be used as a filter for the form.

- The *wherecondition* argument specifies an expression to be used as a filter for the form (you omit the WHERE keyword when specifying a *wherecondition*).

- The *datamode* argument specifies the data entry mode for the form (for example, whether the data is read-only or editable).

- The *windowmode* argument specifies whether the form should be opened normally, hidden, as a dialog box, or as an icon.

- The *openargs* argument enables you to supply arbitrary data to the form's code. You learn more about *openargs* later in the chapter.

At its simplest, the OpenForm method assumes that you want to use default values for all these arguments. For example, you can use this procedure to open the Clients form:

```
Sub OpenClientForm()
  ' Open a form with default values
  DoCmd.OpenForm "Clients"
End Sub
```

In this case, the form will open in its last saved view, displaying all its data, in the saved data mode and window mode. But the power of the VBA code comes in when you decide that you don't want to use the default values. For example, this procedure opens the Clients form in Datasheet view, no matter what view it was saved in:

```
Sub OpenClientFormDataSheet()
  ' Open a form in datasheet view
  DoCmd.OpenForm "Clients", View:=acFormDS
End Sub
```

Closing a Form

After a form is open, you can use the DoCmd.Close method to close it again. This method is used for all sorts of Access objects, not just forms, and it has three optional arguments:

```
DoCmd.Close [objecttype], [objectname], [save]
```

- The *objecttype* argument specifies whether you want to close a form, a report, or some other object.

- The *objectname* argument specifies the name of the object to close.

- The *save* argument controls whether to save changes to the object when closing it.

If the Clients form is already open, this procedure closes it:

```
Sub CloseClientForm()
  ' Close the client form
  DoCmd.Close acForm, "Clients"
End Sub
```

When closing a form, the default is for Access to prompt the user whether to save any changes to the form itself (such as the application of a new filter, or a change in the order of records). You can override this behavior by specifying the constants acSaveNo (to automatically discard the changes) or acSaveYes (to automatically save the changes). To avoid this sometimes-confusing prompt, modify the procedure this way:

```
Sub CloseClientForm()
  ' Close the client form,
  ' automatically saving changes
  DoCmd.Close acForm, "Clients", _
    Save:=acSaveYes
End Sub
```

> **TIP**
> You might have noticed that every argument to the Close method is optional. What happens if you don't specify an object type or an object name? The answer is that VBA closes the object that has the focus when you invoke the method.

10

The Form Module and Event Handling

All the procedures you've seen so far in this chapter have been located in standard modules. But as you've already seen several times in this book, VBA code can also be associated directly with a form. Every form in your Access application can have its own *form module*. The form module is saved as a part of the form so that if (for example) you copy the form to another database, the form comes along with it.

One type of code that is stored within the form module is the event procedures for the form. These procedures are called when something happens to the form or to a control on the form. For example, clicking a button on a form calls the event procedure associated with the button's Click event. Here's how you can add a Close button to the Clients form:

1. Open the Clients form in Design view.

2. Add a command button control to the form. Name the control cmdClose and set its caption to Close.

3. Set the On Click property of the button to [Event Procedure] and click the builder button next to the property to open the form's module.

4. Enter the code to close the form:
   ```
   Private Sub cmdClose_Click()
     DoCmd.Close
   End Sub
   ```

5. Save the form and test the button.

Performing Common Tasks

VBA is very flexible in conjunction with Access. This chapter can't hope to show you everything that you can do with VBA, but it can offer you a selection of techniques to get you started. This section looks at some of the things you can do with forms and VBA:

- Checking for a form's existence
- Determining whether a form is open
- Moving and resizing a form
- Passing arguments to a form
- Populating a form

Checking for a Form's Existence

You might at some point want to know whether a particular form exists in the current database. This is especially useful if you're writing general-purpose code that you plan to use with many databases. Fortunately, Access provides you with a built-in way to determine whether a form exists. Figure 10.1 shows a portion of the Access object model that's useful in this situation.

Figure 10.1
A portion of the Access object model.

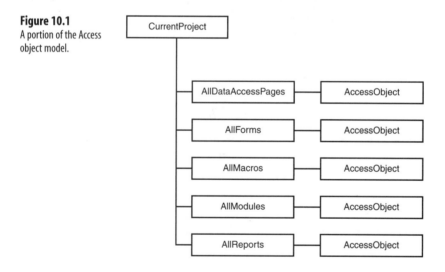

As you can see, Access supplies a built-in object called CurrentProject. This object represents the user interface objects in the current database, and itself contains collections for each of the major classes of objects in the database. These collections contain AccessObject objects.

For example, the AllForms collection contains one AccessObject object for each form in the current database. The AccessObject object is not itself a form; rather, it is an object that indicates the presence of a form.

By combining the `AllForms` collection with error handling, you can easily tell whether a particular form exists:

```
Function DoesFormExist(strName As String) As Boolean
  ' Check for the existence of a form
  On Error GoTo HandleErr
  Dim ao As AccessObject
  Set ao = CurrentProject.AllForms(strName)
  DoesFormExist = True
ExitHere:
  Exit Function
HandleErr:
  DoesFormExist = False
  Exit Function
End Function
```

This procedure starts by setting up an error handler, so that any errors cause VBA to jump to the code after the `HandleErr` label. It then attempts to create an `AccessObject` object corresponding to the form name that the user passed into the procedure. If this attempt succeeds, the form exists, and VBA sets the return value of the procedure to `True`. If the attempt fails, the error handler kicks in, and VBA sets the return value of the procedure to `False`. Either way, VBA next executes the `Exit Function` statement to return control to the caller.

Figure 10.2 shows how you might use this procedure in the Immediate window.

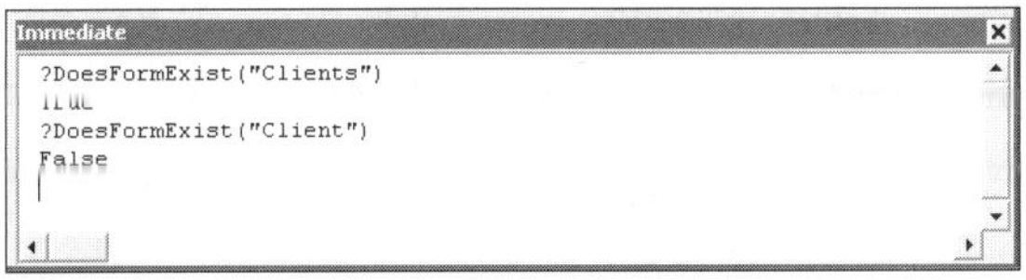

Figure 10.2
Checking for the existence of a form.

```
Immediate
  ?DoesFormExist("Clients")
True
  ?DoesFormExist("Client")
False
```

> **NOTE**
> Sometimes procedures such as `DoesFormExist` seem to worry beginning developers. Isn't it bad to deliberately cause an error in your code? The answer is no. If you're causing the error to collect information and catching it in an error handler, it is a valuable and useful technique.

Determining Whether a Form Is Loaded

Sometimes it's not enough to know whether a database contains a particular form. You might also want to know whether a particular form is open onscreen. In Chapter 8, you learned about the Forms collection, which contains only the open forms. By determining whether a form exists in this collection, you can tell whether the form is open. Here's the code to do this:

```
Function IsFormOpen(strName As String) As Boolean
  ' Check to see whether a form is open
  On Error GoTo HandleErr
  Dim frm As Form
```

```
   Set frm = Forms(strName)
   IsFormOpen = True
ExitHere:
   Exit Function
HandleErr:
   IsFormOpen = False
   Exit Function
End Function
```

This code is almost identical to the code you just saw for checking a form's existence. The only difference is that it uses a different collection.

Resizing a Form

The MoveSize method of the DoCmd object lets you change the position and size of the object that currently has the focus. This method has four optional arguments:

- The *right* argument specifies the new position of the left edge of the form relative to the Access workspace.

- The *down* argument specifies the new position of the top of the form relative to the Access workspace.

- The *width* argument specifies the new width of the form.

- The *height* argument specifies the new height of the form.

Because these arguments include the width and height of the form, you can use the MoveSize method to resize a form without moving it. Here's a practical example. The Clients form in the TimeTrack database currently shows both clients and their projects, a potentially overwhelming amount of information. You'll make use of the MoveSize method to display the projects only when the user clicks on a button.

1. Open the Clients form in Design view.

2. Add a new command button to the form. Set its name to cmdProjects and its caption to "Show Projects".

3. Add this code to the form's module:

```
Private Sub Form_Load()
   ' Make sure the form starts in small size
   DoCmd.MoveSize Height:=3345
End Sub

Private Sub cmdProjects_Click()
   ' Show or hide the projects section
   If cmdProjects.Caption = "Show Projects" Then
      DoCmd.MoveSize Height:=6465
      cmdProjects.Caption = "Hide Projects"
   Else
      DoCmd.MoveSize Height:=3345
      cmdProjects.Caption = "Show Projects"
   End If
End Sub
```

4. Close and open the form. It then opens in condensed mode, as shown in Figure 10.3. Click the new button to switch the form to the expanded mode shown in Figure 10.4. Notice that the button's caption changes as well. Click the button again to return to condensed mode.

Figure 10.3
The Clients form in its original condensed mode.

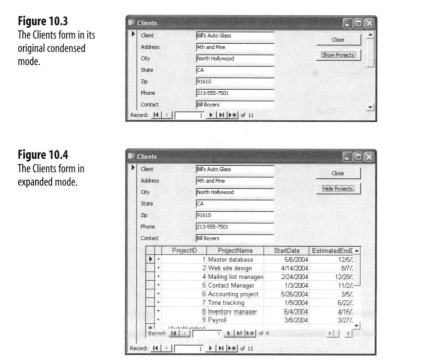

Figure 10.4
The Clients form in expanded mode.

There are a few things in this code worth pointing out. First, the form's Load event occurs when a form is opened and its records are displayed onscreen. You're calling the MoveSize method in this event to control the original size of the form. Second, the code that responds to the button's Click event checks the button's caption to know whether it should expand or contract the form. By using this technique, you don't have to track the form's mode in a separate variable.

Passing Arguments Using OpenArgs

OpenArgs is both an argument to the DoCmd.OpenForm method and a property of the form. The reason for this dual use is that it enables you to pass information into a form at the time that you open it. This section of the chapter concentrates on the syntax of OpenArgs and shows how you can retrieve the information that it contains. Later on, in the "Case Study" section of this chapter, you see a more practical example.

→ Reports also have an OpenArgs argument, which you can read about in "Passing Arguments Using OpenArgs," p. 212.

The idea behind `OpenArgs` is simple: you can use this argument of the `OpenForm` method to pass any arbitrary string data that you want into the form. The value of this argument is then available to any VBA code in the form's module. Here's a quick demonstration:

1. Create a new form in Design mode. Place a single text box control named `txtOpenArgs` on the form.

2. Add this code to the form's module:

```
Private Sub Form_Load()
   txtOpenArgs.SetFocus
   txtOpenArgs.Text = Me.OpenArgs
End Sub
```

3. Save the form as `Chapter10Test`.

4. Close the form.

5. Run this code from the Immediate window to re-open the form:

```
DoCmd.OpenForm "Chapter10Test", OpenArgs:="Pass this data"
```

6. The form will open and display the value that you specified for the `OpenArgs` argument.

> **TIP**
>
> To set most properties of a control, the control must have the focus. Each control that can receive the focus has a `SetFocus` method that you can call to ensure that it is the active control.

In addition to the `OpenArgs` method, there's one other new bit of VBA to note in this example: the `Me` keyword. `Me` is a shortcut for "the object that contains this code." When you're running code in a form's module, the `Me` keyword refers to the form itself. Consequently, `Me.OpenArgs` retrieves the value of the `OpenArgs` property of the form.

Populating the Form

So far you've been working with the appearance of the form, but you can also manipulate the form's data. Suppose, for example, you want to use the same form for more than one data set. As it stands now, the `Timeslips` form displays all the timeslips in the entire database, which is an overwhelming amount of data if you want to focus on what's happened lately. Let's combine the `OpenArgs` property with an extra query to restrict the data on the form:

1. Create a new query in the database and add the `Timeslips` table to the query.

2. Switch to SQL view and enter this SQL for the query:

```
SELECT Timeslips.*
FROM Timeslips
WHERE (((Timeslips.DateWorked) Between Now()-7 And Now()))
ORDER BY Timeslips.DateWorked;
```

3. Save the query as `qryWeeklyTimeslips`.

4. Open the `Timeslips` form in Design mode. Switch to the form's module and enter this code:

```
Private Sub Form_Open(Cancel As Integer)
  ' Set the data source depending on how
  ' the form was called
  Select Case Me.OpenArgs
    Case "All"
      Me.RecordSource = "SELECT Timeslips.* " & _
        "FROM Timeslips ORDER BY Timeslips.DateWorked;"
    Case "Week"
      Me.RecordSource = "qryWeeklyTimeslips"
    Case Else
      Me.RecordSource = "SELECT Timeslips.* " & _
        "FROM Timeslips ORDER BY Timeslips.DateWorked;"
  End Select
End Sub
```

5. Save the form. You can test the code by entering an appropriate `OpenForm` command in the Immediate window. For example, use the first of these lines to open the form with all records displayed, and the second to open the form with only the records for the previous week displayed:

```
Docmd.OpenForm "Timeslips", OpenArgs:="All"
Docmd.OpenForm "Timeslips", OpenArgs:="Week"
```

Of course, you can also call these statements from the user interface[md]for example, you can add a new button to the `Switchboard` form to open the weekly timeslips. By reusing a form this way with multiple data sets, you can make your application easier to maintain.

> **TIP**
>
> It's good practice to supply a `Case Else` with reasonable default behavior. For this form, if the user supplies an unexpected argument, the form will just display all records.

→ The `RecordSource` code is in the form's `Open` event procedure rather than in the `Load` event procedure. In the former, the records are not yet loaded, whereas in the latter it's too late to change the `RecordSource`. To learn more about the order of events, see "The Event Sequence for Forms," p. 167.

The key to the data displayed on the form is the form's `RecordSource` property. You can set this property to a SQL statement or the name of a query, as you saw in this example. You can also set the property to the name of a table if you want to base the form directly on the table without an intervening query.

As an alternative to setting the form's `RecordSource` property, you can apply a filter to the form after it's open. You can use the `DoCmd.ApplyFilter` method to take this approach. Let's modify the `Timeslips` form a bit more:

1. Open the `Timeslips` form in Design view.

2. Add a new command button to the form. Set the button's caption to "Show week" and set its name to `cmdWeek`.

3. Modify the form's module as follows:

```
Option Compare Database
Option Explicit

Private Sub cmdweek_Click()
  'Filter to this week's timeslips
  DoCmd.ApplyFilter "qryWeeklyTimeslips"
End Sub

Private Sub Form_Open(Cancel As Integer)
  ' Set the data source depending on how
  ' the form was called
  Select Case Me.OpenArgs
    Case "All"
      Me.RecordSource = "SELECT Timeslips.* " & _
        "FROM Timeslips ORDER BY Timeslips.DateWorked;"
    Case "Week"
      Me.RecordSource = "qryWeeklyTimeslips"
      cmdWeek.Visible = False
    Case Else
      Me.RecordSource = "SELECT Timeslips.* " & _
        "FROM Timeslips ORDER BY Timeslips.DateWorked;"
  End Select
End Sub
```

4. Save and open the form. Now click the button to filter the records.

> **NOTE**
> The DoCmd object's ApplyFilter method applies a filter, a query, or a SQL WHERE clause to a table, form, or report in order to limit or sort the underlying data. This method takes the form
>
>   DoCmd.ApplyFilter [*filtername*][, *wherecondition*]
>
> Both arguments are optional, but you must specify at least one. If you use both arguments, *where-condition* is applied.

Note the modification to the Form_Open procedure in the case where the record source is already filtered. In that case, there's no point in even showing the new button to the user, because it won't do anything.

→ These examples use SELECT SQL statements to retrieve the appropriate records. You can read about SQL in Appendix A, "Review of Access SQL," p. 347.

Handling Errors at the Form Level

Access forms are the place where your database's users interact directly with the Jet engine. And as such, they are also the places where many things can go wrong. Users might enter data that violates a validation rule, or try to create records with duplicate primary keys, or cause a referential integrity problem.

As you probably already know, Jet is the underlying database engine of Access—the part of the application that actually saves and retrieves data.

None of these errors can be trapped directly in VBA, because VBA does not get involved between the Access user interface and the Jet engine. But there is still a hook to let your VBA code get involved if you like: the Form's `Error` event is called whenever the Jet engine is ready to process a data error of any kind. If you like, you can react to this error to amplify or override Jet's default error message. Here's how:

1. Open the `Timeslips` form and start entering a new record. Enter "Tuesday" for the date worked and press Tab. You'll see the error message shown in Figure 10.5. This error message comes directly from the Jet engine.

Figure 10.5
A Jet error message during data entry.

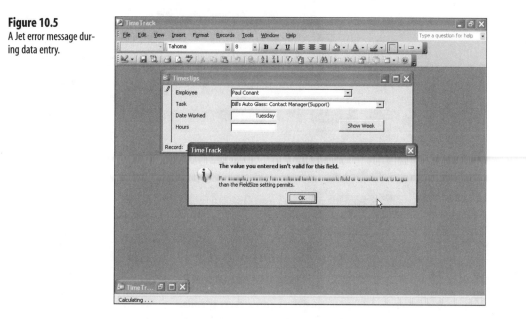

2. Press Esc twice to discard the new timeslip and switch the form to Design mode.

3. Add this code to the form's module:
```
Private Sub Form_Error(DataErr As Integer, _
  Response As Integer)
    ' Respond to Jet errors
    Select Case DataErr
      Case 2113
        ' Data isn't right for the field
        MsgBox "The data you entered isn't right for " & _
          "this field. Please try again, or press the " & _
          "Escape key to undo.", vbInformation
```

```
        ' Suppress the default Access message
        Response = acDataErrContinue
    Case Else
        ' Let Access handle other errors
        Response = acDataErrDisplay
  End Select
End Sub
```

4. Save the form and switch back to Form view.

5. Start entering a new record. Enter "Tuesday" for the date worked and press Tab. You'll see the error message shown in Figure 10.6. This error message comes from the code that you just wrote. When you click OK, the default Access error message is not displayed.

Figure 10.6
A custom error message during data entry.

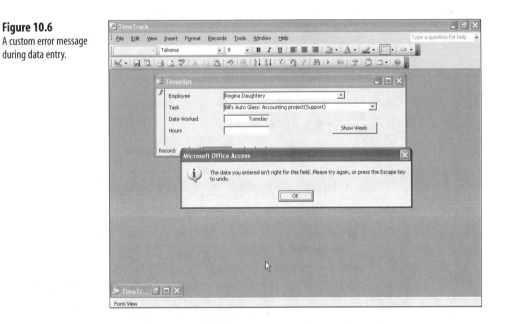

Whenever a Jet error occurs during data entry, Access calls the VBA event handler for the form's Error event. This handler has two arguments. The DataErr argument is the number of the Jet error that triggered the event. In this case, you're looking for event 2113, which corresponds to invalid data. The Response argument is one that you can set when you're done dealing with the error. If you set this argument to the constant acDataErrDisplay, Access displays its own default error message. If you set this argument to the constant acDataErrContinue, Access suppresses its own default error message.

> **TIP**
> There's no master list of Jet errors. But you can set up a skeletal event handler with a breakpoint in it, and then check the value of DataErr in the Immediate window, to determine the error numbers of the errors that you want to deal with.

Working with Multiple Form Instances

Finally, there are some things that you can do in VBA code that you simply cannot do from the Access user interface. One of these is to create more than one copy of the same form. As you learned in Chapter 8, a form object is just an instance of the corresponding form class. Like any other class, this class can be instantiated more than once. But the Access designers didn't choose to make this capability available to end users.

→ To review the code for creating a single instance of a form, see "Creating Your Own Objects," p. 124.

Creating multiple form instances in code is just an extension of the technique for creating a single form instance in code. For example, this code creates two instances of the Projects form:

```
Sub CreateTwoForms()
  ' Create and display two copies
  ' of the Projects form
  Dim frm1 As New Form_Projects
  frm1.Visible = True
  frm1.Move 0, 0
  Dim frm2 As New Form_Projects
  frm2.Visible = True
  MsgBox "Click OK to continue"
End Sub
```

As you can see, the code uses two different form variables to represent the two forms. It also moves the first form to the upper-left corner of the work area (otherwise, the second form would exactly cover the first). Figure 10.7 shows the result of running this code.

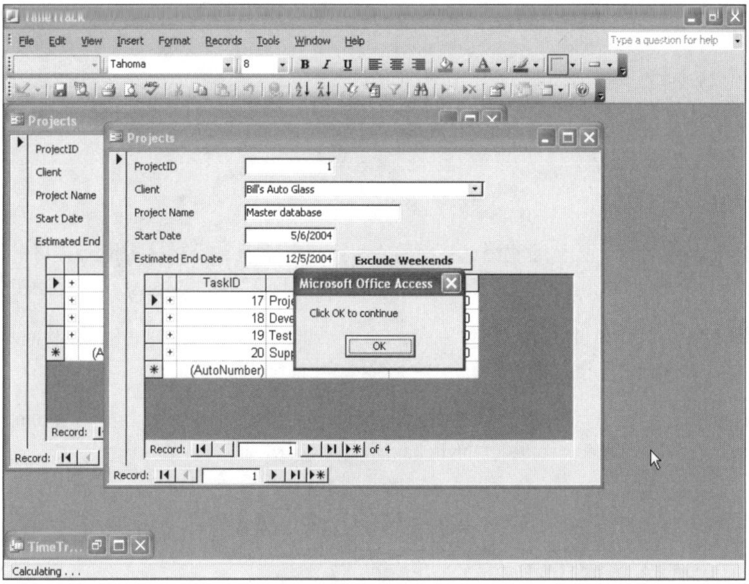

Figure 10.7
Two instances of the same form open in Access.

Multiple form instances behave much like any other form: you can set their properties, navigate their data, and so on. Each instance is a separate member of the Forms collection. However, because you can only create multiple instances in VBA, you need to maintain a form variable for each instance to keep it visible onscreen.

→ For information on maintaining a variable beyond a single procedure, see "Measuring the Lifetime of a Variable or Constant," p. 136.

CASE STUDY

Working with Two Instances of the Same Form

This case study demonstrates a practical use of the capability to create multiple instances of forms, as well as runtime switching of record sources. In the TimeTrack application, the various forms are not well integrated. For example, if the user opens both the Clients and Projects forms, they each show all records in their respective tables. But suppose you want to see just the projects for the current client? You can handle that by basing the Projects form on a query that draws a parameter from the Clients form. As an added twist, though, the code in this case study enables you to open as many of these client-specific project forms as you like.

For starters, here's a query to grab the projects for the current client. To build this object, you can open a new query in Design view, switch to SQL view, and just type in the SQL:

```
SELECT Projects.*
FROM Projects
WHERE (((Projects.ClientID)=[Forms]![Clients]![ClientID]))
ORDER BY Projects.ProjectName;
```

Save the query as qryprojectsForClient. The next step is to slightly modify the code behind the Projects form, by adding a new procedure:

```
Public Sub LoadClient()
  ' Called by the client form to change
  ' the recordsource of this form
  Me.RecordSource = "qryProjectsForClient"
  Me.Refresh
End Sub
```

Remember, a public procedure of a class becomes a method of the class—or in this case, of the form that's based on the class. This means that you can call the procedure from the Clients form, as you see in a moment.

The Refresh method of a form tells it to refresh its records from the database. This is useful any time you change the form's RecordSource property and want to show the new data.

With the changes to the Projects form saved, you can modify the Clients form. Add a new command button named cmdProject. Here's the code for this button:

```
Dim arrProjectForms() As Form_Projects
Dim intProjectFormsCount As Integer
Private Sub cmdProject_Click()
  ' Open the project form, showing
  ' projects for the current client
```

```
' Add a new form variable to the array
intProjectFormsCount = intProjectFormsCount + 1
ReDim Preserve arrProjectForms( _
 1 To intProjectFormsCount)
' Create the new form
Set arrProjectForms(intProjectFormsCount) = _
 New Form_Projects
' Tell it we're opening from here
arrProjectForms(intProjectFormsCount).LoadClient
' And display the new instance
arrProjectForms(intProjectFormsCount).Visible = _
 True
End Sub
```

The first two declaration statements go in the module's Declarations section. This code shows how you can keep track of an arbitrary number of form variables: just put them in an array. Each time the user clicks the button, the code creates a new instance of the form and puts it in the array for safekeeping. It then calls the `LoadClient` method of the new form to set its `RecordSource`, and makes it visible.

→ VBA array functions are covered in Chapter 7, "Working with Arrays," p. 105.

Thus, you can show one client on the Clients form and use `cmdProjects` to open a form showing the projects for just that client. Then, without closing the first projects form, you can move to a different client and repeat the procedure to see the projects for the new client. Figure 10.8 shows the result, with two different client-specific project forms already open.

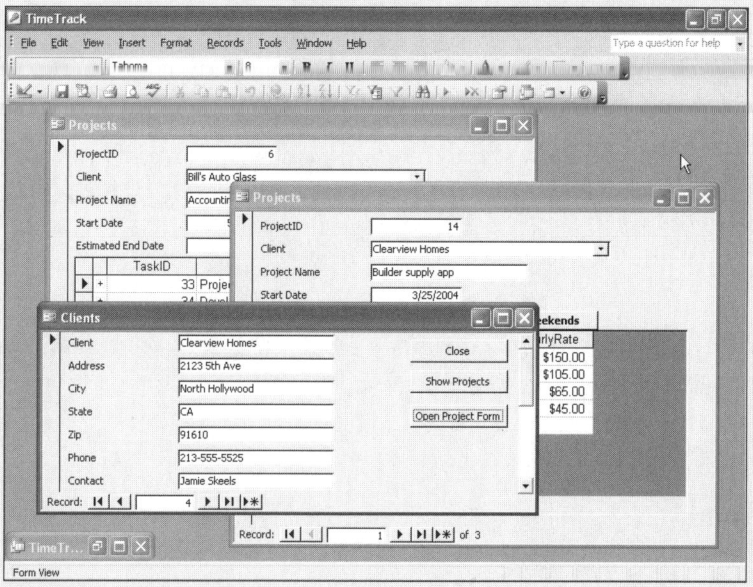

Figure 10.8
Using multiple instances for child forms.

When you close the Clients form, the array goes out of scope. As a result, all the child Projects forms close too.

Analyzing the Access Event Model

Responding to Events

One of the key concepts that Access developers need to understand is that Access is an *event-driven programming* environment. That means that VBA code doesn't just arbitrarily run when it wants to. Rather, code runs in response to events: users clicking buttons, new records being loaded into forms, and so on.

You might have already dug into Access events, depending on how much you did with macro programming in the past. But these topics are so central that this chapter reviews the basics. In particular, you need to understand that events happen in a specific order, and that each one has a specific purpose.

Before the reference topics, it's important to review one more time just how all the pieces fit together. As an example of an event, you look at the Open Report button on the Billing Report Setup form. When you open the form in Design view, you see that the name of the button is cmdOpenReport. Looking at the Properties window for cmdOpenReport, you can then see that the On Click property of this button is set to [Event Procedure]. That tells Access that it should send click events from this button to VBA to be handled.

11

IN THIS CHAPTER

Responding to Events 161

The Event Sequence for Controls 162

Data Events 165

The Event Sequence for Forms 167

The Event Sequence for Reports 170

Canceling Events 171

> **TIP**
> If you see anything other than [Event Procedure] in an event property, it's probably the name of a macro that's called when the event occurs. In that case, VBA isn't involved in handling the event.

Knowing that this event is handled by a VBA event procedure, you need to turn to the VBA editor to see the details. One quick way to get to the appropriate procedure is to click in the On Click property entry in the Properties window, and then click the ellipsis button that shows up next to the [Event Procedure] entry. Click this button to jump to VBA. In this case, you see the following procedure in the Form_BillingReportSetup module:

```
Private Sub cmdOpenReport_Click()
  On Error GoTo HandleErr
  DoCmd.OpenReport "BillingReport", acViewPreview
ExitHere:
  Exit Sub
HandleErr:
  MsgBox "Error " & Err.Number & ": " & _
  Err.Description & " in cmdBillingReport_Click"
  Resume ExitHere
End Sub
```

All the pieces need to be in place for VBA to handle an event:

- The appropriate property must have the [Event Procedure] setting.
- The code must be in the correct module (the one that's attached to the form or report where the event will occur).
- The procedure must be named with the pattern *objectname_eventname*.

> **TIP**
> VBA automatically fills in the [Event Procedure] entries in the Properties window if you write code with the correct procedure name in a module.

There's one more requirement for some events that you'll see later in this chapter: if the event includes arguments, the event procedure declaration must match the arguments that the event sends.

The Event Sequence for Controls

The first set of events that you should be familiar with are events associated with controls (buttons, combo boxes, and so on). Let's look at the general topics of switching focus and changing data first, and then discuss selected events for individual controls.

> **NOTE**
> These lists of events are not comprehensive. There are many events that are of little practical use in most applications. For instance, although the text box control fires a mouse move event, most applications won't respond to this event. We've simplified the presentation so that you can get the big picture.

Focus Events

As the users of your application click and tab around the user interface of your forms, they trigger a flurry of events. You can use code associated with these events to highlight controls, update internal variables, or perform other tasks.

There are four key events here:

- `Enter`—Fired just before a control receives the focus from another control on the same form.
- `Exit`—Fired just before a control loses the focus to another control on the same form.
- `GotFocus`—Fired when a control gets the focus.
- `LostFocus`—Fired when a control loses the focus.

> **TIP**
> The *focus* refers to the indication that a particular control is the active control. Depending on the type of control, the focus might be indicated by a blinking cursor or a dotted outline.

11

To investigate the order in which these various events fire, you can add some code to the Clients form. Open the form in Design mode, open the form's module, and type in this code (or just use the version of the Clients form in the sample database for this chapter):

```
Private Sub Client_Enter()
  Debug.Print "Client Enter"
End Sub

Private Sub Client_Exit(Cancel As Integer)
  Debug.Print "Client Exit"
End Sub

Private Sub Client_GotFocus()
  Debug.Print "Client GotFocus"
End Sub

Private Sub Client_LostFocus()
  Debug.Print "Client LostFocus"
End Sub

Private Sub Address_Enter()
  Debug.Print "Address Enter"
End Sub
```

```
Private Sub Address_Exit(Cancel As Integer)
  Debug.Print "Address Exit"
End Sub

Private Sub Address_GotFocus()
  Debug.Print "Address GotFocus"
End Sub

Private Sub Address_LostFocus()
  Debug.Print "Address LostFocus"
End Sub
```

The purpose of this code is to write messages to the Immediate window as events occur. Save and close the form. Arrange the windows on your screen so that you can see both the Access workspace and the VBA editor. Now open the form and you'll see that two of the events from this set are fired immediately, as shown in Figure 11.1.

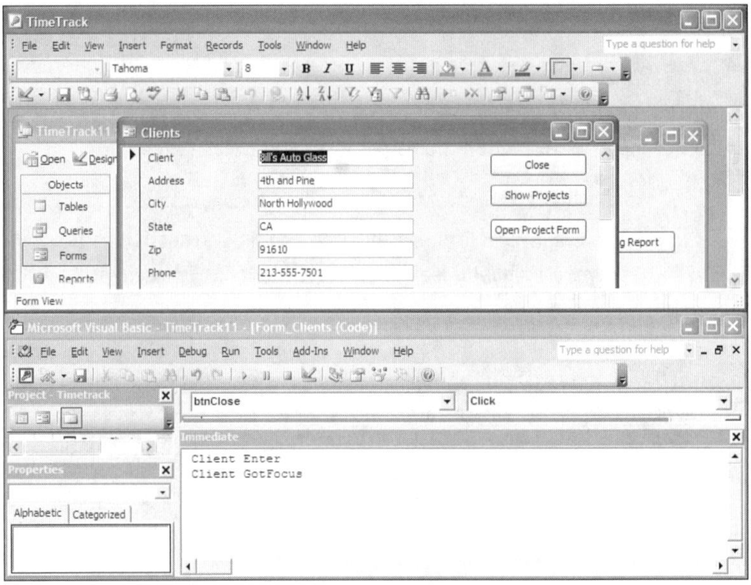

Figure 11.1
Tracing the order of events.

When you open the form for the first time, the focus has to go somewhere. In fact, it goes to the first control in the form's tab order. As you might expect from the earlier discussion, the Enter event is fired before the GotFocus event.

Now press the Tab key to move the focus from the Client text box to the Address text box. You'll see that this fires four more events:

```
Client Exit
Client LostFocus
Address Enter
Address GotFocus
```

Click to activate another form in the `TimeTrack` database, such as the `Switchboard` form, and then click back on the Clients form. This fires two more events:

```
Address LostFocus
Address GotFocus
```

The `Exit` and `Enter` events don't fire in this scenario, because they're only associated with movement to other controls on the same form. But the focus can only belong to one form at a time, so it moves away and then moves back when you switch to the switchboard form and back.

Finally, switch to another application entirely, such as an instance of Microsoft Excel or even Notepad, and then come back to Access. You might be surprised to find that this action does *not* trigger any further focus events. Access events are only concerned with things that happen in Access, not with what's going on in the rest of your computer.

> **NOTE** The `Exit` event is an example of an event that can be canceled. You learn more about this in the section "Canceling Events" later in this chapter.

Data Events

Access being a database, you should not be surprised to discover that many of its events involve the data that the user is entering, or that's being saved to or retrieved from the database. There are actually two sets of data events. The first set applies to any control that is bound to data.

- `BeforeUpdate`—Fired after the user changes data, but before the data is committed to the form.
- `AfterUpdate`—Fired after data changes are committed to the form.

The second set of data events apply only to controls where you can type data (text boxes or combo boxes):

- `KeyDown`—Fired every time the user presses a key.
- `KeyPress`—Fired when the key's value is sent to Access.
- `Dirty`—Fired when the form is marked dirty (the editing pencil appears in the form's record selector).
- `Change`—Fired when the keystroke changes the value displayed onscreen.
- `KeyUp`—Fired when the user releases the key.

To see these events in action, here's some code that you can hook up to the Phone text box on the Clients form:

```
Private Sub Phone_AfterUpdate()
  Debug.Print "Phone AfterUpdate"
End Sub

Private Sub Phone_BeforeUpdate(Cancel As Integer)
  Debug.Print "Phone BeforeUpdate"
End Sub

Private Sub Phone_Change()
  Debug.Print "Phone Change"
End Sub

Private Sub Phone_Dirty(Cancel As Integer)
  Debug.Print "Phone Dirty"
End Sub

Private Sub Phone_KeyDown(KeyCode As Integer, Shift As Integer)
  Debug.Print "Phone KeyDown"
  Debug.Print "  KeyCode = " & CStr(KeyCode)
  Debug.Print "  Shift = " & CStr(Shift)
End Sub

Private Sub Phone_KeyPress(KeyAscii As Integer)
  Debug.Print "Phone KeyPress"
  Debug.Print "  KeyAscii = " & CStr(KeyAscii)
End Sub

Private Sub Phone_KeyUp(KeyCode As Integer, Shift As Integer)
  Debug.Print "Phone KeyUp"
  Debug.Print "  KeyCode = " & CStr(KeyCode)
  Debug.Print "  Shift = " & CStr(Shift)
End Sub
```

Save the form with this code and type a character in the Phone text box. You'll see events similar to this:

```
Phone KeyDown
  KeyCode = 50
  Shift = 0
Phone KeyPress
  KeyAscii = 50
Phone Dirty
Phone Change
```

Type more characters, and you'll see the same events repeat, except for the Dirty event (after the control is dirty, it won't get dirty again until you save its value). Now tab to the next control to see the data events:

```
Phone BeforeUpdate
Phone AfterUpdate
```

You probably noticed that the code for the KeyDown, KeyPress, and KeyUp events prints some extra data. Rather than implement different events for each key on the keyboard, the Access team chose to use the Key events for every key. To allow your code to tell which key was pressed, these events pass in arguments (KeyCode and Shift in the case of KeyDown and KeyUp, KeyAscii in the case of KeyPress) that Access fills in with information on the current key. The KeyCode and KeyAscii parameters tell you the ASCII code of the key that was pressed, whereas the Shift parameter is set to indicate which (if any) of the Ctrl, Alt, and Shift keys were being held down at the same time. Refer to the help on the KeyDown event for details on decoding these parameters.

Control-Specific Events

Some controls have particular events associated closely with them. A good example is the button control, whose Click event you've already seen more than once. Most of a user's interaction with button controls involves clicking the buttons, which fires the Click event.

For toggle buttons, check boxes, and option buttons, the usual event fired by user interaction is the Click event. This event fires when the user clicks on one of these controls. But there's a catch: the click event exists only when these controls are placed directly on a form. If these controls are placed within an option group (which is the more usual way to use them), clicking the controls fires the data events of the parent option group.

Combo box controls have a somewhat peculiar event: the NotInList event. This event is fired when the user types something in the text portion of the combo box that's not contained in the list portion of the combo box. You can use this event to automatically add new data to the list when the user types a new entry. Schematically, you might take these steps:

1. Handle the NotInList event.
2. Ask the users whether they want to add the new entry to the list.
3. If the users agree, run code to add the new entry to the table that supplies data for the combo box.
4. Refresh the combo box.

This sequence is covered in more detail in Chapter 12, "Working with List and Combo Boxes." The NotInList event fires after the KeyUp event.

The Event Sequence for Forms

Combining controls into forms adds another layer of complexity. Forms have their own events, and these are sometimes interlaced with control events. By now, you should understand how to determine the order of events: just add code to print information to the Immediate window whenever an event occurs. So we dispense with the code here, and just explain the events. You can always write your own code to check the work here.

Navigation Events

When you open a form (for example, by calling the `DoCmd.OpenForm` method), five distinct events occur in this order:

1. `Open`

2. `Load`

3. `Resize`

4. `Activate`

5. `Current`

Of these events, the `Open` event marks the earliest point in the form's lifecycle where you can run code. The `Load` event occurs when the data is loaded into the form. The `Resize` event is fired every time a form is resized (including resizing from nonexistence to its initial size). The `Activate` event indicates that the form (or a control on the form) has the focus, whereas the `Current` event is fired whenever a new record is displayed in the form.

> **TIP** If you want to perform some operation for each record that the users navigate to, regardless of how they get there, put your code in the `Current` event handler.

Closing a form leads to a simpler sequence of events:

1. `Unload`

2. `Deactivate`

3. `Close`

As you can probably guess by now, these three events represent unloading the data, removing the focus from the form, and finally closing the form.

If you move from one form to another, the `Deactivate` event for the first form is followed by the `Activate` event for the second form. Note that you won't see the other form events (`Open`, `Load`, `Current`, and so on) if all you're doing is switching focus between forms.

Data Events

Forms have a rich set of data events. After all, forms are where you usually add, edit, and delete records. Let's look at each of those sequences in turn. When you navigate to the empty record on a form and start typing, the very first keystroke triggers five events in order, not counting the keystroke events for the control that you learned about earlier in the chapter:

1. Current
2. Enter for the control
3. GotFocus for the control
4. BeforeInsert
5. AfterInsert

Note the before-and-after pattern of the last two events. The BeforeInsert event is a notification that a record is being created, and at this time the form contains the data that's about to be saved to the new record. You can modify this data during this event, before it is saved. The AfterInsert event is a notification that a record was successfully created, and it contains the data that was actually saved.

You've already seen the events that occur when you're editing data in a single control (BeforeUpdate and AfterUpdate for the control). As you move around a single record and edit data in various controls, each control in turn fires its BeforeUpdate and AfterUpdate events. Then, when you save the data from the record (either by selecting Records, Save Record, or by moving to another record), the BeforeUpdate and AfterUpdate events for the entire form are fired. As with the other before-and-after pairs, the first of these lets you modify the data before it is saved to the table, and the second lets you see the data that was saved.

When you delete an entire record, Access fires three events:

1. Delete
2. BeforeDelConfirm
3. AfterDelConfirm

Each of these events has a specific purpose, of course. The Delete event occurs when the user deletes a record (for example, by clicking on the record selector and then pressing the Del key), but before anything is deleted. The BeforeDelConfirm event occurs just before Access displays the dialog box asking the user to confirm the deletion. In this event, you can cancel the rest of the sequence, preventing the record from being deleted. The AfterDelConfirm event marks the end of the deletion sequence.

Behind the Scenes: Data Buffers

As you edit data on a form, the data is actually stored in several areas in memory (these areas are called *buffers*). Let's trace the life cycle of an edit, using Figure 11.2 as a reference. In this figure, the boxes show the buffers where data can be stored, and the arrows show the flow of data.

Figure 11.2
How data is edited and saved.

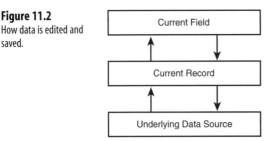

When you first navigate to a record on a form, the data for that record is pulled from the underlying table to the form. This data is stored in a buffer containing a single record. Each control on the form then displays data from that buffer. As soon as you start typing into a control, the data for that single control is pulled into a second buffer.

If you decide to tab to another control, the data from the control buffer is written back to the form buffer, triggering the control's BeforeUpdate and AfterUpdate events. Alternatively, you can press Esc, discarding your changes and wiping out the control buffer. In this case, the control's update events are not fired.

As you edit controls, the entire edited record is still held in the form-level buffer. None of the changes is written back to the database at this point. If you press Esc twice, the form-level buffer is simply discarded. On the other hand, if you save the record, the BeforeUpdate and AfterUpdate events for the form are fired, and the changes are written back to the underlying table.

The Event Sequence for Reports

Reports have events too, although the sequence is somewhat less rich than the event sequence for forms, because reports do not allow the user to interact with the data that they display. When you open a report, Access fires a mere two events in this sequence:

1. Open

2. Activate

As is the case with forms, these events represent the first point where the report is open enough to run code, and the point where it gains the focus onscreen. When you close a report, you see two corresponding events:

1. Deactivate

2. Close

Of course, there's more going on with reports than just opening and closing. In between, Access usually has data to display. For each report section, the event sequence includes up to four events:

1. Format for the section
2. Retreat for the section
3. NoData for the report
4. Print for the section

The Format event occurs after Access determines which data belongs in a particular section of the report, but before the section is actually formatted. The Retreat event is fired only if Access decides it has to "back up" and reformat a previously formatted section. For example, if you have properties set to keep data together on a page, Access might need to revisit a section it's already formatted to honor those properties. The NoData event is fired whenever a bound section does not return any data. And the Print event occurs after the data is formatted, but before it's actually printed.

Finally, Access fires the report's Page event once for each page in the report, just before that page gets printed.

Canceling Events

In some cases, you can cancel an event from your code. When you do so, the action that triggered the event is also cancelled. For example, the Exit event from a control can be cancelled. You can tell which events can be cancelled because their event procedures have a Cancel argument. To cancel an event, set this argument to True somewhere in your event handling code, as in this example:

```
Private Sub Client_Exit(Cancel As Integer)
  Cancel = True
End Sub
```

What happens when you cancel the Exit event? The answer is that whatever action triggered the event is also cancelled by Access. If the users try to tab out of the text box, the cursor won't move. If they try to click elsewhere, they'll still be stuck. So obviously, you don't want to just cancel the event! Typically, you need to add some logic to check the data, and then decide whether to cancel the event based on what the users typed.

Another set of events that you can cancel are the Before events: BeforeUpdate, BeforeInsert, and BeforeDelConfirm. Canceling one of these events stops the corresponding action. For example, if you cancel a BeforeUpdate event, the update does not happen; the data is left in its previous state. This is very useful when you need to perform last-minute data validation before making any changes to the database.

11

CASE STUDY

Validating Data Before Saving It

There are places in the `TimeTrack` application where a little extra data validation can come in handy. For example, consider the Projects form. Two of the key pieces of data on this form are the starting date of the project and the estimated ending date of the project. Obviously, the starting date should occur before the ending date. This case study shows how to add some logic to check for improperly entered data, before the users try to save the data to the database. Of course, you can also use a table-level validation rule for this purpose. But using a validation rule means that the data isn't checked until the user tries to save the entire record.

To add this support, put the Projects form into Design view and then open the form's module. Add this code:

```
Private Sub StartDate_Exit(Cancel As Integer)
  ' Verify that dates make sense
  If DatesAreBad Then
    MsgBox "Start date must be before end date", _
      vbCritical
    Cancel = True
  End If
End Sub

Private Sub EstimatedEndDate_Exit(Cancel As Integer)
  ' Verify that dates make sense
  If DatesAreBad Then
    MsgBox "Start date must be before end date", _
      vbCritical
    Cancel = True
  End If
End Sub

Private Function DatesAreBad() As Boolean
  ' Check to be sure that the start date
  ' is before the end date
  On Error GoTo HandleErr

  ' Assume everything is OK
  DatesAreBad = False

  Dim dtSDate As Date
  Dim dtEDate As Date

  ' Make sure the textboxes hold dates
  dtSDate = CDate(StartDate.Value)
  dtEDate = CDate(EstimatedEndDate.Value)

  ' Check to see if there's a problem
  If dtEDate - dtSDate < 0 Then
    DatesAreBad = True
  End If

ExitHere:
  Exit Function
```

11

```
HandleErr:
  ' In case of any error, assume dates are bad
  DatesAreBad = True
  Resume ExitHere
End Function
```

This code responds to the Exit events on both the starting and ending date controls. After all, a change to either control can cause a problem. Because the validation logic is the same in both cases, it makes sense to put the actual tests in a procedure (DatesAreBad) that's called from both event handlers. This procedure looks at the difference in time between the start and end date, and returns True if the end date is before the start date.

In either event handler, if DatesAreBad returns True, the event handler does two things. First, it displays a message to the users. Second, it sets the Cancel argument to True, which prevents the users from leaving the control until they fix the problem.

11

Working with List and Combo Boxes

Populating a List Control

Controls are interface objects that facilitate communication between the users and the application by either displaying data or accepting input. The list box and combo box controls display a list of items from which the users can select one or many items.

You probably use a wizard to populate a list control (combo box or list box), but doing so limits the list's contents. Sometimes you need more flexibility—allowing the list to determine its contents on the fly (as needed).

Both list controls have two common properties that you can manipulate programmatically to control the list contents:

- **Row Source Type**—Specifies whether the list is based on a table or query, a list of values, or a list of table or query field names.
- **Row Source**—Depends on the Row Source Type setting to determine the type of data displayed by the control.

There are three Row Source Type settings:

- When the Row Source Type setting is Table/Query, the Row Source setting must be a table, query, or SQL statement.
- When the Row Source Type setting is Value List, the Row Source setting must be an explicit list of items separated by the semicolon character.

IN THIS CHAPTER

Populating a List Control 175

Adding to the List–or Not 181

Working with Multiselect Controls 187

Considering Callback Functions 189

- When the Row Source Type setting is Field List, the row Source setting must be a table, query, or SQL statement. You're unlikely to ever use this setting, but Access relies on it for some of the wizards, which are themselves written as Access forms (using VBA as the programming language).

> **NOTE**
> This chapter uses VBA to refer to and manipulate these two controls, and assumes you already know the general purpose and characteristics of both controls.

You're probably familiar with these three properties already because you've set them via the Properties window. You can also set them using VBA code, and in doing so, determine or change the list items.

> **NOTE**
> The ControlSource property isn't all that important to us at this point—a control doesn't need to be bound or unbound to be programmatically manipulated. However, chances are you won't be using VBA to dynamically control a bound control's list items too often.

Although theoretically you can populate a list control most any time, the most logical time to do so is when you load the form or when the control itself gets the focus. Either way, you set the control's RowSourceType property using the following syntax:

```
control.RowSourceType = value
```

where `control` identifies the list control and `value` is one of the string expressions listed in Table 12.1. Use the following syntax to set the RowSource property:

```
control.RowSource = datasource
```

where `datasource` is a table, query, SQL statement, or value list, as determined by the RowSource Type setting.

Table 12.1   Setting the Row Source in VBA

Setting	VBA String
Table/Query	`"Table/Query"`
Value List	`"Value List"`
Field List	`"Field List"`

A Simple Filtering List Control

Let's work through a quick example that builds a filtering combo box for the Employees form. Specifically, you'll add a combo box to the form's header and then use the appropriate VBA code to display a list of employees in the control's drop-down list. (The example uses a combo box, but you can just as easily use a list box—the syntax and properties are identical, but the combo box requires less room.)

To get started, open the Employees form in Design view. Open the form's header and insert a combo box control. Name the combo box control `cboFilter` and set its corresponding label's `Caption` property to `Search For`. Then, complete the following steps:

1. Open the form's module. Add the two property statements shown here between the provided stubs:

```
Private Sub Form_Open(Cancel As Integer)
    cboFilter.RowSourceType = "Table/Query"
    cboFilter.RowSource = "Employees"
End Sub
```

2. Switch to Form view and open the new combo list control's drop-down list as shown in Figure 12.1.

Figure 12.1
The combo box displays the contents of the first column in the Employees table.

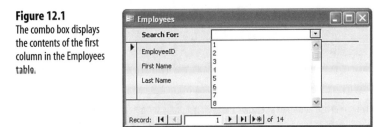

The results might not be what you expected. By default, the combo box list displays only one column—the first column from its data source.

When using VBA, use the `ColumnCount` property to determine how many columns to display and the `ColumnWidths` property to determine how wide each column is. Add the following statements to the form's `Open` event procedure:

```
cboFilter.ColumnCount = 3
cboFilter.ColumnWidths = "0"
```

as shown in Figure 12.2.

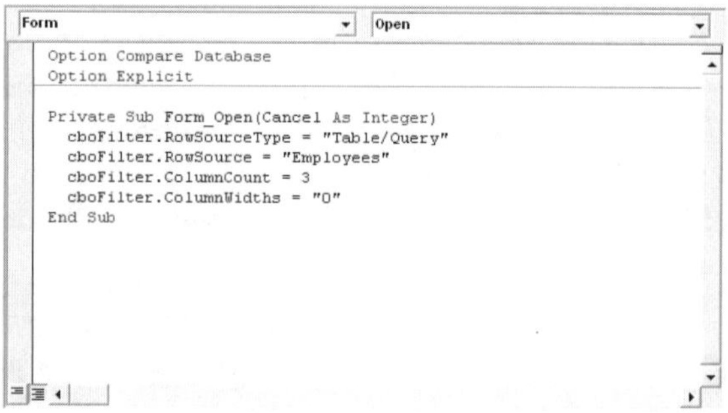

Figure 12.2
Use VBA to manipulate control properties.

```
Form                          ▾   Open                        ▾
  Option Compare Database                                      ▲
  Option Explicit

  Private Sub Form_Open(Cancel As Integer)
      cboFilter.RowSourceType = "Table/Query"
      cboFilter.RowSource = "Employees"
      cboFilter.ColumnCount = 3
      cboFilter.ColumnWidths = "0"
  End Sub
                                                              ▼
```

Save the form and close it. Then, re-open it in Form view and display the control's list a second time. This time, as shown in Figure 12.3, the list displays just the names. However, the employee values in the first column are still available; you just won't see them in the control's list.

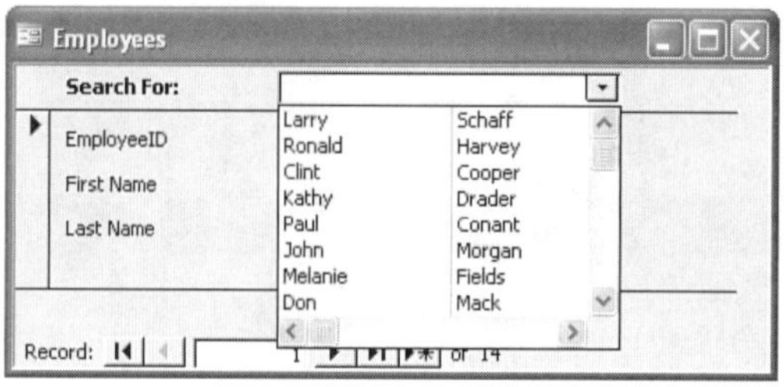

Figure 12.3
Now the list displays just the data you want.

The accompanying exercise automates settings that you generally set manually. When doing so, don't forget that by default, the combo box control's Bound property, and hence, its value, is still the first column in the data source and not the first column of data in the list.

Wouldn't it be nice if the list control you just created actually did something—like display the record for the employee you select? To have it do so, you must add an event procedure that responds when a list item is selected. For the purposes here, the Click event is the least work. To continue the example:

1. Return to the VBE using Alt+Tab or by selecting the appropriate icon on the Windows taskbar.

2. In the form's module, choose cboFilter from the Object control's drop-down list, as shown in Figure 12.4.

Figure 12.4
Choose an object from
the Object control.

Object control

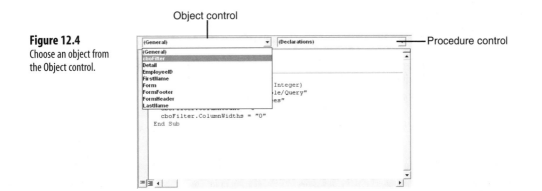

Procedure control

3. Next, choose Click from the Procedure control (the combo box to the right). Doing so enters the appropriate event stub, as shown in Figure 12.5.

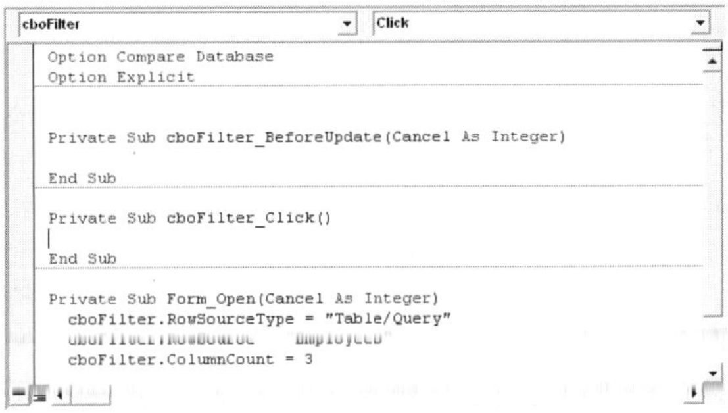

Figure 12.5
Let the editor enter the
event's stub.

4. Insert the following code between the stub's beginning and ending statements (not including the stub statements of course):

```
Private Sub cboFilter_Click()
  Dim strSQL As String
  strSQL = "SELECT * FROM Employees " & _
   "WHERE EmployeeID = " & cboFilter.Column(0)
  Debug.Print strSQL
  Forms!Employees.RecordSource = strSQL
End Sub
```

5. View the form in Form view and choose a name from the list control's drop-down list. Doing so automatically displays that employee's record. Figure 12.6 shows the result of choosing Terry Briggs. If you switch to the VBE, you'll see the modified SQL statement in the Immediate window.

12

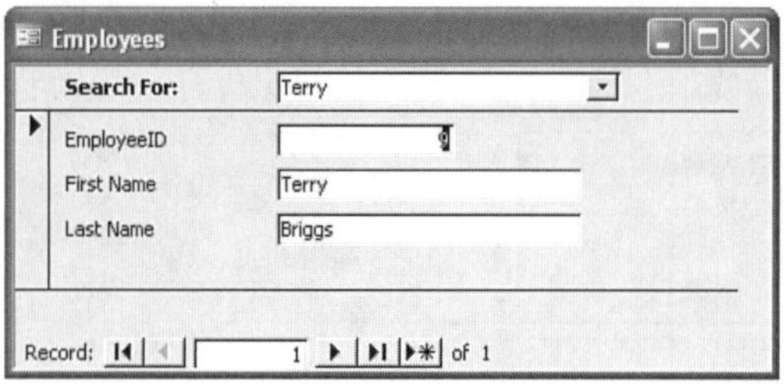

Figure 12.6
Selecting Terry Briggs in the list control displays his employee record.

> **NOTE**
> There are a number of ways to enter VBA code into a module. In the earlier example, you choose the On Open property setting to display and enter the appropriate event's stub. In the accompanying example, you use the Object and Procedure controls in the module window.
>
> After learning all the different ways, you'll slowly slip into a routine that you're comfortable with, but we want to introduce you to all the methods for entering code. That's why you use different methods throughout the examples.

The previous example considers just one type of list—a Table/Query list, which is probably the most common. Creating a field or value list is just as easy. The only key is to make sure you use the right type of RowSourceType setting to accommodate the data. For instance, the following code produces the list shown in Figure 12.7:

```
cboFilter.RowSourceType = "Field List"
cboFilter.RowSource = "Employees"
```

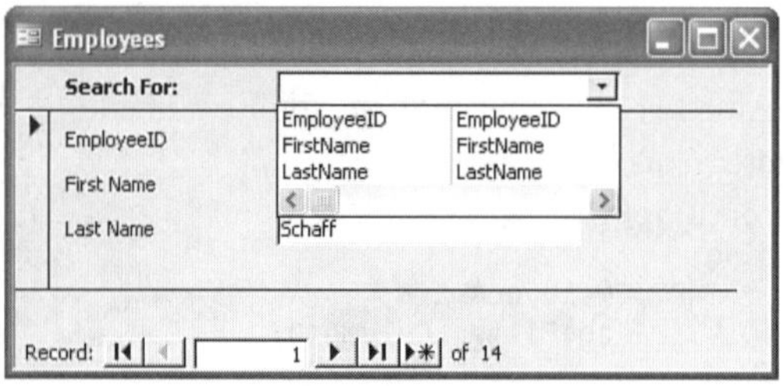

Figure 12.7
This field list displays the names of the fields in the Employees table.

Figure 12.8 displays a value list using this code:

```
cboFilter.RowSourceType = "Value List"
cboFilter.RowSource = "Larry;Ronald;Clint"
cboFilter.ColumnCount = 1
```

Comment out or delete the ColumnWidths property statement (if you've saved the form, you also have to remove the Column Widths setting from the form's Properties window). This last example is impractical in real practice because it isn't dynamic, which means you have to update the RowSource property statement to update the list.

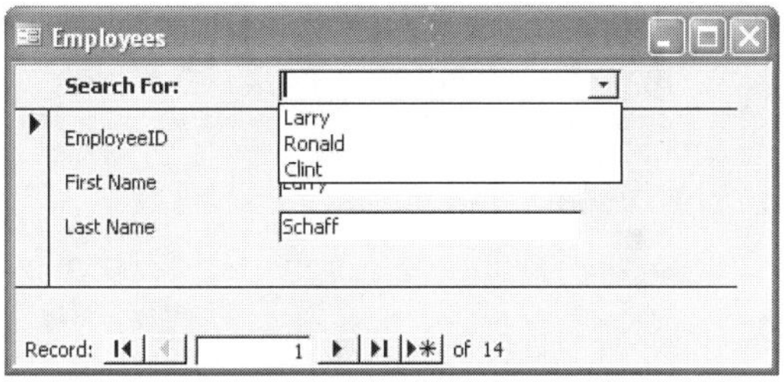

Figure 12.8
Displaying a list of
explicit values in a drop-
down list.

Adding to the List—or Not

The combo box control has a special quality that the list box control lacks. You can enter a value into the text box portion instead of choosing an item from the drop-down list. By default, you can use that value, but you can't add that value to the list. Adding a new item to the control's list takes a bit of work.

Entering a non-list item triggers the combo box control's `NotInList` event. By default, nothing happens when the event is triggered, but the event passes two arguments, `NewData` and `Response`, that you can use to add a value to a list.

`NewData` equals the input value in the combo box control's text box. `Response` indicates how the event was handled by the following intrinsic constants:

- `acDataErrDisplay`—This is the default value and displays a default message. Use this constant when you don't want to allow the users to add a new value to the combo box list.

- `acDataErrContinue`—Displays a custom message to the users, most likely asking them if they want the new value added to the control's list. When the response is Yes, the item is added to the list and the code must set `Response` to `acDataErrAdded`. When the response is No, the code sets the `Response` argument to `acDataErrContinue`.

- `acDataErrAdded`—This value indicates that the value stored by `NewData` has been added to the combo box control's list.

Updating a Value List

The easiest type of list to programmatically update is the value list. There are many ways to approach the problem, so this section takes the path of least resistance for now. Remember, the Row Source property for a value list control is an explicit list of values separated by the semicolon character (;). To update it, you simply need to modify the Row Source property accordingly.

Now let's create a simple unbound value list control that you can quickly update. (Bound value list controls are impractical and as such, are rare.) To create the example control shown in Figure 12.9, do the following:

1. Open a new, blank form in Design view and add a combo box.

2. Name the combo box `cboColors`. Change the caption of the combo box's label to `"Colors:"`.

3. Set the Row Source Type property to `Value List`.

4. Set the Row Source property to the string, `"Red;White;Blue"`.

5. Save the form, and then open it (refer to Figure 12.9) in Form view.

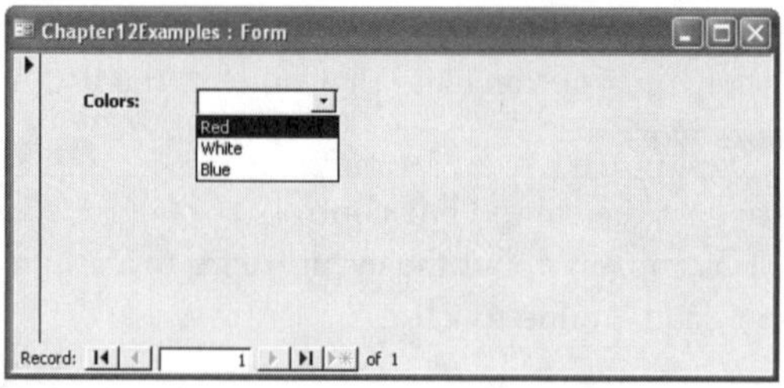

Figure 12.9
This simple combo box displays a fixed list of items.

Now, enter the color Yellow in the text box portion. The text box accepts the value, but does nothing with it. That means, the next time you want to select yellow, you must re-enter it instead of selecting it from the list.

Adding new items to the list takes a bit of VBA. To make the necessary changes, do the following:

1. Return the form to Design view and change `cboColors'` Limit to List property to Yes.

2. Choose [`Event Procedure`] from the On Not in List property. Click the Builder button to open the form's module and enter the `NotInList` event's stub statements.

3. Enter the following code to complete the procedure:

```
Private Sub cboColors_NotInList(NewData As String, Response As Integer)
  Dim bytResponse As Byte
  bytResponse = MsgBox("Do you want to add " & _
    cboColors.Value & " to the list?", vbYesNo)
  If bytResponse = vbYes Then
    Response = acDataErrAdded
    cboColors.RowSource = Me!cboColors.RowSource _
      & ";" & NewData
  Else
    Response = acDataErrContinue
    Me!cboColors.Undo
  End If
End Sub
```

4. Return to the form and click View to display it in Form view.

5. Re-enter Yellow in the text box component.

6. When Access displays the message shown in Figure 12.10, click Yes. Figure 12.11 shows the modified drop-down list, which now includes the string Yellow. If you open the Properties window, you'll see that the Row Source property is also updated to include the string yellow.

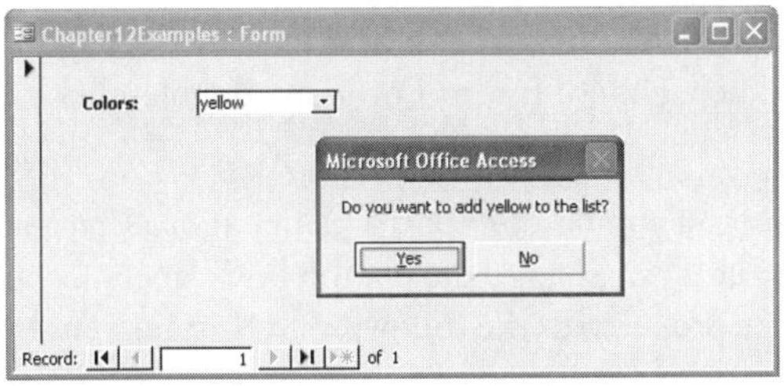

Figure 12.10

The MsgBox statement displays this message when you enter a non-list item.

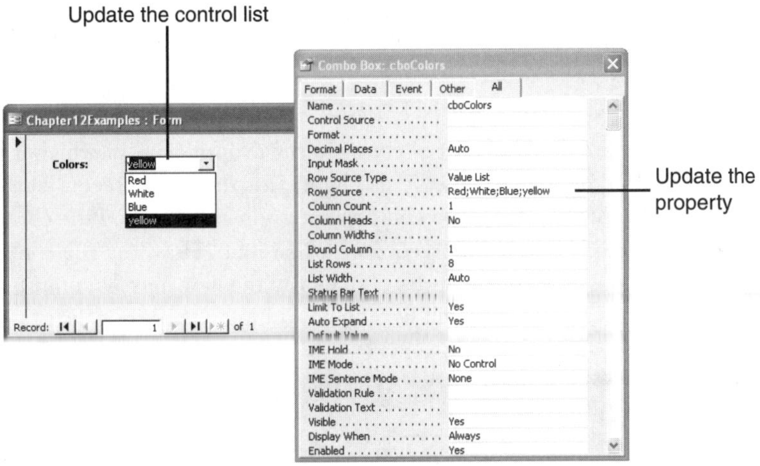

Figure 12.11

Answering Yes to the previous message adds the non-list item to the list.

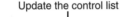

Update the control list

Update the property

Entering a non-list item triggers the NotInList event, which displays the message box (see Figure 12.10) and stores your response in the bytResponse variable. The If statement then adds the new item, or doesn't, depending upon the value stored in bytResponse.

When adding the new item, the procedure also resets the Response argument to acDataErrAdded so the actual insert can be processed (or not) internally. Notice that the Else action resets the Response argument to acDataErrContinue and then uses the Undo method to delete the entry from the text box component.

Updating a Table/Query List

The Table/Query list is probably the most common of the three types of control lists. It's also the most flexible. To display an item in the list, you simply add it to the data source (the table or query). These lists can be bound or unbound and your VBA solution for adding a non-list item will be different for each type.

The simpler solution of the two is with a bound control because all you have to do is save the non-list item to the underlying table and then re-query the control to update its list. To understand this simple process, you need a new combo box control and a table with some data.

First, create a new table named Colors and add one text field named Colors. Enter red, white, and blue into the lone field. Next, bind a new form to the Colors table by selecting Colors in the Tables list. Then, choose Insert, Form and double-click Design View in the New Form dialog box.

In the new, blank form, insert a combo box control, name it cboBound, and set its ControlSource property to Colors. Change the combo box's label's Caption property to Bound. Set the Row Source property to the following SQL statement or use the Query Builder to create the equivalent:

```
SELECT DISTINCT Colors FROM Colors ORDER BY Colors
```

This statement retrieves a unique list of items from the Colors field in the Colors table for the combo box control's list.

→ For a brief review of SQL, see "Review of Access SQL," p. 347.

As is, the control displays a list of colors in the drop-down list, which it gleans from the Colors field in the Colors table. It also highlights the bound record's data as shown in Figure 12.12. At this point, you could enter a non-list item and the control would accept it and update the corresponding record with that item. However, the control won't immediately display the new item in its list. To display the new item, you must close and re-open the form. Then, the control will list any new unique items in its list.

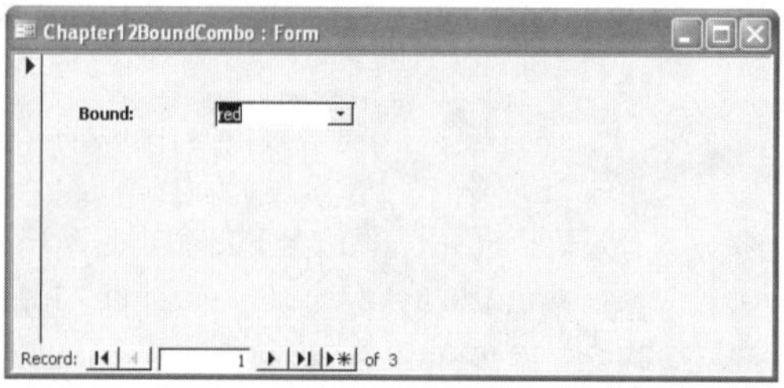

Figure 12.12
The bound control gets its list from the bound data source.

The easiest solution is to control when the input is saved and re-query the control, and you need VBA for that. With the form in Design view, double-click cboBound and choose [Event Procedure] from the After Update property's drop-down list (in the Properties window). Then, click the Builder button to the right. Next, complete the event procedure using the following code:

```
Private Sub cboBound_AfterUpdate()
  DoCmd.RunCommand acCmdSaveRecord
  cboBound.Requery
End Sub
```

TIP Use the `AddItem` method to add the current value to the list when using a Value List control. If you need to be compatible with older systems, keep in mind that the `AddItem` method isn't available in versions earlier than Access 2002.

Return to the form and display it in Form view. Click the New Record button on the Navigation toolbar, enter yellow, and press Enter. Figure 12.13 shows the new list. As you can see, it contains the item you just entered, yellow.

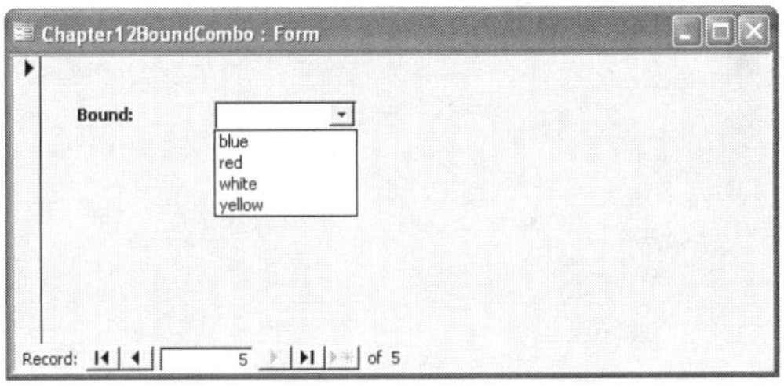

Figure 12.13
Force the control to update as soon as you enter a new item.

This example is extremely simple because it assumes every new item will be added to the list. In addition, keep in mind that list controls aren't generally best for data-entry purposes. It's too easy to choose a new item from the list, and overwrite the existing data for that record when that's not really what you want to do. Use bound list controls wisely.

You can also grab a list of items from an unbound data source, which means you can't accidentally change existing data. But you can update the underlying data source and hence the list. This is a good solution for controls that rely on lookup tables (as opposed to actual stored data).

Insert a new combo box into the unbound example form (the first form you created). Name the combo box cboUnbound and use the following SQL statement as the Row Source property:

```
SELECT DISTINCT Colors FROM Colors ORDER BY Colors
```

Then, set the Limit To List property to Yes.

The SQL statement is identical to the one you used in the bound example. Because the control isn't bound, a more complex solution is needed to update the list's data source. At this point, the list displays a unique list of colors retrieved from the Colors table. If you enter a non-list item, Access rejects it and displays an error message.

12

With the form in Design view, double-click cboUnbound and select [Event Procedure] from the On Not In List event property's drop-down list, and then click the Builder button to launch the form's module. Complete the NotInList event procedure as follows:

```
Private Sub cboUnbound_NotInList(NewData As String, Response As Integer)
  Dim cnn As New ADODB.Connection
  Dim strSQL As String
  Dim bytResponse As Byte
  Set cnn = CurrentProject.Connection
  bytResponse = MsgBox("Do you want to add this new item " _
   & "to the list?", vbYesNo, "New Item Detected")
  If bytResponse = vbYes Then
    strSQL = "INSERT INTO Colors(Colors) VALUES('" _
     & NewData & "')"
    Debug.Print strSQL
    cnn.Execute strSQL
    Response = acDataErrAdded
  ElseIf bytResponse = vbNo Then
    Response = acDataErrContinue
    Me!cboUnbound.Undo
  End If
End Sub
```

Return to the form and display it in Form view. Enter black into the unbound control's text box component, which triggers the control's Not In List event and displays the message box shown in Figure 12.14. Click Yes and the If statement executes the INSERT INTO SQL statement, which inserts the current entry into the list's data source (the Colors table). Figure 12.15 shows the new list. If you open the Colors table, you'll also find the new entry there.

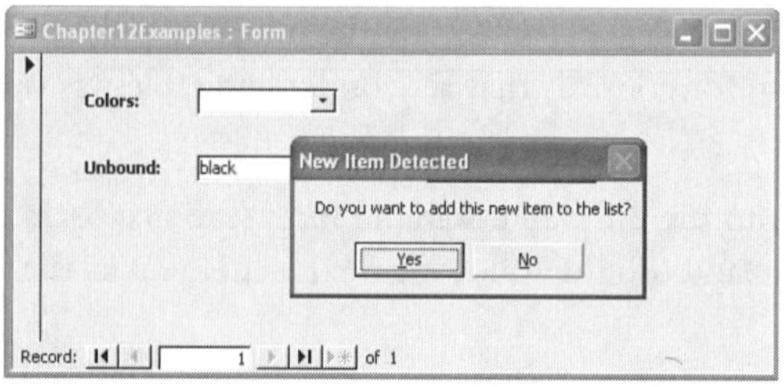

Figure 12.14
The Not In List event displays this message box.

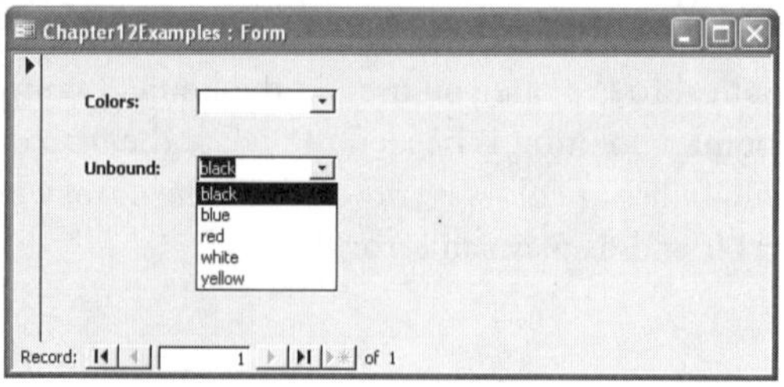

Figure 12.15
The current item has been added to the list.

You don't have to add the item. When Access displays the message box, click No. Setting `Response` to `acDataErrContinue` lets Access continue without making any changes to the data source. In a working situation, you'd probably have some use for entered items that don't make it to the list. To keep this example simple, the `Undo` method just deletes them.

> **NOTE** Another common solution to the accompanying problem is to use a `Recordset` object to update the underlying data source. There's nothing wrong with using a `Recordset` object, but you haven't been introduced to that object yet (see Chapter 17, "Manipulating Data with ADO," for more information on this object). The SQL solution requires less code and performs quicker than the `Recordset` object.

Working with Multiselect Controls

The list box control does something the combo box can't do. You can select multiple items in a list box. By default, the list box control allows only one selected item. By setting the control's Multi Select property to Simple or Extended, you allow the users to select more than one item from the list.

More than likely, you'll set this property when you create the control, but you can use VBA to modify the property using the form

```
listbox.MultiSelect = setting
```

where *setting* is one of the three values listed in Table 12.2.

Table 12.2   Multiselect Property Settings

Setting	Description	Integer Value
None	The default setting, which doesn't allow multiple selections.	0
Simple	Select or deselect multiple items by clicking or pressing the spacebar.	1
Extended	Select or deselect multiple items by holding down the Shift key and using the down arrow to extend the selection. Or, hold down the Ctrl key and click specific items for a noncontiguous selection.	2

Determining What's Selected and What's Not

The value of a combo box or a list box set to a single selection is easy to get by referring to the control's `Value` property in the form

```
control.Value
```

In fact, the `Value` property is the object's default and you don't even have to include the `Value` keyword. However, you probably should include it, because the code's much easier to read with the property.

Getting the value of a multiselect list box takes more work because there's more than one value to handle, which makes it a good candidate for a `For Each` statement. Using this statement, you can cycle through all the control's selected items.

➔ Review the `For Each` statement in "Working with Collections," p. 119.

Let's look at a quick example of a multiselect list box that uses the `For Each` statement to print the selected items to the Immediate window. Open the unbound example form and insert a list box. Name the control `lstCustomers`. Set the Row Source property to the following SQL statement:

```
SELECT Client FROM Clients
```

Then, set the Multi Select property to `Simple`.

Use any of the methods you've learned to open the form's module and enter the following event procedure:

```
Private Sub lstCustomers_LostFocus()
  Dim varItem As Variant
  Dim lst As Access.ListBox
  Set lst = lstCustomers
  'check for at least one selected item
  If lst.ItemsSelected.Count = 0 Then
    MsgBox "Please select a customer", _
      vbOKOnly, "Error"
    Exit Sub
  End If
  'cycle through selected items
  'deselect selected items
  For Each varItem In lst.ItemsSelected
    Debug.Print lst.ItemData(varItem)
    lst.Selected(varItem) = 0
  Next
End Sub
```

Return to the form and view it in Form view. The event procedure uses the Lost Focus event, which occurs when you leave the list box. First, let's see what happens when there are no items selected. Press Tab three times to both give focus to and then move it from the list box (don't select anything in the list box). Access displays the message box shown in Figure 12.16. Click OK to clear it.

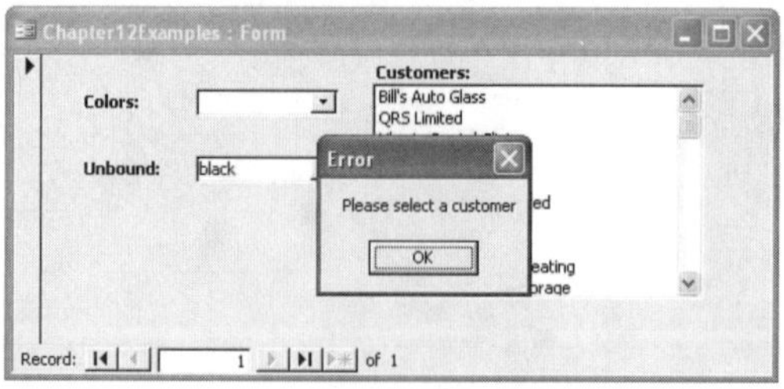

Figure 12.16
The procedure warns you when there isn't at least one item selected.

Before trying to retrieve the selected items, you want to make sure that there is at least one selected item. The `If` statement checks the number of items in the `ItemsSelected` collection. If it's 0, that means there are no items selected.

Tab back to the list box and click the first and third items, as shown in Figure 12.17. Then, select either of the combo boxes from the prior examples to trigger the control's Lost Focus event.

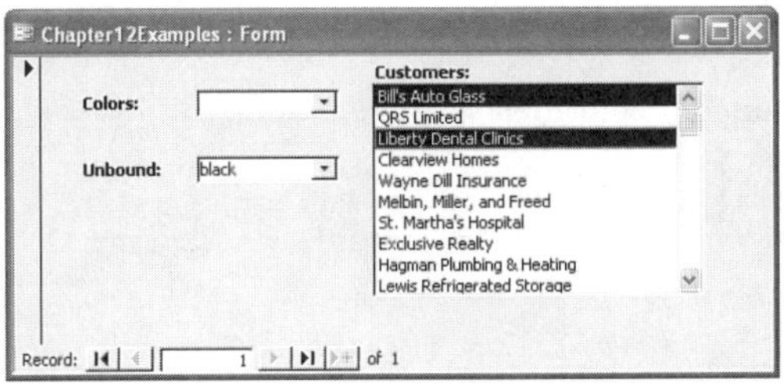

Figure 12.17
Select a couple of items from the multiselect list box.

After determining that there are selected items, the `For Each` statement loops through the `ItemsSelected` collection. The `ItemData` property equals the item text, which the `Debug.Print` statement prints to the Immediate window, as shown in Figure 12.18. Then, the corresponding `Selected` property is set to 0, which has the effect of deselecting the item.

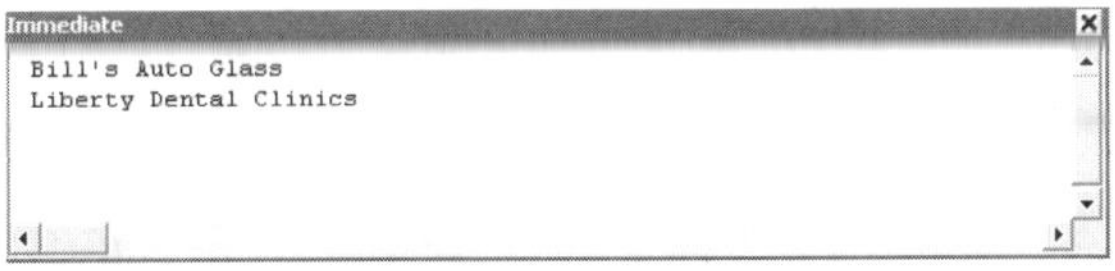

Figure 12.18
Print the selected items to the Immediate window.

Considering Callback Functions

A value list control is easy to create, but it has one limitation you should know about. When you set the control's Row Source Type property to Value List, the Row Source property—the actual list of items—is limited to 2,045 characters or less. Most of the time, this limit will probably be adequate, but when it isn't, you need another solution such as a callback function to populate the list.

For Access to display a list box, certain parameters about that list box must be known first. For instance, Access must know how many rows and columns of data are in the control. The callback function passes these values to Access. A callback function is similar to any other function, but the difference is that you reference the function in the control's Row Source Type property. In addition, the callback function uses DAO, so you must reference that library for this populating method to work. That library is already referenced in the sample database, `TimeTrack.mdb`.

Let's walk through an example that uses a callback function to populate a list box control with all the forms in the current database. To do so, follow these steps:

1. Insert a list box in either of the example forms and name it lstCallback.

2. Enter CallbackList as the control's Row Source Type property. Just write right over the default Table/Query setting. The CallbackList function doesn't exist yet; that's the next step.

3. Click the Code button to launch the VBE and insert a standard module. (Or use the Chapter 12 module.)

4. Enter the following function and then save the module:

```
Function CallbackList(ctrl As Control, id As Variant, _
  row As Variant, col As Variant, code As Variant) As Variant
  Select Case code
    Case acLBInitialize
      CallbackList = 1
    Case acLBOpen
      CallbackList = 1
    Case acLBGetRowCount
      CallbackList = CurrentProject.AllForms.Count
    Case acLBGetColumnCount
      CallbackList = 1
    Case acLBGetColumnWidth
      CallbackList = -1
    Case acLBGetValue
      CallbackList = CurrentProject.AllForms(row).Name
    Case acLBGetFormat
      CallbackList = -1
  End Select
End Function
```

View the form in Form view. Figure 12.19 shows the form and the list control, which displays a list of all the forms.

Figure 12.19
This list box uses a callback function to populate it with a list of forms.

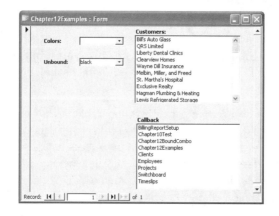

Opening the form in Form view forces the list box to call the `CallbackList` function. There's a lot going on behind the scenes, and you'll want to use the same structure: the arguments passed and the intrinsic constants used in the `Select Case` statement.

The `CurrentProject.AllForms.Count` statement determines the number of rows in the control by counting the number of documents in the Forms collection. Then, the `CurrentProject.AllForms(row).Name` statement determines each item by retrieving the names of all the documents in the Forms collection.

Callback functions are an advanced but powerful technique. They let you take complete control of the data displayed by a list control. Access calls your code each time it wants to retrieve a row for the list, and you can decide dynamically what to supply for the row.

CASE STUDY

Using List Box Controls as Drill-Down Controls

You've seen a few common uses for list controls in this chapter. A combo box makes a good filtering control. In addition, a list box is a good place for listing database objects, such as reports and forms, so users can choose what they need. Now, let's look at an unconventional use for a list control.

Let's suppose you want to use the Employees form to view project information for individual employees. Now, you can use datasheet forms dropped in as subforms or opened with the click of a command button, but list controls make an interesting alternative. In this context, it's easy to apply what's known as the "drill-down" effect to a list control (not so easy with a datasheet form or subform). This term refers to clicking or double-clicking data to display additional data about the clicked or double-clicked item.

The first step is to create the query shown in Figure 12.20 and name it `HoursWorkedByProject`. Notice that the query is a Totals View—so be sure to select the appropriate aggregate functions in each Total cell. In addition, enter the following reference in the EmployeeID column's Criteria cell:

`[Forms]![Employees]![EmployeeID]`

Figure 12.20
This query totals the hours per employee spent on each task.

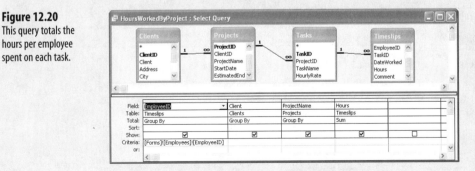

12

The list box shown on the left in the form shown in Figure 12.21 shows the results of the query, but those records are specific to the current employee. Refer to Table 12.3 to add the additional list box controls. Then, launch the form's module, enter the event procedures shown here, and save the form:

```
Private Sub Form_Current()
  lstProjects.Requery
  lstDetails.RowSource = ""
End Sub

Private Sub lstProjects_DblClick(Cancel As Integer)
  Dim strSQL As String
  strSQL = "SELECT Projects.ProjectID, Tasks.TaskName, " _
    & "Tasks.HourlyRate, Timeslips.DateWorked " _
    & "FROM (Projects INNER JOIN Tasks ON Projects.ProjectID=Tasks.ProjectID) " _
    & "INNER JOIN Timeslips ON Tasks.TaskID=Timeslips.TaskID " _
    & "WHERE EmployeeID = " & Forms!Employees!EmployeeID _
    & " AND ProjectName = '" & lstProjects.Column(2) & "'" _
    & "ORDER BY TaskName, ProjectName, DateWorked ASC"
  Debug.Print strSQL
  lstDetails.RowSource = strSQL
End Sub
```

Figure 12.21
Use the list items to learn more about the item.

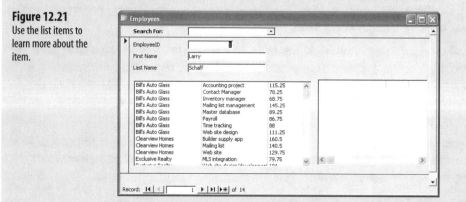

Table 12.3   List Box Control Properties

Object	Property	Setting
list box	Name	lstProjects
	Row Source	HoursWorkedByProject
	Column Count	4
	Column Widths	0";1.5";1.5";0.5"
list box	Name	lstDetails
	Column Count	4
	Column Widths	0";1.5";0.5";0.5"

You can use the form's navigation buttons or the filtering combo box control in the header to browse through the records. The form's Current event re-queries the projects control (on the left) to update it with only records for the current employee. This event also sets the detail displaying the control's Row Source property to " ", so the list displays nothing.

To display more detailed information about an item in the left list box, double-click an item. The control's Dbl Click event sets the blank control's Row Source property to a SQL statement that reflects the current employee and the task you double-clicked in the first list box.

View the form in Form view. The first employee is Larry Schaff. Double-click the third item in the projects control—Inventory Manager with a total of 68.75 hours. The double-click event updates the contents of the second list box, as shown in Figure 12.22.

Figure 12.22
Use the list items to learn more about the item.

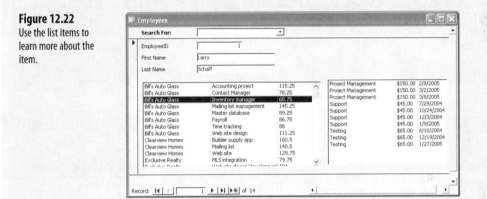

You can see that Larry has clocked hours in project management on the inventory manager project for Bill's Auto Glass on three different days. He spent part of four days on the project in support, and three days in testing. Each task has its own hourly rate, and you can even see the dates on which Larry performed the specific tasks.

Although this approach for displaying data isn't as common as some others, you might find it an approachable and easy alternative after you're familiar with list controls, their properties, and their unique behaviors.

12

Working with Other Controls

13

Working with Text Boxes

Text boxes are the second most common control on most forms (the most common, labels, are pretty uninteresting from the point of view of automation). You saw in Chapter 11's case study how you can use the events of text boxes to prevent users from entering invalid data, but there's much more that you can do with text boxes and VBA. This section of the chapter reviews some of the key properties of text box controls, and then shows you some useful techniques.

Key Properties of Text Boxes

You probably already know most of the properties of text boxes—they're visible in the Properties window when you select a text box in Design mode in the Access user interface. Although you can work with most of these properties in code, some are more useful in code than others. Table 13.1 lists some of the more useful properties.

IN THIS CHAPTER

Working with Text Boxes 195

Using Controls in Option Groups 200

Working with Subforms 202

Working with the Tag Property 202

> **TIP**
>
> Remember, when you refer to things in VBA, there are no spaces in the name. So the `TextBox` object has a `ValidationText` property, which corresponds exactly to the `Validation Text` property of a text box control on the Properties window.

Table 13.1   Selected Properties of the TextBox Object

Property	Description
BackColor	The background color of the text box
BorderColor	The border color of the text box
ControlSource	The field in the record source where the text box gets its data
Enabled	`True` if the text box can accept the focus, `False` if it cannot
FontBold	`True` if the font is bold, `False` if it is not
FontItalic	`True` if the font is italic, `False` if it is not
FontName	The font in the text box
FontSize	The size of the font in the text box
ForeColor	The foreground color of the text box
Locked	`True` if the text box cannot accept input, `False` if it can
OldValue	The original value of a text box that's being edited
SelText	The text that's selected in a text box
Tag	A property that's not used by Access
Text	The current text in the text box
Value	The edited text in a text box
Visible	`True` if the text box is visible, `False` if it's invisible

You can use these properties to adjust the appearance and behavior of a text box at runtime (while the user is working with the form). You might note that there are four properties dealing with the text in a text box. Of these, the `SelText`, `OldValue`, and `Text` properties are valid only for the text box that currently has the focus. The `Text` property is available for any text box on the form. If you try to retrieve, for example, the `Text` property of a text box that doesn't have the focus, VBA reports an error.

The other property that deserves some extra comment is the `Tag` property. This is a property that Access doesn't use. It exists simply to give you a place to store data that's associated with the text box. You see how to use the `Tag` property later in the chapter, in the "Working with the Tag Property" section.

Forms, reports, and all types of controls have a `Tag` property, so you can store arbitrary data with just about everything.

Tracking the Focus

Users of your database might have many different levels of experience. Inexperienced users sometimes have trouble with concepts that you might take for granted. For example, the notion that there is a focus, and that only the control with the focus accepts data, can be challenging when you're first starting with Access. Here's a technique that can help new users understand exactly which part of a form is active.

To start, you need a pair of procedures in a standalone module. One of these procedures sets the `BackColor` property of a control to the code for yellow, and the other sets it to white:

```
Sub HighlightControl(ctl As Control)
  ' Set the background color of the
  ' specified control to yellow, if possible
  On Error Resume Next
  ctl.BackColor = 65535
End Sub

Sub UnhighlightControl(ctl As Control)
  ' Set the background color of the
  ' specified control to white, if possible
  On Error Resume Next
  ctl.BackColor = 16777215
End Sub
```

As you can see, these procedures accept a single argument whose type is `Control`. `Control` is a generic object type that you can use to represent any type of Access control: text boxes, combo boxes, labels, and so on. Access enables you to pass any control to these procedures without raising an error.

However, there's no guarantee that every control you pass in supports a `BackColor` property. That's why the `On Error Resume Next` lines are in these procedures. If the procedure can set the property, great; if not, it exits without any fuss.

To use these procedures, call the `HighlightControl` procedure from the `GotFocus` event of each control on your form, and the `UnhighlightControl` procedure from the `LostFocus` event. For example, here's code to use these procedures with the Timeslips form:

```
Private Sub DateWorked_GotFocus()
  HighlightControl DateWorked
End Sub

Private Sub DateWorked_LostFocus()
  UnhighlightControl DateWorked
End Sub
```

13

```
Private Sub EmployeeID_GotFocus()
  HighlightControl EmployeeID
End Sub

Private Sub EmployeeID_LostFocus()
  UnhighlightControl EmployeeID
End Sub

Private Sub Hours_GotFocus()
  HighlightControl Hours
End Sub

Private Sub Hours_LostFocus()
  UnhighlightControl Hours
End Sub

Private Sub TaskID_GotFocus()
  HighlightControl TaskID
End Sub

Private Sub TaskID_LostFocus()
  UnhighlightControl TaskID
End Sub
```

Save everything and open the form. You'll find that a yellow highlight follows the focus as you tab around the form. Figure 13.1 shows the Timeslips form after clicking in the Date Worked field.

Figure 13.1

Tracking the focus on an open form.

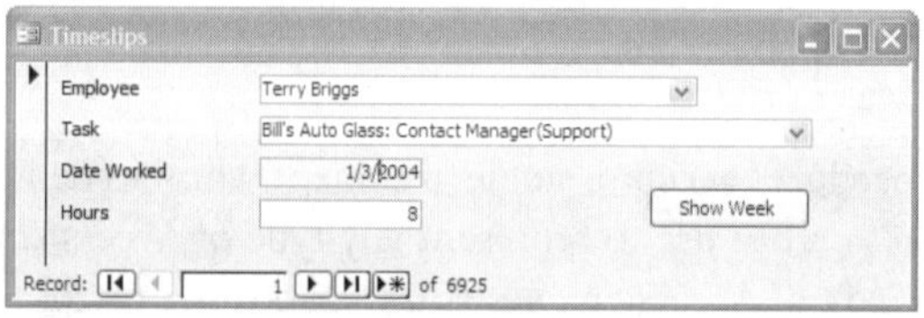

CAUTION

If you use this technique with one form, be sure to use it consistently across your entire application. Inconsistent applications are extremely difficult to use.

Working with Unbound Text Boxes

An *unbound text box* is one that is not connected to a particular field in a database table. Unbound text boxes are useful when you want to allow the users to enter data that's used transiently. For instance, the Billing Report Setup form in the TimeTrack database allows the users to select a client, start date, and end date, and open a report in preview mode. But it doesn't let users filter the results any more specifically than by date. Here's how you might handle that requirement:

1. Open the `BillingReportSetup` form in Design mode.

2. Place the mouse at the bottom of the design area of the form (indicated by the grid of dots), and then click and drag to make the form taller.

3. Add a new text box to the form. Because the form itself is unbound, the text box is automatically unbound. Name the new text box `txtWhere`. Set the attached label to `WHERE` clause.

4. Add a new command button to the form. Name the new button `cmdAdvancedReport` and set its caption to `Advanced Report`.

5. Open the form's module and add this code to handle the `Click` event of the new button:

```
Private Sub cmdAdvancedReport_Click()
  On Error GoTo HandleErr
  DoCmd.OpenReport "BillingReport", acViewPreview, _
   WhereCondition:=txtWhere.Value
ExitHere:
  Exit Sub
HandleErr:
  MsgBox "Error " & Err.Number & ": " & _
   Err.Description & " in cmdAdvancedReport_Click"
  Resume ExitHere
End Sub
```

6. Save the form.

To test the new controls, open the form in Form view. Select Bill's Auto Glass as the client, 5/1/2004 as the start date, and 6/1/2004 as the end date. Then enter `Hours=7` as the `WHERE` clause, and click the Advanced Report button. As you can see in Figure 13.2, the resulting report displays only the timeslips on which exactly seven hours was reported.

Figure 13.2
A report filtered at run-time.

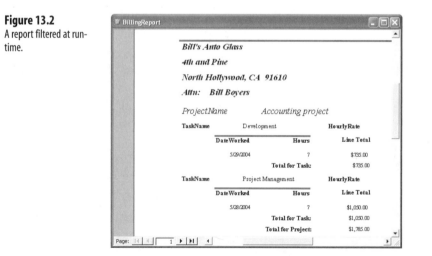

Note that the code uses the Value property to retrieve information from a text box that does not have the focus.

→ For more information on WHERE clauses in reports, see "Populating the Report," p. 213.

Using Controls in Option Groups

Option groups, of course, are controls that can contain other controls. Specifically, you can put any of these controls inside of an option group by dropping the control on the option group when you're designing the form:

- Check box
- Option button
- Toggle button

Only one control within an option group can be selected at a time. When you click on one option button, for example, it becomes selected and all the other controls in the option group become deselected. Each control in the option group has its own Option Value property, and the Value property of the option group is equal to the Option Value of the selected control.

> **TIP**
>
> Because only one control in an option group can be selected at a time, they don't work well when you have a series of check boxes and want to allow the users to check more than one at the same time. In that case, you can construct a fake option group by positioning the check boxes inside of a rectangle control.

None of the fields in the TimeTrack database is especially suited for representation by an option group, so we've constructed the Chapter13OptionGroup form to show you some useful code. Figure 13.3 shows this form.

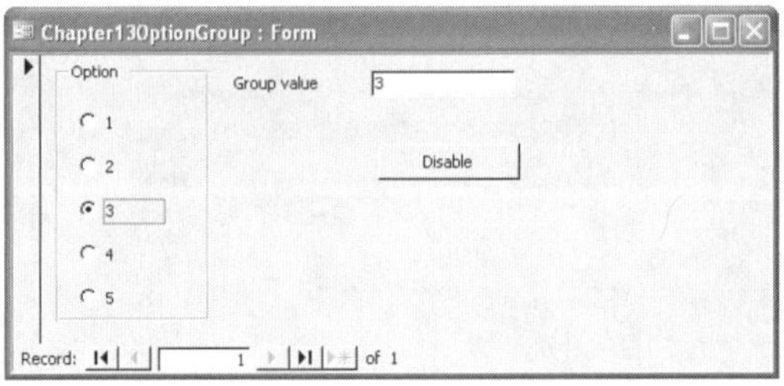

Figure 13.3
Test form for option group code.

The code behind this form shows you how to perform three tasks:

- Report the value of the option group in an unbound text box
- Set the value of the option group by entering a value in the text box
- Disable all the option buttons in the option group as a single operation

To handle the first of these tasks, you have to catch the AfterUpdate event of the option group, which is fired whenever the users click one of the option buttons:

```
Private Sub grpOption_AfterUpdate()
  ' Show the option group value
  ' in the text box
  txtValue = grpOption
End Sub
```

The line of code that does the assignment from the option group to the text box uses the fact that each control has a *default property*. When you specify a control name in a context where only a property makes sense, VBA uses this property. For both the option group and the text box, the default property is the Value property, so this bit of code assigns the value of one to the value of the other.

To handle the second requirement, you need code attached to the Change event of the text box, so that it takes effect whenever the users type a character:

```
Private Sub txtValue_Change()
  ' Update the option group
  ' from the text box
  On Error Resume Next
  grpOption = CInt(txtValue.Text)
End Sub
```

The On Error Resume Next statement takes care of the case where the users type something nonsensical, such as q, in the text box. In that case, the code simply leaves the option group alone.

Finally, disabling all the option buttons at once introduces several new concepts:

```
Private Sub cmdDisable_Click()
  ' Disable the entire option group
  Dim ctl As Control
  For Each ctl In grpOption.Controls
    If ctl.ControlType = acOptionButton Then
      ctl.Enabled = False
    End If
  Next ctl
End Sub
```

13

Controls that contain other controls (like the option group) have their own `Controls` collection. By using a `For Each` loop, the VBA code visits each control in this collection in turn when the users click the button. But if you look at Figure 13.3, you'll see that the option group contains both label controls and option button controls. Trying to disable a label control raises a runtime error. Rather than simply suppress the errors, this code takes a more elegant approach. Every control on an Access form or report has a `ControlType` property that returns a constant indicating the type of the control. So this loop steps through all the controls, tests each one to determine whether it is an option button, and then disables the control only if it is an option button.

Working with Subforms

Subforms are a peculiar sort of control: they contain an entire form. This form, of course, can contain its own controls, including other subforms (although you can't go deeper than sub-subforms in Access).

To work with subforms, you must first know how to refer to the controls that they contain. The general form of control reference for subforms is as follows:

```
Forms![top-levelformname].[subformcontrolname].Form![controlname]
```

For example, the Projects form in the `TimeTrack` database contains a subform control named `Tasks`. To display the value of the `TaskName` field in the current row in this subform, you can type this expression into the Immediate window:

```
?Forms!Projects.Tasks.Form!TaskName
```

Of course, if you're working in code behind the Projects form, you can shorten this reference by using the `Me` shortcut, perhaps assigning the result to a variable:

```
varTaskName = Me.Tasks.Form!TaskName
```

After you understand how to refer to subform controls, working with subforms is exactly like working with forms. The key is the `.Form` property. This property lets you "look inside" the subform to refer to the controls that it contains.

Working with the `Tag` Property

Beginning VBA developers are sometimes confused by the `Tag` property, wondering what good it is to have a property that Access never uses. The answer is that it's very useful indeed to have a property that you can use yourself for whatever you want. Every control on an Access form has a `Tag` property, and it's up to you to decide what to put there and how to use it.

For an example of how to use the `Tag` property, let's modify the `HighlightControl` procedure that you saw earlier in the chapter. As it stands now, this procedure sets controls to a yellow background when you enter them. But what if you don't always want to use that color?

There's no built-in property for Access controls that says "use this color to highlight the control." Fortunately, there is the Tag property. Here's how to make the changes:

1. Open the Timeslips form in Design mode. Set the Tag property of the EmployeeID and TaskID controls to 65535. Set the Tag property of the DateWorked and Hours controls to 16777088.

2. Open the Chapter13 code module and modify the HighlightControl procedure as follows:

```
Sub HighlightControl(ctl As Control)
  ' Set the background color of the
  ' specified control to yellow, if possible
  On Error Resume Next
  If Not IsNull(ctl.Tag) Then
    ctl.BackColor = ctl.Tag
  Else
    ctl.BackColor = 65535
  End If
End Sub
```

Save the form. Switch the form back to Form view and tab through the controls. You'll see that the first two controls turn yellow when they have the focus, which corresponds to a BackColor value of 65535. The second two controls turn a light blue, color 16777088.

> **CAUTION**
>
> Don't confuse the Tag property with the SmartTags property.

Note that the procedure has been written to do something useful (We hope!) whether or not there's a value in the Tag property. If the tag is filled in, the procedure uses that number for the highlighted background color. If there's no tag value, it falls back to the original yellow that was coded in the first version of HighlightControl.

CASE STUDY

13

Creating a Master Viewing Form

This chapter's case study explores an alternative user interface for displaying client, employee, and project information. The idea is to give users a single central form that they can toggle between these three types of information. You also add control highlighting to aid in data entry.

To begin with, you need to build three new forms to act as subforms on the main form. These forms, ClientSub, EmployeeSub, and ProjectSub, are each two inches high and three inches wide. The Tag property of each text box on these forms is set to 65535, and the Tag property of the combo box on the ProjectSub form is set to 12615935 to remind users that it draws its data from another table. Figure 13.4 shows these three forms open in Design mode.

Figure 13.4
Subforms for the alternative user interface.

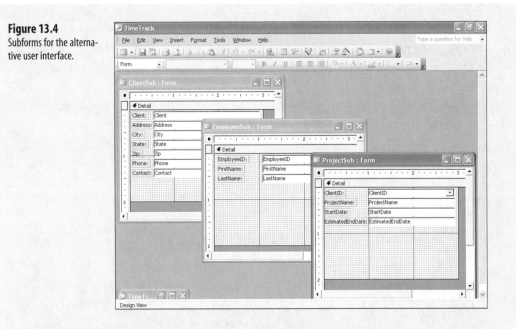

Of course, each of the subforms has the code necessary to handle control highlighting. Here's the code from the `ClientSub` form:

```
Option Compare Database
Option Explicit

Private Sub Address_GotFocus()
  HighlightControl Address
End Sub

Private Sub Address_LostFocus()
  UnhighlightControl Address
End Sub

Private Sub City_GotFocus()
  HighlightControl City
End Sub

Private Sub City_LostFocus()
  UnhighlightControl City
End Sub

Private Sub Client_GotFocus()
  HighlightControl Client
End Sub

Private Sub Client_LostFocus()
  UnhighlightControl Client
End Sub
```

```
Private Sub Contact_GotFocus()
  HighlightControl Contact
End Sub

Private Sub Contact_LostFocus()
  UnhighlightControl Contact
End Sub

Private Sub Phone_GotFocus()
  HighlightControl Phone
End Sub

Private Sub Phone_LostFocus()
  UnhighlightControl Phone
End Sub

Private Sub State_GotFocus()
  HighlightControl State
End Sub

Private Sub State_LostFocus()
  UnhighlightControl State
End Sub

Private Sub Zip_GotFocus()
  HighlightControl Zip
End Sub

Private Sub Zip_LostFocus()
  UnhighlightControl Zip
End Sub
```

Here's the corresponding code for the EmployeeSub form:

```
Option Compare Database
Option Explicit

Private Sub EmployeeID_GotFocus()
  HighlightControl EmployeeID
End Sub

Private Sub EmployeeID_LostFocus()
  UnhighlightControl EmployeeID
End Sub

Private Sub FirstName_GotFocus()
  HighlightControl FirstName
End Sub

Private Sub FirstName_LostFocus()
  UnhighlightControl FirstName
End Sub

Private Sub LastName_GotFocus()
  HighlightControl LastName
End Sub
```

13

```
Private Sub LastName_LostFocus()
  UnhighlightControl LastName
End Sub
```

And finally, the code for the `ProjectSub` form:

```
Option Compare Database
Option Explicit

Private Sub ClientID_GotFocus()
  HighlightControl ClientID
End Sub

Private Sub ClientID_LostFocus()
  UnhighlightControl ClientID
End Sub

Private Sub EstimatedEndDate_GotFocus()
  HighlightControl EstimatedEndDate
End Sub

Private Sub EstimatedEndDate_LostFocus()
  UnhighlightControl EstimatedEndDate
End Sub

Private Sub ProjectName_GotFocus()
  HighlightControl ProjectName
End Sub

Private Sub ProjectName_LostFocus()
  UnhighlightControl ProjectName
End Sub

Private Sub StartDate_GotFocus()
  HighlightControl StartDate
End Sub

Private Sub StartDate_LostFocus()
  UnhighlightControl StartDate
End Sub
```

The next step is to build the master form. This is an unbound form that hosts the three subforms. Follow these steps to create this form:

1. Create a new form in Design mode.

2. Add an option group to the form and name it `grpSub`. Set the default value of `grpSub` to 1.

3. Add three option buttons to the option group. Set their captions to `Clients`, `Employees`, and `Projects`, and set their `Option Value` properties to 1, 2, and 3.

4. Drag the `ClientSub` form from the Database window and drop it on the master form. This is the easiest way to get a subform control sized properly to hold the form.

5. Delete the label that Access creates for the subform.

6. Name the subform control `SwitchForm`. Figure 13.5 shows the master form in Design view.

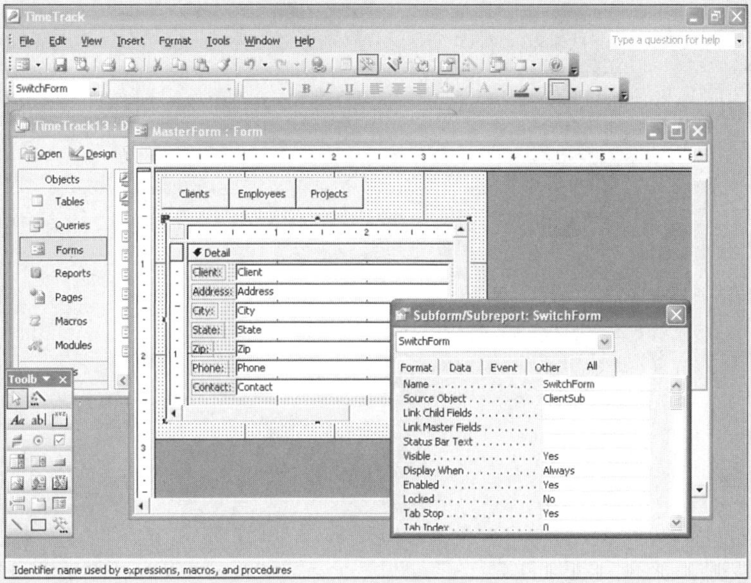

Figure 13.5
Designing the master
form.

7. Add code behind the form to handle switching the contents of the subform:

```
Private Sub grpSub_AfterUpdate()
  ' Switch subforms as buttons as clicked
  Select Case grpSub.Value
    Case 1  ' Clients
      Me!SwitchForm.SourceObject = "ClientSub"
    Case 2  ' Employees
      Me!SwitchForm.SourceObject = "EmployeeSub"
    Case 3  ' Projects
      Me!SwitchForm.SourceObject = "ProjectSub"
  End Select
End Sub
```

Save the form and open it in regular Form view. You'll find that you can use the toggle buttons to switch the embedded subform, and that highlighting follows the cursor through the data-entry fields. Figure 13.6 shows the final form.

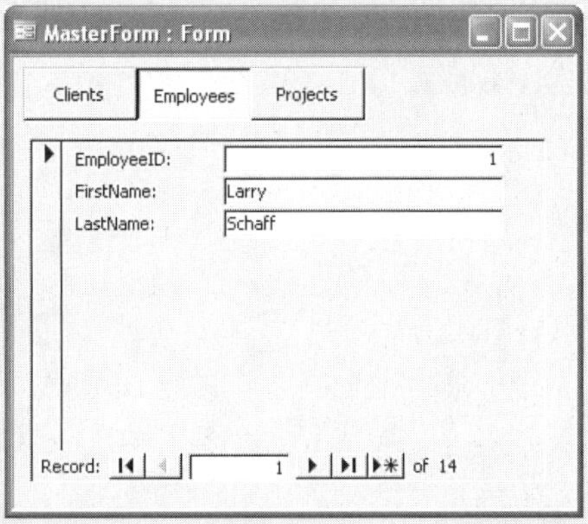

Figure 13.6
The master form in
action.

13

Working with Reports

14

Introducing the Report Module and Events

For the most part, VBA code is stored in one of two module types: standard or object. The object module is a special module attached to a report or a form. The module is saved with the object and supports events and properties that are unique to the object.

Most of the code you enter and store in a report module (or a form module for that matter) comes in the form of event procedures—code that's executed when some action occurs. For instance, code added to the report's Open event is executed when you open the report. Let's look at a quick example that maximizes the report:

1. Select the BillingReport report in the Database window and then click the Code button in the Database toolbar. This launches the VBE with the BillingReport report's module current.

2. Enter the following code:
   ```
   Private Sub Report_Open(Cancel As Integer)
     DoCmd.Maximize
   End Sub
   ```

3. Click the Save button.

4. Return to the Access Database window and close the report.

5. Open the BillingReportSetup form. Remember, this form launches the BillingReport report after you specify a few values that limit the records that make it to the report.

6. Choose Bill's Auto Glass and enter the dates 10/1/04 and 10/31/04.

7. Click the Open Report button, which triggers the report's Open event and maximizes the report window in Print Preview.

IN THIS CHAPTER

Introducing the Report Module
and Events 209

Opening and Closing Reports 210

Passing Arguments Using OpenArgs 212

Populating the Report 213

Handling Report-Level Errors 215

Using VBA to Determine Group
Properties 218

→ Read about report events and their sequence in "The Event Sequence for Reports" on page 170.

Opening and Closing Reports

One of the ways you can lead users through the work process is to open objects for them as the objects are needed and then close them when the users are done with them. Of course, most users can be taught to open and close objects for themselves, but automating the process goes a long way toward keeping users on the right road.

Opening a Report

In the case study found in Chapter 8, "Understanding Objects," you converted the macro that opens BillingReport to an event procedure using the following code:

```
Private Sub cmdOpenReport_Click()
 On Error GoTo HandleErr
 DoCmd.OpenReport "BillingReport", acViewPreview
ExitHere:
 Exit Sub
HandleErr:
 MsgBox "Error " & Err.Number & ": " & _
  Err.Description & " in cmdBillingReport_Click"
 Resume ExitHere
End Sub
```

For now, you're interested in the OpenReport method. It's very similar to the OpenForm method you learned about in Chapter 10, "Working with Forms." Both are methods of the DoCmd object. To open a report, use the OpenReport method in the following form:

DoCmd.OpenReport *reportname* [, *view*] [, *filtername*] [, *wherecondition*] [, *windowmode*] [, *openargs*]

where *reportname* is a string expression that identifies the report you're opening by name. Table 14.1 lists the optional arguments. Tables 14.2 and 14.3 give additional details about the syntax of OpenReport.

Table 14.1 OpenReport **Optional Arguments**

Argument	Data Type	Explanation
view	Constant	One of the intrinsic constants listed in Table 14.2; determines the report's view.
filtername	Variant	A string expression that equals the valid name of a fixed query.
wherecondition	Variant	A string expression that equals a valid SQL statement WHERE clause, without the WHERE keyword.
windowmode	Constant	One of the intrinsic constants listed in Table 14.3; determines the report's mode.
openargs	Variant	A string expression or value that's passed to the report's OpenArgs property.

Table 14.2 `View` **Argument Constants**

Constant	Integer Value	Explanation
`acViewNormal`	0	Prints the report.
`acViewDesign`	1	Opens the report in Design view.
`acViewPreview`	2	Opens the report in Print Preview.

Table 14.3 `Windowmode` **Argument Constants**

Constant	Integer Value	Explanation
`acWindowNormal`	0	Relies on the report's properties.
`acHidden`	1	Opens, but hides, the report.
`acIcon`	2	Opens, but minimizes, the report in the Windows taskbar.
`acDialog`	3	Opens the report as a dialog box when the `Modal` and `PopUp` properties are set to `Yes`.

The `OpenReport` method that you added to the application in Chapter 8

```
DoCmd.OpenReport "BillingReport", acViewPreview
```

opens the `BillingReport` report in Print Preview mode. Although there are several arguments, this particular statement needs only two to get the job done.

The report itself is based on the `BillingReportSource` query, which grabs the values you choose in the form. You can pass the data source in the *filtername* argument, or you can build a `WHERE` clause and use the *wherecondition* argument to limit the resulting report. There are often many ways to accomplish the same task. Normally, you'll find one that accommodates the task a bit better than any other.

Closing a Report

To close a report, use the `DoCmd` object's `Close` method in the form

```
DoCmd.Close [objecttype] [, objectname] [, save]
```

where all the arguments are optional. When all are omitted, VBA closes the object that has the focus. When you're explicitly referencing the report by name, use the *objectname* argument to identify the report and identify the object by type using the `acReport` intrinsic constants. The *save* argument has three constants:

- `acSavePrompt`—The integer value is 0 for this constant. It displays the Save prompt so the users can decide.

- `acSaveYes`—This constant saves changes to the report and equals the integer value of 1.

- `acSaveNo`—This default setting doesn't save changes and equals the integer value of 2.

14

Passing Arguments Using OpenArgs

You learned how to pass values to a procedure using arguments. In a similar way, you can pass values to a report, but outside of the normal procedure structure, using the OpenArgs argument and property.

The OpenArgs argument belongs to the OpenReport method, and handles the actual passing of the value to the report. The property belongs to the report itself and receives and stores the passed value.

→   You can learn how to use the OpenArgs method and property in forms by reviewing "Passing Arguments Using OpenArgs" page 151.

Let's suppose you don't always need to see all the detail records in the billing report; you want just a summary instead. Using the OpenArgs method, you can pass a value to the report that hides the detail records when you want. To add this functionality to TimeTrack, do the following:

1. Open the BillingReportSetup form in Design view and add a check box just below the Open Report command button. (Note that this example is working with the original report opening button and not the Advanced Report button that you added in Chapter 13.) Name the new control chkSummary. Set the caption of the check box to Summary.

2. Set the new control's Default Value property to –1 so it's selected by default.

3. Modify the cmdOpenReport_Click() event procedure by adding the OpenArgs argument to the OpenReport method, as follows:

```
DoCmd.OpenReport "BillingReport", acViewPreview, , , , chkSummary
```

   The OpenArgs argument passes chkSummary's value (checked or unchecked) to the report's OpenArgs property.

4. Save and close the form.

5. Add the following line to the BillingReport report's Open event, immediately following the DoCmd.Maximize statement:

```
Reports("BillingReport").Section(acDetail).Visible = Me.OpenArgs
```

6. Save and close the report.

7. Return to the modified form. Select Bill's Auto Glass and enter 10/1/04 and 10/31/04.

8. Next, uncheck the new check box control as shown in Figure 14.1. Then, click the Open Report button. Figure 14.2 displays the summarized values without the detail records. Close the report and the form when you're done.

Figure 14.1
Add a check box to the setup form.

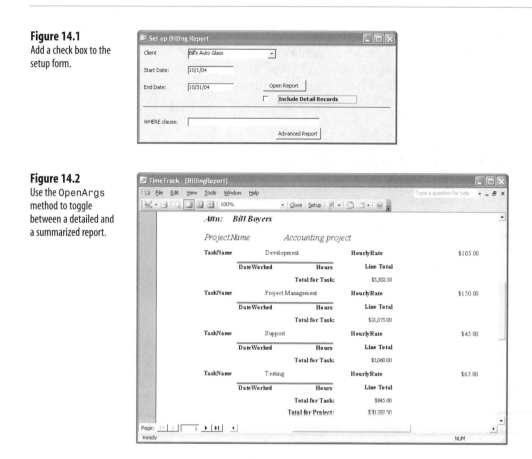

Figure 14.2
Use the OpenArgs method to toggle between a detailed and a summarized report.

Opening the report with the check box checked passes the value –1 or True, which is the section's default setting. That's why you made checked the default. Unchecked, the OpenArgs argument passes 0, or False. When this is the case, the Visible property is set to False and the Detail section is hidden in the previewed report.

Populating the Report

The existing billing report shows one way of limiting the records that populate the report. The report's query grabs values from the setup form. It's a simple technique and requires no VBA code other than the short procedure needed to launch the report from the form.

14

VBA has an alternative to this technique. As mentioned earlier, you can use a couple of the OpenReport method's arguments to specify a particular query or even a WHERE clause. If you choose this route, you need to remove the form references from the report's underlying query and then replace the report opening command button's Click event with the following procedure:

```
Private Sub cmdOpenReport_Click()
 Dim strCriteria As String
 Dim frm As Form
 Set frm = Forms!BillingReportSetup
 On Error GoTo HandleErr
 strCriteria = "Clients.ClientID = " & frm!cboClient.Value & _
 " AND Timeslips.DateWorked Between #" & frm!txtStartDate & _
 "# AND #" & frm!txtEndDate & "#"
 Debug.Print strCriteria
 DoCmd.OpenReport "BillingReport", acViewPreview, , strCriteria

ExitHere:
 Exit Sub
HandleErr:
 MsgBox "Error " & Err.Number & ": " & _
  Err.Description
 Resume ExitHere
End Sub
```

As you can see, this method appears a bit more complex because you must build the WHERE string. There's no right or wrong to the solution you choose. With time, you'll find that each method has its pros and cons and choose according to the requirements.

Applying a Filter and Sort Order

At this point, you've already seen a lot of expressions and literal strings used to limit the records that make it to TimeTrack's billing report. But there's one filtering property you haven't seen yet. Both forms and reports have properties that enable you to apply filters to the underlying recordset:

- Filter—A string expression that identifies the actual filter as a WHERE clause without the WHERE keyword.
- FilterOn—Enables the filter specified in the Filter property.
- OrderBy—Determines how the records are sorted, but the report's native sort order(s) take precedence over this property.
- OrderByOn—Enables the sort specified in the OrderBy property.

Setting the Filter and FilterOn properties through VBA is just one way to automate this process and allow enough flexibility so that you can use the same report to display different recordsets.

To set a filter string, use the following syntax:

```
Me.Filter = filterstring
```

where *filterstring* represents the actual filtering criteria by which you want to filter the report. For instance, if you wanted to filter the billing report by a particular client, you might use the following statement

```
Me.Filter = "ClientID = 1"
```

You would need to follow that statement with the `FilterOn` property in the form

```
Me.FilterOn = True
```

Setting the `FilterOn` property to `False` would disable the current filter.

The sorting properties are similar to the filtering properties in that you specify a SQL `ORDER BY` clause, without using the `ORDER BY` keywords, and then you enable the sort using the following syntax

```
Me.OrderBy = "ClientID, ProjectID DESC"
Me.OrderByOn = True
```

Handling Report-Level Errors

Like forms, you can handle report-specific errors using a special event—the report's `Error` event—when an error occurs at the Jet database engine level. The event has two arguments for passing error values to the event:

- `DataErr`—Stores error code returned by the `Err` object.
- `Response`—Determines whether an error message is displayed using one of the following intrinsic constants: `acDataErrContinue` ignores the error and `acDataErrDisplay` displays the default error message.

The benefit of the `Error` event is that you can glean an error's actual number and then add that error to your list of errors that you need to handle—if a generic handler isn't appropriate. Let's look at a quick example using `BillingReport`:

1. Open `BillingReport` in Design view and change the Record Source property from `BillingReportSource` to `test`.
2. Save the report and close it.
3. Open the `BillingReportSetup` form, choose a client, and then click the Open Report button. Viewing the report in Print Preview generates the error shown in Figure 14.3.

14

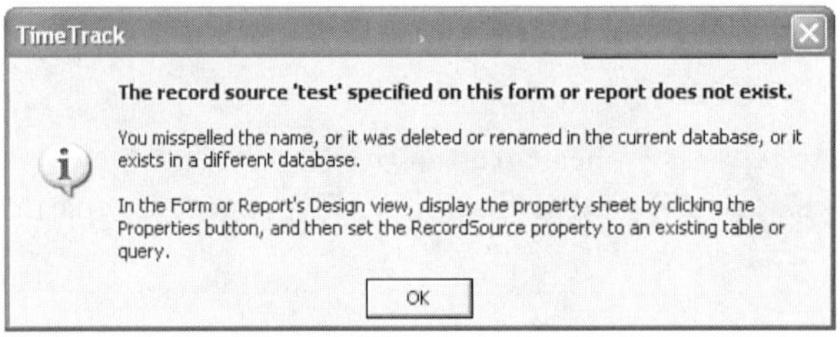

Figure 14.3
Removing a report's data
source produces a Jet
error.

TimeTrack

The record source 'test' specified on this form or report does not exist.

You misspelled the name, or it was deleted or renamed in the current database, or it
exists in a different database.

In the Form or Report's Design view, display the property sheet by clicking the
Properties button, and then set the RecordSource property to an existing table or
query.

OK

4. Click OK to clear the message.

5. Open the report's module and enter the following code in the report's Error event:

```
Private Sub Report_Error(DataErr As Integer, Response As Integer)
 Debug.Print DataErr
End Sub
```

6. View the report in Print Preview to generate the error again.

7. View the Immediate window in the VBE. It contains the Jet error code, as shown in
Figure 14.4.

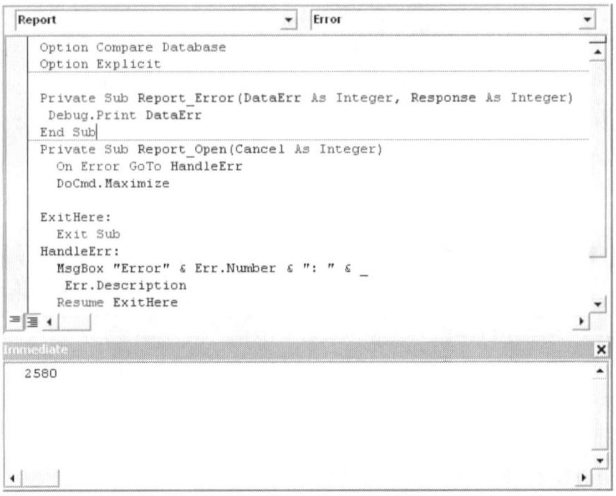

Figure 14.4
You can print the Jet
error code to the
Immediate window.

```
Report                          Error

 Option Compare Database
 Option Explicit

 Private Sub Report_Error(DataErr As Integer, Response As Integer)
  Debug.Print DataErr
 End Sub
 Private Sub Report_Open(Cancel As Integer)
   On Error GoTo HandleErr
   DoCmd.Maximize

 ExitHere:
   Exit Sub
 HandleErr:
   MsgBox "Error" & Err.Number & ": " & _
    Err.Description
   Resume ExitHere
```

Immediate

```
2580
```

8. Now that you know the error code, replace the Debug.Print statement in the error handler with the following code:

```
Private Sub Report_Error(DataErr As Integer, Response As Integer)
 If DataErr = 2580 Then
  MsgBox "The report's data source has been changed or is " & _
   "missing", vbOKOnly, "Error"
  Response = acDataErrContinue
 End If
End Sub
```

14

9. View the report in Print Preview one more time. The same error occurs, but this time, instead of displaying the default message, the Error event displays your custom message shown in Figure 14.5. Click OK to clear the message.

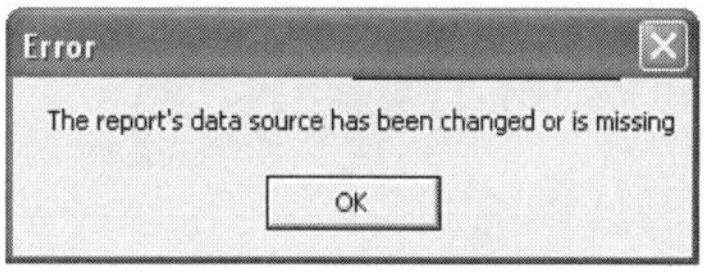

Figure 14.5
Use the Error event to handle Jet errors your way.

10. Return the report to Design view and reset the Record Source property to BillingReportSource.

In this particular case, the custom message you added to the Error event isn't superior to the internal message, but that isn't really the point of the exercise. Now you know how to determine an error's code so you can include it in your own error-handling routine.

What to Do When There's No Data

Reports have a unique problem—what to return when there are no records in the report's underlying record source. That really isn't an error, and Access will still display the report, but most of the time, users won't appreciate or understand what they see. For instance, Figure 14.6 shows the BillingReport report opened from the Database window instead of going through the setup form.

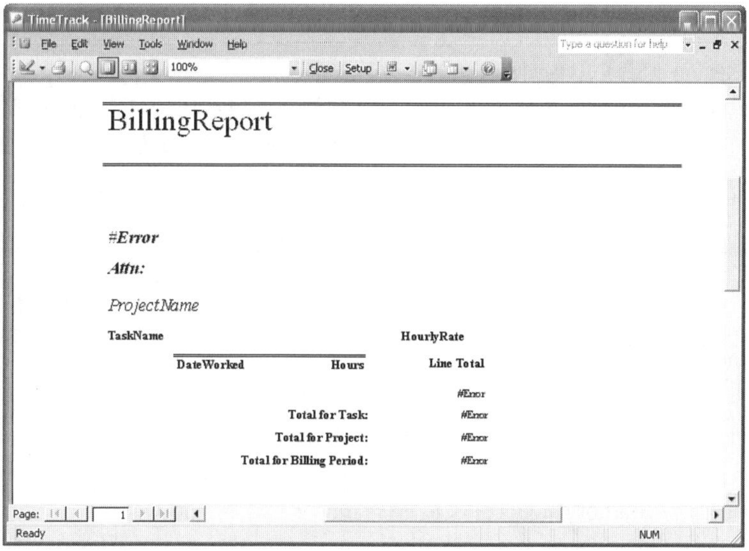

Figure 14.6
Reports with no records to display return error values.

As you can see, the report is full of error values. To avoid this problem, use the report's
`NoData` event to cancel the report or display a custom message. This section uses the billing
report to illustrate a simple solution for this problem. First, open `BillingReport`'s module
and enter the following code:

```
Private Sub Report_NoData(Cancel As Integer)
 MsgBox "There are no records to print", _
  vbOKOnly, "No report"
 Cancel = True
End Sub
```

Preview the report and click OK in response to the parameter prompts. These occur
because Access is trying to resolve references to the form values that are missing. After dis-
missing three parameter prompts, Access displays the message box shown in Figure 14.7.
Click OK to clear the message box.

Figure 14.7
Tell your users when
there's no data to report.

No report

There are no records to print

    OK

Using VBA to Determine Group Properties

You might not realize that a group's header and footer have corresponding events, like other
report sections, and that you can use these events to modify reports on the fly—even adding
new sections as needed.

Referring to Report Components in Code

Whether working with sections or groups, you need to know how to reference the appropriate area or level. To reference
a report section, use the report's name or number. For instance, you can refer to a report's Detail section using the following syntax:

```
Reports(reportname).Detail
```

where `reportname` is a string that identifies the report by name. `Detail` is the actual name of the section. Or, you
can use the following form:

```
Reports(reportname).Section(0)
```

or even

```
Reports(reportname).Section(acDetail)
```

When referencing group levels, use the same form as sections:

```
Reports(reportname).GroupLevel(index).property
```

A group level is actually an object, so you can use an object variable as follows:

```
Dim glGroup As GroupLevel
Set glGroup = Reports("BillingReport").GroupLevel(0)
```

┌─ **CAUTION** ──

When referencing report sections and group levels, you must always explicitly identify the property being read or set. Neither report sections nor group levels offer a default property.
└──

The `GroupLevel` object has a number of properties that you should already be familiar with if you've spent anytime building reports in Access:

- `GroupFooter`
- `GroupHeader`
- `GroupInterval`
- `GroupOn`
- `KeepTogether`
- `SortOrder`
- `ControlSource`

Table 14.4 lists the individual property settings for each of these properties.

Table 14.4   Grouping Property Settings

Property	Possible Settings
`GroupFooter` and `GroupHeader`	True or False
`GroupOn`	Each Value = 0 Prefix Characters = 1 Year = 2 Qtr = 3 Month = 4 Week = 5 Day = 6 Hour = 7 Minute = 8 Interval = 9
`KeepTogether`	No = 0 Whole Group = 1 With First Detail = 2
`SortOrder`	Ascending = False Descending = True

┌─ **CAUTION** ──

You can create new groups only in Design view, but you can set most group properties from the report's Open event.
└──

14

Adding a Daily Report

TimeTrack only has one report and it deals with billing. Suppose, for example, that your developers need to see a revised schedule occasionally. A report is probably the best way to present this information, so you need to give users an easy way to print a schedule grouped by the day, the current week, and even the current month. Doing so requires a form that allows the users to choose one of the three possible schedules—the Switchboard form is the best place for these options—and a new report.

1. Open the Switchboard form in Design view and insert three command buttons. Name them cmdDaily, cmdWeekly, and cmdMonthly and enter the appropriate Caption properties.

2. In the form's module, enter the following event procedures:

```
Private Sub cmdDaily_Click()
 Call GenerateSchedule(6)
End Sub

Private Sub cmdMonthly_Click()
 Call GenerateSchedule(4)
End Sub

Private Sub cmdWeekly_Click()
 Call GenerateSchedule(5)
End Sub

Sub GenerateSchedule(rpt As String)
 DoCmd.OpenReport "Schedule", acViewPreview, , , , rpt
End Sub
```

Each call to GenerateSchedule passes a value, which represents a GroupOn property setting (see Table 14.4). The OpenReport method passes that value to the report using the OpenArgs method. The report doesn't exist yet, but that's okay.

3. Save and close the Switchboard form shown in Figure 14.8.

Figure 14.8
Add three command buttons to the switchboard.

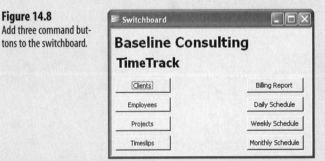

4. Create the new query named Schedule shown in Figure 14.9.

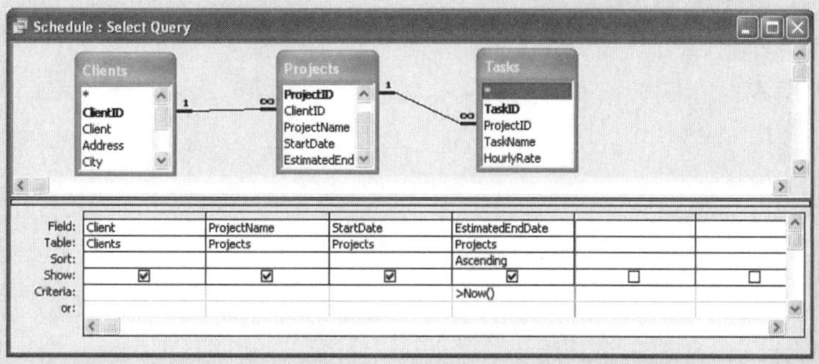

Figure 14.9
Base the scheduling report on this query.

5. Save and close the query.

6. Use the AutoReports: Tabular wizard to create a tabular report based on the `Schedule` query, and name it `Schedule`.

7. Open the new report in Design view and click the Sorting and Grouping tool. Using Figure 14.10 as a guide, set the appropriate group properties. Grouping the schedule by each day (shown as Each Value in the user interface) will be the report's default group. The first and third rows' properties are all defaults. Set the second row's Group Header property to Yes so you can visually tell where one group ends and the next begins.

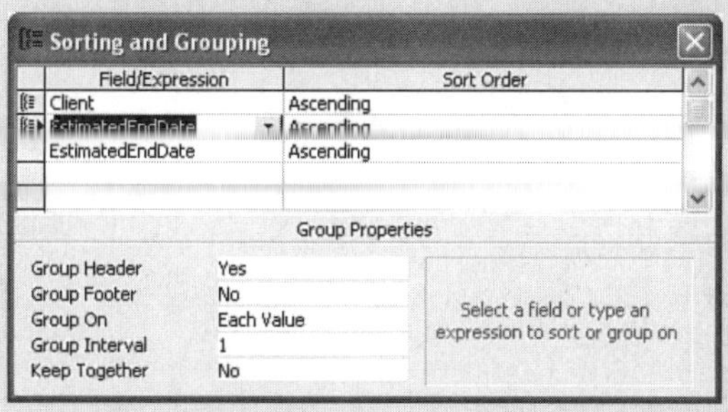

Figure 14.10
Setting the initial grouping properties.

8. In the report's module, enter the following code:

```
Private Sub Report_Open(Cancel As Integer)
 If IsNull(Me.OpenArgs) Then
  Exit Sub
 End If
 Me.GroupLevel(1).GroupOn = CInt(Me.OpenArgs)
End Sub
```

9. Save and close the report.

Open the switchboard and click the new Daily Schedule button to view the schedule grouped by the `EstimatedEndDate` field, as shown in Figure 14.11. (The figure shows only a portion of the report.) The report is grouped by each value (that is, each day gets its own group), which is the same as the default you set earlier. It isn't even necessary to pass the daily value as the sample does, but it doesn't hurt to include it in case you modify the first group level, which is currently based on the Client field (0).

14

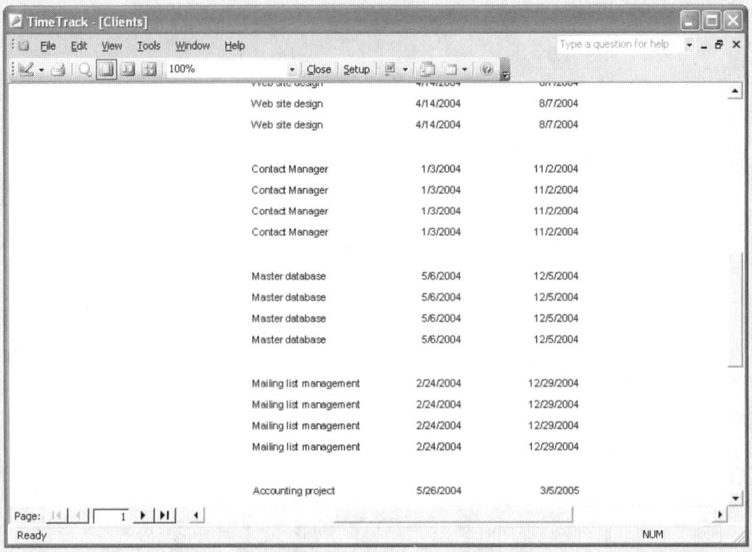

Figure 14.11
This report groups on the `EstimatedEndDate` field by the day.

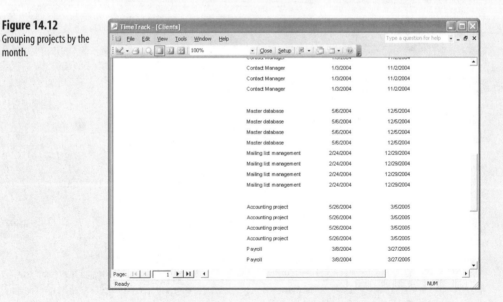

Close the report and click the Monthly Schedule button to see the report shown in Figure 14.12. This report displays the same records as the first, but groups the `EstimatedEndDate` values by the month. As you can see, the records in December are grouped differently for each report. Because of the current dates, the weekly schedule looks the same as the daily schedule, but that won't always be the case.

Figure 14.12
Grouping projects by the month.

Working with the Application Collections

Investigating the Application Collections

You know, of course, that Access has all sorts of objects in each database: tables, forms, macros, and so on. And you've already worked with some of those objects in VBA. For example, you know how to open a form or preview a report from VBA by now. But there are other ways to work with Access objects by using the built-in application collections. Figure 15.1 shows the portion of the Access object model that includes these collections.

The Access `Application` object supplies two main ways to navigate through the object model to individual objects. The `CurrentProject` object leads to collections for each of the user interface objects: `AllDataAccessPages`, `AllForms`, and so on. The `CurrentData` object leads to collections for each of the data-related objects. `AllQueries`, `AllTables`, and so on. Each of these collections in turn contains `AccessObject` objects that represent the individual items in the collection.

IN THIS CHAPTER

Investigating the Application Collections . .233

Retrieving Lists of Objects 225

Working with Object Properties 226

Programmatically Determining
Dependencies 229

Figure 15.1
The application collections and related objects.

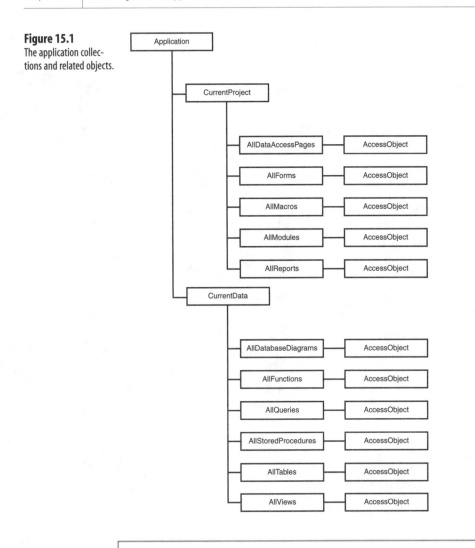

NOTE

Technically, the CurrentProject object gives you the objects maintained by the Access program itself, whereas the CurrentData object leads to the underlying database engine. In regular Access databases, the database engine is Microsoft Jet; in Access projects, it's Microsoft SQL Server. Most of the CurrentData collections (AllDatabaseDiagrams, AllFunctions, AllStoredProcedures, and AllViews) are applicable to Access projects using the SQL Server database engine. We don't discuss those objects in this book.

CAUTION

Don't confuse the AllForms and AllReports collections with the Forms and Reports collections. The former pair contains all their respective objects in the entire database, whereas the latter two contain only open forms and reports.

This chapter shows you what you can do with these objects. They provide ways for your code to work with the information that you see in the Database window when you're interacting directly with Access, and they can be very handy when you're writing tools in VBA. Each of the object collections supports four properties:

- `Application`—This property returns the parent `Application` object.
- `Count`—The number of `AccessObject` objects in the collection.
- `Item`—Indexed property to return individual `AccessObject` objects.
- `Parent`—Pointer to the parent object (such as `CurrentData` or `CurrentProject`).

> **NOTE**
> In some cases, the `Parent` property can return a `CodeProject` or `CodeData` object. These objects are similar to the `CurrentProject` and `CurrentData` objects, but refer to databases loaded in code. You don't run into these objects when just working with normal databases through the user interface; they're important for add-in developers.

Retrieving Lists of Objects

One thing that you can use these collections for is to retrieve lists of objects in the database. You might think that there's little need to do this, because the objects are right there in the Database window. But you'll find that working with your own lists of objects enables you to write friendlier user interfaces for people who find the Database window a bit daunting.

For example, you can use the `AllForms` collection to construct a general-purpose forms launcher for the sample database. Here's how:

1. Create a new form in Design view. Set the form's caption to `Form list`. Place a listbox control named `lstForms` and a command button control named `cmdOpen` on the form. Set the Row Source Type property of the listbox to Value List.

2. Open the form's module and add this code:

```
Option Compare Database
Option Explicit

Private Sub cmdOpen_Click()
  ' Open the selected form
  If Not IsNull(lstForms.Value) Then
    DoCmd.OpenForm lstForms.Value
  End If
End Sub

Private Sub Form_Load()
  ' Stock the listbox with the names of
  ' all forms in the database
  Dim AO As AccessObject
```

```
For Each AO In CurrentProject.AllForms
  lstForms.AddItem (AO.Name)
Next AO

End Sub
```

3. Save the form as `FormList`. Open the `FormList` form and it will list all the forms in the database. Select a form in the listbox and click the button to open the form, as shown in Figure 15.2.

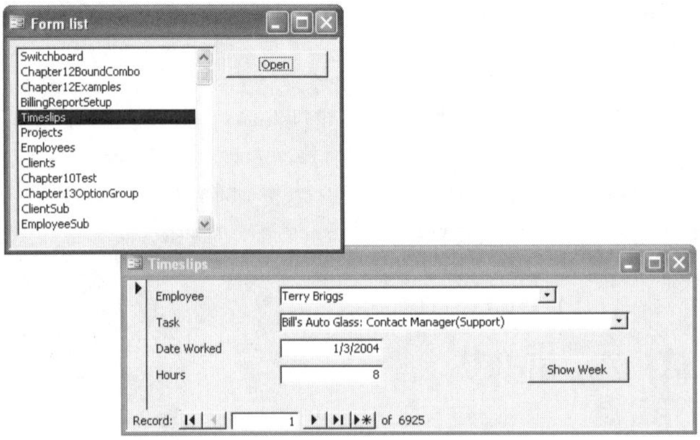

Figure 15.2
A form listing all the forms in the database.

Working with Object Properties

As you've seen, each of the objects in any of the object collections is represented by an `AccessObject` object. This object has a set of built-in properties that tell you a few things about the object:

- `CurrentView`—A constant that tells you the current view of an object (for example, Design view or Datasheet view) if the object is open.
- `DateCreated`—The date that the object was created.
- `DateModified`—The date that the object was last changed.
- `FullName`—The full name (including the path) of the object.
- `IsLoaded`—`True` if the object is currently open, `False` if the object is currently closed.
- `Name`—The name of the object.
- `Parent`—The collection that contains this object.
- `Properties`—A collection of the properties of the object.
- `Type`—A constant representing the type of the object, such as form, report, or table.

> **NOTE**
> The `FullName` property applies only to data access pages, which are stored as external files. It's empty for all other objects.

The `AccessObject` object offers an additional, advanced capability: you can create your own properties for these objects. This is useful in much the same way as the `Tag` property is on a form; you can use your own properties to store custom information that is used in your code.

→ For more information on the `Tag` property, see "Working with the Tag Property," p. 202.

Take another look at the `FormList` form. One problem with it as you initially built it is that it lists all the forms, even ones that you probably don't want to open all by themselves. For example, showing the various sample forms, switchboards, and subforms in the list is more confusing than anything else. To deal with this problem, you can use a custom property to tell the `FormList` form whether to display a particular form.

To start, you need a way to add your own custom property to the forms that you want to display. Typically, this is the sort of thing that you want to do when you're designing a database; there's no need to let the users adjust this property. So you can add a procedure to the sample database to handle the task, like so:

```
Public Sub ShowInFormList(strFormName As String)
   ' Mark the specified form so that it
   ' will be displayed on the FormList
   ' form

   ' Get the AccessObject corresponding to
   ' the specified form
   Dim AO As AccessObject
   Set AO = CurrentProject.AllForms(strFormName)

   ' Create a new property on the object
   AO.Properties.Add "ShowInFormList", True

   Debug.Print "Property set"
End Sub
```

Each `AccessObject` object has its own collection of custom properties named (not surprisingly) `Properties`. This code starts by retrieving the `AccessObject` object that corresponds to the specified form. It then uses the `Add` method of the `Properties` collection to add a new custom property to the `AccessObject`. The two arguments to this method are the name of the property (which must be a string) and the initial value of the property (which can be any variant). So the code as shown adds a new property named `ShowInFormList` and sets its initial value to `True`. Figure 15.3 shows how you might call this procedure from the Immediate window to add the `ShowInFormList` property to the `Clients` form.

> **TIP**
>
> The `Properties` collection of an `AccessObject` object contains only the custom properties that you've added to the object. It doesn't contain any of the standard properties such as `Name` or `DateCreated`.

Figure 15.3
Adding a custom property to a form.

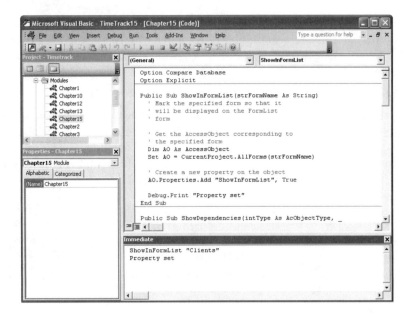

In the sample database, we used the `ShowInFormList` procedure to add the custom property to the `Clients`, `Employees`, `Projects`, and `Timeslips` forms.

The next step is to modify the code behind `FormList` to display only the forms with the custom property present and set to `True`. Here's the revised code:

```
Private Sub Form_Load()
    ' Stock the listbox with the names of
    ' all marked forms in the database
    Dim AO As AccessObject

    ' Keep going if the custom property is missing
    On Error Resume Next

    For Each AO In CurrentProject.AllForms
        If AO.Properties("ShowInFormList").Value = True Then
            If Err = 0 Then
                ' Only add the form if the property is
                ' actually present and set to True
                lbForms.AddItem (AO.Name)
            End If
            Err.Clear
        End If
    Next AO

End Sub
```

You need to exercise some care when working with custom properties. If you try to retrieve a value for a property that doesn't exist, VBA will raise an error. This code shows one way to deal with the situation. First, it sets the error handler to `On Error Resume Next` to make sure that any errors are not fatal. Next, for each form, it tries to retrieve the value of the custom property. There are three possibilities for what happens here:

- If the property doesn't exist, the code proceeds to the next line, but the built-in `Err` variable (which holds the number of the most recent error) is set to some number other than zero. In this case, the line to add the form name is skipped.

- If the property exists and its value is `False`, the check for `True` fails and the line to add the name to the form is also skipped.

- If the property exists and its value is `True`, the check for an error returns zero and the form's name is added to the listbox.

Figure 15.4 shows the `FormList` form after making these code changes. As you can see, it only displays the forms that have the custom `ShowInFormList` property set to `True`.

Figure 15.4
Using a custom form property.

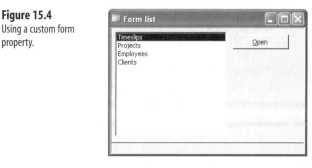

Programmatically Determining Dependencies

Access objects can depend on other objects. For example, a form might use a query as its data source, and the query in turn might draw its information from two or more tables. In this case, the form is directly dependent on the query, and indirectly dependent on the tables. Starting with Access 2003, this information is available through the Access user interface, and also programmatically.

If you haven't looked at this information in the Access user interface, it's easy enough to find. Right-click on any object in the Database window and select Object Dependencies. Doing so opens the Object Dependencies task pane, as shown in Figure 15.5. You can switch between displaying the objects that depend on this object, and the object that this object depends on, by using the radio buttons at the top of the task pane.

Figure 15.5
Viewing object dependencies in the user interface.

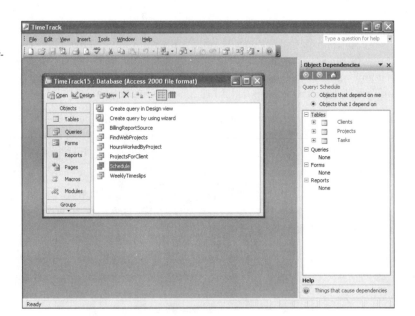

CAUTION

For the object dependencies feature to work, Name AutoCorrect must be on for Access. You can turn on this option using the General tab of the Tools, Options dialog box. You must save and close your objects before Access can generate their dependency information.

To discover object dependencies in VBA, you go through the `AccessObject` object to the `DependencyInfo` object. Here's some code that shows you how this works:

```
Public Sub ShowDependencies(intType As AcObjectType, _
 strName As String)
  ' Show dependency information for the specified object

  Dim AO As AccessObject
  Dim AO2 As AccessObject
  Dim DI As DependencyInfo

  On Error GoTo HandleErr

  ' Get the AccessObject
  Select Case intType
    Case acTable
      Set AO = CurrentData.AllTables(strName)
      Debug.Print "Table: ";
    Case acQuery
      Set AO = CurrentData.AllQueries(strName)
      Debug.Print "Query: ";
```

```vba
    Case acForm
      Set AO = CurrentProject.AllForms(strName)
      Debug.Print "Form: ";
    Case acReport
      Set AO = CurrentProject.AllReports(strName)
      Debug.Print "Report: ";
  End Select
  Debug.Print strName

  ' Get the dependency info
  Set DI = AO.GetDependencyInfo()

  ' Print results
  If DI.Dependencies.Count = 0 Then
    Debug.Print "This object does not depend on any objects"
  Else
    Debug.Print "This object depends on these objects:"
    For Each AO2 In DI.Dependencies
      Select Case AO2.Type
        Case acTable
          Debug.Print "  Table: ";
        Case acQuery
          Debug.Print "  Query: ";
        Case acForm
          Debug.Print "  Form: ";
        Case acReport
          Debug.Print "  Report: ";
      End Select
      Debug.Print AO2.Name
    Next AO2
  End If

  If DI.Dependants.Count = 0 Then
    Debug.Print "No objects depend on this object"
  Else
    Debug.Print "These objects depend on this object:"
    For Each AO2 In DI.Dependants
      Select Case AO2.Type
        Case acTable
          Debug.Print "  Table: ";
        Case acQuery
          Debug.Print "  Query: ";
        Case acForm
          Debug.Print "  Form: ";
        Case acReport
          Debug.Print "  Report: ";
      End Select
      Debug.Print AO2.Name
    Next AO2
  End If

ExitHere:
  Exit Sub

HandleErr:
  MsgBox "Error " & Err.Number & ": " & _
   Err.Description, vbCritical
  Resume ExitHere
End Sub
```

15

That's a big chunk of code, but if you take it one step at a time it will be pretty simple to understand by now. The first order of business is to retrieve the `AccessObject` about which the user requested information. The procedure requires two arguments: the type of object and the name of the object. Because Access already provides an enumeration (`acObjectType`) for the possible object types, you can use that same enumeration here; that's simpler than defining your own. The first `Select Case` statement does two things with this constant. First, it determines which object collection to use to return the correct `AccessObject` object. Second, it prints a message to the Immediate window with the object's name and type.

The next step is to retrieve the `DependencyInfo` object, which you do with the `GetDependencyInfo` method of the `AccessObject`. The `DependencyInfo` object in turn has two collections of its own, each of which also contains `AccessObject` objects. The `Dependencies` collection contains one `AccessObject` object for each object that the current object depends on. The `Dependants` collection contains one `AccessObject` object for each object that depends on the current object.

The remaining code in the procedure simply loops through these two collections and prints their contents to the Immediate window. Here's what the result is for one object in the `TimeTrack` database:

```
ShowDependencies acQuery, "Schedule"
Query: Schedule
This object depends on these objects:
   Table: Clients
   Table: Projects
   Table: Tasks
These objects depend on this object:
   Report: Schedule
```

CASE STUDY

Enhancing the Master Form

To demonstrate how you might use the object collections in a user interface, let's extend the `MasterForm` form assembled in Chapter 13 to include reports. You'll add a listbox to the form to list all the reports in the database, and a button to display the selected report. The tricky thing about this is that some reports can't be displayed without further information. In the `TimeTrack` sample database, the `BillingReport` report requires the `BillingReportSetup` form to be open. You can handle this requirement by attaching a custom property to the report.

Because there's only one report that needs the custom property, it's hardly worth writing a procedure to set it. There's no reason not to do this directly from the Immediate window. This example calls the property `NeedsForm`, and sets it to the name of the required form name. So, to set up `BillingReport` with this property, you execute this code in the Immediate window:

```
CurrentProject.AllReports("BillingReport"). _
  Properties.Add "NeedsForm", "BillingReportSetup"
```

The next step is to add the appropriate controls to the `MasterForm` form: a listbox named `lstReports` and a command button named `cmdOpenReport`. We chose to make the form a bit taller and to add these controls at the bottom of the form. Set the Row Source Type of the listbox control to Value List.

Next comes the code behind the form to populate the listbox and to hook up the command button:

```
Private Sub Form_Load()
    ' Stock the listbox with the names of
    ' all reports in the database
    Dim AO As AccessObject

    For Each AO In CurrentProject.AllReports
        lstReports.AddItem (AO.Name)
    Next AO

End Sub

Private Sub cmdOpenReport_Click()
    ' Open the selected report or the
    ' form required to launch it
    Dim AO As AccessObject
    Dim strForm As String

    On Error Resume Next

    If Not IsNull(lstReports.Value) Then
        ' Retrieve the appropriate AccessObject
        Set AO = CurrentProject.AllReports(lstReports.Value)
        ' Check for the custom property
        strForm = AO.Properties("NeedsForm")
        If Err = 0 Then
            ' Got back a property value, open that form
            DoCmd.OpenForm strForm
        Else
            ' Property doesn't exist, open the report
            DoCmd.OpenReport AO.Name, acViewPreview
        End If
    End If
End Sub
```

When you load the form, it iterates through the `AllReports` collection, adding every report's name to the listbox on the form. You haven't made any provision for selectively hiding reports from this form, but you can use the same technique that you saw earlier on the `FormList` form to do so.

When the user clicks the button to open the report, the code retrieves the `AccessObject` representing the report. It then tries to retrieve a value for the `NeedsForm` property. If it gets a value back, it opens the form with that name. Otherwise, it opens the report in Print Preview view.

Figure 15.6 shows the finished form. If you open the Schedule report, it opens in Print Preview view directly. If you open the Billing report, it opens the appropriate form to prompt you for data instead.

15

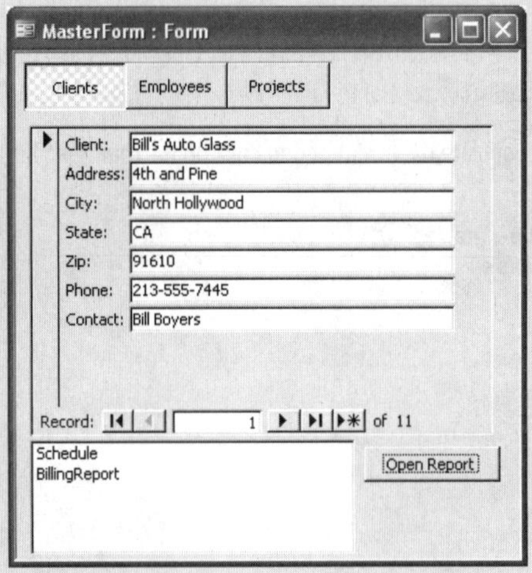

Figure 15.6
The improved
`MasterForm` form.

Working with Access Data

IN THIS PART

16   Retrieving Data with ADO 237

17   Manipulating Data with ADO 253

18   Creating Objects with ADOX 273

19   Performing Advanced Data Operations 287

Retrieving Data with ADO

16

What's ADO and Why Do You Need It?

The data you enter into an Access database isn't actually stored in the database objects. Forms, tables, reports, and even queries are just interface objects by which you input, view, and retrieve data. Fortunately, Access handles the data exchange behind the scenes—you don't need to know what's going on or even that it *is* going on. You benefit from the process, regardless.

Things get a bit more complicated when you start using code to interact with your data. That's where the ActiveX Data Objects (ADO) library comes into the picture. In a nutshell, ADO is an object model that provides a few specialized objects for retrieving data. ADO is your ticket to accessing all types of data, not just Access data.

You don't have to do anything special to get ADO—it's already there. Starting with Windows 2000, ADO comes with and is installed with the operating system. In addition, ADO has been the Access data access library default since Access 2000, so you don't even have to reference the library to use the objects.

The ADO Object Model

Like other object models, the ADO object model is a hierarchy of objects. Figure 16.1 is an illustration of the ADO object model. The model consists of collections of specific object types. King of the ADO hill is the Connection object, which represents a single connection to an OLE DB data source. This chapter reviews the ADO Connection, Command, and Recordset objects.

IN THIS CHAPTER

What's ADO and Why Do You Need It? 237

Using the ADO Connection Object 238

Working with Command Objects 242

Understanding the Different Types of Recordsets 244

Creating and Opening a Recordset 245

Filtering Recordsets 247

Using the Recordset Property 248

> **NOTE**
>
> ADO and OLE DB work together. OLE DB interfaces with the data and translates the data processing components from one format to another using two types of components: providers and consumers.
>
> Providers are programs that talk to one another (expose data). Consumers then use the exposed data.
>
> ADO is a consumer. In other words, OLE DB connections let you actually connect to the data and ADO objects let you retrieve the data after you're connected.

Figure 16.1
The ADO object model consists of objects.

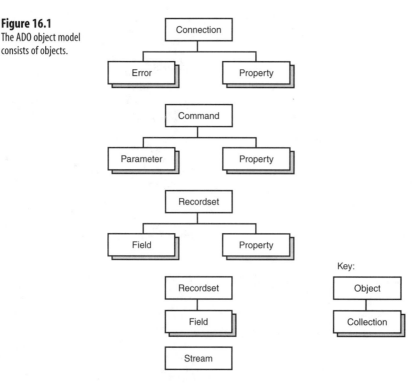

Using the ADO Connection Object

You need a connection to a data source and an object in which to store the data you retrieve from the data source. Technically, an ADO Connection object is a single connection to an OLE DB data source. What that means is that you can use the Connection object to connect to a data source.

You can connect implicitly or explicitly and neither method is more correct than the other. However, if you're going to use the same connection more than once, use an *explicit* Connection object. An *implicit* connection is created whenever you retrieve data without first declaring a Connection object. You might find it less confusing to use explicit Connection objects until you feel comfortable with the ADO object model.

Opening the Connection

An explicit connection actually declares and instantiates a `Connection` object as follows:

```
Dim cnn as ADODB.Connection
Set cnn = New ADODB.Connection
```

We can't really show you an implicit connection because there's no declaration.

The `Connection` object comes with a number of properties that control the object's behavior:

- `ConnectionString`—Specifies the data source.

- `ConnectionTimeout`—Determines how many seconds to wait for a data source to respond. The default is 15, which might not be long enough if you're on a busy network or pulling data across the Internet.

- `Mode`—Sets the permission mode. See Table 16.1 for the intrinsic constants for this property.

- `CursorLocation`—Determines the location of the OLE DB provided cursor. There are two constants: `adUseServer` sets a server-side cursor and `adUseClient` sets a client-side cursor. You can think of a cursor as a set of rows from a table plus an indicator of the current row.

- `DefaultDatabase`—Specifies a specific database on a server to use for all data processes with this particular `Connection` object.

- `IsolationLevel`—Controls how database operations on different connections affect one another. See Table 16.2 for a list of intrinsic constants. You don't need to worry about this unless you're writing code that works with multiple users logged into the database at the same time.

- `Provider`—Specifies an OLE DB provider before opening the connection.

- `CommandTimeout`—Specifies how long to wait before terminating an attempt to connect while executing a command.

Table 16.1 Mode **Property Constants**

Constant	Explanation
adModeRead	Read-only connection
adModeReadWrite	Read-write connection
adModeWrite	Write-only connection
adModeShareDenyRead	Other applications can't open a read connection
adModeShareDenyWrite	Other applications can't open a write connection
adModeShareDenyNone	All applications can open a connection with any permission
adModeShareExclusive	Other applications can't open a connection
adModeRecursive	Subrecords inherit permissions of current record

16

Table 16.2 `IsolationLevel` **Property Constants**

Constant	Explanation
`adXactUnspecified`	Returned when provider can't determine the isolation level
`adXactChaos` `adXactBrowse`	Default setting that protects pending changes from being overwritten
`adXactReadUncommitted` `adXactCursorStability`	Enables you to view but not change uncommitted changes from other transactions
`adXactReadCommitted`	Enables you to view changes from other transactions only after they're committed
`adXactRepeatableRead` `adXacIsolated`	Enables requerying a Recordset to include changes pending from other transactions
`adXactSerializable`	Isolates all transactions from all other transactions

Just remember to set the properties before actually opening the connection. For instance, to set a server side cursor, you use the following code:

```
Dim cnn as ADODB.Connection
Set cnn = New ADODB.Connection
cnn.CursorLocation = adUseServer
```

To open the connection, use the `Connection` object's `Open` method in the form

```
Connection.Open [connectionstring][, userID][, password][, options]
```

All the arguments are optional. The *options* argument is one of two intrinsic constants: `adConnectUnspecified` opens a synchronous connection (one on which only a single operation can proceed at one time) and is the default; `adAsyncConnect` opens an asynchronous connection. Using the default synchronous connection is typically fine for any operation that doesn't involve an extremely large amount of data.

About Connection Strings

There are two opportunities to specify the connection string:

- Use the `Open` method's *connectionstring* argument after creating the `Connection` object.

- Use the `Connection` object's *connectionstring* argument after creating the `Connection` object, but before opening the actual connection.

Either way, certain information can be passed in the form of five arguments that are concatenated together in the connection string:

- `Provider`—Specifies the name of the OLE DB provider; check provider documentation for the exact string. See Table 16.3 for a list of common provider strings.

- `Data Source`—Identifies the file to which you're connecting.

- `Remote Provider`—Specifies the server provider when opening a client-side connection.

- `Remote Server`—Identifies the server.

- `URL`—Identifies the connection string as a URL.

Table 16.3   Common Provider Strings

Application	String
Microsoft Jet 3.51	Microsoft.Jet.OLEDB.3.5.1
Microsoft Jet 4.0	Microsoft.Jet.OLEDB.4.0
ODBC Drivers	MSDASQL
Oracle	MSDAORA
SQL Server	SQLOLEDB

> **TIP**
>
> If you need help constructing a connection string, a visit to `http://www.connection-strings.com/` can likely solve all your problems.

The following connection string connects to the Northwind sample database that comes with Access on your local system from any database, assuming that it's installed in the default location:

```
Private Sub MakeConnection()
  Dim cnn As ADODB.Connection
  Dim strConn As String
  Set cnn = New ADODB.Connection
  strConn = "Provider=Microsoft.Jet.OLEDB.4.0;" & _
    "Data Source=C:\Program Files\Microsoft Office\" & _
    "Office\Samples\Northwind.mdb;"
  cnn.Open strConn
  MsgBox "Connection Made"
  cnn.Close
  Set cnn = Nothing
End Sub
```

Just open a standard module and enter the procedure. Then, press F5. If the connection is made, Access displays the message shown in Figure 16.2. Click OK to clear the message box. This example establishes the data source as it opens the actual connection. (You can use any database as the `Data Source` argument, just be sure to type the complete and correct path.)

Figure 16.2
This message lets you
know the connection
was made.

Closing a Connection

The previous example doesn't do anything but connect to a data source. No data is retrieved. But you might have noticed the Close method at the end of the procedure. It's best to always disconnect the Connection object when you're done by executing the Close method. You don't have to destroy the object, because you might want to use it again.

The Close method takes the form

```
connection.Close
```

where *connection* represents a Connection object.

To reuse a closed Connection object, just execute the Open method. When you're actually done with the Connection object, set it to Nothing after closing the object as follows:

```
Set connection = Nothing
```

> **TIP**
>
> More often than not, you can use a simple connection shortcut. If the data you need is in the current database, use the CurrentProject object to define the connection as follows:
>
> ```
> Dim cnn As ADODB.Connection
> Dim cnn As New ADODB.Connection
> Set cnn = CurrentProject.Connection
> ```
>
> Using this method, you'll share exactly the connection to the data that Access itself is using.

Working with Command Objects

You can use the Connection or the Command object to retrieve and manipulate data. However, the Command object has a few advantages:

- Using a Command object, you can avoid a Recordset object and update data directly, which can be faster with some databases because the changes are made on the server instead of dragging the records across the network.
- The Command object supports parameters; the Connection object doesn't.
- The Command object has more properties than the Connection object, which enables you to fine-tune its behavior.

By way of a definition, you can compare the Command object to a stored procedure or other data access object that returns data because the Command object executes the process that actually returns the data. The object does so by executing code against the OLE DB data source or by retrieving data from the OLE DB data source. This makes the Command object a flexible tool to have around.

Creating a Command Object

Creating a Command object is similar to creating a Connection object: declare it and then define it. But you don't open it, which makes sense given the difference between the two objects. Use the following structure to declare and define a Command object:

```
Dim strConn As String
Dim cmd As ADODB.Command
strConn = connectionstring
Set cmd = New ADODB.Command
cmd.ActiveConnection = strConn
```

The Command's *connectionstring* argument is identical to that used by the Connection object.

Executing the Command Object

The Command object executes code against the data source that manipulates that data in some way—either changing it at the source or retrieving it. Usually, you'll use a Recordset object to retrieve data, you'll read about that object a bit later.

To execute code that updates or retrieves data, use the Command object's CommandText property, which contains the actual instructions executed against the data (technically, the provider). This property is a string expression or value that contains a provider command, which can be a SQL statement, the name of a table, a URL, or a call to a stored procedure.

The following procedure automates a simple update query that increases each of the hourly rate values (in the Timetrack.mdb Tasks table) by three percent using a SQL UPDATE command directly against the data:

```
Private Sub EditCA()
  'Update hourly rate values by 3 percent.
  Dim strConn As String
  Dim cmd As ADODB.Command
  Set cmd = New ADODB.Command
  With cmd
   .ActiveConnection = CurrentProject.Connection
   .CommandText = "UPDATE Tasks " & _
    "SET HourlyRate = HourlyRate + (HourlyRate * .03)"
   .Execute
  End With
  Set cmd = Nothing
End Sub
```

Enter the procedure into a standard procedure (or use Chapter 16's example module). With the cursor inside the procedure, press F5. Nothing seems to happen, but open the Tasks table and you can see that each value has been updated, as shown in Figure 16.3. The first value, $154.50, was $150.00. All the values have been increased.

Figure 16.3

A Command object updated the hourly rate values.

TaskID	ProjectID	TaskName	HourlyRate
17	1	Project Management	$154.50
18	1	Development	$108.15
19	1	Testing	$66.95
20	1	Support	$46.35
21	2	Project Management	$154.50
22	2	Development	$108.15
23	2	Testing	$66.95
24	2	Support	$46.35
25	4	Project Management	$154.50
26	4	Development	$108.15
27	4	Testing	$66.95
28	4	Support	$46.35
29	5	Project Management	$154.50
30	5	Development	$108.15
31	5	Testing	$66.95
32	5	Support	$46.35
33	6	Project Management	$154.50
34	6	Development	$108.15
35	6	Testing	$66.95

Tasks : Table

Record: 1 of 120

Understanding the Different Types of Recordsets

Modifying data at the source is quick and efficient if you don't need to continually review the data. Sometimes you need to actually retrieve the data. For instance, you might want to evaluate specific values before making a change.

Typically, you retrieve data using the Recordset object. You can think of a Recordset object as a simple data container, which you can execute via the Connection or Command object. If you could see it, a Recordset would look very much like an Access table opened in Datasheet view.

On the technical side of things, a Recordset object represents a cursor. A *cursor* is often described as the pointer to the current record, but it's really more. It's all the retrieved data, with a pointer to the current record. There are four types of cursors (Recordset objects):

- A *dynamic cursor* enables you to see changes made by other users. In addition, the cursor (or pointer) can move in all directions. Jet doesn't actually support this type of cursor and defaults to a keyset cursor if you specify a dynamic cursor.

- A *keyset cursor* is dynamic, but you can't see records added or deleted by other users, although you can see changes made to existing data. You can move the cursor in all directions. If only one user opens the database at a time, a keyset cursor and a dynamic cursor are equivalent.

- A *static cursor* creates a copy of the data. You can't change the data or see changes made by other users. You can move the cursor in all directions.

- A *forward-only* cursor is a static cursor that restricts movement. You can only move forward through the records. This is the default ADO cursor.

How you need to use the data determines the type of cursor you choose. The dynamic cursor is the most flexible but requires the most resources (and isn't available in Access). Dynamic cursors can be slow to perform. On the other hand, the forward-only cursor usually responds quickly and requires fewer resources, but it's the most restrictive of the four—you can't change data and you can't move backward through the records.

> **CAUTION**
>
> Microsoft Jet doesn't support dynamic cursors, even though, through ADO, you can request one from Jet. When you do, Jet returns a keyset cursor, which does *not* show you records added by other users that would appear in a true dynamic Recordset. The best workaround is to request your Recordset often so you can work with the most up-to-date data.

Creating and Opening a Recordset

Create a Recordset by using the `Dim` keyword to declare it in the form

```
Dim recordset As ADODB.Recordset
Set recordset = New ADODB.Recordset
```

Populating a Recordset is as simple as opening it. To do so, use the `Open` method in the form

```
recordset.Open source[, activeconnection][, cursortype][, locktype][, options]
```

where *recordset* represents a `Recordset` object. Table 16.4 lists the method's arguments.

Table 16.4   Recordset **Object Arguments**

Argument	Explanation
source	Identifies the data ADO uses to populate the `Recordset` object. This setting can be the name of a `Command` object, a SQL statement, the name of a table, a stored procedure, a persisted Recordset, a `Stream` object or a URL.
activeconnection	Specifies the connection to use to grab the data identified by source. Use a `Connection` object or a connection string.
cursortype	Specifies the type of cursor and is one of four intrinsic constants: `adOpenDynamic`, `adOpenKeyset`, `adOpenStatic`, `adOpenForwardOnly`, which are similar to the cursor types.
locktype	Specifies the record-locking behavior and is one of the intrinsic constants listed in Table 16.5.
options	Supplies additional information that the provider might need. Table 16.6 lists the intrinsic constants for this argument.

Table 16.5 `locktype` **Argument Constants**

Constant	Locking Behavior
adLockReadOnly	This default option creates a read-only Recordset.
adLockPessimistic	Records are locked while being edited.
adLockOptimistic	Records are locked only when updated.
adLockBatchOptimistic	Used with the UpdateBatch method to update multiple records with a single operation.

Table 16.6 `options` **Argument Constants**

Constant	Explanation
adCmdUnknown	The default option; supplies no additional information.
adCmdText	Identifies the CommandText property as a stored procedure (the actual commands, not the name of the procedure).
adCmdTable	Identifies the CommandText property as the name of a table.
adCmdStoredProc	Identifies the CommandText property as the name of a stored procedure.
adCmdFile	Identifies the CommandText property as the name of a file.
adCmdTableDirect	Identifies the CommandText property as the name of a table. The resulting Recordset is the only type that can support the Seek method.
adAsyncExecute	Executes the command asynchronously.
adAsyncFetch	Specifies that the cache should be filled synchronously and then additional rows fetched asynchronously.
adAsyncFetchNonBlocking	Retrieves records asynchronously if possible without blocking the main thread.

As you can see, there can be a lot to consider when opening a Recordset object. However, the good news is that most of the time the operation is really very simple. For instance, the following procedure populates a default Recordset object with the contents of the Clients table:

```
Private Sub ClientsRst()
  Dim rst As ADODB.Recordset
  Set rst = New ADODB.Recordset
  rst.Open "Clients", CurrentProject.Connection
  MsgBox "Connection Made"
  rst.Close
  Set rst = Nothing
End Sub
```

If you decide to run it from a standard module, you'll find that it really doesn't do anything. It creates the `Recordset` object, but it doesn't do anything with the data that the `Recordset` object contains. However, this particular method is probably the most succinct for creating a `Recordset` object.

> **TIP**
>
> If you're just learning ADO, be careful about setting the `Recordset` type. By default, ADO opens a forward-only `Recordset` type, which is different from DAO. DAO defaults to a table, and then a dynaset, and then a snapshot, and finally a forward-only type. ADO retains the forward-only type only for compatibility.
>
> One problem you might run into when trusting defaults is counting records. The forward-only `Recordset` type doesn't support the `RecordCount` property. If you need to use this property, be sure to set a static or keyset cursor.

16

Filtering Recordsets

Searching for specific data in a `Recordset` object is easily accomplished using the `Filter` property. You can submit a new query or even use the `Find` method (which is discussed in the next chapter), but `Filter` is truer to the purpose of a criterion-based search. Submitting a new query completely changes the results of the Recordset and `Find` locates appropriate data one record at a time. The `Filter` property/method temporarily limits access to only those records that meet the filtering criteria. In other words, you end up with a subset of records from your Recordset.

When temporarily restricting the available records in a Recordset, use the `Filter` property in the form

```
recordset.Filter = condition
```

where *recordset* represents a `Recordset` object and *condition* is a criteria string. For instance, the following statement locates all the tasks for employee 1 (Larry Schaff):

```
rstTasks.Filter = 1
```

If the Recordset contained only the employee name fields, you might use one of the following statements:

```
rstTasks.Filter = "LastName = 'Schaff'"
```

or even

```
rstTasks.Filter = "LastName = 'Schaff' AND FirstName = 'Larry'"
```

When using the `Filter` property, the filtered Recordset becomes the current cursor. That means most of the Recordset properties and methods affect only the filtered results, not the original Recordset.

The *condition* expression can specify any field that's in the Recordset and use the following operators: <, >, <=, >=, <>, =, or LIKE. Remember to delimit the value component appropriately using single quotation marks for strings and the pound sign for dates. (Values don't need delimiters.)

To clear a filter, use the following syntax

```
recordset.Filter = adFilterNone
```

The adFilterNone constant is similar to setting the property to a zero-length string. The result is that the current record position moves to the first record in the original Recordset.

CAUTION

Access and VBA support the * and ? wildcard characters, but ADO doesn't. If you use a SQL statement or fixed query to populate an ADO Recordset, you must use ADO's wildcards. The * ADO equivalent is the percent character, %; the ADO ? equivalent is the underscore character, _. Using the * and ? characters won't generate an error. Instead, ADO interprets the characters literally and returns an empty Recordset or perhaps even erroneous data.

Using the Recordset **Property**

Several Access objects—the listbox and combo box controls and the form and report object—support a Recordset property. The result is a control, form, or report that's bound to a Recordset, just as you might bind that same object to a table or query.

The process is simple—create the Recordset as you normally do. Then, use the following syntax to set the object's Recordset property as follows:

```
Set object.Recordset = recordset
```

A few chapters back, you worked through an exercise that added a combo box to the Employees form that filtered the form to a specific employee. If you recall, that form is bound to the Employees table and as such, displays the data for all the employees. The combo box you added temporarily filters the form to the selected employee.

There's always more than one way to accomplish something in Access. You can use this form's Recordset property to limit the form's records in the same say. The difference is that the form, within this context, is bound to a Recordset and not the underlying table. You can still update the data, if you specify the appropriate Recordset type. In addition, the form displays only the record for the specified employee—at no time does this form's recordset contain more than one record.

Open a standard module (or use Chapter 16's example module) and add the following procedure:

```
Sub FilterEmployeeForm(val As Integer)
  Dim rstEmployees As ADODB.Recordset
  DoCmd.OpenForm "Employees"
```

```
   Set rstEmployees = New ADODB.Recordset
   With rstEmployees
     .CursorLocation = adUseClient
     .Open "SELECT * " _
     & "FROM Employees " _
     & "WHERE EmployeeID = " & val, _
     CurrentProject.Connection, adOpenStatic, adLockOptimistic
   End With
   Set Forms("Employees").Recordset = rstEmployees
End Sub
```

Then, in the Immediate window, enter the following statement:

```
FilterEmployeeForm(3)
```

Next, access the newly opened Employees form, which then displays the employee record for Clint Cooper. Notice that the navigation bar displays the value 1 to let you know the form's recordset contains only one record.

Try selecting another employee from the combo box in the header section. Because the Recordset doesn't contain the corresponding record, Access returns an error, as shown in Figure 16.4. Click End to clear the message. If you were to use this form in this fashion, you have to inhibit the combo box control's search capabilities when opened in this manner.

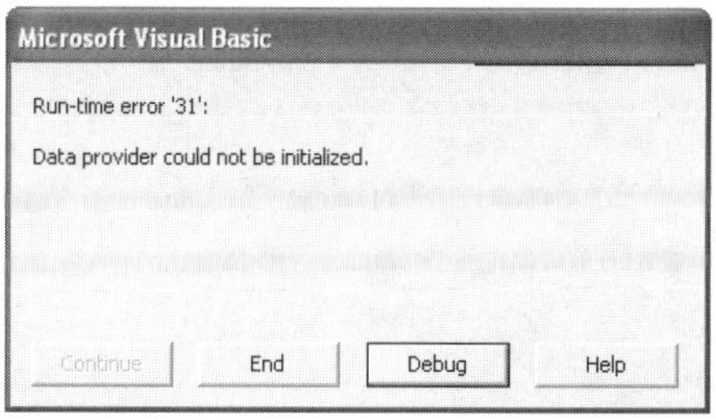

Figure 16.4
The combo box doesn't work when opened from the Recordset property procedure.

> Microsoft Visual Basic
>
> Run-time error '31':
>
> Data provider could not be initialized.
>
> Continue   End   Debug   Help

This example doesn't close or destroy the Recordset object because, as is, you're still using it. In a working example, you need to both close and destroy the Recordset object when you're done with it—most likely when you close the form.

> CAUTION
>
> This example works because the form was originally bound to the underlying data source and you didn't change the control names. That way, the control names still match the Recordset object's field names. If you change the control names, this example won't work until you add code that matches each control to the appropriate Recordset field.

16

CASE STUDY

Who's Connected to the Database?

Let's assume `TimeTrack.mdb` is a shared database. That means the database administrator (or developer) needs to open the database exclusively to make changes and perform general maintenance. Before opening the database exclusively, the administrator must be able to determine who is currently working in the database and ask them to close their connection.

In a small company, you can simply call around, but that won't always be feasible. What happens if someone doesn't answer the phone, or if someone's out for lunch, having left the database open on his or her system? A simple solution is to use ADO to create a list of users currently connected to the database.

To simplify the whole process, you add a command button to the `Switchboard` form that runs the show. Clicking the new button then displays a simple form with a listbox that contains the names of all the currently connected users. For the sake of simplicity, that's all the form will do. However, when applying this technique to your own database, you can easily create a more functional form. Perhaps you might use a `Click` event to send email to the connected users. Or, you might list extension numbers so you can quickly call each user.

This section introduces you to schema recordsets. Normally, a `Recordset` object contains data from a table. A schema `Recordset` contains information about the table or database.

The first step is to add that command button, so open `Switchboard` and add a command button. Name the new button `cmdCurrentUsers` and add an appropriate caption. Enter the following event procedure in the `Switchboard` form's module:

```
Private Sub cmdCurrentUsers_Click()
  On Error GoTo HandleErr
  DoCmd.OpenForm "CurrentUsers"
ExitHere:
  Exit Sub
HandleErr:
  MsgBox "Error " & Err.Number & ": " & _
   Err.Description
  Resume ExitHere
End Sub
```

Don't worry that the `CurrentUsers` form doesn't exist yet; you build that next. For now, save and close the `Switchboard` form.

Open a new blank form and add a listbox. Name the listbox `lstCurrentUsers` and set the Row Source Type property to Value List. Set the form properties listed in Table 16.7. Then, enter the following procedure in the form's module:

```
Private Sub Form_Load()
  'populate list box with current users
  Dim strUsers As String
  On Error GoTo HandleErr
  strUsers = ReturnUsers
  lstCurrentUsers.RowSource = strUsers
```

```
ExitHere:
  Exit Sub
HandleErr:
  MsgBox "Error " & Err.Number & ": " & _
    Err.Description
  Resume ExitHere
End Sub
```

Save the form using the name `CurrentUsers`, and then close the form.

Table 16.7 `CurrentUsers` **Properties**

Property	Setting
Scroll Bars	Neither
Record Selectors	No
Navigation Buttons	No

Next, open a new standard module (or use Chapter 16's example module) and enter the following code:

```
Public Const JET_SCHEMA_USERROSTER = _
 "{947bb102-5d43-11d1-bdbf-00c04fb92675}"

Public Function ReturnUsers() As String
  Dim cnn As ADODB.Connection
  Dim rst As ADODB.Recordset
  Set cnn = New ADODB.Connection
  On Error GoTo HandleErr
  'Open connection to database
  Set cnn = CurrentProject.Connection
  'Open schema recordset to grab user metadata
  Set rst = cnn.OpenSchema(adSchemaProviderSpecific, , _
   JET_SCHEMA_USERROSTER)
  'return current users
  rst.MoveFirst
  Do Until rst.EOF
    ReturnUsers = rst(0) & ";" & ReturnUsers
    rst.MoveNext
  Loop

ExitHere:
  rst.Close
  Set rst = Nothing
  cnn.Close
  Set cnn = Nothing
  Exit Function
HandleErr:
  MsgBox "Error " & Err.Number & ": " & _
    Err.Description
  Resume ExitHere
End Function
```

Be sure that you position the `Public Const` statement in the General Declarations section. Save the module and close it.

To see how it works, open the `Switchboard` form and click the Current Users button to open the new form shown in Figure 16.5. As you can see, the listbox displays the current user, SUSANONE. Actually, SUSANONE is the name of the computer that's currently connected, not the actual user.

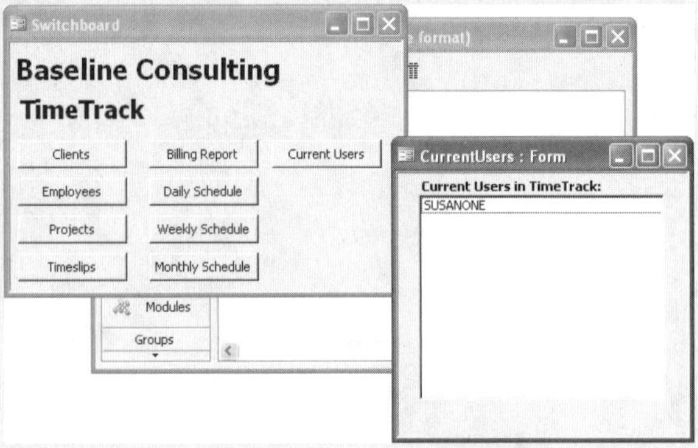

Figure 16.5
This form lists the users currently connected to the database.

You don't really need the switchboard to use this form, but maintenance tasks can just as easily be initiated from the switchboard as any other. Clicking the Current Users button opens the new `CurrentUsers` form. That form's `Open` event calls the `ReturnUsers` procedure.

The `OpenSchema` method tells ADO what kind of information to retrieve. In this case, you used the `JET_SCHEMA_USERROSTER` constant. That long string in the `Public Const` statement is a GUID that identifies the current users schema.

After the `ReturnUsers` procedure returns the list of current users as a single string, the listbox uses that string as its Row Source property.

Manipulating Data with ADO

Moving Through a Recordset

After you retrieve data using an ADO `Recordset` object, you'll want to manipulate that data in some way, even if all you want to do is view the data. A lot of what you learn in this section you can also use to find, add, delete, and edit existing data.

Moving through a `Recordset` actually requires setting the current record pointer within the cursor (the retrieved data). In other words, you point to a specific record making it the current record pointer. To move about the `Recordset`, use these five methods:

- `MoveFirst`—Moves the record pointer to the first record in the `Recordset`.
- `MoveNext`—Moves the record pointer forward to the next record.
- `MovePrevious`—Moves the record pointer backward to the previous record.
- `MoveLast`—Moves the record pointer to the last record in the Recordset.
- `Move`—Moves the record pointer a specific number of records from the current record.

The last method needs a bit more explanation because it supports two arguments

```
Move x[, start]
```

where x is a `Long` value that specifies the number of records to move and *start* is a `String` or `Variant` value that evaluates to a bookmark using one of the enumerate values listed in Table 17.1.

IN THIS CHAPTER

Moving Through a Recordset 253

Finding Data in a Recordset 256

Adding Data Using a Recordset 260

Deleting Data in a Recordset 262

Updating Data in a Recordset 266

Using Transactions to Commit Groups of Records—or Not .266

Table 17.1 *BookmarkEnum*

Constant	Integer Value	Explanation
adBookmarkCurrent	0	Starts at the current record
adBookmarkFirst	1	Starts at the first record
adBookmarkLast	2	Starts at the last record

When *x* is greater than zero, the record pointer moves forward; when *x* is less than zero, the record pointer moves backward. Specifying a negative *x* value is the only way you can move backward in a forward-only Recordset. However, this method is unpredictable because not all providers support this option. If you omit *start*, the move is relative to the current record.

You can't get anywhere in a Recordset if you get stuck in the spot before the first record or after the last record. When looping through records, you need to check for these two place-holders using the BOF and EOF Boolean properties. The BOF (beginning of file) property equals True when the record pointer moves to the spot just before the first record. Similarly, the EOF (end of file) equals True when the record pointer moves to the spot just after the last record.

To illustrate how important these two properties are, take a look at what happens when you ignore them. The following procedure retrieves data from the Clients table and then prints the client name for each record to the Immediate window:

```
Sub PrintClients()
  'Print client name to Immediate window
  Dim rst As ADODB.Recordset
  Set rst = New ADODB.Recordset
  rst.Open "Clients", CurrentProject.Connection
  rst.MoveFirst
  Do
    Debug.Print rst(1)
    rst.MoveNext
  Loop
  rst.Close
  Set rst = Nothing
End Sub
```

You can enter this procedure into a standard module or use Chapter 17's example module. With the cursor anywhere inside the procedure, press F5.

The loop prints the client names in the Immediate window, but when the cursor finally moves beyond the last record, the code returns the error shown in Figure 17.1 because there's nothing beyond the placeholder to print. Click End to clear the error message.

Figure 17.1
Avoid errors by knowing where the cursor is.

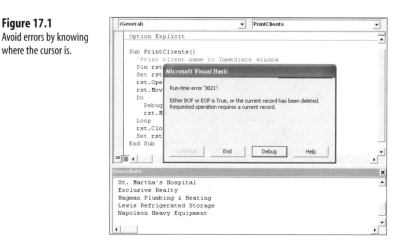

In this case, the solution is simple. Replace the `Do` statement with the following:

`Do Until rst.EOF`

The new `Do Until` statement checks for the `EOF` property before executing the loop code. The `rst.EOF` is `True` when the cursor is at the end of the file placeholder; that's when the loop stops.

Just how you check for either or both properties depends on what you're doing. You can wrap your task code in a `Do Until` loop as in this example or you can use an `If` statement. In addition, you might need to check for both the `BOF` and the `EOF` properties. This time you didn't because the loop stops after the loop's condition equals `True`.

> **TIP**
>
> Use the `EOF` and `BOF` properties to check for an empty Recordset. Both properties return `True` at the same time when the Recordset contains no records. For instance, the combined condition `rst.EOF AND rst.BOF` returns `True` when `rst` is empty.

Also notice that this example uses two of the methods reviewed earlier: `MoveFirst` and `MoveNext`. The `MoveFirst` method just before the `Do Until` loop ensures that you begin the loop at the first record, so you don't need to check the `BOF` property. After executing the loop's code task, the `MoveNext` method moves the record pointer forward to the next record, before the loop repeats its task code.

> **CAUTION**
>
> If you write a loop and your code seems to hang forever, check to make sure that you remembered to put a `MoveNext` call into the loop.

> ┌─ C A U T I O N ───
> │ Keep the cursor type in mind when trying to move through a `Recordset` object because the cur-
> │ sor type determines the direction you can move. For instance, in a forward-only cursor, you can't
> │ move backward using the `MovePrevious` method. For more information about cursor types, read
> │ "Understanding the Different Types of Recordsets" in Chapter 16.

Referencing Recordset Fields

A `Recordset` object contains a `Fields` collection and there's one `Field` object for each column of data. There are a couple of ways to interact with the actual data. First, you use the
`Field` object using the form

```
recordset.Fields(fieldname).Value
```

where *recordset* represents the `Recordset` object and *fieldname* is the column name. For
instance, the following statement returns the data in the Client field for the current record:

```
rst.Fields("Client").Value
```

Alternatively, you can also use the `Fields` collection index value. If you know the Client column is the second column in the Recordset, the following statement gets the same results:

```
rst(1)
```

When using the index value, remember that the left-most column's index value equals 0.
The second column from the left is 1, the third column from the left is 2, and so on.

> ┌───
> │ T I P There's nothing wrong with using the index value to interact with data in a Recordset, but keep two
> │ issues in mind. First, that index value can change if the structure of the underlying data source
> │ changes. For instance, you might add or delete a column. In addition, although the `Fields` collec-
> │ tion method is longer, it is more readable, making it easier to maintain.

Finding Data in a Recordset

Often, you'll need to pinpoint a specific record rather than just move from one record to
another. ADO's `Find` method is flexible and efficient, but it doesn't enable you to combine
multiple conditions using the `And` operator. The `Find` method uses the syntax

```
recordset.Find criteria[, skiprows][, searchdirection][, start]
```

Only the first of these arguments is required:

- *criteria*—A `String` value in the form of a SQL WHERE clause, but without the WHERE
  keyword.
- *skiprows*—A `Long` value that specifies the number of rows from the current row where
  the search will begin. If omitted, `Find` starts with the current row.

- *searchdirection*—One of two intrinsic constants: `adSearchForward` (the default) or `adSearchBackward`.

- *start*—A `Variant` value that specifies an optional bookmark that indicates where the search will begin. If omitted, `Find` starts with the current row. You can use a bookmark or one of the following intrinsic constants: `adBookmarkCurrent`, `adBookmarkFirst`, or `adBookmarkLast`.

> **TIP**
>
> When a search relies on more than one criterion, use the ADO `Filter` property in the form
>
> `recordset.Filter = "condition1 AND condition2"`
>
> Chapter 16 covers the `Filter` property in "Filtering Recordsets," p. 247.

The `Find` method enables you to find a record based on a search string. You supply that search string in the form of a SQL WHERE clause, without the WHERE keyword as follows:

`recordset.Find "field = value"`

The following procedure illustrates the `Find` method:

```
Sub FindClients(str As String)
  'accept string value as search criteria
  'for ADO Find method
  Dim rst As ADODB.Recordset
  Dim strSearch As String
  strSearch = "City = '" & str & "'"
  Set rst = New ADODB.Recordset
  With rst
    .Open "Clients", CurrentProject.Connection, adOpenStatic, _
    adLockPessimistic
    .MoveFirst
    .Find strSearch
    Do Until .EOF
      Debug.Print rst("Client")
      .Find strSearch, 1
    Loop
  End With
  rst.Close
  Set rst = Nothing
End Sub
```

You can enter this procedure in a standard module or use Chapter 17's example module. Then, run the statement

`FindClients("North Hollywood")`

in the Immediate window. Figure 17.2 shows the results—a list of all the clients listed in North Hollywood.

17

Figure 17.2
Locating data with the
Find method.

```
Immediate                                              ×
FindClients("North Hollywood")                          ▲
Bill's Auto Glass
Clearview Homes
St. Martha's Hospital
Napoleon Heavy Equipment
                                                        ▼
◄ |                                               ►
```

After creating and populating the `Recordset` object, the `Find` method locates the first record where the value of the City field equals the value passed by the variable `str`. In this example, that's "North Hollywood." The `Do` loop prints the Client value for that record and then executes a second `Find` using the same criterion. Notice that the `Find` method's *skiprows* argument negates the need to add a `MoveNext` method. If you omit that value, you must precede the `Find` method with a `MoveNext` method. Otherwise, the loop hits a terminal snag and prints the Client value for the current record over and over.

You can also use operators other than = with the `Find` method. For instance, you can use `City > 'Detroit'` to find the first city after Detroit in the data.

An Alternative to `Find`—the ADO `Seek` Method

When circumstances warrant, the ADO `Seek` method is actually a better choice than `Find` because it's faster. However, two important conditions must be met before the Recordset can support the `Seek` method:

- The Recordset type must be a direct table, opened using the `adCmdTableDirect` option. This option is specific to Microsoft Access databases (remember, ADO itself also works with other types of data).

- You must set the Recordset's `Index` property to an index in the underlying table that includes the search field.

> **NOTE**
>
> To use `Seek`, you must know the name of the index on the search field in the underlying table. Most of the time, that's no problem because you name the index when you create it, whether you create the index manually or programmatically. If you fail to name the index when creating it programmatically, Access combines the names of the fields to create a name. Primary key fields are a little different. Access names the primary key index *PrimaryKey*. (You can override that if you create the primary key programmatically.)
>
> You can also use code to discern index names if you don't know the names. To do this, you need to use ADOX, which you learn more about in Chapter 18. As a little preview, you can use the following procedure to return a list of indexes in the Immediate window:
>
> ```
> Sub FindIndex(tblName As String)
>     ' Find all indexes for a table
>     Dim cat As ADOX.Catalog
>     Dim tbl As ADOX.Table
>     Dim idx As ADOX.Index
>     Set cat = New ADOX.Catalog
>     Set cat.ActiveConnection = CurrentProject.Connection
> ```

```
        Set tbl = cat.Tables(tblName)
        For Each idx In tbl.Indexes
            Debug.Print idx.Name
        Next idx
    End Sub
```

CAUTION

When using `Seek`, keep in mind that you can't index a Memo, Hyperlink, or an OLE Object field.

The `Seek` method uses the following syntax:

`recordset.Seek indexname, option`

where *option* is one of the intrinsic constants listed in Table 17.2. Before the constants make sense, you need to understand how `Seek` works. `Seek` doesn't search the entire field for a literal value in what's known as a *table scan*. That's how Access finds data in a field that's not indexed.

Table 17.2   Seek Option Intrinsic Constants

Constant	Explanation
adSeekAfterEQ	Select the index key value that's equal to the search value. If there's no matching value, stop at the key immediately following the key where the match would have occurred (which is only possible because the internal values are sorted).
adSeekAfter	Select the first index key value after the point where a match occurs or would have occurred.
adSeekBefore	Select the first index key value before the point where a match occurs or would have occurred.
adSeekBeforeEQ	Select the index key value that's equal to the search value. If there's no matching value, stop at the key immediately before the key where the match would have occurred.
adSeekFirstEQ	Select the first index key value that's equal to the search value.
adSeekLastEQ	Select the last index key value that's equal to the search value.

The internal workings of an index are complex, but for the purposes here, think of an index as a sorted lookup table that stores key values and pointers to each entry in the indexed field.

The index is really just a list of values with a pointer to the actual row where that data is stored. Because the values are sorted (internally), Access can quickly tell where the value ought to be. `Seek` looks for key values that are equal to the value for which you're searching—without scanning the entire table.

The following procedure uses the Seek method to find a specific client in TimeTrack's Clients table:

```
Sub SeekClient(Clientid As Long)
  'Find client record using
  'ADO Seek method
  Dim rst As New ADODB.Recordset
  With rst
    .Open "Clients", CurrentProject.Connection, _
     adOpenDynamic, adLockOptimistic, adCmdTableDirect
    .Index = "PrimaryKey"
    .Seek Clientid, adSeekAfterEQ
  End With
    If rst.EOF Then
      MsgBox "There are no records for client " _
       & Clientid, vbOKOnly
    Else
      MsgBox "Client " & Clientid & " is " & rst("Client") _
       , vbOKOnly
    End If
    rst.Close
    Set rst = Nothing
End Sub
```

As usual, you can enter the procedure in a standard module or use Chapter 17's example module. In the Immediate window, run the following statement:

```
SeekClient(1)
```

After creating and populating the direct table Recordset object, the Index property is set to the primary key index. Then, the Seek method is used to find the first record with the value 1 in the ClientID field (the primary key field). The If statement displays the corresponding client's name, as shown in Figure 17.3. If there's no match for the value passed by *clientid*, the procedure displays an appropriate message. Either way, click OK to clear the message.

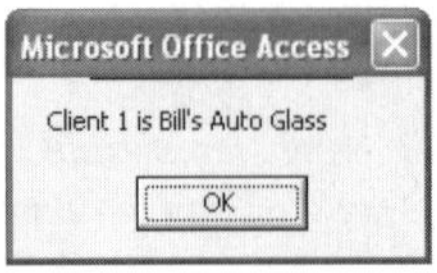

Figure 17.3
You can display the data found by the *Seek* method.

Microsoft Office Access

Client 1 is Bill's Auto Glass

OK

Adding Data Using a Recordset

At some time, you might need to add new data using a Recordset object. The process is a little more involved than just viewing or finding data. Adding a new record requires three actions:

- First, call ADO's AddNew method to create a new row in the Recordset.
- Next, supply the value for each required field.
- Finally, call ADO's Update method to save the new row to the data source. If you forget to call the Update method, the new data is discarded without warning.

TIP A Recordset object isn't the only way to add new data. The ADO Command object can execute a SQL statement directly against the data source. The Command object is covered in "Working with Command Objects," p. 242 in Chapter 16.

Let's look at a simple example that inserts new employees into TimeTrack's Employees table:

```
Sub AddEmployee(fname As String, lname As String)
  'Enter new employee record
  Dim rst As ADODB.Recordset
  Set rst = New ADODB.Recordset
  With rst
    .Open "Employees", CurrentProject.Connection, adOpenDynamic, _
     adLockPessimistic
    .AddNew
    .Fields("FirstName") = fname
    .Fields("LastName") = lname
    .Update
  End With
  rst.Close
  Set rst = Nothing
End Sub
```

Add the procedure to a standard module or use Chapter 17's example module. In the Immediate window, run the statement

```
AddEmployee "Susan", "Harkins"
```

(You can use any names you like.) Then, open the Employees table and you'll find the new employee record, as shown in Figure 17.4.

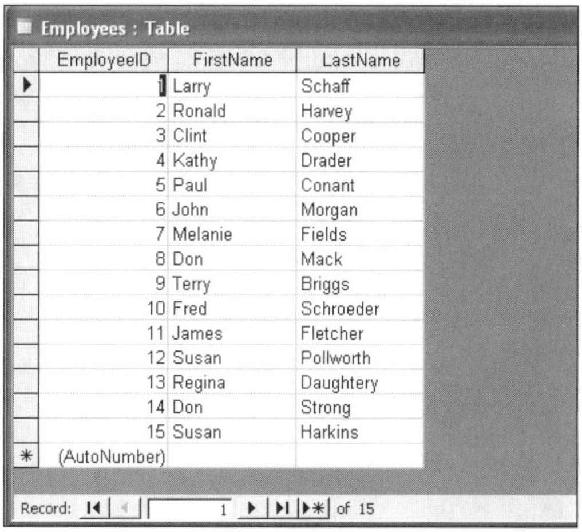

Figure 17.4
You can use an ADO Recordset object to add new records.

	EmployeeID	FirstName	LastName
▶	1	Larry	Schaff
	2	Ronald	Harvey
	3	Clint	Cooper
	4	Kathy	Drader
	5	Paul	Conant
	6	John	Morgan
	7	Melanie	Fields
	8	Don	Mack
	9	Terry	Briggs
	10	Fred	Schroeder
	11	James	Fletcher
	12	Susan	Pollworth
	13	Regina	Daughtery
	14	Don	Strong
	15	Susan	Harkins
*	(AutoNumber)		

Employees : Table

Record: 14 ◀ 1 ▶ ▶I ▶* of 15

After opening and populating the Recordset, the `AddNew` method makes room for the new record. Then, the next two statements supply the values for the new record. Finally, the `Update` method commits the new data. The `Update` method takes the form

```
recordset.Update [fields] [, values]
```

where *fields* identifies the fields you're updating and *values* supplies the data that's replacing the existing value.

You might be wondering why we didn't add a value for the `EmployeeID` field. That field is an AutoNumber field and Access adds the value when the new record is committed. An attempt to add a value to that field returns an error.

When adding new data, you really need to know the underlying data source. Failing to supply a required value or the right data type returns an error. In addition, this example contains no error handling. When you're adding new data, you probably want to include routines for catching common errors. Consider, for instance, whether the record creates a key violation (duplicates), or whether any of the new values violate any validation rules.

Deleting Data in a Recordset

Deleting a record is as simple as finding the record and then executing the `Recordset` object's `Delete` method. Just be careful, because after you delete the record, it's gone. The one trap you need to be aware of is that the current record remains the current record, even after you delete it. To fully commit the delete action and select a valid record, you must execute a `Move`, `Seek`, or `Find` method right after the `Delete` method.

The `Delete` method takes the simple form

```
recordset.Delete
```

First you select the record you want, and then you call the `Delete` method. It's that simple. Let's use the following procedure to delete the new employee record for Susan Harkins added in the last section:

```
Sub DeleteEmployee(emID As Long)
  'Delete employee record
  Dim rst As ADODB.Recordset
  Dim strSearch As String
  Dim strName As String
  Dim bytResponse As Byte
  strSearch = "EmployeeID = " & emID
  Set rst = New ADODB.Recordset
  With rst
    .Open "Employees", CurrentProject.Connection, adOpenDynamic, _
     adLockPessimistic
    .Find strSearch
```

```
      If .EOF = True Then
        MsgBox "There is no employee record for " _
         & emID, vbOKOnly
        Exit Sub
      Else
        strName = rst.Fields("FirstName") & _
         " " & rst.Fields("LastName")
        bytResponse = MsgBox("Do you want to delete the record for " _
         & strName, vbYesNo)
        If bytResponse = vbYes Then
         .Delete
        End If
      End If
  End With
  rst.Close
  Set rst = Nothing
End Sub
```

Enter the procedure in a standard module or use Chapter 17's example module. Then, run the following statement in the Immediate window:

```
DeleteEmployee 15
```

where 15 is the EmployeeID value for Susan Harkins. After creating and populating the Recordset object, the Find method locates the record with the EmployeeID value of 15. Next, the message shown in Figure 17.5 asks you to confirm the deletion. If you click Yes, the If statement executes the Delete method; click No and the Delete method is skipped. If there's no match for the employee value passed by emid, the procedure displays an appropriate message; click OK to clear the message box.

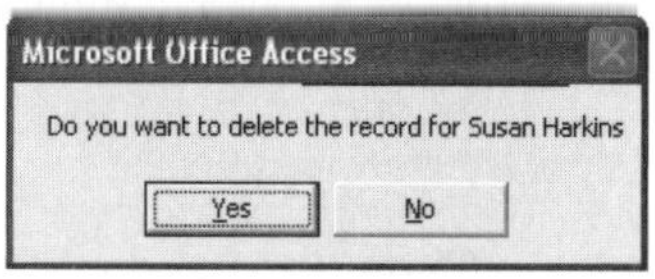

Figure 17.5
It's smart to confirm a delete action before executing it against the data source.

Microsoft Office Access

Do you want to delete the record for Susan Harkins

   Yes   No

Updating Data in a Recordset

Updating (or editing) existing data in a Recordset pulls together parts of most of the previous sections. After creating and populating the Recordset object, you must find the record or records you want to modify. Then, you commit the change by executing an ADO Update method, which you reviewed earlier in the "Adding Data Using a Recordset" section on p. 260.

> ┌─ C A U T I O N ──
> │
> │ Before you can actually run any of the procedures in this section, you must change the Field Size
> │ property of the State field in the Clients table to 10 or greater. If you don't, the procedures will
> │ return an error because the State field won't be large enough to accommodate the string
> │ "California."

First, let's look at an explicit call to Update, which is probably the safest way to approach changes because you control when the update takes place. The following procedure illustrates updates to existing data by changing the State two-letter abbreviations in the Clients table to the state's actual name. This procedure accepts two passed values, *st* and state, which represent the two-letter abbreviation and the full spelling, respectively:

```
Sub ChangeStateExplicit1(st As String, state As String)
  'Explicitly call Update to change state value
  Dim rst As ADODB.Recordset
  Set rst = New ADODB.Recordset
  With rst
    .Open "Clients", CurrentProject.Connection, adOpenDynamic, _
    adLockOptimistic
    .Find "State = '" & st & "'"
    If .EOF = True Then
      MsgBox "There are no matches", vbOKOnly
      Exit Sub
    Else
      .Update "State", state
      MsgBox .Fields("State"), vbOKOnly
    End If
  End With
  rst.Close
  Set rst = Nothing
End Sub
```

Enter the procedure in a standard module or use Chapter 17's example module. In the Immediate window, run the statement

```
ChangeStateExplicit1 "CA", "California"
```

Click OK when the MsgBox function displays the new value for the current record, as shown in Figure 17.6. If you view the Clients table, you'll find that the first record that matched "CA" now equals the string "California," as shown in Figure 17.7.

Figure 17.6
The updating procedure shows the current record's new value.

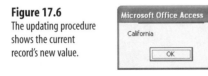

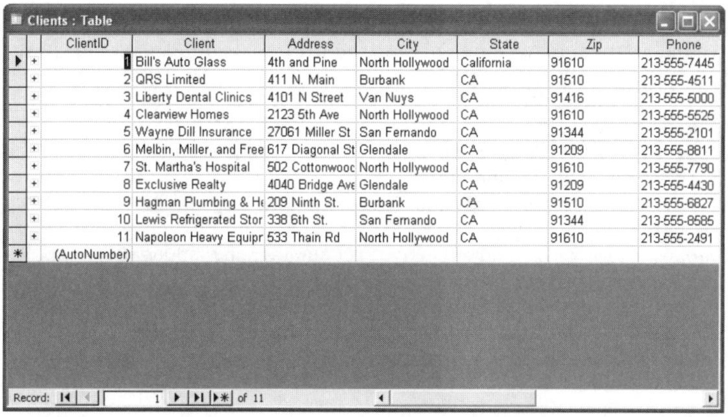

	ClientID	Client	Address	City	State	Zip	Phone
+	1	Bill's Auto Glass	4th and Pine	North Hollywood	California	91610	213-555-7445
+	2	QRS Limited	411 N. Main	Burbank	CA	91510	213-555-4511
+	3	Liberty Dental Clinics	4101 N Street	Van Nuys	CA	91416	213-555-5000
+	4	Clearview Homes	2123 5th Ave	North Hollywood	CA	91610	213-555-5525
+	5	Wayne Dill Insurance	27061 Miller St	San Fernando	CA	91344	213-555-2101
+	6	Melbin, Miller, and Free	617 Diagonal St	Glendale	CA	91209	213-555-8811
+	7	St. Martha's Hospital	502 Cottonwooc	North Hollywood	CA	91610	213-555-7790
+	8	Exclusive Realty	4040 Bridge Ave	Glendale	CA	91209	213-555-4430
+	9	Hagman Plumbing & He	209 Ninth St.	Burbank	CA	91510	213-555-6827
+	10	Lewis Refrigerated Stor	338 6th St.	San Fernando	CA	91344	213-555-8585
+	11	Napoleon Heavy Equipr	533 Thain Rd	North Hollywood	CA	91610	213-555-2491
*	(AutoNumber)						

Figure 17.7
The first *CA* value has been changed to California.

The `Find` method locates the first record to contain `st` in the State field. Then, the `Update` method changes the current value, `st`, to the full spelling in `state`.

Alternatively, you can omit the two arguments and use the `Update` method to commit values stated earlier, as shown in this next procedure:

```
Sub ChangeStateExplicit2(st As String, state As String)
  'Explicitly call Update to change state value
  Dim rst As ADODB.Recordset
  Set rst = New ADODB.Recordset
  With rst
    .Open "Clients", CurrentProject.Connection, adOpenDynamic,
     adLockOptimistic
    .Find "State = '" & st & "'"
    If .EOF = True Then
      MsgBox "There are no matches", vbOKOnly
      Exit Sub
    Else
      .Fields("State") = state
      .Update
      MsgBox .Fields("State"), vbOKOnly
    End If
  End With
  rst.Close
  Set rst = Nothing
End Sub
```

There's little difference between the two processes. Both are explicit calls and both control when the change is actually committed against the data.

You can omit the Update method from the actual code by an implicit call. After supplying a new value, simply change the current record to call the Update method. The following procedure illustrates this process:

```
Sub ChangeStateImplicit(st As String, state As String)
  'Implicitly call Update to change state value
  Dim rst As ADODB.Recordset
  Set rst = New ADODB.Recordset
  With rst
    .Open "Clients", CurrentProject.Connection, adOpenDynamic, _
    adLockOptimistic
    .Find "State = '" & st & "'"
    If .EOF = True Then
      MsgBox "There are no matches", vbOKOnly
      Exit Sub
    Else
      .Fields("State") = state
      .MoveNext
      .MovePrevious
      MsgBox .Fields("State"), vbOKOnly
    End If
  End With
  rst.Close
  Set rst = Nothing
End Sub
```

Notice that there's no call to the Update method in this last example. After stating the new value in the .Fields("State") = state statement, the MoveNext method calls the Update method automatically. You're not committed to a change until you move the current record or explicitly call the Update method. There are two ways to dump changes before they're made:

- Call the CancelUpdate method.
- Close or destroy the Recordset object (by setting it to Nothing).

> **NOTE**
> When creating a Recordset that updates data, remember that the type of lock can matter if more than one user will be using the database at the same time. All the examples in this section use optimistic locking. That means ADO doesn't try to resolve conflicts that can arise when more than one person attempts to edit the same data at the same time. As a rule, your attempt to update the record will fail if another user updates the record first. Use pessimistic locking if you want ADO to resolve conflicts and commit all edits.

Using Transactions to Commit Groups of Records—or Not

Access doesn't support transaction processing directly. However, ADO's Connection object does, so you can benefit from transaction processing even though Access doesn't directly support the process.

Transaction processing involves treating multiple updates to multiple records as one process instead of several. If one update fails, they all fail. If one update is made, they're all made. This type of control is important to business processes where changing one value can have far-reaching results. For instance, let's suppose you commit an order, update the inventory numbers, and update an accounting application for billing purposes, accordingly. Now, what happens if the customer calls to cancel part or even all of the order? Not only must you clear the order from the customer's account, you must also return the items to the inventory. If you do one without the other, the balance sheet will be off somewhere and it might take a long time to find the error.

Not only does transaction processing protect the validity of your data from obvious logic errors, such as in the previous scenario, but transaction processing can also protect your data in the event of a network or power failure. Where Access is concerned, this issue can be touch-and-go. ADO's transaction processing can't be solely trusted in this area, but it's better than nothing. (The technical issues that come into play are well outside the scope of this book.)

You use three methods to implement transaction processing, all three belonging to the `Connection` object:

- `BeginTrans`—This method marks the spot where the provider begins to group the data changes.

- `CommitTrans`—You must execute this method to actually commit the group of changes to the underlying data source.

- `RollbackTrans`—All uncommitted changes are dumped.

In the previous section, you used the `Update` method to change the `CA` values in the Clients table to "California," but only one at a time. Now, let's include a loop that changes all the `CA` values in the table, but wrap the process in a transaction so either all or none of the changes are committed. Enter the following procedure into a standard module or use Chapter 17's example module:

```
Sub ChangeStateTransaction(st As String, state As String)
  'Wrap implicitly call to Update
  'in transaction to committ all changes
  'at one time, or not at all.
  Dim cnn As ADODB.Connection
  Dim rst As ADODB.Recordset
  Dim bytResponse As Byte
  Set cnn = CurrentProject.Connection
  Set rst = New ADODB.Recordset
  With rst
    .Open "Clients", cnn, adOpenDynamic, _
     adLockOptimistic
    .Find "State = '" & st & "'"
    cnn.BeginTrans
    Do Until .EOF
      .Fields("State") = state
      .MoveNext
```

```
      Loop
      bytResponse = MsgBox("Ready to commit changes to " _
       & "State field?", vbYesNo)
      If bytResponse = vbYes Then
        cnn.CommitTrans
      ElseIf bytResponse = vbNo Then
        cnn.RollbackTrans
      End If
    End With
    rst.Close
    Set rst = Nothing
End Sub
```

(If you didn't change the State (Clients table) Field Size property to 10 or greater in the previous section, do so now.)

Run the following statement in the Immediate window:

```
ChangeStateTransaction "CA", "California"
```

After creating and populating the Recordset object, the procedure selects the first record that contains the string "CA" in the State field. Then, the BeginTrans method is executed. Subsequently, all the updates made by the following Do Until loop are gathered, but not committed.

When prompted to commit the changes the first time, click No in the message box shown in Figure 17.8. If you like, open the Clients table to prove to yourself that those changes really weren't made. Then, run the procedure again, clicking Yes. This time when you check the table, you'll see that each State field now contains the string "California" instead of "CA." Unlike the earlier examples, this procedure doesn't warn you if you pass a value that has no matching records in the State field. If there are no matching values, nothing is changed, but there's no warning.

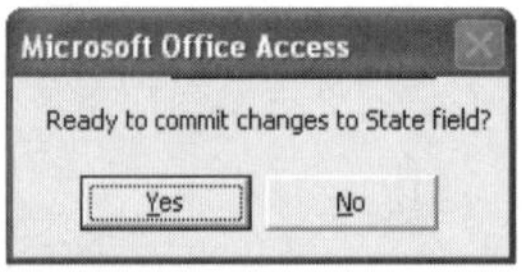

Figure 17.8
Click No to dump the updates.

CASE STUDY

Using a Recordset Object to Add Items to a Combo Box

In Chapter 12, you learned about list controls, including how to add an item to an existing control's list. The examples worked directly with the data source using SQL statements. You can do the same with a Recordset object.

Currently, the project name control in the Projects form shown in Figure 17.9 is a text box control, which means users have to continually re-enter these names. This setup is less efficient and allows typos to creep into the data. One way to limit typos and keep users happy is to provide a combo box that supplies all possible entries for that field.

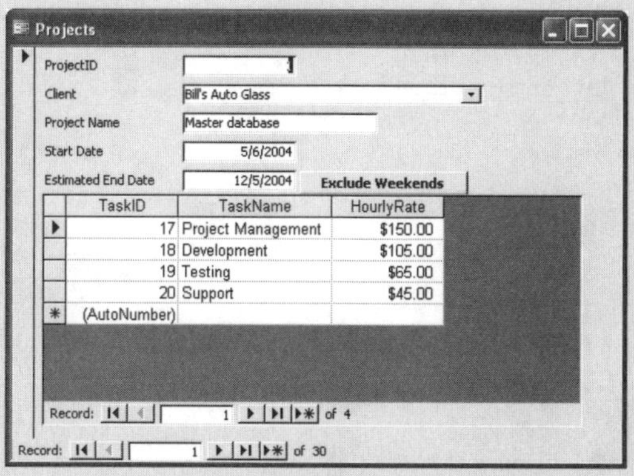

Figure 17.9
Changing the project name text box to a combo box control.

Occasionally, users might need to introduce a new project name. You learned in Chapter 12 that the combo box can accommodate new values. Let's provide a combo box that lists the existing project names and also accepts new ones. To do so, complete the following steps:

1. Open the Projects form in Design view.

2. Right-click the project name text box and choose Change To from the resulting context menu, and then choose Combo Box from the resulting submenu.

3. Refer to Table 17.3 for the new control's properties.

Table 17.3   Combo Box Properties

Property	Setting
Row Source	SELECT DISTINCT Projects.ProjectName FROM Projects ORDER BY Projects.ProjectName
Limit To List	Yes

4. Open the form's module and enter the following event procedure:

```
Private Sub ProjectName_NotInList(NewData As String, Response As Integer)
    'Handle non-list items entered into
    'ProjectName combo box
    Dim bytResponse As Byte
    Dim cnn As ADODB.Connection
    Dim rst As ADODB.Recordset
    'On Error GoTo HandleErr
    bytResponse = MsgBox("Do you want to add " _
     & NewData & " to the list?", vbYesNo)
    Set cnn = CurrentProject.Connection
    Set rst = New ADODB.Recordset
    With rst
      .Open "Projects", cnn, adOpenDynamic, _
         adLockOptimistic
      If bytResponse = vbYes Then
        .AddNew "ProjectName", NewData
        .Update
```

```
        Response = acDataErrAdded
      ElseIf bytResponse = vbNo Then
        Response = acDataErrContinue
        ProjectName.Undo
        GoTo ExitHere
      End If
    End With

ExitHere:
  rst.Close
  Set rst = Nothing
  cnn.Close
  Set cnn = Nothing
  Exit Sub
HandleErr:
  MsgBox "Error " & Err.Number & ": " & _
    Err.Description, vbOKOnly
  Resume ExitHere
End Sub
```

5. Save the form and view it in Form view. Figure 17.10 shows the new combo box with its open list.

Figure 17.10
View the new combo box control's list.

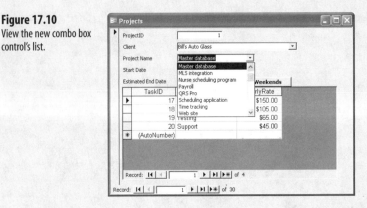

6. Click the New Record button on the form's navigation toolbar.

7. Choose any client from the client list.

8. Instead of choosing an item from the project list, enter Quality Control, and press Tab or Enter. Doing so triggers the control's NotInList event, which displays the message box shown in Figure 17.11.

Figure 17.11
Entering a non-list item triggers the control's NotInList event.

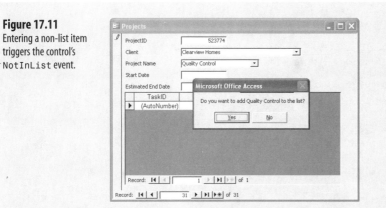

9. Click Yes.

10. Open the drop-down list to view the newly added item shown in Figure 17.12. If you open the Projects table, you'll find a new record with Quality Control as the project name value.

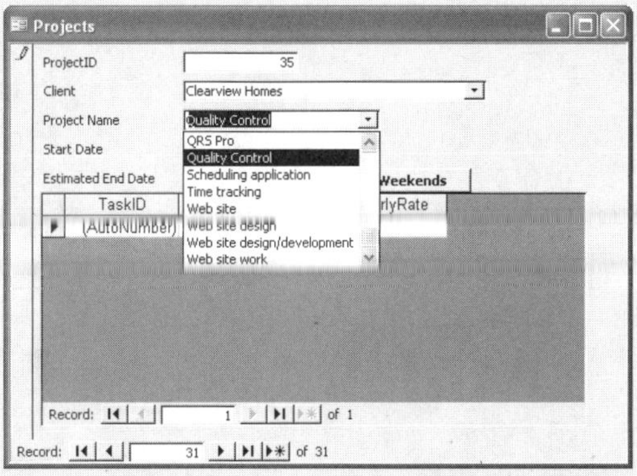

Figure 17.12
The NotInList event adds the new item to the list.

If you click No in response to the message box shown in Figure 17.11, the event removes the non-list item from the control's text box component and does not add the item to the control's data source (the Projects table). Consequently, the item is not added to the control's list.

Creating Objects with ADOX

What Is ADOX?

In the last several chapters, you've learned how to use ADO to explore and manipulate data. But there are limitations to the things that you can do with ADO. One of these limitations is that ADO can work only with objects that already exist in the database. You can't, for example, create a new table or a new query with ADO, no matter what you do with the Connection, Command, or Recordset objects.

Many developers might never feel this limitation, but being able to create new objects from code can be incredibly useful. For example, you might have some tables that you prefer to start with in every database that you create. Wouldn't it be nice to run a procedure to just create these tables, instead of working in the table designer?

That's why Microsoft invented ADOX—more formally, the ADO Extensions for DDL and Security. This is an additional library that hooks in with ADO to enable creating new objects. This chapter exposes you to some of the features and functions of ADOX.

As the name implies, ADOX also enables you to manipulate the security properties of objects in your database, such as who owns an object and who has permission to work with the object.

Figure 18.1 shows the part of the ADOX object model used in this chapter.

IN THIS CHAPTER

What Is ADOX? 273
Creating Tables 274
Securing Objects 279

Figure 18.1
Part of the ADOX object model.

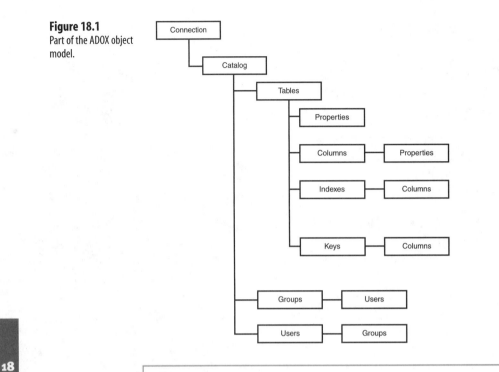

> **NOTE**
> The Connection object shown in Figure 18.1 is not really part of ADOX. Rather, it's the standard ADO Connection object. The two libraries interface by sharing this object.

Creating Tables

There's a pattern that you see over and over again when you're creating objects with ADOX:

1. Instantiate the appropriate ADOX object.
2. Set the properties of the ADOX object.
3. Append the object to the appropriate collection.

Keep this pattern in mind as you work through creating some new tables from code.

> **NOTE**
> As you can see, the pattern for adding objects is very similar to the pattern you've already learned for adding data to a Recordset. The difference is that with ADOX you're working with your database's schema rather than its data.

Creating a Table and Columns

To build a table, you need three ADOX objects:

- The Catalog object represents the design information for an entire Jet database.
- The Table object represents a single table.
- The Column object represents a single field in a table.

To demonstrate how to add tables to a database from code, let's build a pair of tables that you might use to keep track of feature requests in any database. The Users table will consist of an AutoNumber primary key and a username; the FeatureRequests table will consist of an AutoNumber primary key, a foreign key into the Users table, and a text field to hold the feature request.

Being able to create these tables from code is useful if you're a developer who works on many different databases. Instead of building the same tables manually in every database, you can just import the appropriate module and run the procedure. Here's the code that builds these two tables, using ADOX:

```
Sub CreateTables()
  ' Build two new tables in the database

  Dim cat As ADOX.Catalog
  Dim tbl As ADOX.Table
  Dim col As ADOX.Column

  ' Set up a catalog pointing to this
  ' database
  Set cat = New ADOX.Catalog
  Set cat.ActiveConnection = CurrentProject.Connection

    ' Create a table
  Set tbl = New ADOX.Table
  tbl.Name = "Users"

  ' Add some columns to the table
  Set col = New ADOX.Column
  col.Name = "UserID"
  col.Type = adInteger     ' Jet Long Integer type
  ' Associate with the provider so we can set
  ' provider-specific properties
  Set col.ParentCatalog = cat
  col.Properties("Autoincrement") = True
  col.Properties("Description") = "Unique User Number"
  tbl.Columns.Append col

  Set col = New ADOX.Column
  col.Name = "UserName"
  col.Type = adVarWChar
  col.DefinedSize = 50
  col.Attributes = 0  ' Not null
  Set col.ParentCatalog = cat
  col.Properties("Description") = "User Name"
  tbl.Columns.Append col
```

18

```
    ' And save the table
    cat.Tables.Append tbl

    ' Create another table
    Set tbl = New ADOX.Table
    tbl.Name = "FeatureRequests"

    ' Add some columns to the table
    Set col = New ADOX.Column
    col.Name = "FeatureID"
    col.Type = adInteger
    Set col.ParentCatalog = cat
    col.Properties("Autoincrement") = True
    col.Properties("Description") = "Unique Request Number"
    tbl.Columns.Append col

    Set col = New ADOX.Column
    col.Name = "UserID"
    col.Type = adInteger
    Set col.ParentCatalog = cat
    col.Properties("Description") = "User making the request"
    tbl.Columns.Append col

    Set col = New ADOX.Column
    col.Name = "FeatureRequest"
    col.Type = adVarWChar
    col.DefinedSize = 255
    Set col.ParentCatalog = cat
    col.Properties("Description") = "Feature being requested"
    tbl.Columns.Append col

    ' And save the table
    cat.Tables.Append tbl

End Sub
```

> **NOTE**
> You need to set a reference (using the Tools, References menu item) to the Microsoft ADO Ext. for DDL and Security library before you can run this code. Depending on the software on your computer, you might have version 2.5, 2.6, or later available; choose the version with the highest number.

After you instantiate an ADOX Catalog object, you need to set its ActiveConnection property to tell it which database to use for storing newly created objects. In this case, you can just retrieve the connection for the current database from the CurrentProject object.

Creating a table is easy; you just instantiate a new ADOX Table object. From there, you can create Column objects and append them to the table. Note that to use any Access-specific properties on a new column, you need to set the column's ParentCatalog property first. Each Column object has a Name and a Type (types are indicated by a set of constants stored in the ADOX library) and can have other properties as well.

When you've created all the columns for a table, you can add the table to the database by appending it to the appropriate `Tables` collection.

> **TIP**
> If the Tables tab of the database container is open when you run this procedure, you need to select View, Refresh to see the new tables.

Creating Indexes

Just creating tables isn't enough, of course; in most cases, tables need indexes created to help you work with them more effectively. As a rough rule of thumb, create an index for any field that you intend to search or sort on a frequent basis.

In ADOX, you create an index by using the `Index` object, which consists of a collection of `Column` objects representing the indexed columns. A `Table` object has an `Indexes` collection containing all the indexes for the table. Here's some code to add indexes to the newly created tables:

```
Sub CreateIndexes()
  ' Build indexes for the new tables

  Dim cat As ADOX.Catalog
  Dim tbl As ADOX.Table
  Dim idx As ADOX.Index
  Dim col As ADOX.Column

  ' Set up a catalog pointing to this
  ' database
  Set cat = New ADOX.Catalog
  Set cat.ActiveConnection = CurrentProject.Connection

  ' Retrieve a table
  Set tbl = cat.Tables("Users")

  ' Now create an index on the primary key field
  ' As a side effect, this will create the
  ' primary key
  Set idx = New ADOX.Index
  idx.Name = "PrimaryKey"
  idx.PrimaryKey = True
  idx.Unique = True
  ' Specify the column for the index
  idx.Columns.Append "UserID"
  ' And add the index to the table
  tbl.Indexes.Append idx

  ' Create a second index on the name field
  Set idx = New ADOX.Index
  idx.Name = "NameIndex"
  idx.Unique = False
  idx.Columns.Append "UserName"
  tbl.Indexes.Append idx
```

18

```
' Retrieve the other table
Set tbl = cat.Tables("FeatureRequests")

' And create its primary key
Set idx = New ADOX.Index
idx.Name = "PrimaryKey"
idx.PrimaryKey = True
idx.Unique = True
' Specify the column for the index
idx.Columns.Append "FeatureID"
' And add the index to the table
tbl.Indexes.Append idx

End Sub
```

Note a few new things in this code sample:

- Retrieving a table that already exists is just like retrieving an object from any other collection.

- Creating an Index object with its PrimaryKey property set to True builds a primary key for the table.

- You don't have to create the Column objects and then append them to the index's Columns collection. Instead, you can use the Indexes.Append method to do this all in one step.

Make sure you create the columns and append them to the table before you try to use those same columns in indexes. Otherwise, you get a runtime error.

Creating Relationships

Creating a relationship between two tables with ADOX requires creating a primary key on one table and a foreign key on the other. You can represent both of these with Key objects. But as mentioned previously, creating a primary key index automatically creates the primary key. So all that's left to do to build a relationship between these two tables is to create an appropriate foreign key:

```
Sub CreateRelation()
    ' Create a foreign key between the
    ' FeatureRequests and Users tables

    Dim cat As ADOX.Catalog
    Dim tbl As ADOX.Table
    Dim ky As ADOX.Key
    Dim col As ADOX.Column

    ' Set up a catalog pointing to this
    ' database
    Set cat = New ADOX.Catalog
    Set cat.ActiveConnection = CurrentProject.Connection
```

```
' Retrieve the foreign key table
Set tbl = cat.Tables("FeatureRequests")

' Create the key and append it to the table
Set ky = New ADOX.Key
ky.Name = "UserKey"
ky.Type = adKeyForeign
ky.RelatedTable = "Users"
Set col = New ADOX.Column
col.Name = "UserID"
col.RelatedColumn = "UserID"
ky.Columns.Append col
tbl.Keys.Append ky

End Sub
```

The `Key` object representing a foreign key has properties reflecting both sides of the relationship:

- The `Column.Name` property is the name of the column in the foreign key table.
- The `Column.RelatedColumn` property is the name of the column in the primary key table.
- The `Key.RelatedTable` property is the name of the primary key table.
- The key itself is appended to the `Keys` collection of the foreign key table.

Securing Objects

Building tables, indexes, and relationships are activities that affect the *schema* of a database—the design of the objects in the database. That's the "Data Definition" part of the ADOX library name. ADOX also offers facilities for manipulating database security. These facilities match well with the way that Access handles security. ADOX's security features enable you to perform these operations:

- Create a group
- Create a user
- Change object ownership
- Set object permissions

This section shows you the basic code to perform these security operations.

Creating a New Group

Access enables you to secure objects so that they are available only to individual users, or to groups of users. Let's start with groups, because it is often more convenient to manage security with groups. If you have many users for your database, you can set rights for groups and then just assign users to the appropriate groups.

To create a new security Group object using ADOX, you just give it a name and append it to the Groups collection of a catalog, as in this procedure:

```
Sub CreateGroup()
  ' Create a new security group

  Dim cat As ADOX.Catalog

  ' Set up a catalog pointing to this
  ' database
  Set cat = New ADOX.Catalog
  Set cat.ActiveConnection = CurrentProject.Connection

  ' Add a group named Management
  cat.Groups.Append "Management"
  ' And put the Admin user in this group
  cat.Groups("Management").Users.Append "Admin"

End Sub
```

> **CAUTION**
>
> The examples in this section make changes to your default Access workgroup when you actually run them on your computer. The Chapter18 module in the sample database includes a Cleanup procedure to reverse these changes.

After you create a group, you can add users to the group by appending them to the group's Users collection. The users must already exist in the catalog's Users collection. You see how to create users in the next section.

Creating a New User

The code to create a new user is very similar to the code to create a new group:

```
Sub CreateUser()
  ' Create a new security user

  Dim cat As ADOX.Catalog

  ' Set up a catalog pointing to this
  ' database
  Set cat = New ADOX.Catalog
  Set cat.ActiveConnection = CurrentProject.Connection

  ' Add a User named Mike
  cat.Users.Append "Mike", "OriginalPW"
  ' And put them in the Management group
  cat.Users("Mike").Groups.Append "Management"

  ' Change Mike's password
  cat.Users("Mike").ChangePassword "OriginalPW", "Fish"

End Sub
```

After you create users, you can put them in a group by adding that group to the users' Groups collection. The group, of course, must already exist. Alternatively, you can add the users to the group's Users collection. The effect is exactly the same.

When you create a new user, you need to include a password for the user. If you change your mind about the password, you can call the ChangePassword method of the User object to change the password. You must know the old password to use this method.

> **CAUTION**
>
> In an actual application, you shouldn't store the password in the code. Anyone who can get at the source code or the MDB file can read the password in this case. A more secure way to handle things is to prompt the users for their desired password at runtime.

Changing Object Ownership

Every object in Access is initially owned by the user who created the object. Changing the ownership of an object doesn't use the Groups or Users collections at all. Instead, you can retrieve ownership information or assign ownership to a different user with methods of the Catalog object. Here's an example:

```
Sub ChangeOwner()
    ' Change the owner of an object

    Dim cat As ADOX.Catalog
    Dim strOwner As String

    ' Set up a catalog pointing to this
    ' database
    Set cat = New ADOX.Catalog
    Set cat.ActiveConnection = CurrentProject.Connection

    ' Show the current owner of the Clients table
    strOwner = cat.GetObjectOwner("Clients", adPermObjTable)
    Debug.Print "Clients is owned by " & strOwner

    ' Change the ownership
    cat.SetObjectOwner "Clients", adPermObjTable, "Mike"
    Debug.Print "Clients is now owned by Mike"

End Sub
```

Both the GetObjectOwner and SetObjectOwner methods take an object type parameter that indicates the type of database object to work with. When working with Access, this parameter can have any of these values:

- adPermObjProcedure for a query with parameters
- adPermObjTable for a table
- adPermObjView for a query without parameters

18

- `adPermObjProviderSpecific` for other objects

- `adPermObjColumn` for a column

- `adPermObjDatabase` for a database

If you specify `adPermObjProviderSpecific`, you must provide an additional parameter to the `GetObjectOwner` or `SetObjectOwner` method:

```
cat.GetObjectOwner ObjectName, ObjectType, ObjectTypeId
cat.SetObjectOwner ObjectName, ObjectType, UserName, ObjectTypeId
```

In this case, the `ObjectTypeId` is a GUID (globally unique ID) to refer to an object. You can use one of these GUIDs:

- `{C49C842E-9DCB-11D1-9F0A-00C04FC2C2E0}` for a form

- `{C49C8430-9DCB-11D1-9F0A-00C04FC2C2E0}` for a report

- `{C49C842F-9DCB-11D1-9F0A-00C04FC2C2E0}` for a macro

- `{C49C8432-9DCB-11D1-9F0A-00C04FC2C2E0}` for a module

This two-step process—of first choosing `adPermObjProviderSpecific`, and then supplying a GUID—is necessary because ADOX works with databases other than Access (such as SQL Server or Oracle). Those databases don't have objects such as forms or reports, so there's no need for ADOX to include them in its core set of constants.

Setting Object Permissions

To set the permissions on an object, you call the `SetPermissions` method of either a user or a group. Here's an example:

```
Sub SetPermissions()
  ' Set permissions on an object

  Dim cat As ADOX.Catalog

  ' Set up a catalog pointing to this
  ' database
  Set cat = New ADOX.Catalog
  Set cat.ActiveConnection = CurrentProject.Connection


  ' Grant Mike permissions on the Clients table
  cat.Users("Mike").SetPermissions "Clients", adPermObjTable, _
  adAccessSet, adRightFull

End Sub
```

The `SetPermissions` method has four required and two optional arguments:

- `Name` is the name of the object to manipulate.

- `ObjectType` is the type of the object.

- `Action` is `adAccessDeny` to remove the specified permissions, `adAccessGrant` to add the specified permissions to any already in place, `adAccessRevoke` to remove all permissions, or `adAccessSet` to set the exact permissions supplied.

- `Rights` is a constant indicating which permissions to grant. Table 18.1 shows the possible values for this constant.

- The optional `Inherit` parameter can be set to a constant to control whether objects contained within the specified object should inherit the specified permissions. You're unlikely to need this parameter.

- The optional `ObjectTypeId` is used when the `ObjectType` is set to `adPermObjProviderSpecific`, just as it is with the ownership methods.

Table 18.1 Rights Constants for ADOX

Constant	Meaning
`adRightCreate`	Permission to create new objects of the specified type
`adRightDelete`	Permission to delete data
`adRightDrop`	Permission to delete objects of the specified type
`adRightExclusive`	Permission to lock the object exclusively
`adRightExecute`	Permission to execute
`adRightFull`	All possible permissions on the object
`adRightInsert`	Permission to insert data
`adRightMaximumAllowed`	All possible permissions, including provider-specific permissions
`adRightNone`	No permissions on the object
`adRightRead`	Permission to read data
`adRightReadDesign`	Permission to retrieve schema information
`adRightReadPermissions`	Permission to retrieve permission information
`adRightReference`	Permission to reference
`adRightUpdate`	Permission to edit existing data
`adRightWithGrant`	Permission to grant permissions
`adRightWriteDesign`	Permission to modify the design of the object
`adRightWriteOwner`	Permission to change object ownership
`adRightWritePermissions`	Permission to change the specified permissions

18

Creating a Data Dictionary

To demonstrate a practical use for ADOX, we've implemented a simple data dictionary in this chapter's case study. A *data dictionary* is a list of all the fields in a database together with some information about those fields. One of its best uses is to check for inconsistencies. For example, if you discover that some tables define `CustomerID` as a number, whereas others define a field with the same name as text, there's probably something wrong.

This particular data dictionary implementation shows you the column name, table name, and data type for every column in your database. It's built from a single table and a single form. You can use it in any database simply by importing the table and the form to the new database and then opening the form. Here's how you can build this data dictionary from scratch:

1. Create a new table containing three fields, `TableName` (text, 255 characters), `ColumnName` (text, 255 characters), and `Type` (text, 50 characters). Set `TableName` and `ColumnName` together to be a composite primary key for the table. Save the table as DataDictionary.

2. Create a new form and save it as `Data Dictionary`. Set the Record Selectors property to No, the Navigation Buttons property to No, and the Caption property to `Data Dictionary`.

3. Add a ListBox control to the form and name it `lstColumns`. Set the Column Count property of the control to 3 and set the Row Source property to `SELECT DataDictionary.ColumnName,`
   `DataDictionary.TableName, DataDictionary.Type FROM DataDictionary ORDER BY`
   `DataDictionary.ColumnName, DataDictionary.TableName`.

4. Add this code to the form's module:

```
Option Compare Database
Option Explicit

Private Sub Form_Open(Cancel As Integer)
    ' Rebuild the data dictionary on form open

    Dim cnn As ADODB.Connection
    Dim cmdDelete As ADODB.Command
    Dim rstDictionary As ADODB.Recordset
    Dim cat As ADOX.Catalog
    Dim tbl As ADOX.Table
    Dim col As ADOX.Column

    ' Clear the existing dictionary
    Set cnn = CurrentProject.Connection
    Set cmdDelete = New ADODB.Command
    Set cmdDelete.ActiveConnection = cnn
    cmdDelete.CommandText = "DELETE * FROM DataDictionary"
    cmdDelete.Execute

    ' Now stock the new dictionary
    Set rstDictionary = New ADODB.Recordset
    rstDictionary.Open "SELECT * FROM DataDictionary", _
     cnn, adOpenStatic, adLockOptimistic
```

```vba
        ' Set up a catalog pointing to this
        ' database
        Set cat = New ADOX.Catalog
        Set cat.ActiveConnection = CurrentProject.Connection

        ' Iterate through all tables and fields
        For Each tbl In cat.Tables
          ' Block system tables
          If Left(tbl.Name, 4) <> "MSys" And _
            Left(tbl.Name, 4) <> "USys" And _
            Left(tbl.Name, 4) <> "~TMP" Then
            For Each col In tbl.Columns
              rstDictionary.AddNew
                rstDictionary.Fields("TableName").Value = tbl.Name
                rstDictionary.Fields("ColumnName").Value = col.Name
                rstDictionary.Fields("Type").Value = TranslateType(col.Type)
              rstDictionary.Update
            Next col
          End If
        Next tbl

        rstDictionary.Close
End Sub

Public Function TranslateType(intType As Integer) As String
    ' Get the Access data type corresponding to
    ' an ADOX data type
    Select Case intType
      Case adUnsignedTinyInt
        TranslateType = "Byte"
      Case adCurrency
        TranslateType = "Currency"
      Case adDate
        TranslateType = "Date/Time"
      Case adNumeric
        TranslateType = "Decimal"
      Case adDouble
        TranslateType = "Double"
      Case adLongVarWChar
        TranslateType = "Memo"
      Case adSmallInt
        TranslateType = "Integer"
      Case adInteger
        TranslateType = "Long Integer"
      Case adLongVarBinary
        TranslateType = "OLE Object"
      Case adGUID
        TranslateType = "Replication ID"
      Case adSingle
        TranslateType = "Single"
      Case adVarWChar
        TranslateType = "Text"
      Case adBoolean
        TranslateType = "Yes/No"
    End Select
End Function
```

18

```
Private Sub Form_Load()
    ' The underlying table has just been
    ' restocked, so requery the listbox
    lstColumns.Requery
End Sub
```

This code might look complex, but it brings together ADO and ADOX techniques that you've already seen. When you open the form, it starts by using the `Execute` method of a `Command` object to clear out the DataDictionary table. This ensures that the table is refreshed every time that the form is opened. It then uses ADO to open a new Recordset on the now-empty table.

The code switches to ADOX to iterate through all the tables in the database, and through all the columns in each table. There's a rough-and-ready check designed to skip system tables and temporary objects, which starts with one of a small set of prefixes. For each column, the code adds a row to the Recordset.

The `TranslateType` function translates the ADOX column type constants into the more familiar Access data types. When the entire Recordset has been stocked, the form re-queries the listbox. Figure 18.2 shows the result.

Figure 18.2
The Data Dictionary in action.

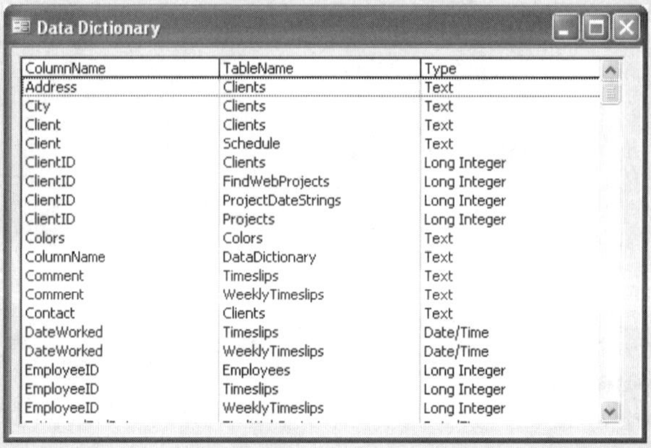

ColumnName	TableName	Type
Address	Clients	Text
City	Clients	Text
Client	Clients	Text
Client	Schedule	Text
ClientID	Clients	Long Integer
ClientID	FindWebProjects	Long Integer
ClientID	ProjectDateStrings	Long Integer
ClientID	Projects	Long Integer
Colors	Colors	Text
ColumnName	DataDictionary	Text
Comment	Timeslips	Text
Comment	WeeklyTimeslips	Text
Contact	Clients	Text
DateWorked	Timeslips	Date/Time
DateWorked	WeeklyTimeslips	Date/Time
EmployeeID	Employees	Long Integer
EmployeeID	Timeslips	Long Integer
EmployeeID	WeeklyTimeslips	Long Integer

TIP

One thing to notice about this technique is that there's no built-in feature or property that sorts an unbound listbox in Access. The easiest way to get a sorted list is to save your data to a table, and then retrieve that same data and sort it using an `ORDER BY` clause.

Performing Advanced Data Operations

19

Coding for Concurrency

Access was designed from the ground up as a multi-user database. That means that two or more users can have the same Access database open at the same time, and nothing bad will happen. This is true from the Access user interface, and it's also true from the code that you write to automate Access.

The key issue in multiuser database use is that of *concurrency*: what happens when two database users try to edit the same record in the database at the same time? This section briefly reviews the way that concurrency works in Access, and then shows you how to handle these issues in your ADO code.

Understanding Concurrency

There are two basic ways in which an Access application (or any other database application, for that matter) can handle concurrency issues. These are normally referred to as *optimistic record locking* and *pessimistic record locking*. Record locking itself is a process of reserving a record for the exclusive use of a single database user. A record lock is always associated with a record in a table and with a particular user. When you have a record locked, no other database user can make changes to that record.

The difference between optimistic record locking and pessimistic record locking lies in precisely when the locks are applied and released. With optimistic record locking, a record is locked only when you save changes. With pessimistic record locking, a record is locked as soon as you begin to edit the data. In either case, the lock is removed when Access finishes saving your changes.

IN THIS CHAPTER

Coding for Concurrency 287

Retrieving a User Recordset 293

Using Other Schema Recordsets 294

> **NOTE**
>
> In earlier versions of Access, page locking was used to implement record locking. With page locking, locking one record locked the nearby records in the database as well. Starting with Access 2000, Access defaults to record locking instead of page locking. You can change this option if you like (choose Tools, Options and uncheck Open Databases Using Record-Level Locking on the Advanced tab), but it's better to leave it set to the default.

Optimistic record locking allows more than one user to be editing a record at the same time. For example, with optimistic locking, this is one possible sequence of actions:

1. Joe begins editing the customer record for Amalgamated Industries.
2. Joe changes the customer's phone number.
3. Mary begins editing the customer record for Amalgamated Industries. She can do this because the record isn't locked when Joe starts to edit it.
4. Mary changes the customer's phone number.
5. Joe saves his change. The record is locked to Joe for the time that it takes for the change to be written to the disk. At this point, the customer record has the phone number that Joe entered.
6. Mary tries to save her change. Mary gets an error message warning her that another user changed the record, so she has to choose between discarding her change or overwriting the other change.

On the other hand, if the table were using pessimistic record locking, the sequence could go like this:

1. Joe begins editing the customer record for Amalgamated Industries.
2. Joe changes the customer's phone number.
3. Mary tries to begin editing the customer record for Amalgamated Industries, but because it is locked to Joe, she can't.
4. After Joe saves his changes, Mary can edit the record to make her changes.

With pessimistic record locking, users of the database can block each other from doing their work. In the previous example, Mary can't make changes until Joe is done, even though they don't want to change the same data. Optimistic record locking has the benefit that users don't tend to get in each other's way.

But there's a drawback to optimistic locking as well: it removes the chance that one user might block another user from working with data, but it increases the chance of losing data. If two users edit the same record, the last one to decide to save changes wins.

> **TIP**
>
> In most cases, choose optimistic locking. That's because in any reasonably large database, users are unlikely to be trying to alter the same data at exactly the same time.

Optimistic Locking in ADO

Optimistic locking is the default locking type for ADO Recordset objects. Here's some code that you can use to test optimistic locking behavior:

```
Public Sub TestOptLock()
  ' Test optimistic locking
  Dim rstOpt As ADODB.Recordset
  Set rstOpt = New ADODB.Recordset

  ' Open a recordset with optimistic locking
  rstOpt.Open "Clients", CurrentProject.Connection, _
   adOpenKeyset, adLockOptimistic, adCmdTable

  ' Pause the code to allow experimentation
  Stop

  ' Make a change and save it
  rstOpt.Fields("State").Value = "Nevada"
  ' The lock is only for the duration of this call
  rstOpt.Update

  rstOpt.Close

End Sub
```

Notice the Stop statement in the middle of this procedure. That statement tells VBA to stop at that point, just as if you had set a breakpoint in your code. This enables you to see just how optimistic record locking works, even without firing up two copies of the application. Follow these steps to investigate:

1. Open Chapter 19's sample module in TimeTrack.mdb (or TimeTrack19.mdb) and run the TestOptLock procedure from the Immediate window. It stops with the cursor at the Stop statement.

2. Now return to the Access user interface and open the Clients table's datasheet directly from the database container.

3. Change the state of the first record in the table to any value you like—for example, "Oregon," but don't save the change or leave the row.

4. Return to the module and press F5 to continue. Access will finish running the code and save the change to the record. At this point, the stored value in the State field is "Nevada." The code can obtain and release the lock it needs, because the user interface practices optimistic locking.

5. Return to the user interface and attempt to save the record. You'll see the error message shown in Figure 19.1.

19

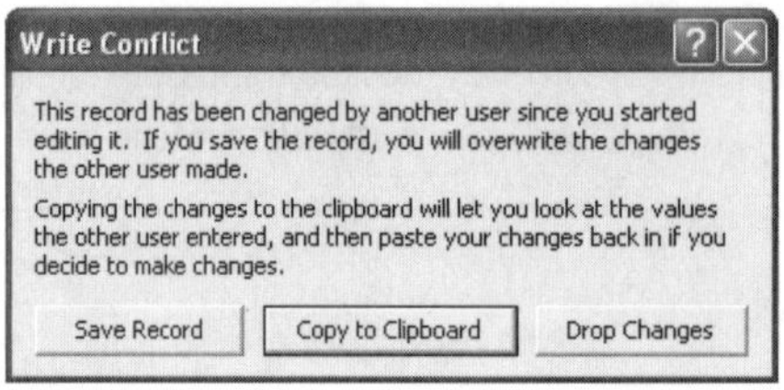

Figure 19.1

Optimistic locking write conflict message.

When you see this error message, you have three choices:

- Save your changes, thus overwriting the changes made by the other user.
- Copy your changes to the Clipboard. Doing so automatically refreshes your view of the data to show the changes made by the other user. If you don't like the user's changes, you can paste yours back in.
- Discard your changes.

Now that you know what a write conflict looks like from the user interface, you can use the TestOptLock2 procedure to investigate it from the code side:

```
Public Sub TestOptLock2()
    ' Test optimistic locking
    Dim rstOpt As ADODB.Recordset
    Set rstOpt = New ADODB.Recordset

    ' Open a recordset with optimistic locking
    rstOpt.Open "Clients", CurrentProject.Connection, _
     adOpenKeyset, adLockOptimistic, adCmdTable

    ' Make a change and save it
    rstOpt.Fields("State").Value = "Nevada"
    ' Pause the code to allow experimentation
    Stop

    ' The lock is only for the duration of this call
    rstOpt.Update

    rstOpt.Close

End Sub
```

The difference between TestOptLock2 and the previous procedure is that now the Stop statement has been moved after the statement that does the edit. You can test the effect of this change by following this procedure:

1. Restore the first record of the Clients table to its original state.

2. Run the TestOptLock2 procedure from the Immediate window. It stops with the cursor at the Stop statement.

3. Now return to the Access user interface and open the Clients table's datasheet directly from the database container.

4. Change the state of the first record in the table to any value you like—for example, "Oregon." Leave the row to save the change. The user interface locks the record just long enough to save the change.

5. Return to the module and press F5 to continue. Access will attempt to finish running the code. But instead of the procedure completing, you'll receive the error message shown in Figure 19.2.

Figure 19.2
Optimistic locking write conflict error in code.

```
Microsoft Visual Basic

Run-time error '-2147217887 (80040e21)':

The Microsoft Jet database engine stopped the process because you
and another user are attempting to change the same data at the same
time.

     Continue        End          Debug          Help
```

Of course, if you add error-handling code to your application, you can trap the error caused by the write conflict. In that case, you can decide what to do about the error in your code, without displaying any errors to the users.

If you inspect the two procedures you've seen so far, you can see how Access detects write conflicts. When you first edit a record, Access saves a copy of the data as it is at that moment. When you try to save the record, Access looks at the data on the hard drive before performing the save. If the data on the hard drive doesn't match the saved copy, someone else must have changed the record, so Access raises a write conflict error.

Pessimistic Locking in ADO

The code to test pessimistic record locking is slightly more complex:

```
Public Sub TestPessLock()
  ' Test pessimistic locking
  Dim cnn As ADODB.Connection
  Dim rstOpt As ADODB.Recordset

  ' Get a new connection to the current project
  Set cnn = New ADODB.Connection
  cnn.Open CurrentProject.BaseConnectionString

  Set rstOpt = New ADODB.Recordset

  ' Open a recordset with pessimistic locking
  rstOpt.Open "Clients", cnn, _
   adOpenKeyset, adLockPessimistic, adCmdTable

  ' Make a change and save it
  ' The lock is taken when the next statement is executed
  rstOpt.Fields("State").Value = "Nevada"
  ' Pause the code to allow experimentation
  Stop
```

19

```
        rstOpt.Update

        rstOpt.Close

    End Sub
```

CAUTION

You'll see that this code opens a new connection to the current project, rather than piggybacking on `CurrentProject.Connection`. That's because you *can't* open a Recordset with pessimistic locking on the current connection. If you try, you don't get an error, but instead Access silently changes the locking type to optimistic.

To see how this code interacts with another attempt to edit data, try this exercise:

1. Restore the first record of the Clients table to its original state.

2. Run the `TestPessLock` procedure from the Immediate window. It stops with the cursor at the `Stop` statement. At this point, the procedure already has the first record locked. With pessimistic locking, the first edit locks the record.

3. Now return to the Access user interface and open the Clients table's datasheet directly from the database container.

4. Change the state of the first record in the table to any value you like—for example, "Oregon." Attempt to leave the row to save the change. You'll receive the error message shown in Figure 19.3. Click OK to dismiss the message. The cursor will still be in the edited record.

5. Return to the module and press F5 to continue. Access will save the change from the code.

6. Return to the user interface and attempt to save the record again. You'll get a write conflict dialog box, because the change from the code was already saved.

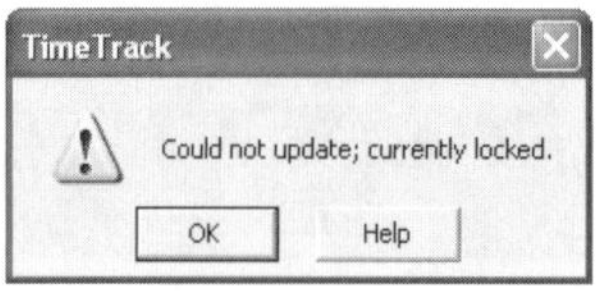

Figure 19.3
Pessimistic locking message.

Access apparently enabled you to edit the locked record. But as you saw in step 4, it doesn't enable you to save the record. When you're editing in Access, you're really editing a local copy of the data until you try to save it. That's the point at which Access checks for write conflicts.

➔ There are two other locking constants you can use besides the ones for optimistic and pessimistic locking. You can find a brief discussion of these constants in "Creating and Opening a Recordset," p. 245.

Retrieving a User Recordset

So far, most of the Recordset objects that you've worked with have contained data from your database. But there's another type of Recordset: the *schema recordset*. A schema recordset is one that contains information on the schema (design) of the database, or some other information maintained by the database engine.

To open a schema recordset, you use the OpenSchema method of the Connection object. This method takes three arguments:

- QueryType—A constant indicating the type of information to retrieve.

- Criteria—An optional filter to tell ADO to return less than a full schema recordset.

- SchemaID—If the QueryType argument is adSchemaProviderSpecific, this argument is required and specifies exactly which schema recordset to return.

Some further explanation might make the use of the SchemaID argument more obvious. The designers of ADO defined a number of standard schema recordsets that they expect most databases to be able to handle (for example, a list of all tables in the database). But the ADO designers couldn't anticipate every schema recordset that an individual database might like to supply. So they supplied adSchemaProviderSpecific as a sort of wildcard. If you call for this schema type, the actual type is determined by the value that you provide for the SchemaID argument; this value is typically a Globally Unique Identifier, or GUID.

You actually saw the use of the SchemaID argument in Chapter 16's case study. In that case study, you constructed the CurrentUsers form. This form uses a schema recordset to retrieve the names of all the users who have the database currently open:

```
Public Const JET_SCHEMA_USERROSTER = _
 "{947bb102-5d43-11d1-bdbf-00c04fb92675}"

Public Function ReturnUsers() As String
  Dim cnn As ADODB.Connection
  Dim rst As ADODB.Recordset
  Set cnn = New ADODB.Connection
  On Error GoTo HandleErr
  'Open connection to database
  Set cnn = CurrentProject.Connection
  'Open schema recordset to grab user metadata
  Set rst = cnn.OpenSchema(adSchemaProviderSpecific, , _
   JET_SCHEMA_USERROSTER)
  'return current users
  rst.MoveFirst
  Do Until rst.EOF
    ReturnUsers = rst(0) & ";" & ReturnUsers
    rst.MoveNext
  Loop

ExitHere:
  rst.Close
  Set rst = Nothing
  cnn.Close
  Set cnn = Nothing
  Exit Function
```

19

```
HandleErr:
  MsgBox "Error " & Err.Number & ": " & _
    Err.Description
  Resume ExitHere
End Function
```

As you can see, the code needs to define the JET_SCHEMA_USERROSTER constant itself; this constant is not built into ADO.

Using Other Schema Recordsets

The Jet database engine can actually supply quite a few schema recordsets other than the user roster. Table 19.1 lists the standard ADO schema recordsets that the Jet engine supports.

Table 19.1   Standard Schema Recordsets Supported by Access

Constant	Description
adSchemaCheckConstraints	A recordset of validation rules in the database.
adSchemaColumns	A recordset of fields in the database.
adSchemaConstraintColumnUsage	A recordset that shows which columns are affected by which constraints.
adSchemaForeignKeys	A recordset of foreign keys in the database.
adSchemaIndexes	A recordset of indexes in the database.
adSchemaKeyColumnUsage	A recordset that shows which columns are included in which keys.
adSchemaPrimaryKeys	A recordset that shows all the primary keys in the database.
adSchemaProcedures	A recordset of queries that have parameters.
adSchemaProviderTypes	A recordset that lists the data types that Jet supports.
adSchemaReferentialConstraints	A recordset of referential integrity constraints.
adSchemaStatistics	A recordset of database statistics.
adSchemaTableConstraints	A recordset of table-level validation rules.
adSchemaTables	A recordset of tables in the database.
adSchemaTrustees	A recordset of users and groups defined in the database.
adSchemaViews	A recordset of queries that do not have parameters.

In addition to the standard schema recordsets, the Jet engine used by Access defines four provider-specific recordsets, each of which is identified by a GUID:

- {8703b612-5d43-11d1-bdbf-00c04fb92675}—Performance statistics recordset
- {947bb102-5d43-11d1-bdbf-00c04fb92675}—User roster recordset

- {e2082df0-54ac-11d1-bdbb-00c04fb92675}—Recordset of partial filters in replicas

- {e2082df2-54ac-11d1-bdbb-00c04fb92675}—List of conflict tables in replicas

As an example of using a schema recordset, here's a procedure that returns some information on the tables in the current database:

```
Public Sub ListTables()
  Dim cnn As ADODB.Connection
  Dim rst As ADODB.Recordset
  Dim fld As ADODB.Field
  Dim i As Integer

  Set cnn = New ADODB.Connection
  On Error GoTo HandleErr

  'Open connection to database
  Set cnn = CurrentProject.Connection
  'Open schema recordset to grab table metadata
  Set rst = cnn.OpenSchema(adSchemaTables)

  ' Now walk through the entire returned recordset
  Do Until rst.EOF
    ' Go through each field in the row
    For i = 0 To rst.Fields.Count - 1
      ' And print the name of the field and its value
      Debug.Print rst.Fields(i).Name & ": " & rst(i)
    Next i
    ' Print a blank line after the row
    Debug.Print
    rst.MoveNext
  Loop

ExitHere:
  rst.Close
  Set rst = Nothing
  cnn.Close
  Set cnn = Nothing
  Exit Sub
HandleErr:
  MsgBox "Error " & Err.Number & ": " & _
    Err.Description
  Resume ExitHere
End Sub
```

If you run this procedure in the sample database, you get back a list of data on each table. For example, here's the data that is returned for the Clients table:

```
TABLE_CATALOG:
TABLE_SCHEMA:
TABLE_NAME: Clients
TABLE_TYPE: TABLE
TABLE_GUID:
DESCRIPTION:
TABLE_PROPID:
DATE_CREATED: 3/13/2004 11:30:57 AM
DATE_MODIFIED: 5/15/2004 5:49:53 PM
```

19

> **NOTE**
>
> The reason that many of the fields are blank is because the schema recordsets are general-purpose, and any given field might not apply to a specific database. For a definition of the fields in each schema recordset, refer to Appendix B of the OLE DB Programmer's Reference, which you can find online at `http://msdn.microsoft.com/library/en-us/oledb/htm/ oledbschema_rowsets.asp`.

CASE STUDY

Using the Form Error Event to Resolve Locking Errors

You saw earlier in this chapter that you can use error handling to trap record-locking errors when working with data in a recordset. But in many applications (including the TimeTrack sample database), users interact with forms rather than with recordsets. What then?

You have two choices for handling locking errors in forms. The first is to allow Access to handle things with its own default messages. If you elect this course of action, the messages shown in Figures 19.1 and 19.3 are presented to users when record-locking problems come up in a multiuser setting.

The alternative is to use the form's `Error` event. This event is raised whenever a data error happens in a form. For this case study, we've added some simple code to the Clients form to handle record-locking errors. Here's the code:

```
Private Sub Form_Error(DataErr As Integer, _
 Response As Integer)
  ' Handle multi-user errors
  On Error GoTo HandleErr

  ' Handle error based on error number
  ' passed in by Access
  Select Case DataErr
    Case 7787 ' Write conflict
      MsgBox "Another user has changed this record. " & _
        "Click OK to see their changes.", vbCritical
      Response = acDataErrContinue
    Case 7878 ' Data Changed
      MsgBox "Another user has changed this record. " & _
        "Click OK to see their changes.", vbCritical
      Response = acDataErrContinue
    Case Else
      ' Let Access handle the error
      Response = acDataErrDisplay
  End Select

ExitHere:
  Exit Sub

HandleErr:
  MsgBox "Error while handling errors", vbCritical
  Resume ExitHere
End Sub
```

When you're working with the form's `Error` event, there are two arguments to deal with. The first, `DataErr`, is passed in by Access and includes the error number of the error that triggered the event. The second, `Response`, enables you to tell Access whether you've handled the error. You can pass back `acDataErrContinue` to tell Access that you've taken care of things, or `acDataErrDisplay` to tell Access to take its own default action (displaying the error).

In this particular case, you're trapping both varieties of locking error, warning the users that their data will get overwritten, and proceeding. Access automatically refreshes the form with the current data from the underlying database after this code runs. If any other data error (such as a validation error) occurs, this procedure just lets Access take its own default action. Finally, if an error occurs in the process of trying to handle some other error, the error handler displays a default message and bails out. This prevents the code from getting stuck in an infinite loop if something should go badly wrong.

Using Advanced VBA Techniques in Access

IN THIS PART

20 Working with Data Files 301

21 Automating Other Applications 313

22 Working with XML Files 325

23 Using the Windows API 337

IV

Working with Data Files

Understanding File I/O

The term *file I/O* refers to file input and output functions, which is one way to manipulate the contents of a file. Although you might never use I/O functions, you might run into them in legacy applications that you must support.

The VBA I/O process is simple:

IN THIS CHAPTER

Understanding File I/O 301

Opening Files 302

Reading from Files 304

Writing to Files 307

Printing to Files 309

- Use the VBA Open function to open a file.
- Use the VBA Input function to retrieve a file's contents.
- Use the VBA Write function to write to a file.
- Use the VBA Print function to write a series of values to an open file.

Before you can use I/O to manipulate a file's contents, you need to know the file's handle. Within this context, a *file handle* is simply a number that uniquely identifies the open files to the operating system.

To open an I/O file, you need an unused file handle. Acquire this value using the FreeFile function in the form

```
hFile = FreeFile
```

where *hFile* is a Long Integer variable.

> **CAUTION**
>
> Chapter 23 is an introduction to using Windows API functions, which also uses file handles. You can't use the result of the VBA `FreeFile` function when working with an API.

Opening Files

The whole process begins with opening a file using the VBA `Open` function in the form

`Open pathname For mode[Access access][lock] As [#]filenumber[Len=recordlength]`

Table 20.1 lists this function's many arguments.

Table 20.1   Open Arguments

Argument	Explanation
pathname	The complete path to the file you want to open.
mode	One of the following: Append, Binary, Input, Output, or Random (the default).
access	One of the following: Read (the default), Write, or Read Write.
lock	One of the following: Shared (the default), Lock Read, Lock Write, or Lock Read Write.
filenumber	Variable that contains the results of a call to the FreeFile function. Use this value to identify the file.
recordlength	When using Random mode, it's the length of the record; when using Append or Output mode, it's the number of bytes buffered.

About mode

The *mode* argument determines how Windows handles the open file and what you can do to it. For the most part, you'll want to perform one of the following actions:

- To review data without editing it or adding to it, use Input mode. Files open in Input mode have read-only access.
- To add or edit values, use Append mode if you want to work with the existing file by adding values to the end of the file.
- To add or edit values, use Output mode when you want to delete the existing file and create a new one with the same name.
- To add or edit values byte by byte, open the file in Binary mode. (You'll mainly use this mode to work with image files.)
- To add or edit values to a file that depends on a fixed record length, open the file in Random mode, using the *recordlength* argument to specify the record's size.

20

About *access*

This argument has three self-explanatory options: Read, Write, and Read Write. Keep in mind that regardless of the option you try to pass, you must have appropriate permission through your system's security settings. For instance, if you try to access a file with Write-level permissions, but Windows security allows you read-only permissions on that file, your request will return an error. For that reason, you'll want to include plenty of error-handling routines in your I/O code.

About *locking*

In a single-user application, locking isn't an issue. In contrast, when working in a multiuser application, the default locking setting is Shared. That means other users can read and write to the file while it's open by someone else. The locking settings with a brief explanation follow:

- Shared—Users with the proper permissions can retrieve values or add values to the file, regardless of who has the file open.

- Lock Read—Users with the proper permissions can write to the file, but they can't retrieve values from a file open by someone else.

- Lock Write—Users with the proper permissions can retrieve values, but they can't write values to a file open by someone else.

- Lock Read Write—Users can't retrieve or write to a file open by someone else.

A Simple Open Example

The following sub procedure accepts a string argument that identifies the path to the file you want to open:

```
Sub OpenFile(fil As String)
  'Open a file using I/O.
  Dim hFile As Long
  hFile = FreeFile
  Open fil For Input Access Read Shared As hFile
  MsgBox fil & " = " & hFile
  Close hFile
End Sub
```

In truth, this procedure really doesn't do anything other than open the file passed to the procedure via the fil argument. The file is opened with Read access using the Shared locking setting. That means you can retrieve data but not write to the file. In addition, any user can read and write to the file while you have it open (with the appropriate permissions of course).

You can test this procedure in TimeTrack.mdb and use Chapter 20's example module or enter the previous procedure into a standard module. In the Immediate window, run the following statement with the appropriate updates to accommodate your system:

```
OpenFile "path\TimeTrack20.mdb"
```

20

Be sure to update *path* accordingly to reflect the location of TimeTrack20.mdb on your own hard drive. After opening TimeTrack.mdb (or TimeTrack20.mdb, depending on the example setup you're using), the procedure displays a message box similar to that shown in Figure 20.1. The message box displays the file you opened with the allocated file handle number. Click OK to clear the message.

Figure 20.1
Now you know the file handle for the opened file.

> **Microsoft Office Access** ⊠
>
> C:\A\AutomatingVBA\Chapter20\TimeTrack20.mdb = 1
>
> OK

> ⎡ **CAUTION** ⎤
>
> When you're done with a file, always close it using the VBA Close statement. Otherwise, you might
> lose data or lock out other users.

Although this is an easy way to discern a file's file handle, it isn't particularly productive or efficient. In a working situation, refer to the hFile variable—you don't need to know the actual number yourself.

> **TIP**
>
> When working with more than one file in an I/O arrangement, open a file using the value returned
> by FreeFile before calling FreeFile again. FreeFile continues to return the same value
> until you actually open a file. Without the proper sequence of events, you can inadvertently assign
> the same value to all the open files, which doesn't work of course.

Reading from Files

The I/O term *read* really means to retrieve. When opening the file in Input, Output or Append mode, use the following read statements:

- Input
- Line Input #
- Input #

Using Input

The easiest way to retrieve data is with the Input function using the form

```
Input(number, [#]filenumber)
```

where *number* specifies the number of characters to return and *filenumber* is any valid file handle. Input returns all the characters it reads, including carriage returns, linefeeds, and spaces.

Let's look at a simple procedure that uses Input to retrieve data from an exported table. To do so, you need to export the table first. Choose <u>F</u>ile, <u>E</u>xport and export the Employees table as a text file (don't change any of the other default settings during the export). Then, enter the following procedure in a standard module (or use Chapter 20's example module):

```
Sub ReadInput(fil As String)
  'Print data from passed file
  'in Immediate window.
  Dim hFile As Long
  hFile = FreeFile
  Open fil For Input Access Read Shared As hFile
  Debug.Print Input(LOF(hFile), hFile)
  Close hFile
End Sub
```

Run the following statement in the Immediate window to retrieve the file's entire contents, as shown in Figure 20.2:

```
ReadInput "path\employees.txt"
```

Remember to update the actual path to the file accordingly. The LOF(hFile) component in the Input function specifies the file's length, and as a result, the function grabs the file's entire content.

Figure 20.2
Use Input to quickly grab an entire file's content.

> **NOTE**
> The exported file, employees.txt, contains line breaks. The Export wizard inserted them when you exported the data and that's why the printed values in the Immediate window are so neatly arranged—one employee, one line. If the file contains no line breaks, Input retrieves the file's contents as one long line, breaking only where forced to by the conventions of the container.

About EOF and LOF

The previous procedure introduced the LOF function. Anytime you actually need to do anything with a file's content, you'll probably use LOF or EOF.

The EOF function determines whether you've reached the end of the file. For the technically minded, the EOF function returns a Boolean value that indicates whether the current byte position is at the end of the file. What all this means is that EOF returns True if you've reached the end of the file and False if you haven't.

The *current byte position* refers to the current pointer in the file, for lack of a better definition. VBA sets this value to 0 when you first open a file—positioning to the very first byte in the file. You might think of this value as representing the spot just before the first value in the first line. For the most part, a byte refers to one character, including spaces.

LOF returns the size of the open file, in bytes. In the previous example, LOF determines the amount of content retrieved by the Input function.

Using Line Input

Like Input, the Line Input # statement reads data from an opened file, but Line Input # grabs the data one line at a time. This statement uses the form

```
Line Input #filenumber, varname
```

where *filenumber* is the file handle and *varname* is the variable to which the statement saves the retrieved data.

The following procedure retrieves the file's entire contents just as the previous Input procedure did:

```
Sub ReadLineInput(fil As String)
  'Print data from passed file
  'in Immediate window.
  Dim hFile As Long
  Dim strLine As String
  hFile = FreeFile
  Open fil For Input Access Read Shared As hFile
  Do Until EOF(hFile)
    Line Input #hFile, strLine
    Debug.Print strLine
  Loop
  Close hFile
End Sub
```

In the Immediate window, run the following statement:

```
ReadLineInput "path\employees.txt"
```

(Be sure to update *path* accordingly.) Instead of retrieving the file's contents as a whole as the Input example did, the Do Until loop retrieves the data line by line. If you remove the Do Until loop, the Debug.Print statement prints only the file's first line.

Using Input

Input # is similar to Line Input #, but it's a little more flexible. This statement retrieves data and assigns the data to variables using the form

```
Input #filenumber, varlist
```

where *varlist* is a list of variables separated by commas. Input # saves each data element in the file to a separate variable. In addition, it deletes the quotation marks that surround text values and converts date strings to VBA dates.

The following procedure returns the same data, but in three separate variables—strID, strFN, and strLN—which the Debug.Print statement then concatenates:

```
Sub ReadInputPoundSign(fil As String)
    'print data from passed file
    'in Immediate window
    Dim hFile As Long
    Dim strID As String
    Dim strFN As String
    Dim strLN As String
    hFile = FreeFile
    Open fil For Input Access Read Shared As hFile
    Do Until EOF(hFile)
        Input #hFile, strID, strFN, strLN
        Debug.Print strID & vbTab & strFN & " " & strLN
    Loop
    Close hFile
End Sub
```

Run the following statement in the Immediate window:

```
ReadInputPoundSign "path\employees.txt"
```

(Don't forget to update *path*.) The data is the same as the previous procedure's data, but is formatted slightly different as shown in Figure 20.3.

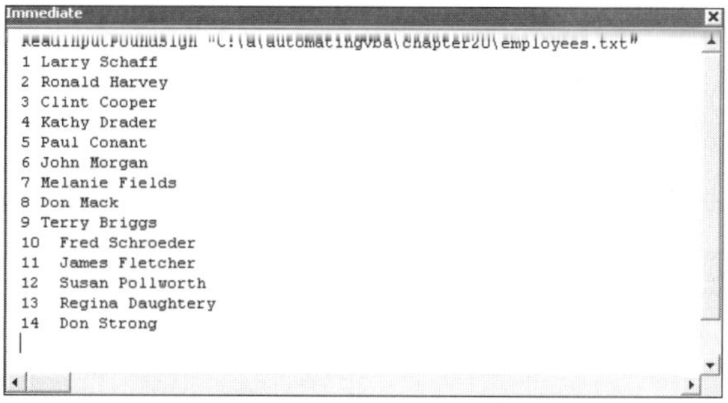

Figure 20.3
You can control the returned data by data elements using Input #.

```
Immediate                                                      [x]
ReadInputPoundSign "C:\a\automatingVBA\chapter20\employees.txt"
1 Larry Schaff
2 Ronald Harvey
3 Clint Cooper
4 Kathy Drader
5 Paul Conant
6 John Morgan
7 Melanie Fields
8 Don Mack
9 Terry Briggs
10   Fred Schroeder
11   James Fletcher
12   Susan Pollworth
13   Regina Daughtery
14   Don Strong
```

Writing to Files

Writing to a file is the process of adding values to that file. When opening the file in Input, Output, or Append mode, use the Print # or Write # statement. For Random and Binary mode, use the Put statement to write to the file.

The Write # statement takes the form

```
Write #filenumber[, outputlist]
```

where *outputlist* is one or more comma-delimited variables or literal values you want to add to the file. Separate these values with a comma, space, or semicolon. If you omit *outputlist* and include a comma character after *filenumber*, the statement adds a blank line to the file.

There are a number of behaviors that might cause you trouble if you don't know about them:

■ All numeric data is written with the period decimal separator.

■ Boolean values are written as #TRUE# or #FALSE#.

■ Dates are written using the universal date format.

■ If *outputlist* is empty, nothing is written to the file.

■ If *outputlist* is Null, the value #NULL# is written.

■ Error values are written as #ERROR errorcode#.

The following procedure enables you to add a new line before retrieving the file's entire contents:

```
Sub InputAndWrite(fil As String, _
 id As Long, fn As String, ln As String)
   'Write to fil and then print data
   'in Immediate window.
   Dim hFile As Long
   Dim strID As String
   Dim strFN As String
   Dim strLN As String
   hFile = FreeFile
   Open fil For Append Access Write As hFile
   Write #hFile, id, fn, ln
   Close hFile
   hFile = FreeFile
   Open fil For Input Access Read Shared As hFile
   Do Until EOF(hFile)
      Input #hFile, strID, strFN, strLN
      Debug.Print strID & vbTab & strFN & " " & strLN
   Loop
   Close hFile
End Sub
```

Run the following statement in the Immediate window to add employee 15, Susan Harkins, to the employees.txt file:

```
InputAndWrite "path\employees.txt", 15, "Susan", "Harkins"
```

The results in Figure 20.4 show the newly added line for employee 15. The Write # statement uses the passed arguments—id, fn, and ln—which supply the new data. Notice that the Open statement is a little different for writing. Specifically, this example uses the Append mode and the Write access setting. To create a new file (that will overwrite an existing file) with the passed data values, use Output mode instead of Append.

Figure 20.4
Use I/O to add new data.

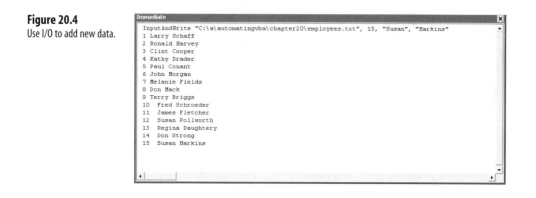

```
Immediate
InputAndWrite "C:\a\automatingvba\chapter20\employees.txt", 15, "Susan", "Harkins"
1 Larry Schaff
2 Ronald Harvey
3 Clint Cooper
4 Kathy Drader
5 Paul Conant
6 John Morgan
7 Melanie Fields
8 Don Mack
9 Terry Briggs
10  Fred Schroeder
11  James Fletcher
12  Susan Pollworth
13  Regina Daughtery
14  Don Strong
15  Susan Harkins
```

Printing to Files

Using the `Print #` statement, you can print data to a file using the following form:

```
Print #filenumber[, outputlist]
```

The information for this statement is basically the same as for `Write #`. The only difference is that `Write #` sends the data to the named file and `Print #` creates a new print file.

To insert a space in *outputlist*, use the `Spc(n)` setting where *n* is the number of spaces to insert. Likewise, to insert a tab, use the `Tab(n)` setting, where *n* represents the absolute value of the column.

The following procedure gleans the entire contents of a file and then creates a new print file:

```
Sub PrintPoundSign(filSource As String, filPrint As String)
  'Print data from passed file
  'in Immediate window.
  Dim hFileSource As Long
  Dim hFilePrint As Long
  Dim strLine As String
  hFileSource = FreeFile
  Open filSource For Input Access Read Shared As hFileSource
  hFilePrint = FreeFile
  Open filPrint For Output Access Write As hFilePrint
  Do Until EOF(hFileSource)
    Line Input #hFileSource, strLine
    Print #hFilePrint, strLine
  Loop
  Close hFileSource
  Close hFilePrint
End Sub
```

To run the procedure, enter the following statement in the Immediate window:

```
PrintPoundSign "path\employees.txt", "PrintFile"
```

Using Word or a text editor, locate the new file named `PrintFile` (which should be in Access's default directory). The contents are the same as the `employees.txt` file, as shown in Figure 20.5.

20

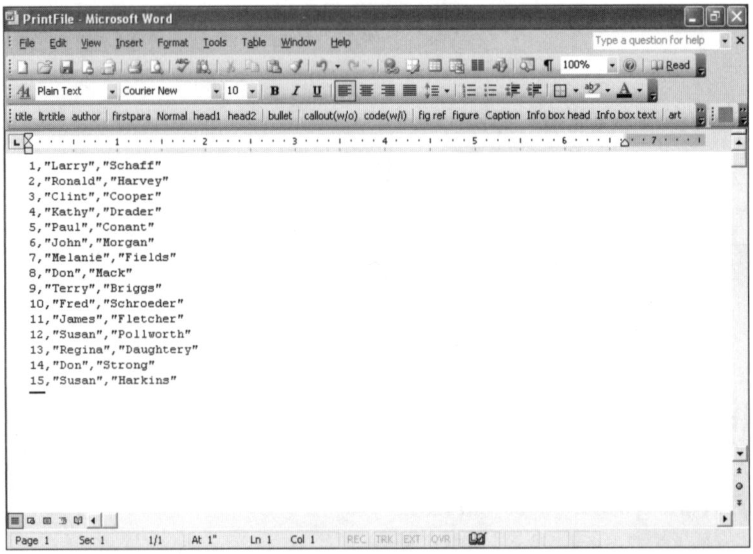

Figure 20.5
The contents of the print file are similar to what you've seen in the Immediate window.

```
1,"Larry","Schaff"
2,"Ronald","Harvey"
3,"Clint","Cooper"
4,"Kathy","Drader"
5,"Paul","Conant"
6,"John","Morgan"
7,"Melanie","Fields"
8,"Don","Mack"
9,"Terry","Briggs"
10,"Fred","Schroeder"
11,"James","Fletcher"
12,"Susan","Pollworth"
13,"Regina","Daughtery"
14,"Don","Strong"
15,"Susan","Harkins"
```

CASE STUDY

Using I/O to Number Lines in a Text File

Your users want to export client information to a text file for sharing, but they also want to add a line number to each line of data in the text file. Users can open the newly created text file and do it manually, but let's automate the process using I/O functions.

First, open the Switchboard form and add a new command button. Name that button `cmdExport` and enter the Caption setting "Export Client Text File." Then, add the following `Click` event procedure to the form's module:

```
Private Sub cmdExport_Click()
  'Export Clients table to
  'delimited text file.
  On Error GoTo HandleErr
  DoCmd.TransferText acExportDelim, , _
    "Clients", "Clients.txt"
  Call NumberClientList
  Exit Sub

HandleErr:
  MsgBox "Error " & Err.Number & ": " & _
    Err.Description
End Sub
```

This procedure is simple in task. It exports the entire Clients table to a file named `Clients.txt`, saving the file in the current directory. You might want to include the entire path in the file's name.

To create the `NumberClientList` function that's called by the `Click` event procedure, open a standard module (or use Chapter 20's example module) and enter the following procedure:

```
Public Sub NumberClientList()
  'Add line numbers to
  'client list in text file.
  Dim hFileSource As Long
  Dim hFilePrint As Long
  Dim strInput As String
  Dim i As Integer
  On Error GoTo HandleErr
  hFileSource = FreeFile
  Open "Clients.txt" For Input Access Read As hFileSource
  hFilePrint = FreeFile
  Open "ClientsPrint.txt" For Output Access Write As hFilePrint
  Do Until EOF(hFileSource)
    i = i + 1
    Line Input #hFileSource, strInput
    Print #hFilePrint, i, strInput
  Loop
  Exit Sub

ExitHere:
  Close hFileSource
  Close hFilePrint
  Exit Sub
HandleErr:
  MsgBox "Error " & Err.Number & ": " & _
   Err.Description
  Resume ExitHere
End Sub
```

Save the module and close it. Open the modified Switchboard form shown in Figure 20.6 and click the new command button. After exporting the Clients table to a new text file, the procedure calls the `NumberClientList` function. This procedure opens the new `Clients.txt` file. The `Do Until` loop does the following:

- Uses the `Line Input` function to cycle through each line in the file.
- Evaluates the expression `i = i + 1` to create the current loop's line number.
- Executes the `Line Input` function to retrieve the data and then to write the line number (i) and the retrieved data to the new print file.

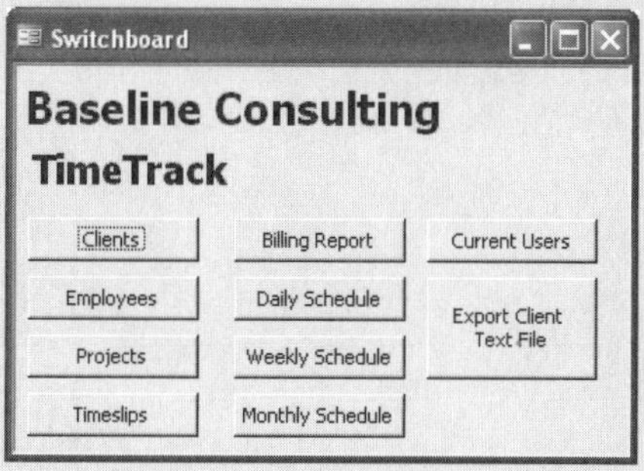

Figure 20.6
Click the Export Client Text File command button to create a text file.

Figure 20.7 shows the new text file with each line numbered. In this case, it's just coincidence that the line numbers equal the client identification values.

Figure 20.7
We used I/O functions to add a line number to each line.

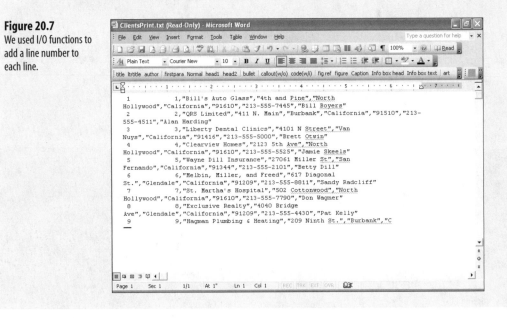

Automating Other Applications

Understanding Automation

The techniques you've used so far in this book have been anchored firmly in the capabilities of Microsoft Access itself. But as you undoubtedly know, Access is part of the Microsoft Office suite, a group of products designed to be used together. That's where *automation* comes in. By writing automation code, you can use one application (such as Access) to control another application (such as Word, PowerPoint, or Excel). This capability isn't limited just to Microsoft Office applications. There are hundreds of other applications, from AutoCAD to XMLSpy, that can be controlled by automation.

Automation code always involves two applications: a client and a server. The client is the application where the VBA code is running; in this case, it's always Access. The server is the application that supplies functionality to the automation code. The client creates one or more objects from the server, and then uses the methods and properties of those objects to do something useful.

For example, an Access application can use automation, with Microsoft Word as the server application, to create a new Word document. Having created the document (by making a new Word.Document object), the Access code can go on to set the document's properties, add and format text, and save it with a particular filename. The result is the creation of a Word .doc file without ever leaving Access.

Automation doesn't bring objects from one application into another. Rather, it lets one application control objects that are supplied by another application. This is an important distinction. If you're using Microsoft Word as an automation server, for example, the users must still have Word installed on their computers to run your code. But they don't have to open Word and manipulate it by hand. Your automation code can do that for them.

IN THIS CHAPTER

Understanding Automation 313

Setting Object References 314

Creating Objects in an Automation Server . . .315

Talking to Excel from Access 318

Talking to Word from Access 320

C A U T I O N _____

If there's any chance that users might try to run your automation code on a system that doesn't have the required server application installed, be sure to include error trapping to prevent the inevitable errors from terminating your application.

Setting Object References

Automation clients need a way to determine which objects they can use from any given automation server. This information is stored in files called *type libraries*, which normally have a .tlb or .olb extension. A type library contains information on:

- Objects
- Methods
- Properties
- Events

Although it's not absolutely necessary to use a type library to use objects from an automation server, it's normally a very good idea. For one thing, without using the type library, you don't get the benefits of IntelliSense or the Object Browser when writing automation code. So, we recommend that you always use a type library. To use a type library for automation, you need to set a reference to the type library. Here's how to do that for the Microsoft Word and Microsoft Excel type libraries that you use in this chapter:

1. Open the Visual Basic Editor by pressing Alt+F11 from Access.

2. Choose Tools, References to open the References dialog box, shown in Figure 21.1.

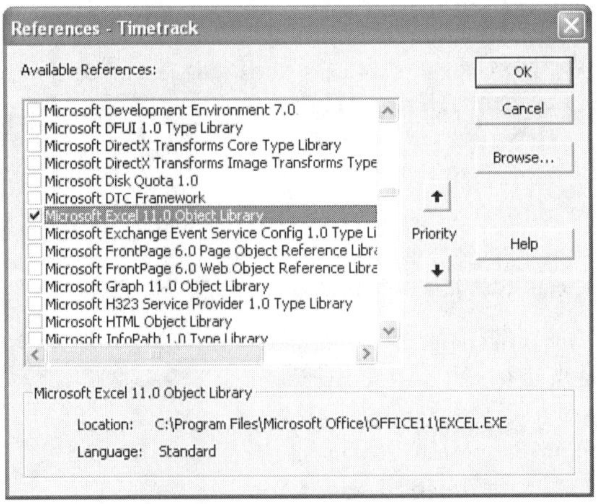

Figure 21.1
Adding a reference to a type library.

3. Locate the Microsoft Excel 11.0 Object Library and the Microsoft Word 11.0 Object Library in the list of available references, and click the checkbox for each of them.

4. Click OK to add references to these type libraries to the current Access database.

After you've added a reference to a type library, you'll find that type library's objects in the Object Browser. Press F2 to open the Object Browser, and then choose the type library you want to inspect from the Project/Library combo box. Figure 21.2 shows some of the objects in the Excel type library. You can see that these objects deal with such things as cells and charts, even though you're inspecting the type library from within an Access database.

Figure 21.2
Using Object Browser to inspect a type library.

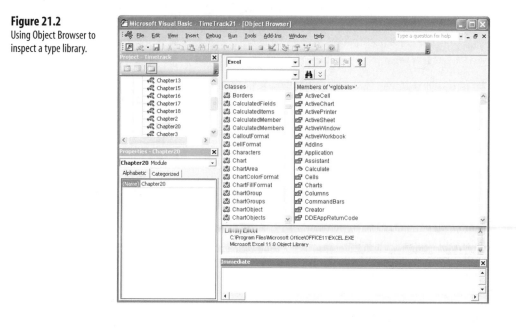

> **NOTE** There's nothing really different about using the Object Browser on Access itself; it's still looking at a type library. The only difference is that Access automatically sets a reference to its own type library.

Creating Objects in an Automation Server

To work with objects from other applications, you must first create those objects in your Access code. There are three ways to do this:

- Using the CreateObject function
- Using the GetObject function
- Using early binding

We show you each of these ways in turn.

21

Using CreateObject

The CreateObject function enables you to specify an object by its name, and creates an instance of that object. Here's a short example:

```
Sub CreateObjectDemo()
  ' Use Word as as automation server
  ' via CreateObject
  Dim objWord As Object
  Set objWord = CreateObject("Word.Application")
  objWord.Visible = True
  objWord.Quit
End Sub
```

As you can see, this code uses the special variable type Object to refer to the object that it creates. Object is a variable type that can refer to any object: a Word document, an Excel chart, an Access form, or anything else.

The CreateObject function turns this generic Object variable into a particular type of object. The argument to CreateObject is what's known as a ProgID: a value that signifies the type of object that you want to create. You can put together most ProgIDs that you need from the name of the application plus the name of the object within that application. So, Word.Application refers to the Application object supplied by Word (as distinct from, say, the built-in Application object provided by Access).

As soon as you run the line of code that calls CreateObject, the variable objWord now refers to an instance of the Word Application object. This object represents all of Microsoft Word (just as the Access Application object represents an entire Access session). But if you put a breakpoint in the code and execute this line, you won't find Word anywhere. That's because Word, like most automation servers, starts itself invisibly when it's launched from an automation call. The next line of code sets the Visible property of the Word application to True; that line causes the application to become visible on your screen.

Finally, the code calls the Quit method of the Word Application object. This is the equivalent of choosing Exit from the File menu within Word, and causes Word to vanish again.

Note that, apart from CreateObject itself, there's no new syntax here. After you have retrieved an automation object, you can use its methods and properties just like those of any other object within Access.

Using GetObject

The GetObject function is very close to the CreateObject function. Here's a sample that uses GetObject:

```
Sub GetObjectDemo()
  ' Use Word as as automation server
  ' via GetObject
  Dim objWord As Object
  Set objWord = GetObject("", "Word.Application")
  objWord.Visible = True
  objWord.Quit
End Sub
```

If you run this code, you'll find that it works the same as CreateObjectDemo. But there are two differences between CreateObject and GetObject:

- CreateObject always creates a new instance of the automation server. GetObject uses an existing instance if there's one running on your system.

- GetObject takes an optional first parameter specifying a document. If you call GetObject("c:\temp\doc1.doc", "Word.Application"), it will load the specified document into the Word application as well as create the Application object, if necessary.

GetObject is useful when you want to work with specific documents, or when you're concerned with minimizing the resource impact of your automation code on a low-memory system (because it won't launch extra copies of the server unnecessarily).

Using Early Binding

Both CreateObject and GetObject use what's known as *late binding*. With late binding, you don't specify in your code which object type to use; instead, you use the generic Object for your variables and let VBA figure it out. The third way to create objects, using early binding, enables you to use the native variable types from an automation server directly in your VBA code.

> **TIP**
> Late binding works with or without a reference to the type library for an automation server. Early binding requires a reference to the appropriate type library. Although VBA provides a way to add a reference (using the References collection), our experience has been that this is unreliable in practice.

Here's the sample code converted to use early binding:

```
Sub EarlyBindingDemo()
  ' Use Word as as automation server
  ' via early binding
  Dim objWord As Word.Application
  Set objWord = New Word.Application
  objWord.Visible = True
  objWord.Quit
End Sub
```

With early binding, you actually use the object's native type in your VBA code. This is made possible by having a reference set to the object's automation server. After you've done this, you can declare and instantiate the automation object using exactly the same code as you use with a native Access object.

We recommend using early binding for these reasons:

- You don't have to remember two different syntaxes for creating objects.

- You get the benefit of IntelliSense when you're writing code, which means you can catch errors before they affect your users.

- Early binding is faster than CreateObject or GetObject.

21

Talking to Excel from Access

As you can see, the syntax for automation coding is not difficult to learn. You just set the appropriate reference and then use objects from the automation server just like native Access objects. The real learning curve in automation comes in discovering what you can do with other applications. If you've installed a reasonable amount of software on your computer, you probably have dozens or even hundreds of automation servers available.

We can't possibly give you a comprehensive look at what all those applications can do via automation. Instead, we just show you a couple of examples, one using Microsoft Excel and the other using Microsoft Word.

> **TIP**
>
> The Microsoft Office applications make all their functions available to other programs via automation, so they're a good place to start.

For the first example, we show how to get the results of the WeeklyTimeslips query to Excel. This is a typical use of automation: moving data from one application to another so that it can be further analyzed. Excel makes it easy to get a total for a set of records while still viewing the detail, for example, which is difficult in Access.

To export the data to Excel, you can open the Chapter21 sample module and run the `QueryToExcel` procedure directly from the Immediate window. Here's the code:

```
Sub QueryToExcel()
    ' Send the Weekly Timeslips results to Excel
    ' for further analysis

    Dim rstWeeklyTimeslips As ADODB.Recordset
    Dim objXL As Excel.Application
    Dim objWS As Excel.Worksheet
    Dim fld As ADODB.Field
    Dim intCol As Integer
    Dim intRow As Integer

    Set rstWeeklyTimeslips = New ADODB.Recordset

    ' Get the desired data into a recordset
    rstWeeklyTimeslips.Open _
      "WeeklyTimeslips", CurrentProject.Connection

    ' Launch Excel
    Set objXL = New Excel.Application
    ' Create a new worksheet
    objXL.Workbooks.Add
    Set objWS = objXL.ActiveSheet

    ' Copy the data
```

```
' First the field names
For intCol = 0 To rstWeeklyTimeslips.Fields.Count - 1
  Set fld = rstWeeklyTimeslips.Fields(intCol)
  objWS.Cells(1, intCol + 1) = fld.Name
Next intCol
' Now the actual data
intRow = 2
Do Until rstWeeklyTimeslips.EOF
  For intCol = 0 To rstWeeklyTimeslips.Fields.Count - 1
    objWS.Cells(intRow, intCol + 1) = _
      rstWeeklyTimeslips.Fields(intCol).Value
  Next intCol
  rstWeeklyTimeslips.MoveNext
  intRow = intRow + 1
Loop

' Make the worksheet visible
objXL.Visible = True

' Don't call the Excel Quit method, so the
' worksheet will hang around after this
' procedure exits
End Sub
```

This procedure might look a bit complex, but the complexity is there only because it's manipulating both ADO and Excel objects simultaneously. After declaring variables, it begins to do its work by opening a Recordset on the WeeklyTimeslips query. We haven't bothered to specify a lock type or cursor type for the Recordset, so it opens as a forward-only, read-only Recordset. This is the fastest type and perfectly appropriate here, because all you want to do is read through the data one time.

The next step is to launch Excel and create a new worksheet where the data can go. When you launch Excel from the Start menu it automatically creates a default workbook with three worksheets for you, but that doesn't happen when you launch it by automation. Instead, you need to call the Add method of the Excel Workbooks collection to do so. After that, the ActiveSheet property of the Application object provides a handy reference to the default worksheet.

Copying the data involves two parts. First, the code loops through the Fields collection of the Recordset to set up column heads in Excel. After that, it moves through the Recordset itself to move the values in the data over. The Cells object, a child of the Excel Worksheet object, enables you to refer to individual cells on a worksheet by using the row and column numbers as indexes. Note that there's some adjustment necessary because the columns of a Recordset are numbered starting at zero, whereas those of a worksheet are numbered starting at one.

After creating the worksheet and moving the data over, the procedure makes it visible. It's faster to do this than to make it visible before writing, so the screen doesn't have to be updated constantly. The final step is simply to exit. Although this causes the objXL variable to go out of scope, it doesn't dispose of the automation server that it pointed to. Excel remains running, and displays the data as shown in Figure 21.3.

21

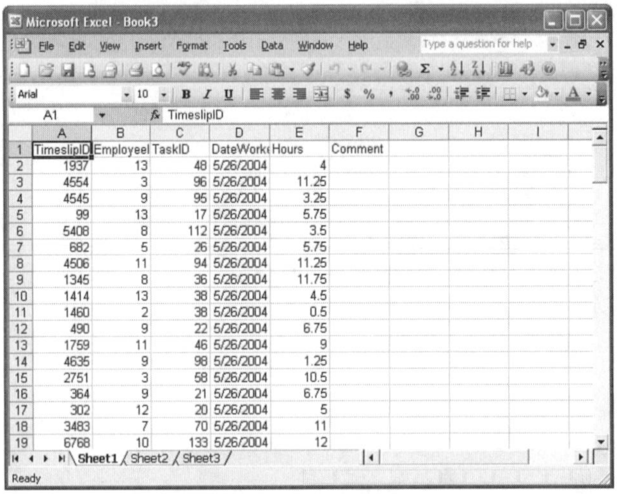

Figure 21.3
Access data exported to
Excel via automation.

Talking to Word from Access

Access offers many benefits, but it doesn't have a good way to create a report containing arbitrary text and formatting. With automation, it's easy to work around that limitation; Microsoft Word is perfect for creating whatever reports you might like, and it's an automation server. Figure 21.4 shows a simple Access form that enables you to enter any text you like and a filename. When you click the button, it creates a Word document containing the specified text and saves it to the filename that you supply.

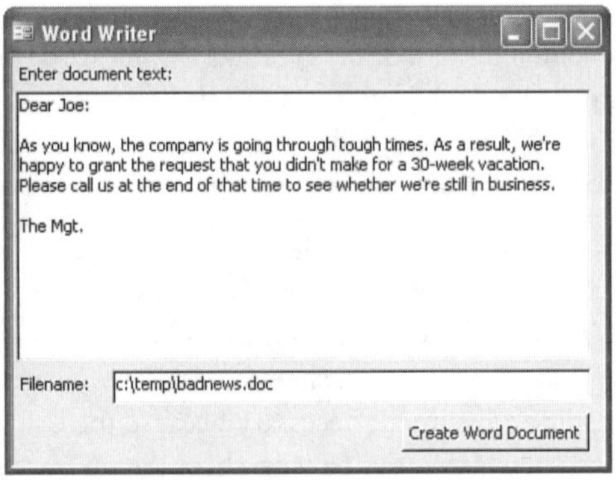

Figure 21.4
Access form to create a
Word document.

The code behind the button is once again straightforward:

```
Private Sub cmdCreate_Click()
    ' Copy the text to a Word document
    Dim objWord As Word.Application
```

```
' Instantiate Word and a new document
Set objWord = New Word.Application
objWord.Documents.Add

' Insert the text after the default range,
' which is the start of the document
objWord.ActiveDocument.Range.InsertAfter (txtText.Value)

' Save the file
objWord.ActiveDocument.SaveAs (txtFileName.Value)

' And show it
objWord.Visible = True
End Sub
```

The only trick here is knowing enough of Word's object model to make it do what you want. The key steps are creating a document and adding text to the document. To create a document, you call the Add method of the Documents collection. Adding text is a bit trickier. Word documents contain a Range object, which represents the range of text that's currently selected. The Range object has a variety of methods for adding text, including InsertAfter and InsertBefore. When you first create a document there's no text in it, so of course the Range object just points to the very start of the document. Inserting text after this point does the job that you want. Figure 21.5 shows the results.

Figure 21.5
Word document created from Access.

CASE STUDY

Using Excel Chart Features from Inside Access

To show how automation can be used to enhance an application, this case study adds a button to TimeTrack's switchboard form. This button opens Excel and creates a chart showing how the hours worked divides among the various employees of the company. The code, of course, uses automation to Excel:

```
Sub ChartInExcel()
  ' Send the Weekly Timeslips results to Excel
  ' for further analysis

  Dim rstHoursByEmployee As ADODB.Recordset
  Dim objXL As Excel.Application
  Dim objWS As Excel.Worksheet
  Dim objChart As Excel.Chart

  Dim fld As ADODB.Field
  Dim intCol As Integer
  Dim intRow As Integer

  Set rstHoursByEmployee = New ADODB.Recordset

  ' Get the desired data into a recordset
  rstHoursByEmployee.Open _
   "HoursByEmployee", CurrentProject.Connection

  ' Launch Excel
  Set objXL = New Excel.Application
  ' Create a new worksheet
  objXL.Workbooks.Add
  Set objWS = objXL.ActiveSheet

  ' Copy the data
  ' First the field names
  For intCol = 0 To rstHoursByEmployee.Fields.Count - 1
    Set fld = rstHoursByEmployee.Fields(intCol)
    objWS.Cells(1, intCol + 1) = fld.Name
  Next intCol
  ' Now the actual data
  intRow = 2
  Do Until rstHoursByEmployee.EOF
    For intCol = 0 To rstHoursByEmployee.Fields.Count - 1
      objWS.Cells(intRow, intCol + 1) = _
      rstHoursByEmployee.Fields(intCol).Value
    Next intCol
    rstHoursByEmployee.MoveNext
    intRow = intRow + 1
  Loop

  ' Add a new chart
  objXL.Charts.Add
  Set objChart = objXL.ActiveChart
```

```
    ' Set up the chart
    objChart.ChartType = xl3DPieExploded
    objChart.SetSourceData _
     Source:=objWS.Range("A1:B" & CStr(intRow - 1)), _
     PlotBy:=xlColumns
    objChart.Location Where:=xlLocationAsNewSheet
    objChart.HasTitle = True
    objChart.ChartTitle.Characters.Text = "Hours By Employee"

    ' Make the worksheet visible
    objXL.Visible = True

    ' Don't call the Excel Quit method, so the
    ' worksheet will hang around after this
    ' procedure exits
End Sub
```

Much of this code should look familiar from earlier in the chapter: it opens a Recordset using the `HoursByEmployee` query, and then moves the data over to Excel. Then creating the chart is an exercise in using the Excel object model. First, you call the `Add` method of the `Charts` collection to add a new chart. Excel keeps a pointer to the active chart, which you save in the `objChart` object to make things easier.

The `Chart` object has many methods and properties, but you need to set only a few of them to make an attractive chart. In this case, we've chosen a 3D exploded pie chart, with the data taken from the range of cells that we just wrote. The chart is saved as a new worksheet, with a specified title.

Figure 21.6 shows the results of running this code. It might not be the clearest chart in the world, but it's colorful enough to impress lots of people.

Figure 21.6
Excel chart from Access.

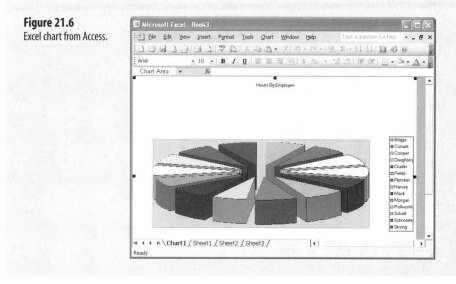

Working with XML Files

An Introduction to XML

If you've ever resorted to hair pulling because you couldn't get the data you needed in a format that Access could understand, Extensible Markup Language (XML) might be for you. Technical gurus define XML as a platform-independent markup language for structured documents. That definition might not mean much to you, and because this is a chapter on automating the entire process anyway, we won't discuss XML basics at great length. All you really need to know is that XML is a technology that makes sharing data easy, regardless of the data's original format. If the application can export the data as an XML file, Access can import it. XML takes the hair pulling out of data-sharing tasks.

Although XML has been around for a while, Access only began to support it in version 2002. Access 2003 supports the following XML file types:

- **XML**—A formatting standard for structured files. An XML file uses tags to organize the actual data into data blocks.

- **XSL**—A standard for modifying imported or exported data. Use an XSL file to format the data in the XML file. Often, these two files are combined by embedding the XSL data into the XML file.

- **XSD**—A standard that defines or describes a database structure in XML terms. These *schema definition* files contain data type and constraint information about the tags and data in a corresponding XML file.

In the course of this chapter, you learn how to work with all three of these file types. You'll see how XML can be used to carry data, how XSL is used to add formatting, and how XSD is used to capture information about the structure of data.

22

IN THIS CHAPTER

An Introduction to XML 325
Using ExportXML 326
Using ImportXML 330

> **NOTE**
>
> A *structured file* is a type of text file that uses what's known as tags to identify the data and meta-data. For instance, an XML file that contains customer data might contain the tags `<CustomerName>`, `<CustomerAddress>`, and so on. Access can interpret these tags as column headings. Most likely, the actual data for these columns would follow the corresponding tag.

In addition, the features of Access XML can create a Web-ready HTML document. You learn more about that later in this chapter ("Exporting a Web-Ready File").

Using ExportXML

You can export Access data to an XML file by executing VBA's `ExportXML` method, which takes the form

```
application.ExportXML objecttype, datasource[, datatarget] _
 [, schematarget],[presentationtarget] _
 [, imagetarget][, encoding][, otherflags]_
 [, filtercriteria][, additionaldata]
```

where *application* represents the Access model. Table 22.1 lists this function's many arguments. Although *datatarget*, *schematarget*, and *presentationtarget* are optional, you must specify at least one. Tables 22.2 and 22.3 further define the constants that you can use with some of the `ExportXML` arguments.

Table 22.1 ExportXML Arguments

Argument	Explanation
objecttype	An intrinsic constant that defines the type of object being exported (see Table 22.2).
datasource	A string value that identifies the object being exported by name.
datatarget	The path and filename for the XML file to which the Access data is being exported.
schematarget	The path and filename for the exported schema data (XSD file).
presentationtarget	The path and filename for the exported presentation information (XSL file).
imagetarget	The path for exported graphics and image files.
encoding	One of two constants, acUTF16 and acUTF8, that determines text encoding.
otherflags	A bit mask value (see Table 22.3). You can add the values to specify more than one option.
filtercriteria	A String value that limits the records actually exported by applying criteria.
additionaldata	Specifies additional tables for the export, but is ignored if *otherflags* is set to acLiveReportSource.

Table 22.2   Object Constants

Object	Constant
Form	acExportForm
Function	acExportFunction
Query	acExportQuery
Report	acExportReport
View	acExportServerView
Stored Procedure	acExportStoredProcedure
Table	acExportTable

Table 22.3   Values for the *otherflags* Argument

Value	Constant	Description
1	acEmbedSchema	Embed schema information with data in the XML document (specified by *datatarget*).
2	acExcludePrimaryKeyAndIndexes	Exclude primary key and indexes from exported schema document.
4	acRunFromServer	Create an Active Server Page (ASP) wrapper for exported report.
8	acLiveReportSource	Create a live link to remote SQL Server 2000 database for exported report.
16	acPersistReportML	Persist the exported object as ReportML, a type of XML that was specifically designed for Access reports.

> **CAUTION**
>
> VBA's ExportXML function writes over existing files. If you don't want to overwrite existing files, you must check for the file before beginning the export process and then rename the existing file, specify a new name for the file you're about to create, or cancel the task.

An Export Example

The simplest XML export creates a single XML file. For instance, the following procedure exports the client data to an XML file:

```
Sub ExportTable(source As String, path As String, _
  target As String)
```

```
'Export source to XML file
  Access.Application.ExportXML acExportTable, source, path & target
End Sub
```

Enter the procedure in a standard module or use Chapter 22's sample module. When executing the procedure, pass the name of the table that contains the data you're exporting and the complete path and filename to which you want the data exported. For instance, in the Immediate window, run the following statement to export client data:

```
ExportTable "Clients", path, "Clients.xml"
```

Be sure to update *path* to accommodate your own system's directory structure, and include the .xml extension in the *target* argument (otherwise, the exported file won't be recognized as XML by editors and other utilities). (Remember, *path* is a string, so be sure to enclose it in double quotation marks.) Figure 22.1 shows the exported XML file in Word 2003, which can display XML files.

Figure 22.1
The XML file contains tags and actual data, but isn't particularly viewable in any meaningful way.

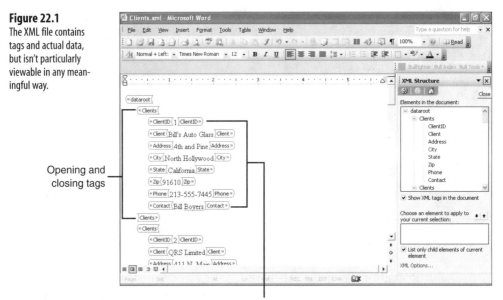

Opening and closing tags

The data in between is one client record

The XML format, as is, doesn't produce a particularly readable file. You'll probably never view files in this format unless you're editing the content.

This procedure handles only tables. You can add an argument and enable the users to pass the object type.

Exporting a Web-Ready File

You can quickly create a Web-ready document by simply changing the extension in the *target* argument from .xml (or whatever standard you're using) to .html. The results aren't perfect, but your browser will display just the data instead of the tags and data.

To illustrate, run the previous statement in the Immediate window, but change the .xml extension to .html as follows:

```
ExportTable "Clients", path, "Clients.html"
```

Next, view clients.html in your browser. (Use Windows Explorer to locate the file in the current directory and double-click it to open it in your system's default browser.) Figure 22.2 shows this file in Internet Explorer. It isn't perfect, but the quick result is impressive.

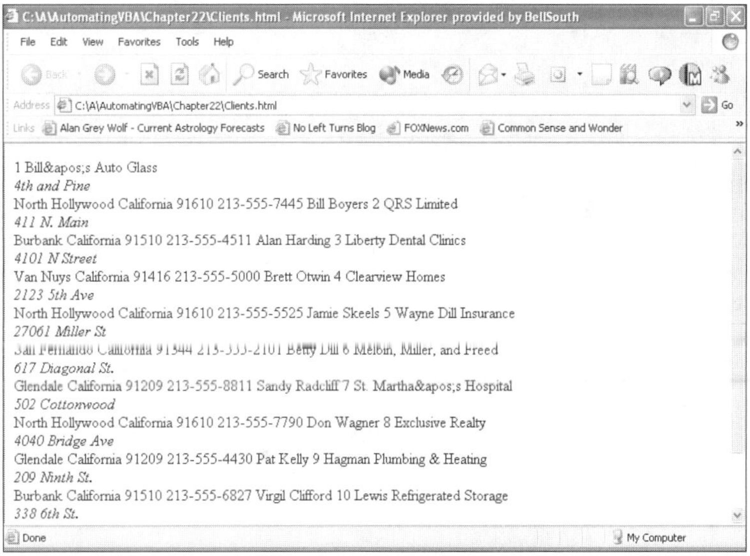

Figure 22.2
Quickly produce Web-quality results by simply changing the extension.

Exporting Related Data

Exporting related data via the user interface is fairly simple. Automating the process presents a bit of a challenge. The ExportXML method's *additionaldata* argument enables you to specify additional tables to export, but you can't just add the table's name. Instead, you append the table using the AdditionalData object.

To export related data, you must identify the related table as an AdditionalData object and then use that reference as the *additionaldata* setting. The following procedure creates an AdditionalData object and then uses that object's Add method to append addtable to the collection:

```
Sub ExportMultipleTables(source As String, path As String, _
  target As String, addtable As String)
```

```
'export related tables to XML file
Dim objAddTable As AdditionalData
Set objAddTable = Application.CreateAdditionalData
objAddTable.Add (addtable)
Access.Application.ExportXML acExportTable, source, path & target, _
  , , , , , , objAddTable
End Sub
```

To illustrate this procedure, run the following statement in the Immediate window (after updating *path*):

```
ExportMultipleTables "Clients", path, "ClientsAndProjects.html", "Projects"
```

Figure 22.3 shows each client with its current projects in a browser. Although the format is lacking a bit in structure, you can see that the data's all there.

Figure 22.3

Export related data programmatically to an XML file.

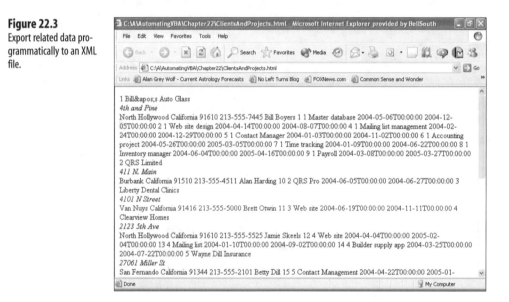

Using ImportXML

Data isn't always conveniently stored in the current database. Occasionally, you have to import foreign data. Fortunately, the Import Wizard does a good job of handling a number of formats. However, you won't use this wizard to import XML data. Use the ImportXML method to import XML data and schema information using the form

```
Application.ImportXML datasource[, importoptions]
```

where *datasource* is a required String value that identifies the complete path and filename to the XML file you're importing and *importoptions* is one of the optional intrinsic constants listed in Table 22.4.

Table 22.4   ImportXML Constants

Constant	Integer Value	Explanation
acStructureOnly	0	Import only the table's structure.
acStructureAndData	1	The default option, which imports both the file's structure and data.
acAppendData	2	Append the data into an existing table.

Importing XML data isn't quite as complicated as exporting. For the most part, you just identify the XML file that by default, Access imports into its own new Access table. Occasionally, you might need to import just the file's structure or append the data to an existing table, and then specify one of the constants listed in Table 22.4.

An Import Example

Let's review how the three constants change the result of importing the same file by importing the client data exported in the previous section. First, enter the following procedure in a standard module or use Chapter 22's sample module:

```
Sub ImportXMLData(source As String, Optional impopt As Variant)
  'import XML file
  'include entire path if necessary
  If IsMissing(impopt) = True Then
    impopt = acStructureAndData
  End If
  Access.Application.ImportXML source, impopt
End Sub
```

This procedure enables you to pass the XML file's name and the constant. You can pass the actual text constant or the Integer value. The second argument is optional, but if you omit it, the procedure assumes you want to use the default, acStructureAndData.

Before you import anything, be sure to close all your browser and Word windows that contain the .xml and .html files from previous examples. An open .xml file can return an error in some cases.

In the Immediate window, run the following statement:

```
ImportXMLData "path\clients.xml"
```

(If you didn't save clients.xml to the current directory, you might need to include *path*.) After running the statement, check the Database window for the new table, Clients1. Figure 22.4 shows the new table in Datasheet view—it is identical to Clients. The only difference is that the imported table doesn't contain a primary key or any indexes. During the import process, Access concatenates the 1 because the database already contains a table named Clients.

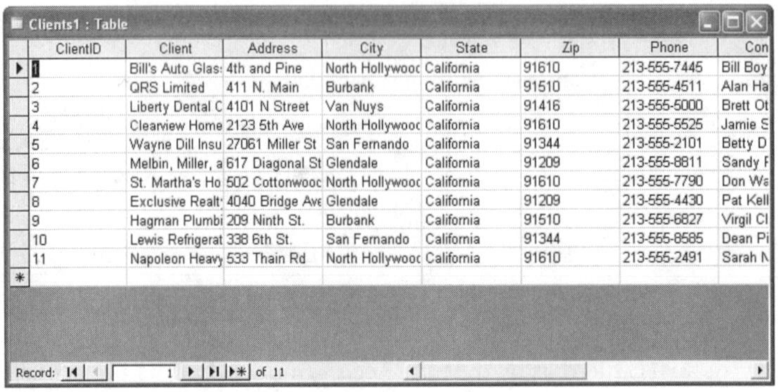

ClientID	Client	Address	City	State	Zip	Phone	Con
1	Bill's Auto Glas:	4th and Pine	North Hollywooc	California	91610	213-555-7445	Bill Boy
2	QRS Limited	411 N. Main	Burbank	California	91510	213-555-4511	Alan Ha
3	Liberty Dental C	4101 N Street	Van Nuys	California	91416	213-555-5000	Brett Ot
4	Clearview Home	2123 5th Ave	North Hollywooc	California	91610	213-555-5525	Jamie S
5	Wayne Dill Insu	27061 Miller St	San Fernando	California	91344	213-555-2101	Betty D
6	Melbin, Miller, a	617 Diagonal St	Glendale	California	91209	213-555-8811	Sandy F
7	St. Martha's Ho	502 Cottonwooc	North Hollywooc	California	91610	213-555-7790	Don Wa
8	Exclusive Realt	4040 Bridge Ave	Glendale	California	91209	213-555-4430	Pat Kell
9	Hagman Plumbi	209 Ninth St.	Burbank	California	91510	213-555-6827	Virgil Cl
10	Lewis Refrigerat	338 6th St.	San Fernando	California	91344	213-555-8585	Dean Pi
11	Napoleon Heavy	533 Thain Rd	North Hollywooc	California	91610	213-555-2491	Sarah N

Figure 22.4
The *ImportXML* method easily imports XML data into a new table.

As is, you can't import `clients.xml` using the `acAppendData` option because doing so would create duplicate values and violate the existing constraints (indexes), as shown in Figure 22.5. Access imports records that don't trigger a key violation. If a record creates a problem and returns an error, Access logs error information in a table named ImportErrors.

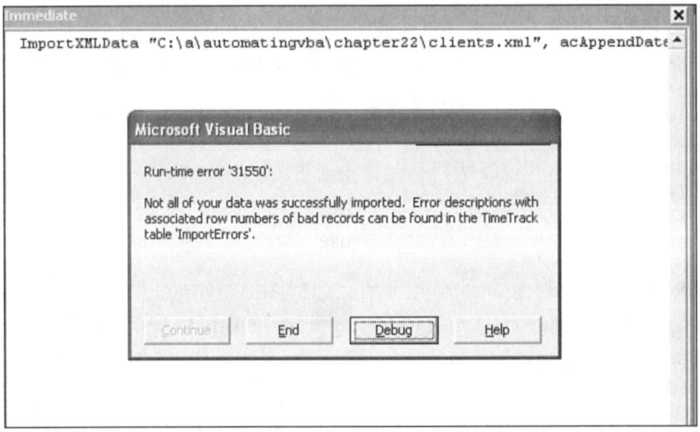

Figure 22.5
If importing the data violates key constraints, Access returns an error and doesn't import the offending records.

The problem in this case is the `ClientID` (primary key) values; there's already a `ClientID` 1 in the Clients table. If you open `clients.xml` (using Word or some other XML editor) and change the `ClientID` value of 1 to 100, Access imports the record for Bill's Auto Glass even though the record is actually a duplicate.

To import just the table's structure, run the following statement:

```
ImportXMLData pathtoclients.xml acStructureOnly
```

Be sure to update *`pathtoclients.xml`* so that it includes the entire pathname and the .xml filename. Figure 22.6 shows the results—a new table with no data. Notice that the new table's name is Clients2. As before, Access concatenates the next consecutive value to the table's name because Clients and Clients1 already exist.

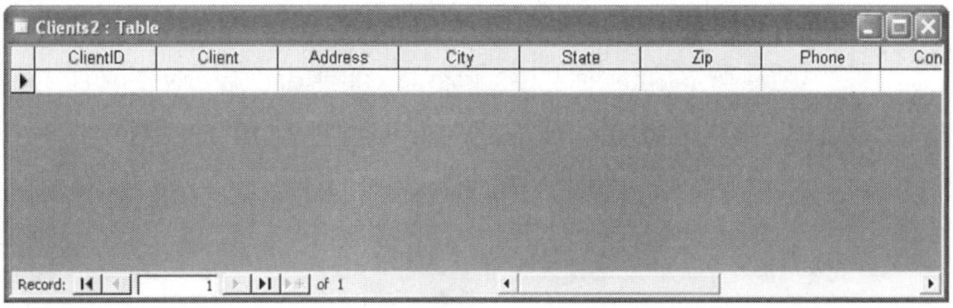

Figure 22.6
You can import just the table's structure.

CAUTION

Importing the XML file's structure creates a new table with the same fields and properties. However, the process does *not* copy the original file's primary key or indexes.

In the previous section on exporting, you learned how to export related tables to an XML file using the `AdditionalData` object. Importing related tables is much easier because Access handles the entire process internally. The XML file knows the data is related and it is imported as such, without any additional information from you. To illustrate the ease with which Access handles related data, run the following statement in the Immediate window:

```
ImportXMLData "path\clientsandprojects.html"
```

(Include *path* if the file isn't in the current directory.) The results are shown in Figure 22.7—Clients3 and Projects1. Notice that the example imports the previously exported .html file and not an actual .xml file. The `ImportXML` method is flexible enough to handle .html data, although most likely you'll use the method to import .xml data.

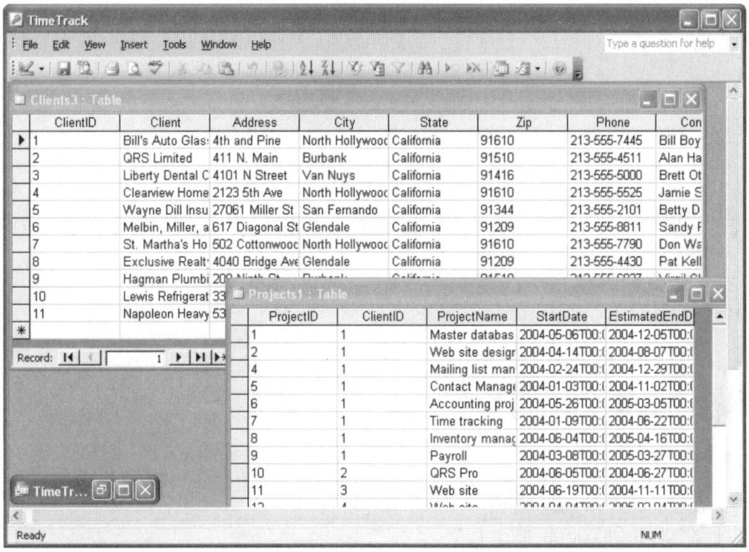

Figure 22.7
The *ImportXML* method easily handles related data.

CAUTION

Access can import related data from an XML file and can even separate the data into tables, accordingly. However, Access can't create a permanent relationship between the new tables. You must create the relationship yourself.

CASE STUDY

Exporting Up-to-Date Project Information

Let's suppose your developers often spend days at a time on site at a client's office. During that time, the developer might want to access the most current project data. To do so, you can export the appropriate client records to an XML or HTML file and then email that file to the developer in the field. If your setup is sophisticated enough, you can automate the email process or even allow the developer Internet access to the database (although this example doesn't do either).

First, create a new blank form with a list box and two command buttons. Refer to Table 22.5 for the appropriate form and control properties.

Table 22.5   Form and Control Properties

Object	Property	Setting
form	Name	Export
	Caption	Export Client Projects
	Scroll Bars	Neither
	Record Selectors	No
	Navigation Buttons	No
list box	Name	lstClients
	Row Source	SELECT Clients.ClientID, Clients.Client FROM
	ClientsColumn Count	2
	Column Widths	0"
command button	Name	cmdCancel
	Caption	Cancel
command button	Name	cmdExport
	Caption	Export

Enter the following code in the form's module:

```
Private Sub cmdCancel_Click()
  'Set selection to nothing
  lstClients.Value = ""
End Sub
```

```
Private Sub cmdExport_Click()
   'Export projects for selected client to HTML file
   'to current directory
   Dim objProjects As AdditionalData
   On Error GoTo HandleErr
   Set objProjects = Application.CreateAdditionalData
   objProjects.Add ("Projects")
   Application.ExportXML acExportTable, _
    "Clients", "ClientsAndProjects.HTML", _
    , , , , , "ClientID = " & lstClients, objProjects
   Exit Sub

ExitHere:
   Set objProjects = Nothing
   Exit Sub
HandleErr:
   MsgBox "Error " & Err.Number & ": " & _
    Err.Description
   Resume ExitHere
End Sub
```

Save the form and then open it in Form view, as shown in Figure 22.8.

Figure 22.8
Use this simple form to
select a client.

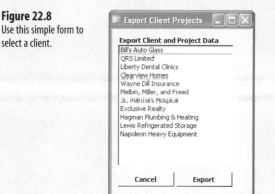

Select Bill's Auto Glass in the list box. Right now, the technique handles just one client. We used a list box so you can easily adapt the technique to handle multiple clients.

After selecting a client, click the Export button. Nothing seems to happen, but the Export button's Click event just exported (to the current directory) the client and related project records for Bill's Auto Glass (or the client you selected) to an HTML file. Check the current folder for a file named ClientsAndProjects.html.

At this point, you'd email the resulting HTML file to the developer in the field. However, because you really can't do that, go ahead and launch the file in your default browser as shown in Figure 22.9. The file contains project data for only the client selected in the Export form.

22

Figure 22.9
Launch the HTML file in your browser to quickly view the client's projects.

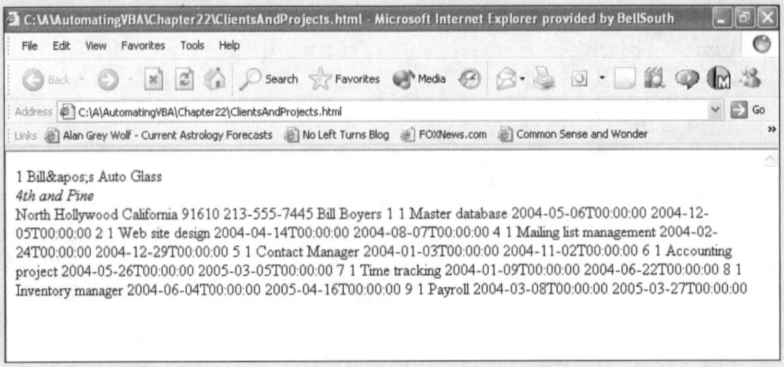
C:\A\AutomatingVBA\Chapter22\ClientsAndProjects.html - Microsoft Internet Explorer provided by BellSouth
File Edit View Favorites Tools Help
Back Search Favorites Media
Address C:\A\AutomatingVBA\Chapter22\ClientsAndProjects.html Go
Links Alan Grey Wolf - Current Astrology Forecasts No Left Turns Blog FOXNews.com Common Sense and Wonder
1 Bill's Auto Glass
4th and Pine
North Hollywood California 91610 213-555-7445 Bill Boyers 1 1 Master database 2004-05-06T00:00:00 2004-12-05T00:00:00 2 1 Web site design 2004-04-14T00:00:00 2004-08-07T00:00:00 4 1 Mailing list management 2004-02-24T00:00:00 2004-12-29T00:00:00 5 1 Contact Manager 2004-01-03T00:00:00 2004-11-02T00:00:00 6 1 Accounting project 2004-05-26T00:00:00 2005-03-05T00:00:00 7 1 Time tracking 2004-01-09T00:00:00 2004-06-22T00:00:00 8 1 Inventory manager 2004-06-04T00:00:00 2005-04-16T00:00:00 9 1 Payroll 2004-03-08T00:00:00 2005-03-27T00:00:00

CAUTION

The export process writes over the existing file of the same name that you created earlier. If you want more control, you need to add code that checks the directory for an existing file of the same name before executing the export. You can cancel the export or change the name of either file.

Using the Windows API

Declaring API Calls

You probably know that VBA is not the only programming language that can be used by Windows applications. In fact, there are hundreds of alternatives, including C#, C++, Visual Basic .NET, and others. You can't use the other languages within an Access application like VBA, but they do show the variety of programming languages available for Windows.

Although the various computer languages offer different ways of doing things, they all share one key feature: they all work on Windows. This is made possible by a layer of software called the Windows Application Programming Interface, or Windows API. The Windows API, supplied by Microsoft, contains thousands of functions for performing tasks such as drawing windows, sending information over networks, and so on.

Sometimes a particular part of the Windows API isn't available directly through a particular programming language. For example, VBA doesn't enable you to directly retrieve the name of the computer where the code is running, even though that function is part of the Windows API. But VBA provides something almost as good: a general-purpose mechanism that enables you to call procedures from the Windows API, usually referred to as API calls. This chapter shows you the basics of this mechanism.

Using a Windows API call is a two-step process. First, you need to *declare* the API call that you're going to use. This sets up a connection between VBA and the underlying Windows software. After that, you can call the procedure like any other procedure.

23

IN THIS CHAPTER

Declaring API Calls 337

Using API Calls 338

API Calls That You Can Use From Access 340

Knowing When to Use the Windows API ...343

> **NOTE** Calling the Windows API directly is a rather advanced topic, and many developers might never need to use this facility. But we suggest that you at least skim this chapter so that you understand the power that is available if and when you need it.

For example, the Windows API call to retrieve the name of the local computer is named `GetComputerName`. Here's how you can declare it in the declarations section of a VBA module:

```
Declare Function GetComputerName _
 Lib "kernel32" Alias "GetComputerNameA" _
 (ByVal lpBuffer As String, nSize As Long) _
 As Long
```

This declaration tells VBA a number of things:

- The name of the function in VBA code is `GetComputerName`.
- The actual function is contained in a Windows library named `kernel32`.
- The name of the function within the Windows library is `GetComputerNameA`.
- The function takes two arguments, one `String` and one `Long`.
- The function returns a single `Long` value.

> **TIP** The VBA help files don't contain any information on Windows API calls. Instead, you have to go to the Windows Platform Software Developers Kit, usually just called the Platform SDK. The entire Platform SDK is available online. You can find documentation on `GetComputerName`, for example, at `http://msdn.microsoft.com/library/default.asp?url=/library/en-us/sysinfo/base/getcomputername.asp`.

Using API Calls

As far as your other code is concerned, there's no difference between a procedure declared in VBA (using the `Sub` or `Function` keywords) and one declared using the `Declare` keyword. Here's a VBA function that gets the computer name using the API call just declared:

```
Function GetThisComputerName() As String
    ' Retrieve the name of this computer using
    ' the Windows API
```

```
    Dim strName As String
    Dim lngChars As Long
    Dim lngRet As Long

    strName = Space(255)
    lngChars = 255

    lngRet = GetComputerName(strName, lngChars - 1)
    If lngChars > 0 Then
      GetThisComputerName = Left(strName, lngChars)
    Else
      GetThisComputerName = "Unable to retrieve name."
    End If
End Function
```

23

Although `GetComputerName` is just another function as far as this code is concerned, there are two other points to be aware of. First, you need to be careful when passing `String` arguments to API calls, because the API definition of a string differs from the VBA definition. API strings are a fixed length, whereas VBA strings are variable. So, when you're passing in a string to an API call, you pass a string that you've initialized to a specified length, and another variable to tell the API how long the string is. The API call passes back, in the second variable, the number of characters that it actually used in the fixed-length string.

> **TIP**
>
> The VBA `Space()` function returns a string consisting of the specified number of spaces—an ideal way to initialize a string argument for an API call.

The API needs one extra position in the string to hold its own end-of-string marker. That's why, when you pass in a 255-character long string, you must tell the API that it has 254 characters to work with.

When the string comes back, you can use the VBA `Left` function to trim off the characters past the length that the API call specified. This section of the code also indicates the second point that you need to be aware of: most API calls return zero if all is well, or a non-zero value if something went wrong.

Figure 23.1 shows the result of running this function on the testbed system. Of course, on your own computer, the return value will be different.

Figure 23.1
Using the Windows API to get the computer name.

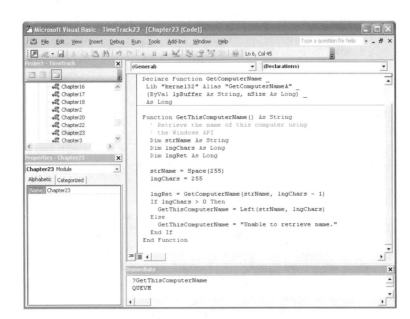

API Calls That You Can Use From Access

The Windows API is a huge collection of functions and sub procedures. There's no way that we can give you even a cursory overview in a single chapter. Instead, we've chosen to just demonstrate a few of the things that you can do with the API:

- Determine whether an application is running
- Retrieve the current username
- Get the executable for a data file

Determining Whether an Application Is Running

Sometimes you might like to know whether a particular application is already running on a user's system. For example, if you're using automation with Microsoft Excel, you can check to see whether Excel is already running before making automation calls. The FindWindow API call does this for you:

```
Declare Function FindWindow Lib "user32" Alias _
 "FindWindowA" (ByVal lpCLassName As String, _
 ByVal lpWindowName As String) As Long
Function IsAppRunning(strClassName As String, _
 strwindowname As String) As Boolean
  ' Determine whether an application is running
  ' by class name or title bar text
  If strClassName = "" Then
    IsAppRunning = ( _
      FindWindow(vbNullString, strwindowname) <> 0)
```

```
   Else
     IsAppRunning = ( _
       FindWindow(strClassName, vbNullString) <> 0)
   End If
End Function
```

`FindWindow` takes either a class name or a window caption and checks to see whether it can find a matching window. If it finds one, it returns the window handle of the window. Window handles are numbers that Windows itself uses to keep track of things. The important thing here is that a window handle is never zero.

Any window on the screen is identified to Windows by its class name. This is a name assigned by the developers of the application. For example, Excel's class name is `xlMain`, whereas Word's is `OpusApp` (Opus the Penguin was the mascot of the original Word development team). If you don't know the class name for an application, you can query by the title bar text instead. However, in this case, you must exactly match what's displayed on the screen. For example, with Excel open and a new default workbook loaded, you might get the following results:

```
?IsAppRunning("","Excel")
False
?IsAppRunning("","Microsoft Excel - Book1")
True
```

`FindWindow` expects you to pass it a null string for the argument that you're not using. VBA doesn't use null strings, but it provides the `vbNullString` constant for precisely this reason.

Retrieving the Current Username

Suppose you're writing VBA code that needs to maintain an audit trail of which actions happened when. One important piece of information for such a procedure is the current username. Here again the Windows API can come to the rescue:

```
Declare Function GetUserName Lib "advapi32.dll" Alias _
  "GetUserNameA" (ByVal lpBuffer As String, _
  nSize As Long) As Long
Function GetCurrentUserName() As String
   ' Retrieve the name of this user using
   ' the Windows API
   Dim strName As String
   Dim lngChars As Long
   Dim lngRet As Long

   strName = Space(255)
   lngChars = 255

   lngRet = GetUserName(strName, lngChars - 1)
   If lngChars > 0 Then
     GetCurrentUserName = Left(strName, lngChars)
   Else
     GetCurrentUserName = "Unable to retrieve name."
   End If
End Function
```

As you can see, the code for returning the username is almost identical to the code for returning the computer name. The only difference is in knowing which API call to use and which library it's found in. The overall pattern of setting up a string argument, passing its length, and determining the valid string on return remains the same.

TIP You might be wondering why so many actual function names end in A. Actually, there are two versions of these functions. For example, Windows supplies `GetUserNameA` and `GetUserNameW`. The A version uses ANSI characters, whereas the W version uses Unicode characters. VBA works only with ANSI characters, so that's the version that you want.

Getting the Executable for a Data File

Does a user have Word installed, or might .doc files on their system be opened by WordPad? If they open an .html file, which Web browser is it displayed in? Both of these questions can be answered by using the `FindExecutable` API call, which tells you which application is associated with a particular data file.

```
Declare Function FindExecutable Lib "shell32.dll" _
 Alias "FindExecutableA" (ByVal lpFile As String, _
 ByVal lpDirectory As String, ByVal lpResult As String) _
 As Long
Function GetMatchingApp(strDataFile As String, _
 strDir As String) As String
 ' Get the executable for the specified
 ' data file in the specified location

 Dim strApp As String
 Dim lngRet As Long

 strApp = Space(260)
 lngRet = FindExecutable(strDataFile, strDir, strApp)

 If lngRet > 32 Then
   GetMatchingApp = strApp
 Else
   GetMatchingApp = "No matching application found."
 End If
End Function
```

To use this function, you supply the name of a data file (which must actually exist) and the name of the working directory. The result is the name and path of the application that is launched when you go to Explorer and double-click on the data file:

```
?GetMatchingApp("c:\temp\foo.txt","c:\temp")
C:\WINDOWS\system32\NOTEPAD.EXE
```

Notice the magic number 260 that we used when setting up the string to hold the return value. This is the maximum length of a path and filename under Windows. As you can see, `FindExecutable` also breaks one of the previous rules; instead of returning zero for failure, it returns some number less than 32 for failure.

Knowing When to Use the Windows API

The hardest thing about using the Windows API is not understanding how to use it but knowing when to use it. A few guidelines:

- Use the Windows API only when you must. If there's a VBA way to do something, don't spend time looking for an API alternative.
- Use the Windows API to manipulate applications other than Access.
- Use the Windows API to retrieve information from Windows itself.
- Use the Windows API to interact with things (such as network messages) that are inaccessible from VBA.

If you get seriously interested in advanced VBA programming, there are several books available that discuss the Windows API in depth. A good starting point is Dan Appleman's *Visual Basic Programmer's Guide to the Win32API* (Sams, 1999).

Appendix

A Review of Access SQL 347

IN THIS PART

V

Review of Access SQL

An Introduction to SQL

VBA isn't the only language Access understands. Structured Query Language (SQL) is the de facto language of relational databases, and as such, Access also speaks SQL. Specifically, Access speaks a dialect known as Jet SQL. Although you'll often hear Jet SQL called Access SQL, SQL speaks to Jet, not Access. This appendix covers general information about Jet SQL as well as syntax instructions and a short language reference. This short appendix is meant to serve as a simple introduction to the most common and basic statements and certainly isn't inclusive of all SQL statements and rules.

SQL is the industry's standard support language for relational databases. There are a number of relational databases on the market and each has its own version of SQL. As mentioned, Access uses Jet SQL. Originally, SQL was called Structured English Query Language, pronounced *sequel*. Because of a legal conflict with the name, the language was renamed to SQL, pronounced "s-q-l".

You'll still hear it pronounced *sequel*, but don't be so quick to correct someone—they might be showing their many years of experience in the product. Many were around when it was actually called *sequel*, and thus still do out of habit, not ignorance.

IN THIS APPENDIX

An Introduction to SQL 342

SQL Structure and Syntax 348

Retrieving with SQL SELECT 350

Modifying with SQL UPDATE 354

Deleting with SQL DELETE 355

Appending With SQL INSERT INTO 355

Making Tables With SQL SELECT INTO 356

Creating a Crosstab Query with
SQL TRANSFORM 357

> **TIP**
>
> Many standards, including the standard for SQL, are adopted, coordinated, and maintained by the American National Standards Institute (ANSI). For more information on SQL standards, visit www.ansi.org.

> **CAUTION**
>
> Although there is a standard for SQL, no product actually implements the full SQL standard. This appendix discusses the Jet version of SQL; the statements demonstrated here might not work in any other database.

You use Jet SQL to interact with the actual data via Jet. As such, statements are broken into two distinct areas:

- **Data Manipulation Language**—Use DML to retrieve, modify, and delete existing data or add new data.
- **Data Definition Language**—Use DDL to manage the objects in your database. This appendix doesn't cover DDL.

> **CAUTION**
>
> Throughout this appendix, you'll find literal examples that correspond with data and tables in the TimeTrack sample database. These examples are illustrative only. Please don't actually run them against your sample database, because doing so might affect the outcome of working chapter examples. If you really want to see the examples at work, create a copy of the finished database and run the examples against the copy.

SQL Structure and Syntax

You'll find SQL simple to learn and use if you know the proper syntax for passing data. For the most part, SQL consists of *keywords*—individual words with a predefined meaning. Most keywords can include arguments, just like functions and procedures. A keyword with arguments is known as a *clause*.

Combined clauses that make a request of the database engine are called *statements*. A statement can consist of just one clause, but usually, there is more than one.

The most basic and general statement form is the following:

`action fieldlist FROM datasource`

where `action` is one of many keywords that defines the statement's purpose, `fieldlist` defines the fields to act upon, and `datasource` identifies the table in which the data is stored.

You can limit the records acted upon by adding a WHERE clause in the form

```
action fieldlist FROM datasource
[WHERE condition]
```

Table A.1 lists the most common *action* SQL keywords. Table A.2 lists several SQL keywords that act as predicates that supply more information to the statement.

Table A.1 Common SQL `action` Keywords

Keyword	Purpose	Syntax
SELECT	Retrieve data	SELECT *fieldlist* FROM *datasource*
UPDATE SET	Modify data	UPDATE *datasource* SET *col = expression*
DELETE	Delete records	DELETE FROM *datasource*
INSERT INTO	Insert (or append) records into any existing table	INSERT INTO *target* SELECT *datasource*
SELECT INTO	Copy an existing table's structure and data to a new table	SELECT *fieldlist* INTO *newtable* FROM *datasource*

Table A.2 Additional Information Keywords and Predicates

Keyword	Purpose	Syntax
ALL	Predicate that retrieves or acts upon all the rows in the data source	SELECT ALL FROM *datasource*
DISTINCT	Predicate that returns unique values in specified fields	SELECT DISTINCT *fieldlist* FROM *datasource*
DISTINCTROW	Predicate that returns unique records	SELECT DISTINCTROW *fieldlist* FROM *datasource*
FROM	Identifies the data source	FROM *datasource*
TOP	Limits the number of records retrieved or acted upon	TOP *number*
WHERE	Condition expression that conditionally limits records	WHERE *conditionalexpression*
GROUP BY	Arranges records by similar values	GROUP BY *fieldlist*
ORDER BY	Sorts records by a field or fields	ORDER BY *fieldlist*
HAVING	Determines which records make it to a group	HAVING *condition*

A

Retrieving with SQL SELECT

By far, the most often used SQL statement is the SELECT statement, which retrieves data so you can view or otherwise use data. SELECT, in and of itself, does not act upon the data in any way.

The SELECT statement can do a lot and is very flexible. Consequently, its syntax structure can be complex:

```
SELECT ALL ¦ DISTINCT ¦ TOP fieldlist ¦ *
FROM datasource
[WHERE condition]
[GROUP BY col1[, col2...]]
[HAVING condition]
[ORDER BY col1 [ASC ¦ DESC] [, col2... [ASC ¦ DESC]]
```

If you omit the All ¦ DISTINCT component, SQL assumes ALL. Similarly, ASC is assumed in an ORDER BY clause if omitted. The asterisk character (*) in the SELECT clause retrieves all columns in the underlying data source, but it's better to avoid doing so unless that's what you really mean to do. The more data you retrieve, the slower the query performs. The FROM clause is the only mandatory clause.

The simplest SELECT uses none of the optional clauses:

```
SELECT *
FROM datasource
```

The `fieldlist` argument represents a list of field names from the underlying data source, separated by a comma character, as follows:

```
SELECT col1[AS alias][, col2 [AS alias]...]
```

where `col1`, `col2`, and so on represent the list of field names. You can list as many field names as you want to return. The AS clause in the SELECT clause is optional and allows you to refer to the field using some name other than the column's actual field name. For instance, the following statement refers to the LName and FName fields as LastName and FirstName:

```
SELECT LName AS LastName, FName AS FirstName
FROM Employees
```

The SQL Predicates

The ALL, DISTINCT, and TOP predicates determine which records are retrieved. ALL is the default and retrieves all the records in the underlying data source. DISTINCT limits the results to unique records in the fields listed. For instance, the following statement limits the results to only one record for each record that contained the same values in both the LName and FName fields:

```
SELECT DISTINCT LName AS LastName, FName AS FirstName
FROM Employees
```

In other words, if there were two Mary Smiths listed in the Employees table, the resulting recordset would contain only one record for both.

> **CAUTION**
>
> The DISTINCT predicate returns a recordset that can't be updated, so don't use this predicate when modifying data.

The difference between DISTINCT and DISTINCTROW is this: DISTINCTROW eliminates duplicates based on all the columns in the data source, regardless of the fields retrieved. DISTINCT eliminates duplicates only in the retrieved fields.

SQL's TOP predicate lets you limit the number of records retrieved using the following syntax:

```
SELECT TOP n [PERCENT] col1[, col2...]
```

where *n* is the number of records you want to retrieve. For instance, the following state-ment retrieves the first and last name values for the first 10 records in the Employees table:

```
SELECT TOP 10 LName, FName
FROM Employees
```

The PERCENT keyword interprets *n* as a percentage of records instead of a literal number. The following statement retrieves 10 percent of the records:

```
SELECT TOP 10 PERCENT LName, FName
FROM Employees
```

The first example always retrieves 10 records, whereas the number of records retrieved by the second statement varies, depending upon the total number of records in the data source. If there are 50 employee records, the second statement retrieves just the first five records; if there are 1,000 records, the second statement retrieves the first 100.

The SQL FROM **Clause**

The FROM clause is mandatory and its full form follows:

```
FROM datasource ¦ onetable join manytable ON onetable.primarykey =
manytable.foreignkey
```

where *onetable* and *manytable* refer to two related tables in a one-to-many relationship. The more complicated form lets you retrieve data from related tables. The *join* argument identifies the type of join as INNER JOIN, RIGHT, and LEFT. There are other SQL joins, but these are the three supported by Jet SQL. For instance, the following statement retrieves all the client records and all the projects for each client whereby ClientID and ClientIDFK match:

```
FROM Clients INNER JOIN Projects ON Clients.ClientID = Projects.ClientIDFK
```

A

If a client doesn't have a project, the INNER JOIN won't retrieve that client record. Similarly, if a project isn't attached to a particular client (which really shouldn't happen), that project won't appear in the resulting recordset.

To return all clients, even those without a project, you use a LEFT join. Similarly, to return all projects, even those not assigned to a client, you use a RIGHT join. The LEFT join returns all records from the one table *and* any matching records from the many table. The RIGHT join returns all records from the many side *and* any matching records from the one table.

The SQL WHERE **Clause**

Often, the data retrieved or otherwise acted upon depends on some condition that you express in the way of criteria. In similar fashion, the SQL WHERE clause lets you narrow down the data that's retrieved, updated, deleted, and so on.

This clause takes the form

```
WHERE conditionalexpression
```

where *conditionalexpression* can take many forms, but the gist is that *conditionalexpression* expresses some value or condition that the stored value in question must meet to be included in the query's result. This expression can be a simple comparison to a literal value such as

```
SELECT *
FROM Clients
WHERE ClientID = 1
```

which returns any record whereby the ClientID value equals the value 1. On the other hand, this argument can be an extremely complex set of conditions combined by the SQL And and Or operators. For instance, let's suppose you want all the records for a specific client whose project start dates occur in the month of January, 2004. In that case, you use the statement

```
SELECT *
FROM Projects
WHERE ClientID = 1 And StartDate Between #1/1/2004# And #1/31/2004#
```

Note that you need to use pound signs to delimit dates and quotation marks to delimit strings. SQL's WHERE clause is flexible enough to handle criteria that refers to columns that aren't in the SELECT clause, as long as the columns are in the underlying data source. For instance, you can limit the previous statement to just the client information, but still retrieve the same records using this statement

```
SELECT ClientID, ProjectName
FROM Projects
WHERE ClientID = 1 And StartDate Between #1/1/2004# And #1/31/2004#
```

To see records that contain a Null value, you must include an expression that explicitly says so. For instance, the expression

```
WHERE ClientID = 1 And StartDate Between #1/1/2004# And #1/31/2004# Or StartDate
Is Null
```

returns records for client 1 whereby the StartDate is Null.

The SQL ORDER BY **Clause**

Grabbing the right records isn't always enough; order is important in many cases. SQL's ORDER BY clause sorts by text, numeric, and date/time values. Don't even bother referencing any other type of column, because the effort will return an error. To specify a sort order, use the ORDER BY clause in the following form:

```
ORDER BY col1 [ASC ¦ DESC][, col2 [ASC ¦ DESC],...]
```

The ASC ¦ DESC component specifies an ascending or descending sort, where ascending is the default. If you omit this component, SQL applies an ascending sort. For instance, the following statement returns client records sorted by the start date value, in ascending order:

```
SELECT ClientID, ProjectName
FROM Projects
WHERE ClientID = 1 And StartDate Between #1/1/2004# And #1/31/2004#
ORDER BY StartDate
```

Like the WHERE clause, you can sort by a column that isn't specified in the SELECT clause, as long as the column is in the underlying data source. Keep in mind that the sort columns take precedence from left to right.

The SQL GROUP BY **Clause**

Like an aggregate function, the GROUP BY clause defines a group and most often performs some type of calculation that summarizes that group. For instance, you might use a GROUP BY clause to return subtotals for each client rather than returning all the detail values for each client.

The syntax for the GROUP BY clause follows.

```
GROUP BY col1[, col2...]
```

where col1, col2, and so on reference actual columns or calculated fields. The one condition with the calculated fields is that the expression cannot contain an aggregate function or constant. Another condition is that all fields in the SELECT clause must be present as follows:

- An argument to an aggregate function
- In the GROUP BY clause as a column reference

What isn't apparent at first is that each column in the resulting recordset either defines the group or evaluates the group. It's important to note that a column doesn't have to be part of the SELECT clause to be included in the GROUP BY clause as long as the column is in the underlying data source. Like the ORDER BY clause, precedence is given from left to right. For an example, suppose you want to group client project records by start date to count them. In this case, you might use the following statement:

```
SELECT Projects.ClientID, Projects.ProjectName,
 Count(Projects.StartDate) AS CountOfStartDate
FROM Projects
WHERE (((Projects.ClientID)=1) AND
 ((Projects.StartDate) Between #1/1/2004# And #1/31/2004#))
GROUP BY Projects.ClientID, Projects.ProjectName
```

A

Notice that each column in the SELECT clause appears either as part of an aggregate function (in this case, the Count function) or is listed in the GROUP BY clause.

The SQL HAVING Clause

SQL's HAVING clause limits the results of a group produced by a GROUP BY clause. You'll not see a HAVING clause in an SQL statement without an accompanying GROUP BY clause. However, a statement can contain a GROUP BY clause without a HAVING clause. The most important thing to remember about the HAVING clause is that Jet applies the clause after the data is grouped. That means you can use this clause to eliminate records after the fact, which is helpful when you're summarizing a grouped column and want to use summarized values as a condition for eliminating specific records.

The HAVING clause takes the form

```
HAVING condition
```

which is certainly simple enough. The *condition* argument can be one or more expressions combined using the SQL And and Or operators in the more complex form

```
HAVING expression1 AND ¦ OR expression2...
```

The following expression is a good example of using the HAVING clause to limit a group:

```
SELECT EmployeeID, DateWorked, Sum(Hours) AS SumOfHours
FROM Timeslips
GROUP BY EmployeeID, DateWorked
HAVING Sum(Hours) > 8
```

The group is based on EmployeeID and DateWorked. However, the HAVING clause retrieves only those records where the sum of the Hours field is greater than eight hours for any given day. Notice that the HAVING clause evaluates the result of the Sum aggregate function Sum(Hours) in the SELECT clause. Doing so isn't absolutely necessary, but it's a common way to use it.

> **TIP**
>
> You can use the WHERE and HAVING clauses to limit the results of a grouped recordset, but keep in mind that they work differently. WHERE eliminates records before they're grouped and HAVING eliminates records after they're grouped. Often, you'll get the same results using either clause, but be careful because they're not interchangeable.

Modifying with SQL UPDATE

A SQL UPDATE statement is the same as the update query executed by the Access user interface to modify existing data. This statement uses the following syntax:

```
UPDATE datasource
SET col1 = expression[, col2 = expression, ...]
[WHERE condition]
```

Given the nature of the statement's purpose, you don't use the GROUP BY, HAVING, or even the ORDER BY clauses with this statement. In addition, UPDATE doesn't return a resultset, but Access displays a message telling you how many records will be updated and asking you to confirm the action. For instance, this simple UPDATE changes all the occurrences of California in the State field in the Clients table to CA:

```
UPDATE Clients SET State = "CA"
WHERE State = "California"
```

> **TIP**
>
> Before updating data via an action query, such as UPDATE, create a copy of the data source. That way, if something goes wrong, you have a copy of the unchanged data. After confirming that the changes are correct, you can delete the copy.

Modifying data won't usually violate referential integrity, unless you're changing a primary or foreign key value, which you shouldn't do anyway. However, changes must respect properties and validation rules in place. When running updates via code, include error handling for these potential errors.

Deleting with SQL DELETE

SQL's DELETE statement deletes records and is basically the same as a Delete query created through the Access user interface. The main thing to remember is that you're deleting the entire record, which is why the DELETE clause has no field list argument. This statement takes the form

```
DELETE
FROM datasource
[WHERE condition]
```

You can specify a field, but doing so is unnecessary and meaningless; the DELETE clause will accept the asterisk character (*), but it's irrelevant and SQL always deletes the entire record. The following statement deletes the record for Don Strong from the Employees table. You probably shouldn't delete this data, because doing so can affect the results of chapter exercises.

```
DELETE
FROM Employees
WHERE EmployeeID = 14
```

Appending With SQL INSERT INTO

Adding new records is a common task, and you can use SQL's INSERT INTO statement to copy data from one table to another or insert a new record into an existing table. When copying records from one table to another, use the form

```
INSERT INTO target
SELECT source
```

A

where *target* is the table you're copying the data to and *source* is the original data you're copying. This statement supports both the WHERE and ORDER BY clauses.

INSERT INTO won't create a new table, so *target* must exist prior to executing the statement. In addition, the columns you're inserting must exist in *target*—SQL won't create new columns either.

> **CAUTION**
>
> Using the asterisk character (*) in the INSERT INTO clause can return an error if both tables are using AutoNumber fields to produce the primary key value. That's because there's a likelihood that primary key values are duplicated in both tables.

The second form of this statement appends data to an existing table, one record at a time:

```
INSERT INTO target [col1[, col2, ...]]
VALUES (val1[, val2, ...])
```

There are a few rules you must comply with to use this form successfully:

- Column references are optional. When omitted, you must include a value for each column in the target table.
- The arguments in the VALUES clause must occur in the same order as their corresponding columns in the target table. This order doesn't have to match the order in which the columns occur in the table's design.

The simple statement

```
INSERT INTO Employees (LastName, FirstName)
VALUES ('Harkins', 'Susan')
```

adds a new record for Susan Harkins to the Employees table. Notice that the EmployeeID field isn't referenced. That's because that field is an AutoNumber field, so Access generates its value automatically. If you attempt to apply a value to an AutoNumber field, Access returns an error.

Making Tables With SQL SELECT INTO

SQL doesn't just manipulate existing data. You can use an SQL SELECT INTO statement to create a new table. Instead of copying data from one table to another as the INSERT INTO statement does, SELECT INTO copies data from a source table into a new table that the statement creates.

A

To create a new table based on existing data, use this statement in the form

```
SELECT * ¦ col1[, col2, …] INTO newtable
FROM source
```

`SELECT INTO` supports the `WHERE`, `GROUP BY`, `HAVING`, and `ORDER BY` clauses, which you can use to limit and arrange the data in *newtable*.

To copy a table's structure to a new table, but copy no data, use the form

```
SELECT * INTO newtable
FROM source
WHERE False
```

Because no record can equal `False`, the SQL statement copies no data to the new table. Keep in mind that this statement copies just the table's column structure. It doesn't set a primary key or create any indexes for the new table.

CAUTION

`SELECT INTO` replaces an existing table of the same name (*newtable*). Be careful to check for existing tables of the same name *before* running the `SELECT INTO` statement and act accordingly. Simply reacting to the confirmation request that warns you that continuing will delete the table isn't enough because Access deletes the existing table even if you cancel the action.

Creating a Crosstab Query with SQL TRANSFORM

A crosstab query is a great way to present a lot of data in a consistent and easy-to-read format. These queries summarize data by categories, generally using an aggregate function for the summary calculations. The general rule of thumb is that the query must have at least one column heading and one summary column.

Crosstab queries are produced by SQL's TRANSFORM statement, which takes the form

```
TRANSFORM aggregate
SELECT statement
PIVOT column
```

where *aggregate* is one of many aggregate functions used to evaluate a column, *statement* is any valid SQL statement, and *column* identifies the column heading(s). TRANSFORM doesn't support the SQL HAVING clause.

A

> **TIP**
>
> Crosstabs can be a bit intimidating, but there's an easy way to get the results you want:
>
> 1. Start with a grouped SELECT statement using an aggregate function to evaluate the grouped column.
>
> 2. Insert a TRANSFORM clause before the SELECT statement and move the aggregate function from the SELECT clause to the TRANSFORM clause.
>
> 3. Follow the SELECT clause with a PIVOT clause and move a column from the GROUP BY clause to the new PIVOT clause.
>
> There's no guarantee the results will be exactly what you want, but they will probably be very close. After you have the basic structure, you can more easily add column headings and column-evaluating aggregate functions.

The following statement presents a lot of information:

```
TRANSFORM Sum([HourlyRate]*[Hours]) AS Total
SELECT Clients.Client, Projects.ProjectName
FROM Clients INNER JOIN Projects ON Clients.ClientID = Projects.ClientID
 INNER JOIN Tasks ON Projects.ProjectID = Tasks.ProjectID
 INNER JOIN Timeslips ON Tasks.TaskID = Timeslips.TaskID
GROUP BY Clients.Client, Projects.ProjectName
PIVOT Projects.StartDate
```

The results show a list of clients and projects with a total of labor hours listed by columns according to start dates. In other words, you can quickly see how much money has been spent thus far on each project for each client, while quickly discerning when the project began. Because this query retrieves data from more than one table, the references include table and column names, which prevent ambiguous references, such as the ClientID column in the Clients and Projects tables.

INDEX

Symbols

& (ampersand), 85

' (apostrophe), 30, 76

@ (at symbol), 85

\ (backslash), 83

! (bang character), 43

[] (brackets), 44

, (comma), 49

& (concatenation operator), 49

> (greater than symbol), 85

< (less than symbol), 85

" (quotes), 76

% (percent sign), 83

(pound sign), 76, 83

; (semicolon), 181

0 format, 83

A

a/p format, 84

Abs function, 70

Absolute Beginner's Guide to Microsoft Office Access 2003, 11

absolute values, returning, 70

Access databases. *See also* **TimeTrack sample database**

accessing Excel from, 318-319, 322-323

accessing Word from, 320-321

application collections, 223-225

  AllForms, 225

  case study, 232-233

  object dependencies, 229-232

  object properties, 226-229

  objects, retrieving lists of, 225-226

  properties, 225

commands, 242-244

compared to Excel spreadsheets, 9-10

compared to OneNote, 11

concurrency, 287

  locking errors, resolving, 296-297

  optimistic record locking, 288-291

  pessimistic record locking, 288, 291-292

  schema recordsets, 2 93-295

connections, 238

  closing, 242

  connection strings, 240-241

  opening, 239-240

control events, 162, 167

crosstab queries, 357-358

data events, 165-167

exporting databases to XML (Extensible Markup Language)

  example, 327-328

  exporting related data, 329-330

  ExportXML function, 326-327

  up-to-date project information, 334-335

  Web ready files, 329

focus events, 163-165

forms

  AllForms collection, 148

  arguments, 151-152

  checking existence of, 148-149

  checking for open forms, 149-150

  closing, 146-147

  error handling, 154-156

  event handling, 147, 168-170

  form modules, 147

  multiple form instances, 157-159

opening, 145-146
populating, 152-154
resizing, 150-151
list controls, 175-176
  adding items to, 181
  callback functions,
    189-191
  drill-down controls,
    191-193
  filtering list control,
    177-180
  MultiSelect controls,
    187-189
  row source type, 175
  row sources, 175
  Table/Query list con-
    trols, 183-187
  value list controls,
    181-183
macros, 12
objects, 114
  AccessObject, 226
  CurrentProject, 224
  dependencies, 229-232
  DependencyInfo, 232
  properties, 226-229
  retrieving lists of,
    225-226
records
  adding, 355-356
  deleting, 355
  locking errors, resolving,
    296-297
  optimistic record lock-
    ing, 288-291
  pessimistic record lock-
    ing, 288, 291-292
  updating, 354-355
recordsets, 244-245
  adding data to, 260-262
  combo boxes, adding
    items to, 268-271
  creating, 245-247

current users, displaying,
  250-252
cursors, 244-245
deleting data in, 262-263
fields, 256
filtering, 247-248
finding data in, 256-260
moving through,
  253-255
opening, 245-247
populating, 245-246
Recordset property,
  248-249
schema recordsets,
  293-295
transactions, 266-268
updating data in,
  263-266
report events, 170-171
retrieving data with
  SELECT statements
  ALL predicate, 350-351
  DISTINCT predicate,
    350-351
  FROM clause, 351-352
  GROUP BY clause,
    353-354
  HAVING clause, 354
  ORDER BY clause, 353
  syntax, 350
  TOP predicate, 350-351
  WHERE clause, 352
schemas, 279
tables
  creating with ADOX,
    274-277
  creating with SELECT
    INTO statement,
    356-357
  indexes, 277-278
  relationships, 278-279
updating, 354-355

XML files, importing
  import example, 331-333
  ImportXML function,
    330-333

AccessObject object, 226

acDialog constant, 211

**acEmbedSchema constant,
331**

**acExcludePrimaryKeyAndIn
dexes constant, 327**

acHidden constant, 211

acIcon constant, 211

**acLiveReportSource con-
stant, 327**

**acPersistReportML con-
stant, 327**

**acRunFromServer constant,
327**

acSaveNo constant, 211

acSavePrompt constant, 211

acSaveYes constant, 211

**acStructureAndData con-
stant, 331**

**acStructureOnly constant,
331**

Activate event, 168

**ActiveX Data Objects. See
ADO**

acViewDesign constant, 211

acViewNormal constant, 211

**acViewPreview constant,
211**

**acWindowNormal constant,
211**

**adAsyncExecute constant,
246**

adAsyncFetch constant, 246

adAsyncFetchNonBlocking constant, 246

adBookmarkCurrent constant, 254

adBookmarkFirst constant, 254

adBookmarkLast constant, 254

adCmdFile constant, 246

adCmdStoredProc constant, 246

adCmdTable constant, 246

adCmdTableDirect constant, 246

adCmdText constant, 246

adCmdUnknown constant, 246

AddEmployee procedure, 261

AdditionalData object, 329

AddNew method, 260

Address_Enter procedure, 163

Address_Exit procedure, 164

Address_GotFocus procedure, 164

Address_LostFocus procedure, 164

adFilterNone constant, 248

adLockBatchOptimistic constant, 246

adLockOptimistic constant, 246

adLockPessimistic constant, 246

adLockReadOnly constant, 246

adModeRead constant, 239

adModeReadWrite constant, 239

adModeRecursive constant, 239

adModeShareDenyNone constant, 239

adModeShareDenyRead constant, 239

adModeShareDenyWrite constant, 239

adModeShareExclusive constant, 239

adModeWrite constant, 239

ADO (ActiveX Data Objects), 237. *See also* ADOX (ADO Extensions for DDL and Security)
   Command object, 242-244
   Connection object, 238
      closing connections, 242
      connection strings, 240-241
      opening connections, 239-240
   object model, 237-238
   optimistic record locking, 289-291
   pessimistic record locking, 291-292
   Recordset object, 244-245
      adding data to, 260-262
      combo boxes, adding items to, 268-271
      creating, 245-247
      cursors, 244-245
      deleting data in, 262-263
      fields, referencing, 256

      filtering, 247-248
      finding data in, 256-260
      moving through, 253-255
      opening, 245-247
      populating, 245-246
      Recordset property, 248-249
      transactions, 266-268
      updating data in, 263-266

ADOX (ADO Extensions for DDL and Security), 273
   data dictionary case study, 284-286
   groups, creating, 279-280
   object ownership, 281-282
   object permissions, 282-283
   tables, creating, 274-277
      indexes, 277-278
      relationships, 278-279
   users, creating, 280-281

adRightCreate constant, 283

adRightDelete constant, 283

adRightDrop constant, 283

adRightExclusive constant, 283

adRightExecute constant, 283

adRightFull constant, 283

adRightInsert constant, 283

adRightMaximumAllowed constant, 283

adRightNone constant, 283

adRightRead constant, 283

adRightReadDesign constant, 283

adRightReadPermissions constant, 283

adRightReference constant, 283

adRightUpdate constant, 283

adRightWithGrant constant, 283

adRightWriteDesign constant, 283

adRightWriteOwner constant, 283

adRightWritePermissions constant, 283

adSchemaCheckConstraints constant, 294

adSchemaColumns constant, 294

adSchemaConstraintColumn Usage constant, 294

adSchemaForeignKeys constant, 294

adSchemaIndexes constant, 294

adSchemaKeyColumnUsage constant, 294

adSchemaPrimaryKeys constant, 294

adSchemaProcedures constant, 294

adSchemaProviderTypes constant, 294

adSchemaReferentialConstraints constant, 294

adSchemaStatistics constant, 294

adSchemaTableConstraints constant, 294

adSchemaTables constant, 294

adSchemaTrustees constant, 294

adSchemaViews constant, 294

adSeekAfter constant, 259

adSeekAfterEQ constant, 259

adSeekBefore constant, 259

adSeekBeforeEQ constant, 259

adSeekFirstEQ constant, 259

adSeekLastEQ constant, 259

adXactBrowse constant, 240

adXactChaos constant, 240

adXactCursorStability constant, 240

adXactIsolated constant, 240

adXactReadCommitted constant, 240

adXactReadUncommitted constant, 240

adXactRepeatableRead constant, 240

adXactSerializable constant, 240

adXactUnspecified constant, 240

AfterDelConfirm event, 169

AfterInsert event, 169

AfterUpdate event, 165

ALL predicate (SELECT statement), 350-351

AllForms collection, 148, 225

am/pm format, 84

American National Standards Institute (ANSI), 76, 348

ampersand (&), 85

annuities
future values, 72-73
interest rates, 74
number of annuity periods, 73
payments, 73
principal payments, 73-74

ANSI (American National Standards Institute), 76, 348

apostrophe ('), 30, 76

Append mode, 302

appending database records, 355-356

application collections, 223-225
AllForms, 225
case study, 232-233
object dependencies, 229-232
object properties, 226-229
objects, retrieving lists of, 225-226
properties, 225

Application property (collections), 225

applications, checking whether applications are running, 340-341

ApplyFilter method, 154

arguments
 default values, 50
 forms, 151-152
 optional arguments, 50
 passing, 49
  by reference, 50-51
  by value, 51
  to reports, 212-213

arrays, 105
 adding elements to, 108
 changing dimensions of, 110-111
 declaring, 105-106
 defined, 105
 dynamic arrays, 110-111
 examples, 106
 fixed-size arrays, 110
 index values, 106-107
 multiple dimensions, 110
 Option Base statement, 107
 ReDim statement, 110-111
 referencing elements in, 109
 upper/lower bounds, 106

Asc function, 76

at symbol (@), 85

automation, 313
 Excel, accessing from Access, 318-319, 322-323
 object creation, 315
  CreateObject function, 316
  early binding, 317
  GetObject function, 316-317
  late binding, 317
 object references, 314-315
 Word, accessing from Access, 320-321

B

BackColor property (text boxes), 196

backslash (\), 83

bang character (!), 43

BeforeDelConfirm event, 169

BeforeInsert event, 169

BeforeUpdate event, 165

beginning transactions, 267

BeginTrans method, 267

Billing Report, 15

billing work in progress, 102-104

Binary mode, 302

binding, 317

Boolean data type, 40
 converting values to, 59-60

BorderColor property (text boxes), 196

bounds (arrays), 106

brackets ([ ]), 44

branching and looping, 91
 case study, 102-104
 Do loops
  conditions, 100-101
  simple example, 99-100
  terminating, 101
 For Next statements, 95-96
  loop counter variables, 97
  looping in reverse, 96-97
  nesting, 98
  terminating, 99
 GoTo statements, 101-102

If Then Else statements
 conditions, 92-93
 Else statement, 93
 ElseIf statement, 93-94
 simple If statement, 91-92
Select Case statements, 94

Break command (Standard toolbar), 19

break mode, 54-55

breakpoints, 56

buffers, 169-170

business days, estimating, 88-90

Byte data type, 40
 converting values to, 60

C

callback functions, 189-191

CallbackList function, 190

calling
 functions, 47-48
 methods, 117-118
 sub procedures, 46

canceling events, 171

case of strings, changing, 77

case studies
 application collections, 232-233
 combo boxes, adding items to, 268-271
 current database connections, displaying, 250-252
 daily reports, 220-222
 data dictionaries, creating, 284-286

data validation, 172-173

error handling, 128-130

Excel, accessing from Access, 322-323

forms, opening, 128-130

list controls as drill-down controls, 191-193

master viewing form, 203-207

multiple form instances, 158-159

record locking errors, resolving, 296-297

text files, numbering lines in, 310-312

up-to-date project information, exporting, 334-335

Catalog object, 275

cboBound_AfterUpdate procedure, 184

cboColors_NotInList procedure, 182

CBool function, 58-60

cboUnbound_NotInList procedure, 186

CByte function, 58, 60

CDate function, 58, 61

Change event, 165

ChangeOwner procedure, 281

ChangeStateExplicit1 procedure, 264

ChangeStateExplicit2 procedure, 265

ChangeStateImplicit procedure, 266

ChangeStateTransaction procedure, 267-268

ChartInExcel procedure, 322-323

Chr function, 76

CInt function, 58, 62

classes, 114

clauses, 348

FROM, 351-352

GROUP BY, 353-354

HAVING, 354

ORDER BY, 353

WHERE, 352

Click event, 167

Client_Enter procedure, 163

Client_Exit procedure, 163

Client_GotFocus procedure, 163

Client_LostFocus procedure, 163

ClientSub form, 204-205

Close event, 168

Close method, 146, 211, 242

CloseClientForm procedure, 146

closing

database connections, 242

forms, 146-147

reports, 211

cmdDisable_Click procedure, 201

cmdExport_Click procedure, 335

code

comments, 30-31

debugging

breakpoints, 56

run and break mode, 54-55

single-stepping, 55-56

entering, 22-23

error handling, 52-54

indenting, 30

naming conventions, 28-30

saving, 24-25

collections, 119-121, 223-225

AllForms, 148, 225

case study, 232-233

Groups, 280

Indexes, 277

object dependencies, 229-232

object properties, 226-229

objects, retrieving lists of, 225-226

properties, 225

Users, 281

Column object, 275

columns

Column object, 275

creating with ADOX, 275-277

combo boxes. *See also* list controls

adding items to, 181, 268-271

filtering combo boxes, 177-180

comma (,), 49

Command object, 242-244

CommandTimeout property (Connection object), 239

comments, 30-31

committing transactions, 267

CommitTrans method, 267

comparing strings, 79

concatenation operator (&), 49

concurrency, 287
locking errors, resolving, 296-297
optimistic record locking, 288-291
pessimistic record locking, 288, 291-292
schema recordsets
retrieving, 293-294
standard schema record-sets, 294-295

conditions
Do loops, 100-101
If statements, 92-93

Connection object, 238
closing connections, 242
connection strings, 240-241
opening connections, 239-240

ConnectionString property (Connection object), 239

ConnectionTimeout property (Connection object), 239

Const statement, 37

constants
declaring, 37
intrinsic constants, 38
public constants, 134-135

control flow. *See* **flow-of-control statements**

control-specific events, 167

controls
combo boxes
adding items to, 181
filtering combo boxes, 177-180
control-specific events, 167
data events
AfterUpdate, 165
BeforeUpdate, 165
Change, 165
Dirty, 165
examples, 166-167
KeyDown, 165
KeyPress, 165
KeyUp, 165
defined, 43
focus events, 163-165
list controls, 175-176
adding items to, 181
callback functions, 189-191
drill-down controls, 191-193
filtering list control, 177-180
MultiSelect controls, 187-189
row source type, 175
row sources, 175
Table/Query list controls, 183-187
value list controls, 181-183
option groups, 200-202
subforms, 202
Tag property, 202-203

text boxes
focus, tracking, 197-198
properties, 195-196
unbound text boxes, 198-200

ControlSource property (text boxes), 196

converting data types, 58-59
to Boolean data types, 59-60
to Byte data types, 60
CDate function, 58
conversion example, 63-65
to Date data types, 61
to Integer data types, 62
null values, 63
to String data types, 62
to Variant data types, 62

Count property (collections), 225

counting characters in strings, 77

CreateGroup procedure, 280

CreateIndexes procedure, 277-278

CreateObject function, 316

CreateObject1 procedure, 114

CreateObject2 procedure, 115

CreateObjectDemo procedure, 316

CreateRelation procedure, 278-279

CreateTables procedure, 275-276

CreateTwoForms procedure, 157

CreateUser procedure, 280

crosstab queries, 357-358

CStr function, 58, 62

Currency data type, 39-40

Currency format, 82

current database connections, displaying, 250-252

Current event, 168-169

current usernames, retrieving, 341-342

CurrentProject object, 224

CurrentView property (AccessObject object), 226

CursorLocation property (Connection object), 239

cursors, 244-245

custom object properties, 227-229

CVar function, 58, 62

D

d format, 83

daily reports, 220-222

data buffers, 169-170

Data Definition Language (DDL), 348

data dictionaries, 284-286

data events, 165-169
    AfterUpdate, 165
    BeforeUpdate, 165
    Change, 165
    Dirty, 165
    examples, 166-167
    KeyDown, 165
    KeyPress, 165
    KeyUp, 165

Data Manipulation Language (DML), 348

data types
    Boolean, 40
    Byte, 40
    comparison of, 39-40
    converting
        to Boolean data types, 59-60
        to Byte data types, 60
        conversion example, 63-65
        to Date data types, 61
        to Integer data types, 62
        null values, 63
        to String data types, 62
        to Variant data types, 62
    Currency, 39-40
    Date, 41
    Decimal, 40-41
    Double, 41
    function return values, 51-52
    Integer, 39-41
    Long, 41
    Object, 41
    Single, 39-41
    String. See strings
    type conversion functions
        CBool, 58-60
        CByte, 58-60
        CDate, 58, 61
        CInt, 58, 62
        conversion example, 63-65
        CStr, 58, 62
        CVar, 58, 62
        Nz, 63
    Variant, 42

data validation, 172-173

databases. See Access databases

DataErr argument (Error event), 215

Date data type, 41
    converting values to, 61

Date function, 65

date user-defined formats, 83-84

DateAdd function, 66

DateCreated property (AccessObject object), 226

DateDiff function, 66-67

DateModified property (AccessObject object), 226

DatePart function, 68

dates
    adding to/subtracting from, 66
    creating from components, 68
    creating from strings, 69
    date/time named formats, 82
    date user-defined formats, 83-84
    extracting date components, 68
    finding different between, 66-67
    formatting, 81-84
    functions
        Date, 65
        DateAdd, 66
        DateDiff, 66-67
        DatePart, 68
        DateSerial, 68
        DateValue, 69

Day, 69
    example, 69-70
    Hour, 69
    Minute, 69
    Month, 69
    Second, 69
    Year, 69
    returning, 65, 69

DatesAreBad function, 172

DateSerial function, 68

DateValue function, 69

Day function, 69

dd format, 83

Ddb function, 72

ddd format, 83

dddd format, 83

ddddd format, 83

dddddd format, 83

DDL (Data Definition Language), 348

Deactivate event, 168

Debug menu commands
    Run to Cursor, 56
    Step Into, 55
    Step Out, 55
    Step Over, 55
    Toggle Breakpoint, 56

Debug toolbar (VBE), 20

debugging
    breakpoints, 56
    run and break mode, 54-55
    single-stepping, 55-56

Decimal data type, 40-41

declaring
    arrays, 105-106
    constants, 37
    procedures
        functions, 47
        private procedures, 48
        public procedures, 48
        sub procedures, 45
    variables, 33-34
    Windows API functions, 337-338

default argument values, 50

DefaultDatabase property (Connection object), 239

Delete event, 169

Delete method, 262-263

DELETE statement, 355

DeleteEmployee procedure, 262-263

deleting
    breakpoints, 56
    database records, 355
    recordset data, 262-263

delimiters, 76

dependencies (object), 229-232

DependencyInfo object, 232

depreciation, calculating, 72-74

Design Mode command (Standard toolbar), 19

Dim statement, 33-34, 106

dimensions of arrays, changing, 110-111

Dirty event, 165

DISTINCT predicate (SELECT statement), 350-351

DML (Data Manipulation Language), 348

Do loops
    conditions, 100-101
    simple example, 99-100
    terminating, 101

documentation of Windows API functions, 338

DoesFormExist function, 149

Double data type, 41

drill-down controls, 191-193

dynamic arrays, 110-111

dynamic cursors, 244

E

E-/E+ formats, 83

early binding, 317

EarlyBindingDemo procedure, 317

Edit toolbar (VBE), 20

EditCA procedure, 243

editor. *See* **VBE (Visual Basic Editor)**

elements of arrays
    defining, 108
    referencing, 109

Else clause, 93

ElseIf clause, 93-94

Employees form, 14

EmployeeSub form, 205

Enabled property (text boxes), 196

End Function statement, 47

End Sub statement, 46

Enter event, 163, 169

entering code, 22-23

EOF function, 305-306

Error event, 215

error handling, 52, 128-130
forms, 154-156
locking errors, resolving, 296-297
On Error Goto statement, 53-54
On Error Resume Next statement, 53
report-level errors, 215-217

EstimatedEndDate_Exit procedure, 172

event-driven programming environments, 161

events, 126-127, 161-162
canceling, 171
control events
control-specific events, 167
data events, 165-167
focus events, 163-165
event-driven programming environments, 161
event procedures, 127
form events, 147
data buffers, 169-170
data events, 168-169
navigation events, 168

report events, 170-171
Error, 215
NoData, 217-218

Excel spreadsheets, 9-10
accessing from Access, 318-319, 322-323

exclamation point (!), 43

executables, 342

executing Command objects, 243-244

existence of forms, checking, 148-149

Exit Do statement, 101

Exit event, 163

Exit For statement, 99

Exit Function statement, 53

exiting
Do loops, 101
For, Next loops, 99

exporting to XML (Extensible Markup Language)
example, 327-328
exporting related data, 329-330
ExportXML function, 326-327
up-to-date project information, 334-335
Web-ready files, 329

ExportMultipleTables procedure, 329

ExportTable procedure, 327

ExportXML function, 326-327

Extensible Markup Language. See XML files

F

fg format, 84

fields
defined, 43
referencing, 256

file handles, 301

File menu commands, Save, 24

files
file handles, 301
numbering lines in, 310-312
opening
access permissions, 303
file modes, 302
locking settings, 303-304
printing, 309
reading
EOF function, 305-306
Input # statement, 306-307
Input function, 304-305
Line Input # statement, 306
LOF function, 306
structured files, 326
type libraries, 314
Web-ready files, exporting to, 329
writing to, 307-308
XML (Extensible Markup Language) files
exporting Access data to, 326-330, 334-335
importing into Access
import example, 331-333
ImportXML function, 330-333
XSD, 325
XSL, 325

Filter property (reports), 214

filtering
 recordsets, 247-248
 reports, 214-215

filtering list control, 177-180

filtername argument (OpenReport method), 210

FilterOn property (reports), 214

financial functions
 Ddb, 72
 example, 74-75
 FV, 72-73
 IPmt, 73
 NPer, 73
 Pmt, 73
 PPmt, 73-74
 Rate, 74
 Syd, 74

Find command (Standard toolbar), 19

Find method, 256-258

FindExecutable function, 342

finding
 data in recordsets
  Find method, 256-258
  Seek method, 258-260
 executables, 342

FindWindow function, 340-341

Fixed format, 82

fixed-size arrays, 110

flow-of-control statements, 91
 case study, 102-104
 Do loops
  conditions, 100-101
  simple example, 99-100
  terminating, 101
 For Next 95-96
  loop counter variables, 97
  looping in reverse, 96-97
  nesting, 98
  terminating, 99
 GoTo, 101-102
 If Then Else
  conditions, 92-93
  Else clause, 93
  ElseIf clause, 93-94
  simple If statement, 91-92
 Select Case, 94

focus events, 163-165

focus, tracking, 197-198

FontBold property (text boxes), 196

FontItalic property (text boxes), 196

FontName property (text boxes), 196

FontSize property (text boxes), 196

For, Next statement, 95-96
 loop counter variables, 97
 looping in reverse, 96-97
 nesting, 98
 terminating, 99

ForeColor property (text boxes), 196

form modules, 147

Format function, 81-85
 date user-defined formats, 83-84
 date/time named formats, 82
 numeric named formats, 82
 numeric user-defined formats, 83
 string user-defined formats, 85

formatting
 dates/times, 81-84
 Format function, 81-85
  date user-defined formats, 83-84
  date/time named formats, 82
  numeric named formats, 82
  numeric user-defined formats, 83
  string user-defined formats, 85
 numbers, 81-84
 strings, 85

forms
 AllForms collection, 148, 225
 arguments, 151-152
 checking existence of, 148-149
 checking for open forms, 149-150
 ClientSub, 204-205
 closing, 146-147
 Employees, 14
 EmployeeSub, 205
 error handling, 154-156
 events, 147
  data buffers, 169-170
  data events, 168-169
  navigation events, 168

form modules, 147

master viewing forms, 203-207

multiple form instances, 157-159

opening, 128-130, 145-146

option groups, 200-202

populating, 152-154

Projects, 14

ProjectSub, 206

resizing, 150-151

subforms, 202

Switchboard, 14

text boxes
  focus, tracking, 197-198
  properties, 195-196
  unbound text boxes, 198-200

Timeslips, 15

forward-only cursors, 245

FreeFile function, 304

FROM clause (SELECT statement), 351-352

FullName property (AccessObject object), 226

Function statement, 47

functions. *See also* **methods; procedures; statements**
  Abs, 70
  Asc, 76
  callback functions, 189-191
  CallbackList, 190
  calling, 47-48
  CBool, 58-60
  CByte, 58, 60
  CDate, 58, 61
  Chr, 76
  CInt, 58, 62

CreateObject, 316
creating, 47
CStr, 58, 62
CVar, 58, 62
Date, 65
DateAdd, 66
DateDiff, 66-67
DatePart, 68
DatesAreBad, 172
DateSerial, 68
DateValue, 69
Day, 69
Ddb, 72
defined, 47
DoesFormExist, 149
EOF, 305-306
ExportXML, 326-327
Format, 81-85
FreeFile, 304
FV, 72-73
GetObject, 316-317
Hour, 69
ImportXML, 330-333
Input, 304-305
InputBox, 86
Int, 71
IPmt, 73
IsArray, 85
IsDate, 85
IsEmpty, 85
IsError, 85
IsFormOpen, 149
IsMissing, 85
IsNull, 85
IsNumeric, 85
IsObject, 85
LCase, 77
Left, 77
Len, 77

LOF, 306
LTrim, 79
Mid, 78
Minute, 69
Month, 69
MsgBox, 86-88
NPer, 73
Nz, 63
Open, 240, 302-304
Pmt, 73
PPmt, 73-74
Rate, 74
Replace, 78
return values, 48
Right, 77
Rnd, 71
RTrim, 79
Second, 69
Space, 78
Split, 79
StrComp, 79
Syd, 74
TranslateType, 286
Trim, 79
UCase, 77
Windows API functions
  declaring, 337-338
  documentation, 338
  FindExecutable, 342
  FindWindow, 340-341
  GetThisComputerName, 338-339
  GetUserName, 341-342
  string arguments, 339
  when to use, 343
Year, 69

future annuity values, calculating, 72-73

FV function, 72-73

G

General Date format, 82

General Number format, 82

GetDependencyInfo method, 232

GetObject function, 316-317

GetObjectDemo procedure, 316

GetObjectOwner method, 281

GetThisComputerName function, 338-339

GetUserName function, 341-342

GotFocus event, 163, 169

GoTo statement, 101-102

greater than symbol (>), 85

GROUP BY clause (SELECT statement), 353-354

Group object, 280

GroupLevel object, 219

groups
creating with ADOX, 279-280
Groups collection, 280
Group object, 280
properties, 218-219

Groups collection, 280

grpOption_AfterUpdate procedure, 201

grpSub_AfterUpdate procedure, 207

H

h format, 84

HAVING clause (SELECT statement), 354

help
documentation, 58
Task pane, 25
Visual Basic Help pane, 25

Help menu commands, Microsoft Visual Basic Help, 25

hh format, 84

HighlightControl procedure, 197, 203

Hour function, 69

Hungarian convention, 29

I

I/O (input/output), 301
numbering file lines, 310-312
opening files
access permissions, 303
example, 303-304
file modes, 302
locking settings, 303
printing files, 309
reading files, 304-307
writing to files, 307-308

identifiers, 42

Immediate window (VBE), 18

importing XML (Extensible Markup Language) files, 330-333

ImportXML function, 330-333

indenting code, 30

Index object, 277

index values (arrays), 106-107

indexes
creating with ADOX, 277-278
Indexes collection, 277

Input # statement, 306-307

input boxes, 86

Input function, 304-305

Input mode, 302

InputAndWrite procedure, 308

InputBox function, 86

INSERT INTO statements, 355-356

Insert menu commands, Procedure, 22

Insert Module command (Standard toolbar), 19

Insert Procedures dialog box, 22

instantiating objects, 114

Int function, 71

Integer data type, 39, 41
converting values to, 62

integers, returning, 71

IntelliSense, 26-27

interacting functions, 86-88

interest payments, calculating, 73

interest rates, calculating, 74

interval string settings, 66

intrinsic constants, 38

InvokeMethod procedure, 117

invoking methods, 117-118

IPmt function, 73

IsArray function, 85

IsDate function, 85

IsEmpty function, 85

IsError function, 85

IsFormOpen function, 149

IsLoaded property (AccessObject object), 226

IsMissing function, 85

IsNull function, 85

IsNumeric function, 85

IsObject function, 85

IsolationLevel property (Connection object), 239

Item property (collections), 225

J-K

keyboard shortcuts, 22

KeyDown event, 165

KeyPress event, 165

keyset cursors, 244

KeyUp event, 165

keywords. *See* statements

L

late binding, 317

LCase function, 77

Left function, 77

Len function, 77

less than symbol (<), 85

libraries, 314

lifetime of variables, 136
    module-level variables, 137-138
    procedure-level variables, 137
    public variables, 138-139

Line Input # statement, 306

list controls, 175-176
    adding items to, 181
    callback functions, 189-191
    drill-down controls, 191-193
    filtering list control, 177-180
    MultiSelect controls, 187-189
    row source type, 175
    row sources, 175
    Table/Query list controls, updating, 183-187
    value list controls, updating, 181-183

ListCollection1 procedure, 119

ListCollection2 procedure, 120

ListCollection3 procedure, 120

ListControls procedure, 121

lists. *See* list controls

ListTables procedure, 295

Load event, 168

LoadClient method, 159

local scope, 131

Lock Read locking setting, 303

Lock Read Write locking setting, 303

Lock Write locking setting, 303

Locked property (text boxes), 196

locking records
    locking errors, resolving, 296-297
    optimistic record locking, 288-291
    pessimistic record locking, 288, 291-292

LOF function, 306

Long data type, 41

Long Date format, 82

Long Time format, 82

loops, 91
    case study, 102-104
    Do loops
        conditions, 100-101
        simple example, 99-100
        terminating, 101
    For Next statements, 95-96
        loop counter variables, 97
        looping in reverse, 96-97
        nesting, 98
        terminating, 99
    GoTo statements, 101-102

If Then Else statements
  conditions, 92-93
  Else clasue, 93
  ElseIf clause, 93-94
  simple If statement,
    91-92
Select Case statements, 94

LostFocus event, 163

lower bounds (arrays), 106

**lstCustomers_LostFocus
  procedure, 188**

LTrim function, 79

M

M format, 83

macros, 12

**MakeConnection procedure,
  241**

**master viewing forms,
  203-207**

MasterForm, 232-233

math functions
  Abs, 70
  example, 72
  Int, 71
  Rnd, 71

Medium Date format, 82

Medium Time format, 82

memory buffers, 169-170

message boxes, 86-88

methods. *See also* functions;
  procedures; statements
  AddNew, 260
  ApplyFilter, 154

BeginTrans, 267
Close, 146, 211, 242
CommitTrans, 267
Delete, 262-263
Find, 256-258
GetDependencyInfo, 232
GetObjectOwner, 281
invoking, 117-118
LoadClient, 159
Move, 253
MoveFirst, 253
MoveLast, 253
MoveNext, 253
MovePrevious, 253
MoveSize, 150-151
Open, 240, 302-304
OpenArgs, 151-152
OpenForm, 145-146, 151
OpenReport, 210-211
RollbackTrans, 267
Seek, 258-260
SetObjectOwner, 281
Update, 262-266

**Microsoft Visual Basic Help
  command (Help menu), 25**

Mid function, 78

Minute function, 69

mm format, 83

mmm format, 84

mmmm format, 84

**Mode property (Connection
  object), 239**

**models, object models,
  121-122**

modes (file), 302

module scope, 131

module-level variables
  lifetimes, 137-138
  scope, 133

modules
  class modules, 21
  form modules, 147
  module-level variables
    lifetimes, 137-138
    scope, 133
  object modules, 21
  report module, 209
  saving, 24-25
  standard modules, 21

Month function, 69

Move method, 253

MoveFirst method, 253

MoveLast method, 253

MoveNext method, 253

MovePrevious method, 253

MoveSize method, 150-151

**moving through recordsets,
  253-255**

MsgBox function, 86-88

**multiple array dimensions,
  110**

**multiple form instances,
  157-159**

**MultiSelect controls,
  187-189**

N

n format, 84

**Name property
  (AccessObject object), 226**

naming conventions, 28-30
  natural naming system, 29
  variables, 37

navigating recordsets, 253-255

navigation events, 168

nesting For Next loops, 98

nn format, 84

NoData event, 217-218

NotInList event, 167

NPer function, 73

null values, converting, 63

number of annuity periods, calculating, 73

NumberClientList procedure, 311

numbering lines in text files, 310-312

numbers. *See also* **financial functions; math functions**
  formatting, 81-84
  numeric named formats, 82
  numeric user-defined formats, 83
  random numbers, generating, 71

Nz function, 63

O

Object Browser, 123-124

Object Browser command
  Standard toolbar, 19
  View menu, 123

Object data type, 41

object models, 121-122

objects, 113-114. *See also* **ADO (ActiveX Data Objects); controls**
  AccessObject, 226
  AdditionalData, 329
  application collections, 223-225
    AllForms, 225
    object dependencies, 229-232
    object properties, 226-229
    objects, retrieving lists of, 225-226
    properties, 225
  Catalog, 275
  collections, 119-121
  Column, 275
  Command, 242-244
  Connection, 238
    closing connections, 242
    connection strings, 240-241
    opening connections, 239-240
  creating, 114-115, 124-126, 315-317
  CurrentProject, 224
  dependencies, 229-232
  DependencyInfo, 232
  enclosing in brackets, 44
  events, 126-127
  Group, 280
  GroupLevel, 219
  Index, 277
  instantiating, 114
  methods, invoking, 117-118
  Object Browser, 123-124
  object models, 121-122
  ownership, 281-282
  permissions, 282-283

  prefixes, 29
  properties, 116-117, 226-229
  real-world example, 113-114
  Recordset
    adding data to, 260-262
    combo boxes, adding items to, 268-271
    creating, 245-247
    cursors, 244-245
    deleting data in, 262-263
    fields, referencing, 256
    filtering, 247-248
    finding data in, 256-260
    moving through, 253-255
    opening, 245-247
    populating, 245-246
    Recordset property, 248-249
    transactions, 266-268
    updating data in, 263-266
  references, 42-43, 122-123, 314-315
  retrieving lists of, 225-226
  Table, 275

.olb filename extension, 314

OldValue property (text boxes), 196

On Error Goto HandleErr statement, 53

On Error Goto statement, 53-54

On Error Resume Next statement, 53

On/Off format, 82

OneNote, 11

Open event, 168

open forms, checking, 149-150

Open function, 240, 302-304

openargs argument (OpenReport method), 210

OpenArgs method, 151-152

OpenFile procedure, 303

OpenForm method, 145-146, 151

opening
  database connections, 239-240
  files
    access permissions, 303
    example, 303-304
    file modes, 302
    locking settings, 303
  forms, 128-130, 145-146
  recordsets, 245-247
  reports, 210-211
  schema recordsets, 293-294

OpenReport method, 210-211

operators, 42

optimistic record locking, 288-291

Option Base statement, 107

Option Explicit statement, 34-36

option groups, 200-202

optional arguments, 50

ORDER BY clause (SELECT statement), 353

OrderBy property (reports), 214

OrderByOn property (reports), 214

Output mode, 302

ownership of objects, 281-282

P

page locking, 288

Parent property
  AccessObject object, 226
  collections, 225

passing arguments, 49
  default values, 50
  optional arguments, 50
  passing by reference, 50-51
  passing by value, 51
  to reports, 212-213

payments, calculating, 73-74

Percent format, 82

percent sign (%), 83

permissions, 282-283, 303

pessimistic record locking, 288, 291-292

Phone_AfterUpdate procedure, 166

Phone_BeforeUpdate procedure, 166

Phone_Change procedure, 166

Phone_Dirty procedure, 166

Phone_KeyDown procedure, 166

Phone_KeyPress procedure, 166

Phone_KeyUp procedure, 166

Pmt function, 73

populating
  forms, 152-154
  recordsets, 245-246
  reports, 213-214

pound sign (#), 76, 83

PPmt function, 73-74

predicates (SQL), 350-351

prefixes, 29-30

Preserve statement, 111

principal payments, calculating, 73-74

Print # statement, 309

PrintBillingChart procedure, 102-104

PrintClients procedure, 254

printing files, 309

PrintPoundSign procedure, 309

private procedures, 48

Private statement, 48

Procedure command (Insert menu), 22

procedure-level variables
  lifetimes, 137
  scope, 131-132

procedures, 45-46. *See also* functions; methods; statements
  AddEmployee, 261
  Address_Enter, 163
  Address_Exit, 164
  Address_GotFocus, 164
  Address_LostFocus, 164
  arguments
    default values, 50
    optional arguments, 50

passing, 49

passing by reference, 50-51

passing by value, 51

cboBound_AfterUpdate, 184

cboColors_NotInList, 182

cboUnbound_NotInList, 186

ChangeOwner, 281

ChangeStateImplicit, 266

ChangeStateExplicit1, 264

ChangeStateExplicit2, 265

ChangeStateTransaction, 267-268

ChartInExcel, 322-323

Client_Enter, 163

Client_Exit, 163

Client_GotFocus, 163

Client_LostFocus, 163

CloseClientForm, 146

cmdDisable_Click, 201

cmdExport_Click, 335

CreateGroup, 280

CreateIndexes, 277-278

CreateObject1, 114

CreateObject2, 115

CreateObjectDemo, 316

CreateRelation, 278-279

CreateTables, 275-276

CreateTwoForms, 157

CreateUser, 280

creating, 22-23

debugging

breakpoints, 56

run and break mode, 54-55

single-stepping, 55-56

defined, 22, 45

DeleteEmployee, 262-263

EarlyBindingDemo, 317

EditCA, 243

error handling, 52-54

EstimatedEndDate_Exit, 172

event procedures, 127

ExportMultipleTables, 329

GetObjectDemo, 316

grpOption_AfterUpdate, 201

grpSub_AfterUpdate, 207

HighlightControl, 197, 203

InputAndWrite, 308

InvokeMethod, 117

ListCollection1, 119

ListCollection2, 120

ListCollection3, 120

ListControls, 121

ListTables, 295

lstCustomers_LostFocus, 188

MakeConnection, 241

NumberClientList, 311

OpenFile, 303

Phone_AfterUpdate, 166

Phone_BeforeUpdate, 166

Phone_Change, 166

Phone_Dirty, 166

Phone_KeyDown, 166

Phone_KeyPress, 166

Phone_KeyUp, 166

PrintBillingChart, 102-104

PrintClients, 254

PrintPoundSign, 309

private procedures, 48

ProjectName_NotInList, 269

property procedures, 125

public procedures, 48

QueryToExcel, 318-319

ReadInput, 305

ReadInputPoundSign, 307

ReadLineInput, 306

ReadProperties, 116

SeekClient, 260

SetPermissions, 282

ShowDependencies, 230-231

ShowInFormList, 227

StartDate_Exit, 172

TestExcel, 122

TestOptLock, 289

TestOptLock2, 290

TestPessLock, 291-292

txtValue_Change, 201

UnhighlightControl, 197

UseTimeWeek, 126

WriteProperties, 116

Project Explorer, 18-19

ProjectName_NotInList procedure, 269

Projects form, 14

ProjectSub form, 206

properties, object properties, 116-117

Properties property (AccessObject object), 226

Properties window (VBE), 18

Properties Window command (Standard toolbar), 19

property procedures, 125

Provider property (Connection object), 239

public constants, 134-135

public procedures, 48

public scope, 131

Public statement, 48

public variables
lifetimes, 138-139
scope, 134-135

Q

qualifiers, 42

queries. *See* SQL (Standard Query Language)

QueryToExcel procedure, 318-319

quotes , 76

R

Random mode, 302

random numbers, generating, 71

Rate function, 74

reading
files
EOF function, 305-306
Input # statement, 306-307
Input function, 304-305
Line Input # statement, 306
LOF function, 306
object properties, 116-117

ReadInput procedure, 305

ReadInputPoundSign procedure, 307

ReadLineInput procedure, 306

ReadProperties procedure, 116

records
adding, 355-356
deleting, 355
locking
locking errors, resolving, 296-297
optimistic record locking, 288-291
pessimistic record locking, 288, 291-292
updating, 354-355

Recordset object. *See* recordsets

Recordset property, 248-249

recordsets, 244-245
adding data to, 260-262
combo boxes, adding items to, 268-271
creating, 245-247
cursors, 244-245
deleting data in, 262-263
fields, referencing, 256
filtering, 247-248
finding data in
Find method, 256-258
Seek method, 258-260
moving through, 253-255
opening, 245-247
populating, 245-246
records
adding, 355-356
deleting, 355
locking, 288-292, 296-297
updating, 354-355
Recordset property, 248-249

schema recordsets
retrieving, 293-294
standard schema recordsets, 294-295
transactions, 266-268
updating data in, 263-266

ReDim statement, 110-111

Redo command (Standard toolbar), 19

reference, passing by, 50-51

references, 122-123
array elements, 109
object references, 42-43, 314-315
recordset fields, 256
reports, 218

References command (Tools menu), 122, 314

References dialog box, 122, 314

relationships, 278-279

Replace function, 78

replacing string characters, 78

report module, 209

report-level errors, 215

reports
closing, 211
daily reports, 220-222
displaying in MasterForm, 232-233
events, 170-171
filtering, 214-215
group properties, 218-219
NoData event, 217-218
opening, 210-211
passing arguments to, 212-213

populating, 213-214

referencing, 218

report events, 217-218

report-level errors, 215-217

report module, 209

sort order, 214-215

Reset command (Standard toolbar), 19

Resize event, 168

resizing forms, 150-151

resolving locking errors, 296-297

Response argument (Error event), 215

Resume Next statement, 54

Resume statement, 54

return values (functions), 48

Right function, 77

Rnd function, 71

RollbackTrans method, 267

rolling back transactions, 267

RowSource property (list controls), 175

RowSourceType property (list controls), 175

Rtrim function, 79

Run Sub/UserForm command (Run menu), 54

Run to Cursor command (Debug menu), 56

running

    functions, 47-48

    sub procedures, 46

S

s format, 84

Save As dialog box, 24

Save command (File menu), 24

saving modules, 24-25

schema recordsets

    retrieving, 293-294

    standard schema recordsets, 294-295

schemas, 279

Scientific format, 82

scope

    local scope, 131

    module-level variables, 133

    module scope, 131

    procedure-level variables, 131-132

    public scope, 131

    public variables, 134-135

    static variables, 139-141

searching recordsets

    Find method, 256-258

    Seek method, 258-260

Second function, 69

security (ADOX)

    data dictionary case study, 284-286

    groups, 279-280

    object ownership, 281-282

    object permissions, 282-283

    users, 280-281

Seek method, 258-260

SeekClient procedure, 260

Select Case statement, 94

SELECT INTO statement, 356-357

SELECT statement

    ALL predicate, 350-351

    DISTINCT predicate, 350-351

    FROM clause, 351-352

    GROUP BY clause, 353-354

    HAVING clause, 354

    ORDER BY clause, 353

    syntax, 350

    TOP predicate, 350-351

    WHERE clause, 352

SelText property (text boxes), 196

semicolon (;), 181

SetObjectOwner method, 281

SetPermissions procedure, 282

Shared locking setting, 303

Short Date format, 82

Short Time format, 82

shortcuts (keyboard), 22

ShowDependencies procedure, 230-231

ShowInFormList procedure, 227

Single data type, 39, 41

single-stepping, 55-56

sizing forms, 150-151

sorting reports, 214-215

Space function, 78

Split function, 79

splitting strings, 79

spreadsheets (Excel), 9-10
accessing from Access, 318-319, 322-323

SQL (Standard Query Language), 12-13, 347-348
DDL (Data Definition Language), 348
DELETE statement, 355
DML (Data Manipulation Language), 348
INSERT INTO statement, 355-356
SELECT INTO statement, 356-357
SELECT statement
ALL predicate, 350-351
DISTINCT predicate, 350-351
FROM clause, 351-352
GROUP BY clause, 353-354
HAVING clause, 354
ORDER BY clause, 353
syntax, 350
TOP predicate, 350-351
WHERE clause, 352
standards, 348
structure and syntax, 348-349
TRANSFORM statement, 357-358
UPDATE statement, 354-355

ss format, 84

Standard format, 82

Standard Query Language. See SQL

standard schema recordsets, 294-295

Standard toolbar (VBE), 18, 20

StartDate_Exit procedure, 172

statements, 349. *See also* functions; methods; procedures
branching and looping, 91
compared to functions, 58
Const, 37
defined, 45
DELETE, 355
Dim, 33-34, 106
Do loops
conditions, 100-101
simple example, 99-100
terminating, 101
Else, 93
ElseIf, 93-94
End Function, 47
End Sub, 46
Exit Do, 101
Exit For, 99
Exit Function, 53
For, Next, 95-96
loop counter variables, 97
looping in reverse, 96-97
nesting, 98-99
Function, 47
GoTo, 101-102
If Then Else
conditions, 92-93
Else clause, 93
ElseIf clause, 93-94
simple If statement, 91-92
Input #, 306-307
INSERT INTO, 355-356
Line Input #, 306
On Error Goto, 53-54
On Error Goto HandleErr, 53

On Error Resume Next, 53
Option Base, 107
Option Explicit, 34-36
Preserve, 111
Print #, 309
Private, 48
Public, 48
ReDim, 110-111
Resume, 54
Resume Next, 54
SELECT
ALL predicate, 350-351
DISTINCT predicate, 350-351
FROM clause, 351-352
GROUP BY clause, 353-354
HAVING clause, 354
ORDER BY clause, 353
syntax, 350
TOP predicate, 350-351
WHERE clause, 352
Select Case, 94
SELECT INTO, 356-357
Sub, 45
TRANSFORM, 357-358
UPDATE, 354-355
Write #, 307-308

static cursors, 244

static variables, 139-141

Step Into command (Debug menu), 55

Step Out command (Debug menu), 55

Step Over command (Debug menu), 55

StrComp function, 79

string arguments, passing to Windows API functions, 339

String data type. *See* strings

string user-defined formats, 85

strings, 42
  changing case of, 77
  comparing, 79
  connection strings, 240-241
  counting characters in, 77
  converting values to, 62
  creating dates from, 69
  formatting, 85
  functions
    Asc, 76
    Chr, 76
    example, 80
    LCase, 77
    Left, 77
    Len, 77
    LTrim, 79
    Mid, 78
    Replace, 78
    Right, 77
    RTrim, 79
    Space, 78
    Split, 79
    StrComp, 79
    Trim, 79
    UCase, 77
  interval string settings, 66
  replacing characters in, 78
  returning characters from, 77
  splitting, 79
  trimming, 79
  user-defined formats, 85
structured files, 326

stubs, 23

sub procedures. *See* procedures

subforms, 202

subtracting dates, 66

sum-of-years' depreciation, calculating, 74

Switchboard form, 14

Syd function, 74

T

Table object, 275

Table/Query list controls, 183-187

tables
  creating with ADOX, 274-277
  creating with SELECT INTO statement, 356-357
  indexes, 277-278
  relationships, 278-279

Tag property (controls), 196, 202-203

Task pane (VBE), 25

terminating
  Do loops, 101
  For Next loops, 99

TestExcel procedure, 122

TestOptLock procedure, 289

TestOptLock2 procedure, 290

TestPessLock procedure, 291-292

text boxes
  focus, tracking, 197-198
  properties, 195-196
  unbound text boxes, 198-200

Text property (text boxes), 196

TextBox objects. *See* text boxes

times. *See also* dates
  date/time named formats, 82
  formatting, 81-84
  returning, 69

Timeslips form, 15

TimeTrack sample database
  application collections, 232-233
  Billing Report, 15
  business days, estimating, 88-90
  current users, displaying, 250-252
  daily reports, 220-222
  data dictionary, 284-286
  data validation, 172-173
  drill-down controls, 191-193
  Employees form, 14
  error handling, 128-130
  Excel, accessing from Access, 322-323
  forms, opening, 128-130
  master viewing form, 203-207
  multiple form instances, 158-159
  overview, 13-15
  Projects form, 14

record locking errors, resolving, 296-297

reports, displaying in MasterForm, 232-233

Switchboard form, 14

text files, numbering lines in, 310-312

Timeslips form, 15

work in progress, billing, 102-104

.tlb filename extension, 314

Toggle Breakpoint command (Debug menu), 56

toolbars (VBE), 18-20

Toolbars command (View menu), 20

Toolbox command (Standard toolbar), 19

Tools menu commands, References, 122, 314

TOP predicate (SELECT statement), 350-351

tracking focus, 197-198

transactions, 266-268

TRANSFORM statements, 357-358

TranslateType function, 286

Trim function, 79

trimming strings, 79

True/False format, 82

ttttt format, 84

txtValue_Change procedure, 201

type libraries, 314

Type property (AccessObject object), 226

types. *See* data types

U

UCase function, 77

unbound text boxes, 198-200

Undo command (Standard toolbar), 19

UnhighlightControl procedure, 197

uninitialized variables, 62

Unload event, 168

Until condition (Do loops), 100

up-to-date project information, exporting, 334-335

Update method, 262-266

UPDATE statement, 354-355

updating

database records, 354-355

recordset data, 263-266

Table/Query list controls, 183-187

value list controls, 181-183

upper bounds (arrays), 106

user interaction

InputBox function, 86

MsgBox function, 86-88

UserForms toolbar (VBE), 20

users

creating with ADOX, 280-281

usernames, retrieving, 341-342

Users collection, 281

UseTimeWeek procedure, 126

V

validating data, 172-173

value list controls, updating, 181-183

Value property (text boxes), 196

value, passing by, 51

variables. *See also* arrays; data types; objects

declaring, 33-34

lifetimes, 136

module-level variables, 137-138

procedure-level variables, 137

public variables, 138-139

module-level variables

lifetimes, 137-138

scope, 133

naming conventions, 37

Option Explicit, 34-36

prefixes, 30

procedure-level variables

lifetimes, 137

scope, 131-132

public variables

lifetimes, 138-139

scope, 134-135

scope

local scope, 131

module-level variables, 133

module scope, 131

procedure-level variables, 131-132

public scope, 131

public variables, 134-135

static variables, 139-141

uninitialized variables, 62

Variant data type, 42

converting values to, 62

VBA (Visual Basic for Applications), 13. *See also* forms; functions; procedures

arrays
adding elements to, 108
changing dimensions of, 110-111
declaring, 105-106
defined, 105
dynamic arrays, 110-111
examples, 106
fixed-size arrays, 110
index values, 106-107
multiple dimensions, 110
Option Base statement, 107
ReDim statement, 110-111
referencing elements in, 109
upper/lower bounds, 106
branching and looping
case study, 102-104
Do loops, 99-101
For Next statements, 95-99
GoTo statements, 101-102
If Then, Else statements, 91-94
Select Case statements, 94
classes, 114
comments, 30-31
constants
declaring, 37
intrinsic constants, 38
public constants, 134-135

data types
Boolean, 40
Byte, 40
comparison of, 39-40
converting, 59-65
Currency, 39-40
Date, 41
Decimal, 40-41
Double, 41
function return values, 51-52
Integer, 39-41
Long, 41
Object, 41
Single, 39-41
String. *See* strings
Variant, 42
debugging
breakpoints, 56
run and break mode, 54-55
single-stepping, 55-56
delimiters, 76
error handling, 52-54, 128-130
events, 126-127
file I/O (input/output)
file handles, 301
numbering file lines, 310-312
opening files, 302
access permissions, 303
example, 303-304
file modes, 302
locking settings, 303
printing files, 309
reading files, 304-307
EOF function, 305-306
Input # statement, 306-307
Input function, 304-305
Line Input # statement, 306

LOF function, 306
writing to files, 307-308
help, 25
identifiers, 42
indents, 30
IntelliSense, 26-27
modules
class modules, 21
object modules, 21
saving, 24-25
standard modules, 21
naming conventions, 28-30
objects
Access objects, 114
collections, 119-121
creating, 114-115, 124-126
events, 126-127
instantiating, 114
methods, 117-118
Object Browser, 123-124
object models, 121-122
prefixes, 29
properties, 116-117
real-world example, 113-114
references, 122-123
referencing, 42-43
operators, 42
qualifiers, 42
referencing syntax, 42-43
reports
closing, 211
daily reports, 220-222
events, 215-218
group properties, 218-219
NoData event, 217-218
opening, 210-211
passing arguments to, 212-213
populating, 213-214

referencing, 218
report module, 209
report-level error,
    215-217
sort order, 214-215
scope
    local scope, 131
    module-level variables,
        133
    module scope, 131
    procedure-level vari-
        ables, 131-132
    public scope, 131
    public variables, 134-135
statements
    compared to functions,
        58
    Const, 37
    defined, 45
    Dim, 33-34, 106
    Do, 99-101
    Else, 93
    ElseIf, 93-94
    End Function, 47
    End Sub, 46
    Exit Do, 101
    Exit For, 99
    Exit Function, 53
    For Next, 95-99
    Function, 47
    GoTo, 101-102
    If Then Else, 91-94
    On Error Goto, 53-54
    On Error Goto
        HandleErr, 53
    On Error Resume Next,
        53
    Option Base, 107
    Option Explicit, 34-36
    Preserve, 111
    Private, 48
    Public, 48
    ReDim, 110-111

Resume, 54
Resume Next, 54
Select Case, 94
Sub, 45
variables
    declaring, 33-34
    lifetimes, 136-139
    module-level variables,
        133, 137-138
    naming conventions, 37
    Option Explicit, 34-36
    prefixes, 30
    procedure-level vari-
        ables, 131-132, 137
    public variables,
        134-135, 138-139
    static variables, 139-141
    uninitialized variables,
        62
VBE (Visual Basic Editor),
    17-18
    Debug toolbar, 20
    Edit toolbar, 20
    Immediate window, 18
    IntelliSense, 26-27
    modules, 21
    Project Explorer, 18
    Properties window, 18
    Standard toolbar, 18-20
    Task pane, 25
    UserForms toolbar, 20
    VBA code, entering,
        22-23
    VBA code, saving, 24-25
    Visual Basic Help pane,
        25

VBA Help command
(Standard toolbar), 19

VBE (Visual Basic Editor),
17-18
    Debug toolbar, 20
    Edit toolbar, 20

Immediate window, 18
IntelliSense, 26-27
modules, 21
Project Explorer, 18
Properties window, 18
Standard toolbar, 18, 20
Task pane, 25
UserForms toolbar, 20
VBA code
    entering, 22-23
    saving, 24-25
Visual Basic Help pane, 25

view argument (OpenReport
method), 210

View menu commands
    Object Browser, 123
    Toolbars, 20

Visible property (text boxes),
196

Visual Basic Editor. See VBE

Visual Basic for
Applications. See VBA

W

w format, 84

Web-ready files, exporting
to, 329

WHERE clause (SELECT
statement), 352

wherecondition argument
(OpenReport method), 210

While condition (Do loops),
101

windowmode argument
(OpenReport method), 210

Windows API functions
declaring, 337-338
documentation, 338
FindExecutable, 342
FindWindow, 340-341
GetThisComputerName, 338-339
GetUserName, 341-342
string arguments, 339
when to use, 343

Word, accessing from Access, 320-321

work in progress, billing, 102-104

Write # statement, 307-308

WriteProperties procedure, 116

writing
to files, 307-308
object properties, 116

ww format, 84

X-Z

XML (Extensible Markup Language) files, 325-326
exporting Access data to
export example, 327-328
exporting related data, 329-330
ExportXML function, 326-327
up-to-date project information, 334-335
Web-ready files, 329

importing into Access
import example, 331-333
ImportXML function, 330-333
XSD, 325
XSL, 325

Year function, 69

Yes/No format, 82

yy format, 84

yyyy format, 84

business solutions